COMPUTER SCIENCE, TECHNOLOGY AND APPLICATIONS

FACE RECOGNITION

METHODS, APPLICATIONS AND TECHNOLOGY

COMPUTER SCIENCE, TECHNOLOGY AND APPLICATIONS

Additional books in this series can be found on Nova's website under the Series tab.

Additional E-books in this series can be found on Nova's website under the E-books tab.

MECHANICAL ENGINEERING THEORY AND APPLICATIONS

Additional books in this series can be found on Nova's website under the Series tab.

Additional E-books in this series can be found on Nova's website under the E-books tab.

COMPUTER SCIENCE, TECHNOLOGY AND APPLICATIONS

FACE RECOGNITION

METHODS, APPLICATIONS AND TECHNOLOGY

ADAMO QUAGLIA
AND
CALOGERA M. EPIFANO
EDITORS

Nova Science Publishers, Inc.
New York

Library of Congress Cataloging-in-Publication Data

Face recognition : methods, applications, and technology / editors, Adamo Quaglia and Calogera M. Epifano.
p. cm.
Includes bibliographical references and index.
ISBN 978-1-61942-663-4 (hardcover)
1. Human face recognition (Computer science) I. Quaglia, Adamo. II. Epifano, Calogera M.
TA1650.F34 2012
006.3'7--dc23

2011051149

Published by Nova Science Publishers, Inc. † New York

Contents

PREFACE

Face recognition has been an active area of research in image processing and computer vision due to its extensive range of prospective applications relating to biometrics, information security, video surveillance, law enforcement, identity authentication, smart cards, and access control systems. Topics discussed in this compilation include two-dimensional principal component analysis algorithms for face recognition; principal component analysis (PCA) and artificial immune networks in face recognition; multi-class learning facial age estimation and forensic face recognition.

Chapter 1 – Although we have an excellent ability to recognise familiar faces even under challenging viewing conditions (e.g., low-quality and old images), people are remarkably poor at identifying unfamiliar faces even under optimal circumstances (e.g., high-quality and recent images). This chapter discusses unfamiliar face identification accuracy and reports convergent evidence from several research fields including face recognition, eye-witness identification, and change blindness. In addition, recent face perception experiments suggest that the limitatons of unfamiliar face recognition might be arised during encoding faces in the first place, rather than processing them into memory. Importantly, however, there are quite large individual differences in unfamiliar face perception, but only few studies tried to predict these variabilities.

Chapter 2 – Two-dimensional (2-D) principal component analysis (PCA) algorithms for face recognition are an attractive alternative to the traditional one-dimensional (1-D) PCA algorithms because they are able to provide higher accuracy in extracting facial features for human face identification with reduced computational complexity. The improved performance and efficiency are gained largely because the 2-D PCA algorithms treat facial images more naturally and effectively as matrices rather than vectors and, as a result, one can employ a covariance matrix of much reduced-size for analysis and algorithmic development. This chapter presents an extended 2-D PCA algorithm for improving rate of face recognition. The new algorithm is deduced based on an analysis in which a pair of (rather than a single) covariance matrices are defined and utilized for extracting both row-related and column-related features of facial images. In addition, by incorporating a pre-processing procedure, which was recently developed by the authors based on perfect histogram matching, the performance of the proposed 2-D PCA algorithm can be considerably enhanced. Experimental results are presented to examine the performance of the proposed algorithms and their robustness to noise, face occlusion, and illumination conditions.

Chapter 3 – This chapter complements our paper: "Spectral optimized asymmetric segmented phase-only correlation filter ASPOF filter" published in Applied Optics (2012).

Chapter 4 – This study proposes a face recognition method based on Principal Component Analysis (PCA) and artificial immune networks. The PCA extracts principal eigenvectors of the face image to get best feature description, consequently to reduce the size of feature vectors of the artificial immune networks. Hereafter these reduced-dimension image data are input into immune network classifiers to be trained. Subsequently the antibodies of the artificial immune networks are optimized using genetic algorithms. The performance of the proposed method was evaluated employing the ORL (ATandT Laboratories Cambridge) face database. The results show that this method gains higher recognition rate in contrast with most of the developed methods even for single training sample problem.

Chapter 5 – This work addresses the problem of distributed face recognition. In this problem, the training data does not reside on a single computer; it resides in multiple computers which are distributed geographically. The challenge is to develop a face recognition system where the dimensionality reduction and classification modules have access to only a small portion (few classes) of the entire training data. Such problems will arise when face recognition are employed at a large scale such as automatic client authentication in bank ATMs or automatic employee authentication in offices. Popular dimensionality reduction methods such as Principal Component Analysis (PCA), Linear Discriminant Analysis (LDA) etc. are data-dependent and so are classification algorithms like Neural Networks and Support Vector Machines. Therefore these methods are not suitable for this problem. This paper proposes a novel solution of the problem based on recognizing faces from video sequences.

For dimensionality reduction, we employ random projections as a data-independent alternative to PCA or LDA. The classification is carried out in parallel by the Hidden Markov Model (HMM) and our newly proposed Nearest Subspace Classifier (NSC). The classifiers are designed in such a way that they can be applied to each class separately; therefore they can operate on the smaller portions (few classes) of the data that reside on individual computers. The results from the two classifiers are finally fused to arrive at the final classification decision.

We have identified a new problem in face recognition. Therefore there are no previous studies that can address this problem. However, in order to see how our proposed method works with previous ones we have compared our results with a few previous works in video based face recognition. Our method shows better results than the ones we have compared with.

Chapter 6 – *Aim.* A growing interest has been directed to evaluate whether a symptom-based remitted state, based on standardized criteria for schizophrenia, also corresponds to an overall good functioning. This study aimed to examine the relationships between remission status and two outcome parameters in a group of schizophrenic patients: face processing (facial identity and facial emotion recognition) and basic cognitive abilities. *Methods.* Ninety patients in stable phase were enrolled, of whom 28 patients attained "cross-sectional" remission, and 62 patients failed to. Facial emotion perception performances were assessed with the Comprehensive Affect Testing System, a standardized measure of emotion processing. Cognitive functions were evaluated by a wide battery of tests for attention, verbal memory/learning, perceptual-motor speed and executive functions. *Results.* The two groups of patients were homogeneous in demographic and clinical variables (age of onset, length of illness, previous relapses, dose equivalent to 100 mg/day of chlorpromazine, type of antipsychotics). Emotion perception was not different between the two groups, nevertheless the ability to discriminate facial identity was better in patients with symptomatic remission. Compared to non-remitted patients, remitted ones obtained higher scores in the executive functions task. No differences were detected in attentive functions, verbal memory/learning, and perceptual-motor speed. Among the significant variables of the groups comparison, only facial identity discrimination was a contributing factor to the remission status. *Conclusion.* These data suggest that remission criteria for schizophrenia can only partially be considered an index of "functional" remission and that other aspects of social functioning, such as cognitive impairments, must be considered in order to focus on recovery from the illness.

Chapter 7 – Many studies have investigated cognitive and social competences of newborn infants as face recognition, ability to imitate facial gestures and communicative skills. The preferential looking paradigm showed that newborns prefer to look at a human face-like stimulus compared to any other non human face-like stimulus. Furthermore, it is highlighted a newborn preference to look at a new face compared to a face previously seen from the habituation procedure (novelty effect); to explain this effect, it is assumed that the newborns are able to build a *perceptive representation* of the face that they looked at, *like an expression of a motivation for novelty.* This effect disappeared if the known face is the mother's face which is looked at more when it is compared to a new face (familiarity effect); it is assumed that the newborns are able to build a *dynamic "social" representation* of the face through few communicative interactions with their mother in the first hours of life. The studies about the novelty effect and the familiarity effect are based on a preference-task, where a new face is compared with a known face. These studies show a large heterogeneity of the encoding methods related to the gazing behaviour of the newborns. The most widely used methods in literature are summarized in three big classes: live encoding, frame by frame video encoding, real time video encoding. This chapter will focus on the differences among encoding methods of the gazing behaviour of the newborns. Moreover the findings of an empirical study on the comparisons among different encoding methods will be reported.

Chapter 8 - Face image-based age estimation is an approach to classify a face image into one of several pre-defined age-groups. It is a challenging problem because the aging variation is specific to a given individual and is determined by not only the person's gene, but also by many external factors, such as exposure, weather conditions (e.g. ambient humidity), health, gender, living style and living location. Age estimation is a multiclass problem. One of the Adaptive Boosting (AdaBoost) or Support Vector Machine (SVM) extensions for solving the multiclass problem is the combination of the method of Error-Correcting Output Codes (ECOC) with boosting using a decision tree based classifier or binary SVM classifier. In this paper, we apply this extension to solve the age estimation problem. Gabor and LBP aging features are combined at the feature level to represent the face images. Experimental results on FG-NET and Morph database are reported to demonstrate its effectiveness and robustness. The ECOC can achieve nearly similar results when it was combined with AdaBoost or SVM. However, ECOC plus AdaBoost is much faster than ECOC plus SVM. The results obtained using the fused LBP and Gabor features are better than the one when using either LBP or Gabor alone.

Chapter 9 – Majority of systems whose primary interest is face recognition emphasizes on the analysis of the spatial representation of the images i.e. the intensity value of images, however the use of frequency domain approach sometimes achieves better performance with respect to speed and robustness. Frequency domain techniques are executed by cross-correlating the Fourier transform of test face image with a synthesized template or filter,generated from Fourier transform of training images and processing the resulting correlation output via inverse fast Fourier transforms. The correlation output is searched for peaks and the relative heights of these peaks are analysed to determine whether the test face is recognized or not. Correlation filters offer several advantages. Correlation filters are shift-invariant and are based on integration operation and thus offer graceful degradation in any impairment to the test image. Correlation filters can be designed to exhibit noise tolerance and high discrimination ability. The main purpose of the chapter is to review the status of the several general purpose correlation filters and compare their performance for face recognition task under various facial expressions and varying lighting conditions. Correlation filters like maximum average correlation height (MACH), unconstrained minimum average correlation energy (UMACE), Optimal Trade-off MACH (OTMACH), quad phase UMACE (QPU MACE), phase only UMACE (POUMACE) and distance classifier correlation filter (DCCF) are synthesized and tested over several databases including AMP, Cropped YaleB, PIE and AR. The photonics instrumentation technique offers advantages of parallel noninteractive high speed processing in optical domain and therefore is a better candidate for hardware implementation of frequency domain algorithms. However, the need of optics to electronics conversion and vice-versa limits the achievable speed of operations. Hardware implementation of the frequency domain systems for face recognition using photonic architectures along with the device constraints which limit the speed are also discussed in this chapter.

Chapter 10 – The improvements of automatic face recognition during the last 2 decades have disclosed new applications like border control and camera surveillance. A new application field is forensic face recognition. Traditionally, face recognition by human experts has been used in forensics, but now there is a quickly developing interest in automatic face recognition as well. At the same time there is a trend towards a more objective and quantitative approach for traditional manual face comparison by human experts. Unlike in most applications of face recognition, in the forensic domain a binary decision or a score does not suffice as a result to be used in court. Rather, in the forensic domain, the outcome of the recognition process should be in the form of evidence or support for a prosecution hypothesis verses a defence hypothesis. In addition, in the forensic domain, trace images are often of poor quality. The available literature on (automatic) forensic face recognition is still very limited. In this survey, an overview is given of the characteristics of forensic face recognition and the main publications. The survey introduces forensic face recognition and reports on attempts to use automatic face recognition in the forensic context. Forensic facial comparison by human experts and the development of guidelines and a more quantitative and objective approach are also addressed. Probably the most important topic of the survey is the development of a framework to use automatic face recognition in the forensic setting. The Bayesian framework is a logical choice and likelihood ratios can in principle be used directly in court. In the statistical evaluation of the trace image, the choice of databases of facial images plays a very important role.

Chapter 11 – Independent component analysis (ICA) models, describing a given signal as a linear combination of various independent sources, have proven to be a fruitful endeavor. One prominent example deals with audio applications in order to separate the speaker's voice from environmental noises disturbing it. However, very few ICA based systems are available for biometric encryption applications. For that specific purpose, the ICA method can be easily adapted to add noise to a target image in order to encrypt it. In this chapter, at first, we discuss biometric recognition systems based on the ICA and correlation approaches. Next, we explore an ICA-based algorithm for face recognition. Basically, it consists of building a base of independent components using a learning database that contains several chosen reference images. Then, the target image (image to be recognized) is projected on the independent component base, and the similarity between the target image and each of the reference images is studied. Discrimination tests between the proposed technique and alternate methods are conducted by using the Pointing Head Pose Image Database (PHPID). In this chapter we report some of the recent developments dealing with the ICA method for face recognition applications. As part of our analysis, we precisely determine a set of metrics aimed at better understanding the role of the number and choice of the reference images on the performance of the proposed technique.

In: Face Recognition
Editors: Adamo Quaglia and Calogera M. Epifano
ISBN 978-1-61942-663-4

Chapter 1

ACCURACY OF FACE RECOGNITION

Ahmed M. Megreya[*]
Department of Psychology, Menoufia University, Egypt
Umm Al-Qura University, University College in Qunfudah, KSA

ABSTRACT

Although we have an excellent ability to recognise familiar faces even under challenging viewing conditions (e.g., low-quality and old images), people are remarkably poor at identifying unfamiliar faces even under optimal circumstances (e.g., high-quality and recent images). This chapter discusses unfamiliar face identification accuracy and reports convergent evidence from several research fields including face recognition, eye-witness identification, and change blindness. In addition, recent face perception experiments suggest that the limitatons of unfamiliar face recognition might be arised during encoding faces in the first place, rather than processing them into memory. Importantly, however, there are quite large individual differences in unfamiliar face perception, but only few studies tried to predict these variabilities.

INTRODUCTION

For several reasons, faces have been received remarkable interests by cognitive psychologists (Goldstein, 1983), cognitive neuroscientists (Gobbini and Haxby, 2007), and engineers (Li and Jain, 2005). First, faces have biological importance. For example, they involve some organs (e.g., the eyes, nose, etc), which serve a range of biological functions (e.g., vision, smelling, etc). Second, unlike all other visual objects, faces require within-category discrimination and this specialty seems to suggest that they might rely more functionally and anatomically on distinct mechanisms than those required for other kinds of pattern recognition (Farah, 1996; Kanwisher, 2000). Third, faces are the most encountered stimuli in our daily live, not only for adults, but also for newborn infants, who show

[*] Address Correspondence to Ahmed M. Megreya. Department of Psychology, Faculty of Arts, Menoufia University, Shebin El-Kom, Egypt; E-mail: amegreya@yahoo.com

preferential tracking of faces and face-like stimuli (e.g., Johnson, Dziurawiec, Ellis, and Morton, 1991). Last, and perhaps the most important, faces convey a wealth of information such as sex, race, and emotion. Identity is also one of the most important information that could be extracted from faces. Therefore, we do need an accurate estimate for how well humans could identify faces in real-world situations.

Examining face recognition accuracy has important implications in the forensic settings too, in spite of some early criticism which states that person recognition is "*more than a pretty face*" (Patterson, 1978), and eyewitnesses also "*have ears*" (Bull, 1978). More recent studies suggest that faces provide the most reliable cues for identification. For example, Burton, Wilson, Cowan and Bruce (1999) asked subjects to identify personally familiar identities from their faces without bodies, bodies without faces, gaits without faces, and whole persons. In each condition, targets were seen on motion in video clips, each of which lasted for 3 seconds. When faces were obscured, identification rates were significantly worse than any other condition. Therefore, Burton et al (1999) concluded that information received from faces is more useful for person identification than information received from the gait or the body. Pryke, Lindsay, Dysart and Dupuis (2004) supported this conclusion using unfamiliar faces. Namely, Pryke et al (2004) found that identification of a target seen live was significantly worse from a body line-up than from a face-line-up.

Ear-witness identification is also not as reliable as face identification. Evidence seems to indicate that identification from voices is significantly worse than identification from faces (Pryke et al., 2004; Yarmey, Yarmey and Yarmey, 1994). Moreover, it is thought that faces are dissociable from voices (e.g. Neuner and Schweinberger, 2000). Thus, listening to someone's voice, while studying the face, has no effect on the accuracy of facial identification (McAllister, Dale, Bregman, McCabe and Cotton, 1993), and seeing someone's face, while listening to the voice, does not improve the accuracy of voice recognition (Legge, Grosmann and Pieper, 1984). On the contrary, it impairs voice recognition (Cook and Wilding, 1997).

Overall, the aim of this chapter is to discuss how accurate is face recognition. In fact, to provide a good answer for this critical question, we do need to differentiate between familiar and unfamiliar face recognition. Therefore, I will begin with reviewing evidence on the dissociation between familiar and unfamiliar face processing. Then I will review evidence from different research fields on the accuracy of familiar and unfamiliar face perception *and* memory. Eventually, I will discuss the role of individual differences in face perception and recognition.

Familiar versus Unfamiliar Face Processing

Now, there is good evidence that familiar and unfamiliar faces are processed rather differently from one another. Perhaps the most convincing evidence for this dissociation comes from the neuropsychological literature. For example, Malone, Morris, Kay and Levin (1982) reported two surgically recovered cases of prosopagnosia, a specific disorder of the face recognition system (McNeil and Warrington, 1993). The first case could readily recognize familiar faces, but was impaired in matching unfamiliar faces. The second case, on the other hand, failed to recognize familiar faces but preserved the ability to match unfamiliar faces. This intriguing dissociation between familiar and unfamiliar face processing is not limited to Malone et al's (1982) patients, but it has also been observed for patients suffering from other neurological impairments (Benton, 1980; Tranel, Damasio and Damasio, 1988; Warrington and James, 1967; Young, Newcombe, de Hann, Small and Hay, 1993).

There is also evidence that familiar and unfamiliar face processing can be dissociated in neurological normal participants. For example, this dissociation may be reflected in the relative importance of the internal and external facial features. Internal features refer to the central region of a face that contains the eyes, brows, nose and mouth. External features refer to the face outline, hair, ears and chin. When a face is unfamiliar, it is easier to match and recognize from external features (Bonner, Burton, and Bruce, 2003; Bruce et al., 1999; Frowd, Bruce, McIntyre, and Hancock, 2007; Nachson and Shechory, 2002; Want, Pascalis, Coleman, and Blades, 2003; but see Ellis, Shepherd and Davies (1979) for a different pattern of results). After familiarization, however, internal features dominate face matching and recognition performance (Bonner et al., 2003; Campbell et al., 1999; Clutterbuck and Johnston, 2002; Ellis et al., 1979; Young, Hay, McWeeny, Flude, and Ellis, 1985). Therefore, some researchers suggest that the differences in familiar and unfamiliar face recognition may be located in the way the internal features are encoded (Clutterbuck and Johnston, 2002). Consistently, Bonner et al (2003) found that familiarization improves the accuracy of matching internal features for originally unfamiliar faces but it does not affect matching external features. This internal-feature advantage is, therefore, considered as an index of familiarity (Clutterbuck and Johnston, 2002, 2004, 2005; Osborne and Stevenage, 2008). However, this notion is recently challenged (Megreya and Bindemann, 2009).

Another piece of evidence seems to suggest that familiar and unfamiliar faces are processed in a qualitatively different manner. For example, Hancock, Bruce and Burton (2000) suggest that unfamiliar face processing relies on image-based processes, whereas familiar face recognition engages a more specialized type of processing that transcends individual images. Consistently, Megreya and Burton (2006b) found no correlation between recognizing familiar and unfamiliar faces. Furthermore, recognizing inverted faces was the best predictor of the individual differences in unfamiliar face recognition, regardless of whether the inverted faces were familiar or unfamiliar. These results suggest that the processes involved in upright unfamiliar face processing appear to be qualitatively similar to those underlying the recognition of inverted familiar and unfamiliar faces, but very different to those responsible for upright familiar face processing. This dissociation between familiar and unfamiliar face processing and the surprising association between matching upright unfamiliar faces and inverted familiars are further replicated by a more recent study (Megreya and Burton, 2007), where a short familiarization procedure was found to be successful in producing the mirror effect (a negative correlation between hits and false positives) in recognizing upright unfamiliar faces. However, this effect disappeared when targets were presented upside down. Accordingly, Megreya and Burton (2006b) suggest that unfamiliar faces are perceived and recognized as images. Perhaps unsurprisingly then, recognition memory for familiar faces is not sensitive to changes of viewpoint or expression between study and test phase, whereas recognition memory for unfamiliar faces is highly image-based (Bruce, 1982).

There are further suggestions for dissociation between familiar and unfamiliar face processing, but these are not as convincing as the above mentioned evidence. For example, Begleiter, Porjesz and Wang (1995) found that the visual memory potential (VMP) component of event-related brain potentials (ERPs) also differs significantly, albeit weakly, between the recognition of familiar and unfamiliar faces. Mohr, Landgrebe and Schweinberger (2002) also found a weak but significant effect of interhemispheric cooperation for familiar but not for unfamiliar face processing. In addition, a few brain-imaging studies report different activation patterns for familiar and unfamiliar faces, suggesting that both types of stimuli may be processed by distinct neural substrates (e.g. Leveroni, Seidenberg, Mayer, Mead, Binder and Rao, 2000; but see also Rossion, Schiltz, Robaye, Pirenne and Crommelinck, 2001).

ACCURACY OF UNFAMILIAR FACE MEMORY

Several procedures have been used for examining the accuracy of face recognition memory including: face recognition memory task, eye-witness identification test, immediate memory procedure, and change blindness paradigm.

RECOGNITION MEMORY

Recognition memory task is very common on face processing literature. This task requires subjects to learn some faces and then to recognize them from a larger set of faces. Early face recognition research proposed that people are experts in recognizing unfamiliar faces. For example, recognition memory rates of more than 90% have been reported (e.g. Hochberg and Galper, 1967; Nickerson, 1965; Yin, 1969). Importantly however, it is now known that this high level of accuracy represents memory for the *images* of faces, rather than the faces themselves. For example, Bruce (1982) found that recognition memory rates dropped from 90% correct, when the same images were used in study and test, to only 60% when different images were used. Subsequent research confirmed that changing photos between the study and test had a detrimental effect on face recognition accuracy (e.g., Read, Vokey, and Richard, 1990).

Indeed, unfamiliar face recognition memory is highly error-prone such that, in many occasions, people frequently miss some "old" (learned) faces and false positively accept some "new" (unlearned) ones (e.g., Bruce, 1982).

This low level of recognition memory for unfamiliar faces was also replicated using alternative forced-choice recognition tests, in which subjects are asked to select a previously studied face among some distractors.

For example, in Cambridge Face Memory Test (CFMT: Duchaine and Nakayama, 2006) participants are asked to learn six target faces. Then, they are given forced-choice recognition displays consisting of three faces. Each display contains the target and two distractors, and each target is presented in three conditions (identical images, novel images, and novel images with Gaussian noise). Figure 1 shows examples. Correct recognition on this test ranges from 60% to 100%, with an average of roughly 80%.

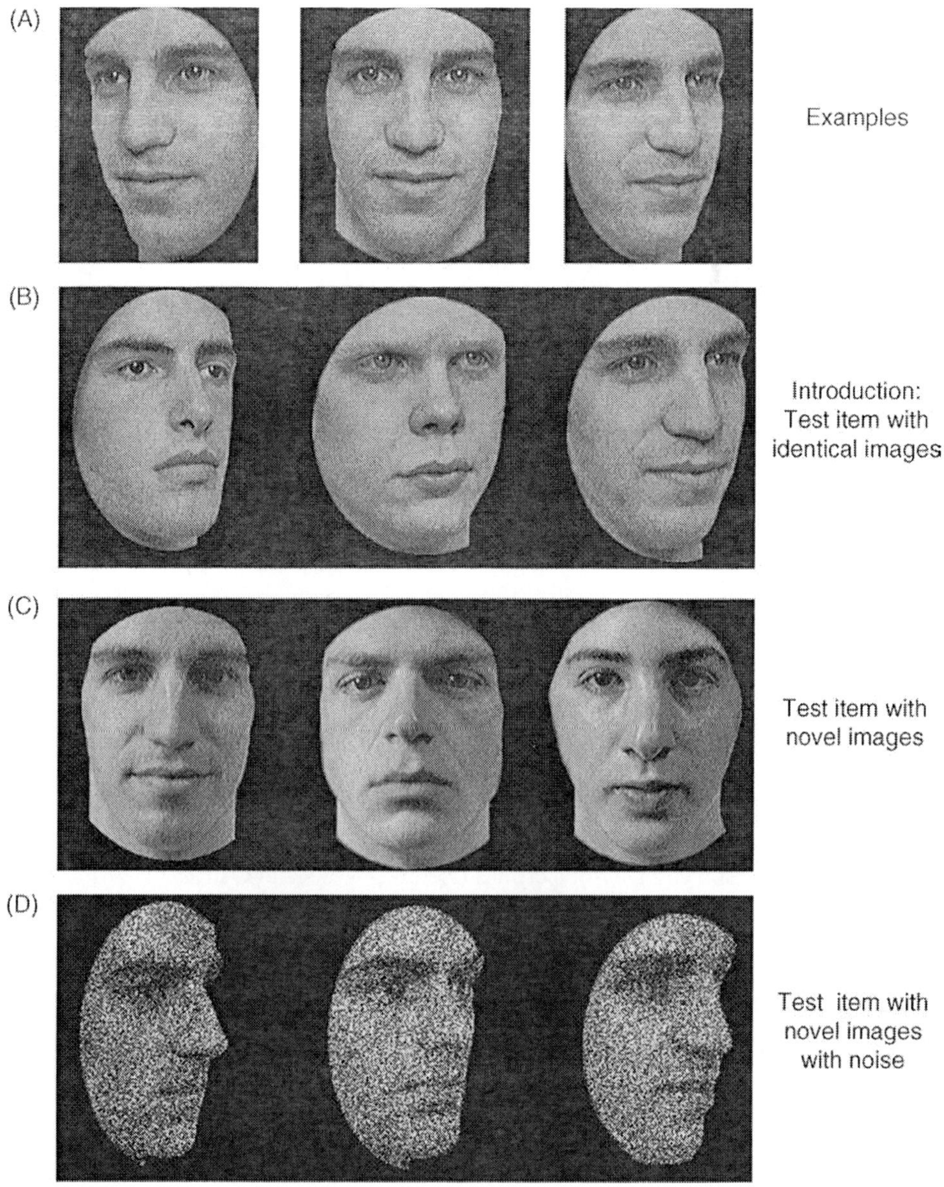

Figure 1. Examples of The Cambridge face recognition test.

Eye-Witness Memory

The reliability of eyewitness identification has been under question for more than a century. For example, Hugo Münsterberg (1908) concluded that eyewitnesses are fallible, and Edwin Borchard (1932) found that eyewitness misidentification is the most important cause of wrongful conviction of innocents. Indeed, it is now documented that more than 75% of wrongful imprisonment cases, in which the accused are subsequently exonerated by DNA evidence, involve eyewitness misidentifications (see The Innocence Project, n.d.). In eye-witness identification paradigm, subjects are presented with a staged crime (video or live).

Following a retention interval (filler task), they are asked to identify the culprit from a target-present or target-absent line-ups (e.g., Megreya, Memon, and Havard, in press). In addition to this line-up identification test, some studies used a show-up test, in which the eye-witnesses are presented with a single person and are asked to decide whether or not this person is the culprit (e.g., Steblay, Dysart, Fulero, and Lindsay, 2003). A large corpus of research has reported that eyewitness identification is highly error-prone. For example, in a meta-analysis, Steblay et al (2003) found that line-up tests produced means of 45% and 57% correct decisions when the targets were present or absent; respectively. In addition, Steblay et al (2003) found that showup presentation produced means of 47% and 85% correct decisions when the test person was actually the culprit or an innocent distractor. Although the overall rates of correct identification in eyewitness literature are generally low, they are highly variable as many factors could affect eye-witness identification, besides the low ability to recognise unfamiliar faces (Megreya and Burton, 2008). For example, a large body of work investigating the effects of many situational factors on identification accuracy indicated:

(i) An advantage for longer exposure duration (Memon, Hope and Bull, 2003).
(ii) A disadvantage for the presence of weapon (Maass and Kohnken, 1989).
(iii) A disadvantage for being alcohol intoxicated while witnessing the crime (Dysert, Lindsay, MacDonald and Wicke, 2002).
(iv) A disadvantage for longer retention intervals (Behrman and Davey, 2001; Flin, Boone, Knox and Bull, 1992).
(v) An advantage for expectation (Kerstholt, Raaijmakers and Valenton, 1992).
(vi) A disadvantage for multiple perpetrator-crimes (Megreya and Burton, 2006a).
(vii) A disadvantage for violent crimes (Clifford and Hollin, 1981).
(viii) An advantage for high serious crimes (Leippe, Wells and Ostrom, 1978).

In addition, research that examined the effects of system variables (the factors that are directly under the control of the criminal justice system) indicates that identification could be significantly impaired by:

(i) Biased instructions (e.g. Malpass and Devine, 1981).
(ii) Presenting the line-up members sequentially, rather than simultaneously (Memon and Bartlett, 2002), though this significantly reduces false positives (Lindsay and Wells, 1985).
(iii) Investigator bias (Garrioch and Brimacombe, 2001; Haw and Fisher, 2004; Phillips, McAuliff, Kovera and Cutler, 1999).
(iv) Misleading information such as wrong composites (Comish, 1987; Gibling and Davies, 1988; Jenkins and Davies, 1985).
(v) Mugshots exposure (Davies, Shepherd and Ellis, 1979; Dysart, Lindsay, Hammond and Dupuis, 2001; Memon, Hope, Bartlett and Bull, 2002).
(vi) Verbal descriptions of targets (e.g. Schooler and Engster-Schooler, 1990), though this effect seems to be not universal (Lyle and Johnson, 2004; Memon and Bartlett, 2002).
(vii) Line-up bias (e.g. Luus and Wells, 1991).
(viii) Clothes bias (Lindsay, Wallbridge and Drennan, 1987).

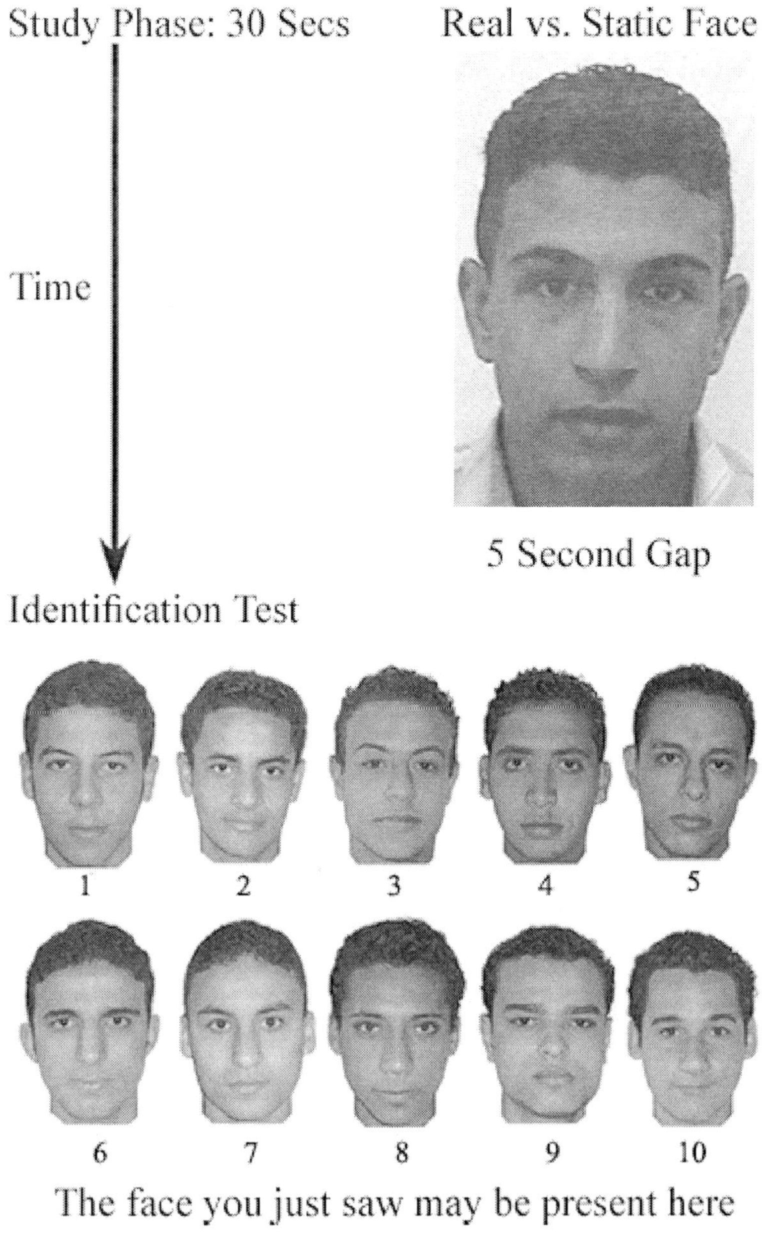

Figure 2. An example of immediate memory test for unfamiliar face recognition.

Immediate Memory

Megreya and Burton (2006a) have developed an immediate face memory task, in which subjects view a single face or two simultaneously-presented target faces until they feel confident that they can identify them subsequently. This learning phase is followed by a simultaneous ten-face identification line-up, in which just one or neither of the targets appears. In this immediate memory test, correct identification rates drop from 59% for the single target condition to just 34% for two-target displays. In a further experiment, Megreya and Burton (2008) have asked subjects to study unfamiliar faces seen either in static video images or in real-life situations. After a very short gap, they are given a photo line-up identification test, consisting of 10 faces, and are informed that targets might or might not be present in the line-ups (see Figure 2 for a schematic representation of this procedure).The results show a very poor overall performance. Accuracy rates for target-present line-ups were roughly 60%, and for target-absent line-ups roughly 80%. These poor levels of performance replicate our previous research with a different database of photographic targets (Megreya and Burton, 2006a), but what is striking about the present results is that there is no improvement at all when presented with live targets. Notably, this immediate face memory task represents an ideal-case for estimating baseline performance in an identification task. The memory requirement is minimal, with only a short gab between the disappearance of the target and the presentation of the test array. In addition, the task do not involve many of the factors thought to be significant sources of eyewitness misidentifications (which are reported above).This suggests that the processing of unfamiliar faces, rather than effects on memory or interventions between encoding and test, might form a significant component in understanding the difficulty of eyewitness memory (Megreya and Burton, 2008).

CHANGE BLINDNESS

Change blindness studies have provided further evidence that the immediate memory for unfamiliar faces is highly error-prone. Change blindness refers to the phenomenon that people often fail to notice large changes of visual scenes (see Rensink, 2002; Simons, 2000 for reviews). Simons and Ambinder (2005) suggest that it may result from the difficulty in encoding, retaining and comparing visual information from one glance to the next. Intriguingly, one of the largest changes that people often fail to notice is the *replacement* of identities. For example, 50% of observers failed to notice a change of heads in a picture of two cowboys sitting on a bench (Grimes, 1996). In another study, Levin and Simons (1997) show subjects a video clip, in which one actor is replaced by another person. In more details, an actor is sitting at a desk and then rises to answer the wall-phone. Unknown to the viewers, the actors are exchanged during this sequence. Although subjects were able to provide detailed descriptions of this sequence after viewing the video clip, two thirds of subjects failed to notice this change in identity.

Subsequently, Simons and Levin (1998) also replicated these change blindness effects in a real-life experiment. In this, an experimenter carrying a map approached pedestrians on a university campus to ask for directions. During conservation, two other people carrying a large door seemingly inadvertently passed between them, and the experimenter was replaced by another person (see Figure 3). Surprisingly, more than 50% of pedestrians failed to notice this replacement, and continued the conversation as if nothing had happened. Moreover, when they were asked if they had noticed anything unusual, they often only reported that "*the people carrying the door were rude*" (p. 646). Importantly, in spite of this alarming fallibility, people usually over-estimate their ability to detect changes, specifically changes in identity. Levin, Momen, Drivdahl and Simons (2000) termed this over-estimation "*change blindness blindness*", and described it as a meta-cognitive error.

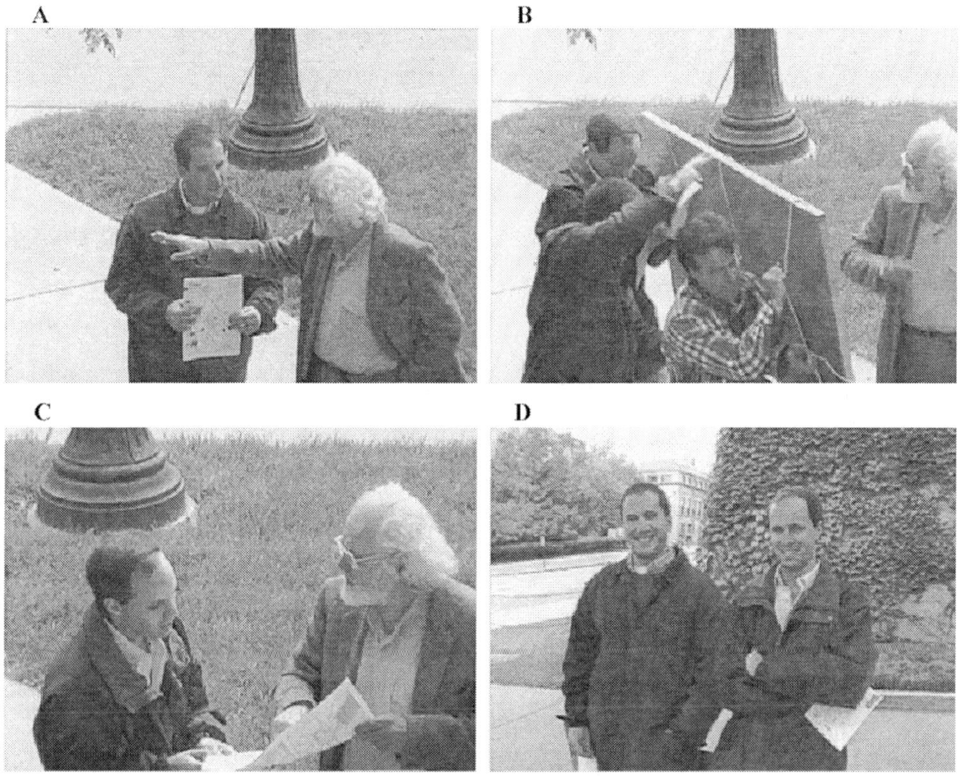

Figure 3. Change blindness of identity replacement.

Levin, Simons, Angelone and Chabris (2002) replicated the change blindness of identities using another real-life scenario, but with no distraction (e.g. giving direction) or unusual disruption (e.g. the door). This time, an experimenter approached participants and asked them if they would like to participate in a psychology experiment. The participants were given a consent form to read and sign. The experimenter then took the forms and briefly disappeared behind a counter, where the replacement was made. A second person then rose and handed the participants a packet of questions and continued conversation. Although the original experimenter and the replaced person had similar clothes, they were dissimilar in their facial appearance. However, three-quarter of participants failed to notice this change in identity. In a further experiment, Levin et al (2002) examine the relationship between recognition memory and change detection with a real-life person change. Participants who missed the identity change failed to identify both the pre- and post- change targets (37% and 32%, respectively) from a 4-person line-up. Notably, this finding does not support the rather simple *over-writing* hypothesis of change blindness (see Simons, 2000 for a review), as there was no advantage for recognizing the post-change target. On the other hand, Participants who have noticed the change correctly identified both the pre- and post- change targets (81% and 73%, respectively) above chance levels. Consequently, Levin et al (2002) conclude that the inability to detect changes in identity is caused by a representation failure. Participants who missed the change, compared to those who noticed it, were more likely to insufficiently represent both targets. This conclusion was confirmed by a subsequent study (Angelone, Levin and Simons, 2003).

The four strands of research reviewed so far in this chapter – the low levels of face recognition memory, the fallibility of eye-witness identification, the poor immediate face memory, and the inability to detect changes in identities – provide convincing evidence that unfamiliar face memory is quite problematic. Thus, the question that raises itself now is whether these problems rise during the processing of faces into memory or occur during face encoding in the first place? In the next section, therefore, I will review relevent evidence from face perception literature.

ACCURACY OF UNFAMILIAR FACE PERCEPTION

Recent face perception experiments suggest that encoding identity from unfamiliar face images is rather a difficult task. For example, Bruce, Henderson, Greenwood, Hancock, Burton and Miller (1999) showed subjects arrays consisting of a target face above a line-up of 10 faces, in which a different image of the target person could or could not be included (see Figure 4). The subjects' task was to decide whether or not the target face was present, and if so to pick the correct match. Performance on this task was *surprisingly* poor. When the target was present, subjects picked the right person on only about 70% of trials (hits), whereas they incorrectly decided that the target was not present on roughly 20% of occasions (misses) and picked a wrong person on roughly 10% of trials (misidentifications). When the target was absent, subjects still choose a person from the line-up on roughly 30% of trials (false positives), despite knowing that half of all arrays would not contain the target. Intriguingly, there was dissociation between performance on target-present and target-absent arrays. For example, Megreya and Burton (2007) presented subjects with the normal 1-in-10 face matching task, in which the targets were present only in the half of the arrays. Immediately after completing this task, subjects were presented with an identical task, except that targets that had been seen in target-present trials in the first task were now seen in target-absent trials. Similarly, targets seen in target-absent trials in the first task were now seen in target-present trials. The results showed no reliable association between hits and FPs in matching the faces within *and* across both sets, suggesting that faces that were easy to match in target-present arrays did not retain this advantage in target-absent trials.

In fact, the difficulty of matching unfamiliar faces has been replicated under different task constraints. For example, it persists when the targets are always present in all arrays (Burton, Miller, Bruce, Hancock, and Henderson, 2001; Bruce et al., 1999), or when the heavy demands of the 1 in 10 arrays were reduced to a 1 in 2 task (Henderson, Bruce, and Burton, 2001) or to simple match/mismatch pairs (Bindemann, Avetisyan, and Blackwell, 2010; Burton, White, and McNeil, 2010; Bruce, Henderson, Newman, and Burton, 2001; Henderson et al, 2001; Megreya and Burton, 2006b and 2007; 2008; Megreya and Bindemann, 2009; Megreya, Bindemann, and Havard, 2011), in which there was also no relationship between performance on match and mismatch pairs. Importantly, this poor face matching performance has been replicated using rather different face matching databases including British police officers (Bruce et al., 1999), British university students (Burton et al., 2010), and Egyptian university undergraduates (Megreya and Burton, 2008). Figure 5 shows examples of face matching pairs from these databases. Therefore, the difficulty of matching unfamiliar faces is not *artificial* to any characteristics of face matching database.

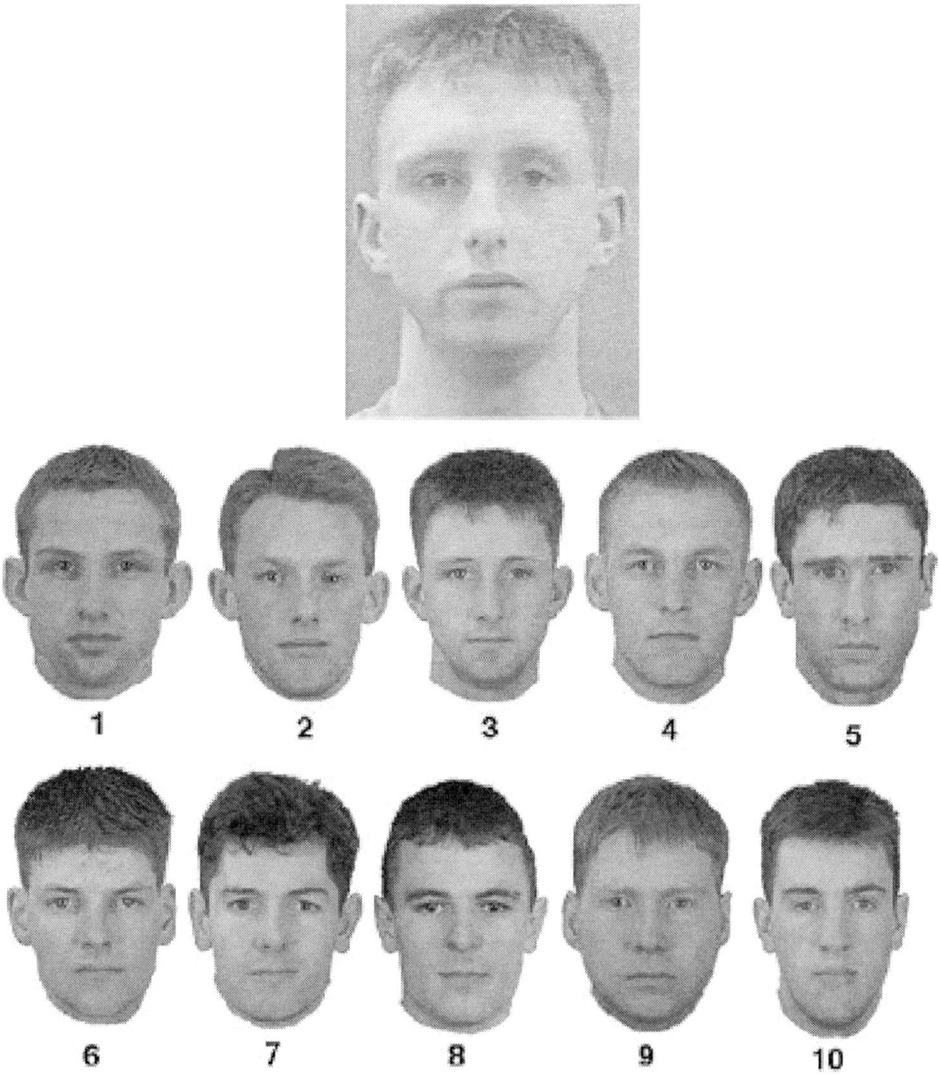

Figure 4a. An example of Bruce's et al (1999) face matching arrays.

This level of face matching performance is particularly striking, because the arrays used in these face matching databases were designed in several dimensions to optimize subjects' performance.

For instance, there was no memory load and no time constraints. Moreover, all images were taken in good lighting, from a very similar full-face pose, on the same day and under the same conditions, thereby eliminating any transient differences in hairstyle, weight, age or health. In fact, the biggest difference between these face images was that they were taken with different cameras.

Target stills were taken from a high quality video camera, whereas the line-up images were photographs captured with a high quality studio camera. According to Bruce et al (1999), this causes some superficial differences in the quality and the general appearance of faces that makes matching difficult.

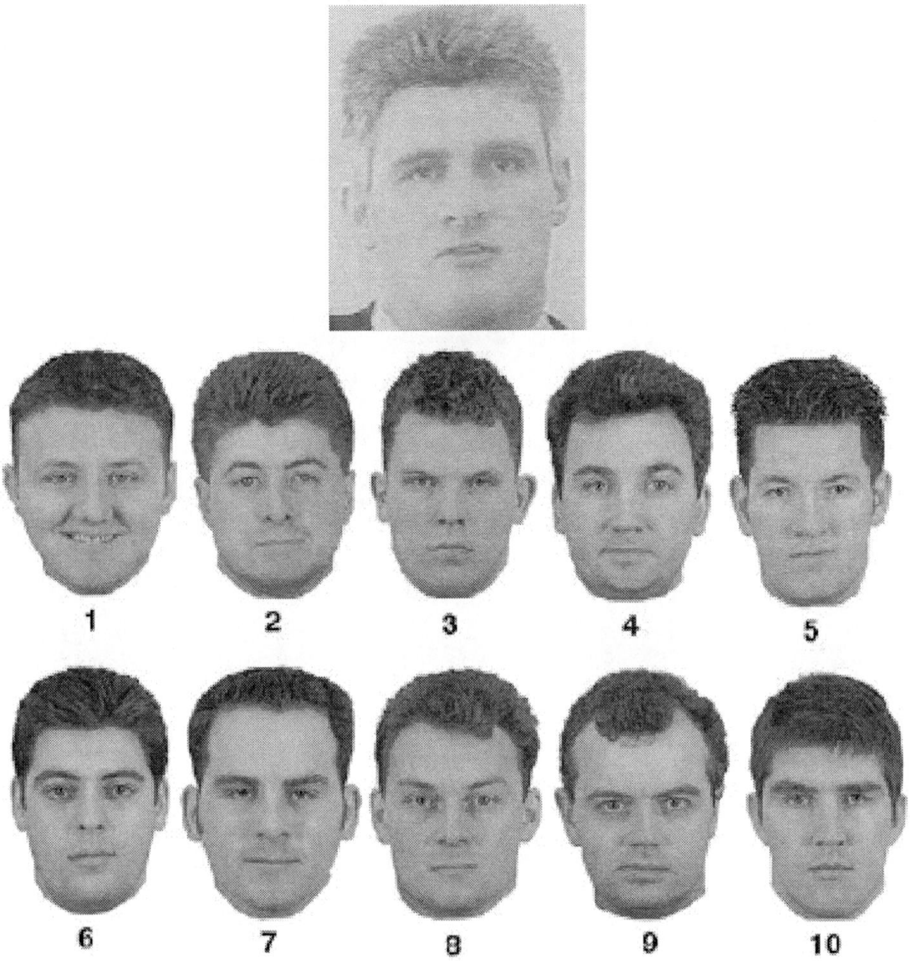

Figure 4b. An example of Bruce's et al (1999) face matching arrays.

To this point, Hancock et al (2000) suggest that matching unfamiliar faces does not engage processes specializing on face perception (which are used for the processing of familiar faces), but it employs mechanisms that are used for matching simple visual patterns and that do not require any domain-specific expertise. Consistently, Megreya and Burton (2006b) found that the best predictor for matching upright unfamiliar faces was matching inverted faces, regardless of whether they were familiar or unfamiliar. Notably, turning the faces upside down *disproportionately* impairs recognition (Yin, 1969). Indeed, faces suffer considerable performance deficits, across a number of measures, when inverted. For example, it has been suggested that this might reflect a disruption of the processes normally engaged in face recognition, and particularly configural processing (Bartlett and Searcy, 1993; Farah, Drain andTanaka, 1995; Freire, Lee and Symons, 2000; Rhodes, Brake and Atkinson, 1993; Searcy and Bartlett, 1996; Tanaka and Farah, 1993; Tanaka and Sengco, 1997; Young, Hellawell and Hay, 1987). For this reason, inverted faces are thought to be processed in a manner more similar to the general object processing system than to the normal face recognition system (de Gelder and Rouw, 2000; Farah, Wilson, Drain and Tanaka, 1995; Haxby, Ungerleider, Clark, Schouten, Hoffman and Martin, 1999; Moscovitch, Winocur and Behrmann, 1997). Therefore, the strong positive correlation between matching upright and inverted faces suggests that faces in the unfamiliar face matching task are treated as "images" or "simple visual patterns", and matched on this basis without domain-specific expertise (Megreya and Burton, 2006b; 2007).

Figure 5. Examples of match/mismatch pairs from different face matching databases: Bruce's et al (1999) top; Burton's et al (2010) Middle; Megreya and Burton (2008) bottom.

Outside the laboratory, the difficulty of matching unfamiliar faces has also been first demonstrated by Kemp and associates in a real-life scenario. Kemp, Towell and Pike (1997) examined the accuracy of identity verification of people bearing photo-credit cards. The experiment was run in a genuine supermarket setting, and participants were six highly experienced cashiers, who were asked to verify the identities of shoppers to decide whether to accept or reject their credit cards. Each shopper had four credit cards: (i) an unchanged appearance card, which contains an image showing the same general appearance of the shopper as on the day of shopping; (ii) changed appearance cards, which includes an image of the shopper with a minor paraphernalia such as the addition or removal of eyeglasses; (iii) matched foil cards, which contains an image of a different person who was previously judged to look like the shopper; and (iv) unmatched foil cards, which includes an image of a different person who was previously judged to be dissimilar to the shopper. All cards were produced by a credit card manufacturer, and were very similar to the normal credit cards except that they include a small 2cm x 2cm photographs. The photographs were taken by a Polaroid passport camera a few days prior to the experiment, and were presented in color, and full-face view. Surprisingly, cashiers falsely accepted 64% of matched foil cards and 34% of unmatched foil cards, forcing Kemp et al. (1997) to conclude that security would not be enhanced by the introduction of photo-credit cards.

More recently, Megreya and Burton (2008) examined how well Egyptian participants could match their own-race faces seen "live" or in static video images using a 1 in 10 matching task (see Figure 6). Participants' performance in both conditions was very low. When a target was present, participants picked the correct face on only roughly 70% of occasions. When it was absent, they identified a wrong match on about 35% of occasions. Importantly, there is no advantage for matching live faces as compared to matching photos. Rather, it appears that there is quite high correspondence between the faces when presented as photos or live. In a further experiment, Megreya and Burton (2008) reduced this 1-in-10 face matching procedure to a simple match/mismatch task using live versus static faces. In the live condition, participants are simply shown a person and an image at the same time, and they are asked whether the image matches the person. In the static image condition, participants are shown two different images, and they are asked whether they are the same person. For overall accuracy, participants made over 15% errors in both match and mismatch trials. In fact, this is a very high rate. For example, those checking photo-IDs in security settings would not probably find this an acceptable error rate. When performance on match and mismatch trails was separately analyzed, there was a response bias in the live condition, such that participants tended to claim that two faces match. Interestingly, this bias was also reported by Kemp et al (1997) in their supermarket photo-ID study. Furthermore, the fallibility of matching a real face to a recent and high-quality image has also been replicated by Davis and Valentine (2009) using British faces. Therefore, a significant part of the problem of eyewitness memory may involve problems of unfamiliar face encoding in the first place (Megreya and Burton, 2008).

The face matching tests described for far are all devised from images of faces belonging to the same race as the subjects. However, there are many great situations where people routinely make face-matching decisions to individuals of another race. This is particularly prevalent in international airport security, and people perform this task routinely as part of their daily work in many forensic and security settings. Megreya, White, and Burton (in press) have recently examined the ability to match other-race compared to the same-race faces. Participants from UK and Egypt were presented with a set of 1 in 10 face matching arrays, which consisted of unfamiliar British or Egyptian faces. In addition, the targets were either presented upright or inverted. The results replicated the other-race effect using this face matching task. This effect refers to the phenomenon that people recognize faces of their own race significantly better than those of other races (for a meta-analysis, see Meissner and Brigham, 2001). Indeed, Egyptian participants matched their own-race faces more accurately than British faces, whereas British participants matched their own-race faces more accurately than Egyptian ones. Interestingly, the other-race effect was divergent between British and Egyptian subjects as a function of whether targets were present in the line-ups or not. UK participants showed the other race effect only when targets were absent from the line-ups, showing a problem of cross-identity differentiation. On the other hand, Egyptian subjects showed the other-race effect only when targets were present in the arrays, showing a problem of within-identity differentiation. Thus, the separate analyses of subjects' performance on target-present and target-absent trials were successful in picking up different components of the other-race effect, confirming the dissociation of hits and FPs (Megreya and Burton, 2007). Furthermore, the other-race effect significantly interacted with the face inversion effect, keeping with the same pattern of divergence between British and Egyptian subjects on hits and FPs. UK subjects showed a larger inversion effect for their own-race faces only when targets were absent from the line-ups. On the other hand, Egyptian participants revealed a larger inversion effect for their own-race faces, but only when targets were present in the arrays. This interaction confirmed the suggestion that own-race faces are processed configurally, whereas other-race faces are processed featurally (Michel, Caldera and Rossion, 2006a; Michel, Rossion, Han, Chung, and Caldera, 2006b; Rhodes, Brake, and Taylor, 1989; Tanaka, Kiefer and Bukach, 2004).

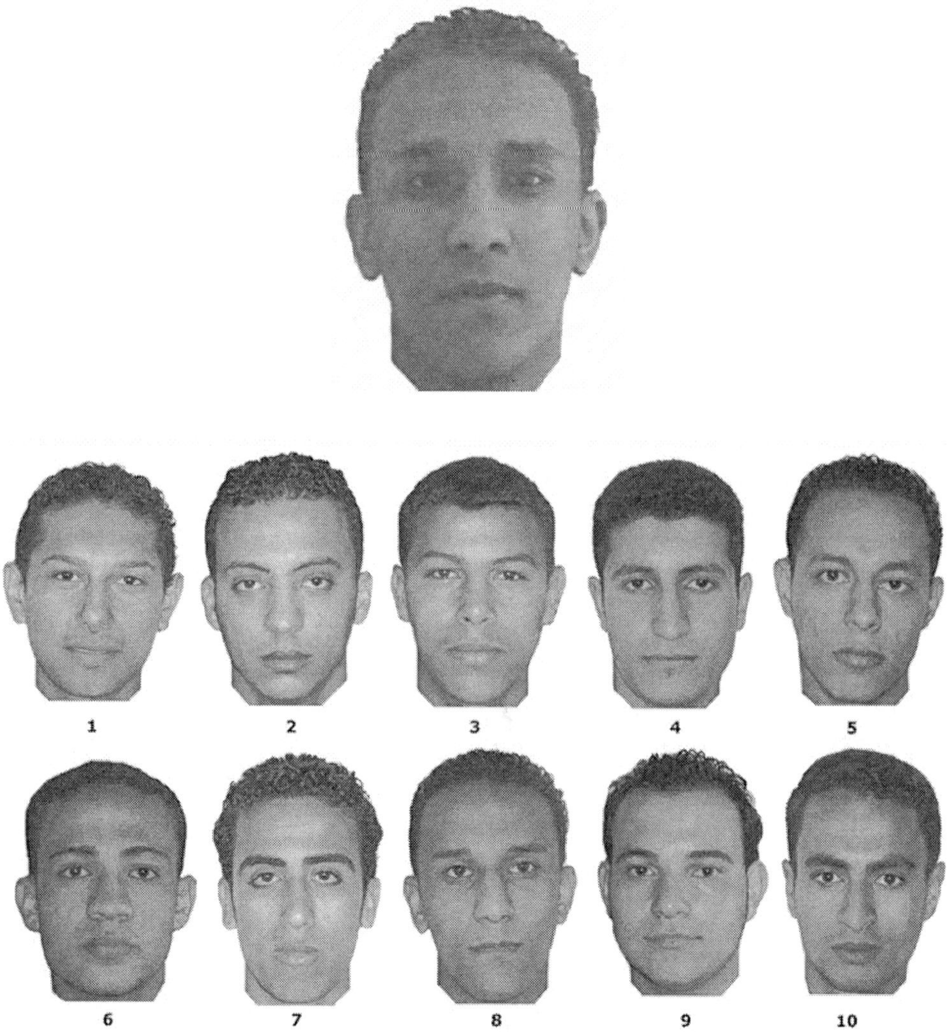

Figure 6a. An example of the Egyptian face matching arrays.

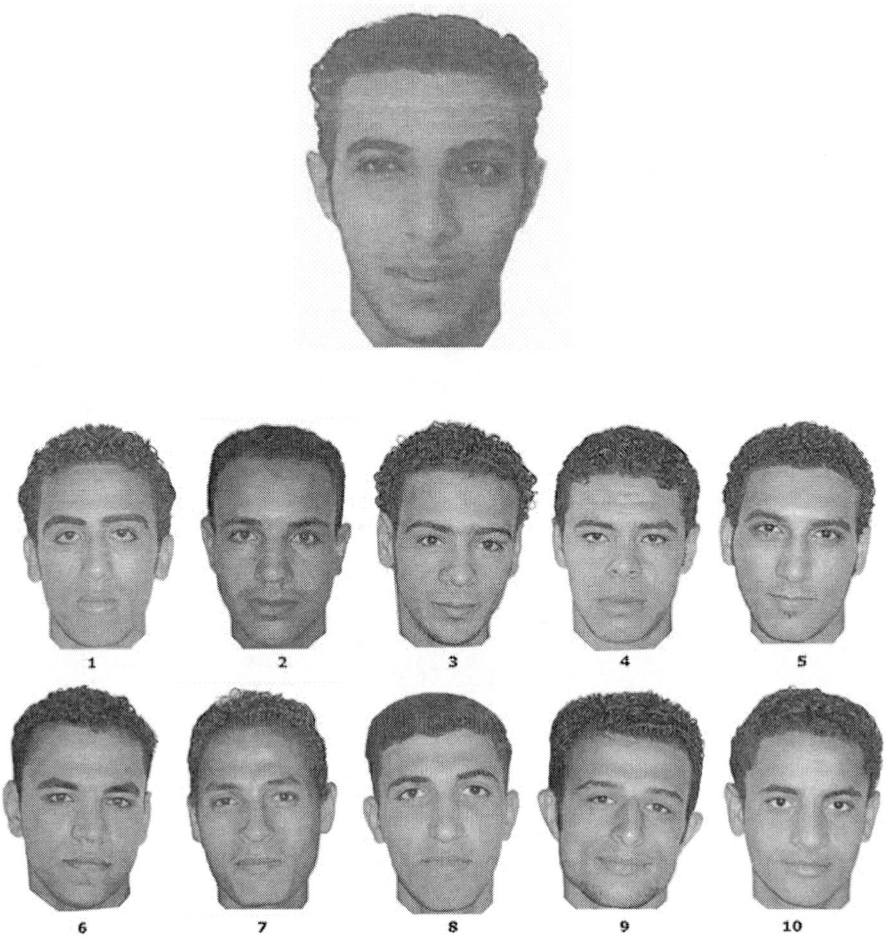

Figure 6b. An example of the Egyptian face matching arrays.

Our recent research further addressed some cross-cultural differences between British and Egyptian observers in face perception. For example, Megreya and Bindemann (2009) examined the ability of Egyptian and British adults to match the internal and external features of unfamiliar Egyptian and British faces. Egyptian observers showed an internal-feature advantage for Egyptian *and* British (Caucasian) faces, while British participants consistently showed an external-feature advantage for all of these face stimuli. Megreya and Bindemann (2009) attributed these cross-cultural differences to the extensive experience of Egyptian adults at recognizing female faces with headscarves, which are commonly worn in Egypt (and in many other countries) and completely cover external facial features. This so-called headscarf effect has been recently confirmed in a subsequent experiment using eye-witness identification paradigm (Megreya, Memon, and Havard, in press).

Megreya and Havard (2001) reported a further difference between British and Egyptian participants in face perception. They found a left face matching bias using both native readers of left-to-right English scripts (British) and native readers of right-to-left Arabic scripts (Egyptian). However, the magnitude of the bias was almost three times stronger amongst the British participants. Accordingly, they suggested that the interaction between the right hemisphere dominance and scanning habits is important for the well-established leftward face processing bias (e.g., Butler and Harvey, 2008; Coolican, Eskes, McMullen and Lecky, 2008; Failla, Sheppard and Bradshaw, 2003).

Individual Differences in Unfamiliar Face Recognition

Although the recognition of unfamiliar faces is generally poor, there are quite large individual differences. For example, Woodhead and Baddeley (1981) reported that the *d'* scores of unfamiliar face recognition memory ranged from –0.5 to 6.8. In addition, Megreya and Burton (2006b) found that the overall face matching accuracy ranges from 50% to 96%. Research reported several biases in face processing including own-race bias (e.g., Meissner and Brigham, 2001), own-sex bias especially for female faces (e.g., Lewin and Herlitz, 2002; Megreya et al., 2011), and own-age bias (e.g., Wright and Stroud, 2002). However, there are further individual differences among people who are belonging to the same race, sex, and age group.

For example, Woodhead and Baddeley (1981) found that people who were good at face recognition memory were also good at object and scene recognition. Fagan (1985) replicated this positive association, and further reported that face recognition memory correlated positively with intelligence. Furthermore, face memory correlated positively with the speed of processing in infants (Rose, Feldman and Jankowski, 2003), and with perceptual speed in 11 year-olds (Rose and Feldman, 1995). Research examined the relationship between field dependence and face recognition memory produced rather inconclusive results. Witkin, Dyk, Faterson, Goodenough and Karp (1974) predicted that field dependents would be more accurate in face recognition than field independents; as they are giving more attention to the social content of their surroundings. Some findings have supported this prediction (Messick and Damarin, 1964); and some have found the precise converse pattern (Lavrakas, Buri and Mayzner, 1976), while others show no relationship between field dependence and face recognition (Courtois and Mueller, 1982; Ryan and Schooler, 1998).

This inconsistency is also apparent for anxiety. Mueller, Bailis and Goldstein, (1979) found that anxiety predicted false positives (the incorrect identification of new faces as being old), but not hits (the correct identification of new faces as being new). However, Nowicki, Winograd and Millard (1979) found anxiety to predict hits (negatively), but to be uncorrelated with false positives. In addition, Brigham, Maass, Martinez and Whittenberger (1983) found that subjects in a moderate arousal condition made higher hits and lower false positives than those in the high arousal condition. More recently, Mograss, Guillem, and Stickgold (2010) examined individual differences in face recognition memory using habitual short, average, and long sleepers. Mograss et al (2010) found that the short sleepers were more accurate than the average and long ones, and they further reported a negative correlation between face recognition and sleep durations in the short sleepers.

Other research linked between face processing and personality (Li, Tian, Fang, Xu, Li, and Liu, 2010; Saito, Nakamura, Endo, 2005) showed that participants with higher levels of extraversion and emotional stability were more accurate at face recognition than those with higher levels of introversion and neuroticism. Inconsistently, however, other studies found no role for extraversion on face recognition memory (Thompson and Mueller, 1984) and eyewitness identification (Trouvé and Libkuman, 1992; Ward and Loftus, 1985), even though neuroticism consistently had a negative effect on eye-witness identification (Bothwell, Brigham, and Pigott, 1987). In addition, Bate, Parris, Haslam, and Kay (2010) found that participants with high levels of socio-emotional empathy were more accurate, at face recognition memory, than those with low levels. On the other hand, shyness had no effect on eye-witness performance (Pozzulo, Crescini, Lemieux, and Tawfik, 2007).

Megreya and Burton (2006b) found that participants' performance on the 1-in-10 face matching task could be predicted using a variety of cognitive tests including visual-short term memory, perceptual speed, and matching objects. This positive association between matching faces and objects was also replicated by Burton, White, and McNeill (2010). Furthermore, Megreya and Burton (2006b) found that the best predictor of face matching was performance on a version of the same test in which the target face alone or the whole display (the target and the line-up) was presented upside down. In addition, Schretlen, Pearlson, Anthony and Yates (2001) found that performance of normal adults on the Benton Facial Recognition Test (BFRT) correlated positively with perceptual speed and total cerebral volume. Alexander, et al. (1999) found that individual differences in PET activation of the general object perception and attention system predicted the accuracy of face matching.

Accuracy of Familiar Face Recognition

The low level of performance for unfamiliar face recognition is in stark contrast to our excellent ability to recognize familiar faces. In one notable study, Burton, Wilson, Cowan and Bruce (1999) asked subjects to learn some identities from video clips captured by low quality CCTV security camera.

Two thirds of subjects were students, who were either familiar or unfamiliar with the targets, and the remaining subjects were highly experienced police officers, who were also unfamiliar with the targets.

At test, subjects were presented with high quality photographs, half of which showed the targets and half of which showed new persons, and were asked to indicate whether or not each face had been previously seen on video. Subjects were extremely accurate in recognizing persons' faces *only* when the faces belonged to someone familiar. Subjects who were unfamiliar with the targets performed poorly, regardless of whether they were students or police officers.

More recently, Liu, Seetzen, Burton and Chaudhuri (2003) replicated these results with images that were either congruent or incongruent in resolution between study and test phase. Other studies that have compared memory for familiar and unfamiliar faces with high quality images also provide similar results: recognition memory is superior for familiar than for unfamiliar faces (e.g. Klatzky and Forrest, 1984).

Memory for familiar faces is also remarkably robust over long intervals. Bahrick, Bahrick and Wittlinger (1975) conducted a real-life study to examine whether people could recognize familiar faces across long retention intervals, which ranged from 2 weeks to 57 years, using photographs of faces taken from high school yearbooks. They found that graduates could successfully recognize more than 90% of their old classmates, even after retention periods of

15 to 34 years. In fact, 48 years after graduation, subjects could still recognize 73% of their classmates' faces.

Note, however, that the accuracy of memory for familiar faces over such long retention interval seems to be mediated by the *level* of familiarity. Bahrick (1984) examined the ability of college teachers to recognize students of introductory university classes, which lasted for 10 weeks and were held 3-4 times per week. Here teachers could 'only' recognize 69%, 48%, 31%, and 26% of the students after 3 months, and one, four, and eight years, respectively.

Figure 7a. The image-averaging technique using a familiar face. The face at the middle represents the average of John Travola's face.

Therefore, it seems reasonable to suggest that the processing of familiar faces, unlike familiars, does not rely on pictorial representations. The image-averaging technique provides further support for this suggestion. Burton, Jenkens, Hancock, and White (2005) developed new representations based on "averages" of a large number of highly variable images for a familiar face (see Figure 7).

Intriguingly, the quality of the average image improves as more images are used to derive it. Burton et al (2005) found that this image averaging technique improved both the automatic and human face recognition. Importantly, however, this technique was not successful for improving unfamiliar face perception (unpublished data form Mike Burton's Lab). Figure 7 shows examples of averages for a familiar (John Travolta) and unfamiliar (if the reader does not know Mike Burton) faces.

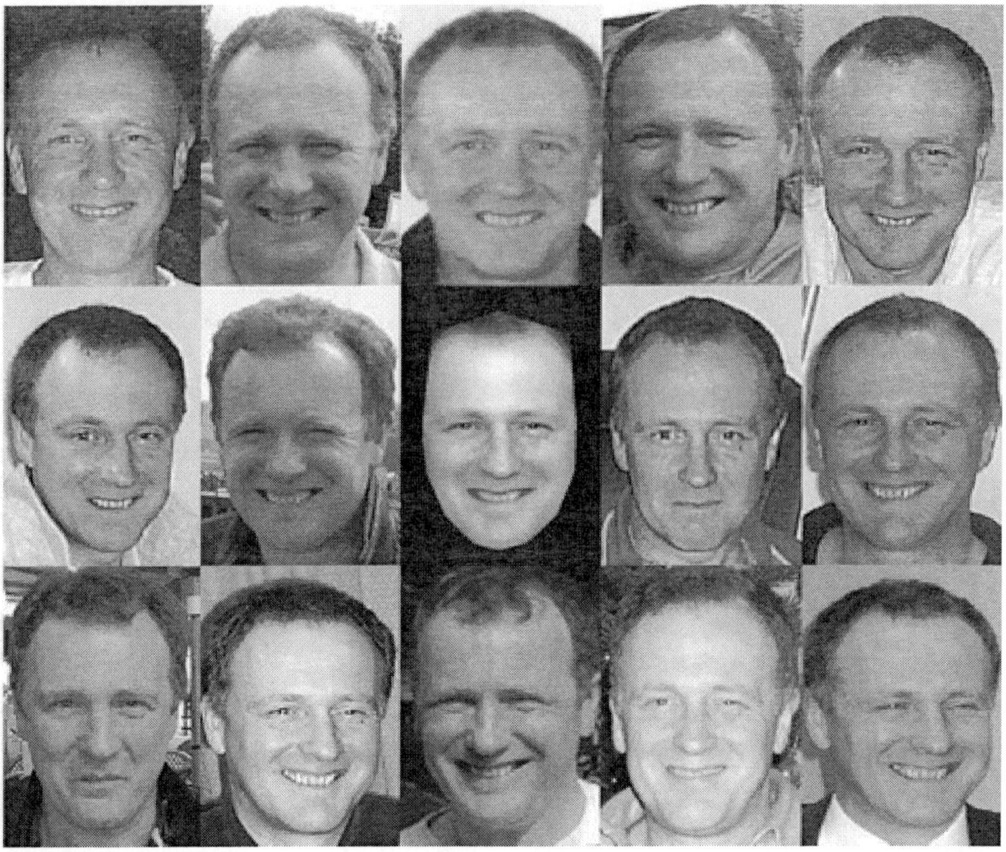

Figure 7b. The image-averaging technique using an unfamiliar face. The face at the middle represents the average of Mike Burton's face.

CONCLUSION

Evidence seems to suggest dissociation between familiar and unfamiliar face processing. The strongest evidence for this argument comes from the double dissociation between familiar and unfamiliar face recognition. On one hand, some brain-damaged patients have a severe impairment in recognizing unfamiliar faces, but they perform normally in recognizing familiar faces. On the other hand, some patients are significantly impaired in recognizing familiar faces, but they retain the ability to recognize unfamiliar faces (e.g., Malone et al., 982). Further evidence for this dissociation is concerned with the accuracy of familiar and unfamiliar face recognition. Several lines of research in memory and perception literature report that the recognition of unfamiliar faces is highly error-prone even under optimal task demands, such as matching high-quality full-face images that are taken on the same day and under the same lighting conditions (e.g., Bruce et al., 1999), and matching the faces of live actors to concurrently shown high-quality full-face images (e.g., Megreya and Burton, 2008). In stark contrast, the recognition of familiar faces is robust even under challenging viewing conditions, such as poor-quality closed-circuit television (CCTV) images taken from difficult viewing angles (e.g., Burton et al., 1999). This contrast suggests that unfamiliar face processing relies on image-based processes, whereas familiar face recognition engages a more specialized type of processing (e.g., Megreya and Burton, 2006b) that transcends superficial characteristics of individual images (Burton et al., 2005).

References

Alexander, G. E., Mentis, M. J., Van Horn, J. D., Grady, C. L., Berman, K. F., Furey, M. L., Pietrini, P., Rapoport, S. I., Schapiro, M. B., and Moeller, J. R. (1999). Individual differences in PET activation of object perception and attention systems predict face matching accuracy. *NeuroReport, 10*, 1965-1971.

Angelone, B. L., Levin, D. T., and Simons, D. J. (2003). The relationship between change detection and recognition of centrally attended objects in motion pictures. *Perception, 32*, 947-962.

Bahrick, H. P. (1984). Memory for people. In J. E. Harris and P. E. Morris (Eds.). *Everyday memory, actions and absent-mindedness* (pp. 19-34). London: Academic Press.

Bahrick, H. P., Bahrick, P. O., and Wittlinger, R. P. (1975). Fifty years of memory for names and faces: A cross-sectional approach. *Journal of Experimental Psychology: General, 104*, 54 – 75.

Bartlett, J.C., and Searcy, J. (1993). Inversion and configuration of faces. *Cognitive Psychology, 25*, 281-316.

Bate, S., Parris, P., Haslam, C., and Kay, J. (2010). Socio-emotional functioning and face recognition ability in the normal population. *Personality and Individual Differences 48*, 239–242.

Begleiter, H., Porjesz, B., and Wang, W. (1995). Event-related brain potentials differentiate priming and recognition to familiar and unfamiliar faces. *Electroencephalography and Clinical Neurophysiology, 94*, 41-49.

Behrman, B. W., and Davey, S. L. (2001). Eyewitness identification in actual criminal cases: An archival analysis. *Law and Human Behavior, 25*, 475-491.

Benton, A. L. (1980). The neuropsychology of face recognition. *American Psychologist, 35*, 176-186.

Bindemann, M., Avetisyan, M., and Blackwell, K. (2010). Finding needles in haystacks: Identity mismatch frequency and facial identity verification. *Journal of Experimental Psychology: Applied, 16*, 378-386.

Bonner, L., Burton, A.M., and Bruce, V. (2003). Getting to know you: How we learn new faces. *Visual Cognition, 10*, 527-536.

Borchard , E. M. (1932). *Convicting the Innocent*. New York. Garden City Pub. Co.

Bothwell, R. K., Brigham, J. C., and Pigott, M. A. (1987). An exploratory study of personality differences in eyewitness memory. *Journal of Social Behavior and Personality, 2*, 335-343.

Brigham, J. C., Maass, A., and Martinez, D. (1983). The effect of arousal on facial recognition. *Basic and Applied Social Psychology, 4*, 279-293.

Bruce, V. (1982). Changing faces: Visual and non-visual coding processes in face recognition. *British Journal of Psychology, 73*, 105-116.

Bruce, V., Henderson, Z., Greenwood, K., Hancock, P.J.B., Burton, A.M., and Miller, P. (1999). Verification of face identities from images captured on video. *Journal of Experimental Psychology: Applied, 5*, 339-360.

Bruce, V., Henderson, Z., Newman, C., and Burton, A.M. (2001). Matching identities of familiar and unfamiliar faces caught on CCTV images. *Journal of Experimental Psychology: Applied, 7*, 207-218.

Bull, R. (1978). Eyewitness also have ears. In M. M. Guneberg, P. E. Morris, and R. N. Sykes (Eds.). *Practical aspects of memory* (pp. 210-218). London: Academic press.

Burton, A. M., Miller, P., Bruce V., Hancock, P. J. B., and Henderson, Z. (2001). Human and automatic face recognition: A comparison across image format. *Vision Research, 41*, 3185-3195.

Burton, A. M., Wilson, S., Cowan, M., and Bruce, V. (1999). Face recognition in poor-quality video: Evidence from security surveillance. *Psychological Science, 10*, 243-248.

Burton, A.M., Jenkins, R., Hancock, P.J.B., and White, D. (2005). Robust representations for face recognition: The power of averages. *Cognitive Psychology, 51,* 256-284.

Burton, A.M., White, D., and McNeill, A. (2010). The Glasgow Face Matching Test. *Behavior Research Methods. 42*, 286-291.

Butler, S. H. and Harvey, M. (2008) Effects of aging and exposure duration on perceptual biases in chimeric face processing. *Cortex, 6,* 665-672.

Clifford, B. R., and Hollin, C. R. (1981). Effects of the type of incident and the number of perpetrators on eyewitness memory. *Journal of Applied Psychology, 66*, 364-370.

Clutterbuck, R., and Johnston, R.A. (2002). Exploring levels of face familiarity by using an indirect face-matching measure. *Perception, 31*, 985-994.

Clutterbuck, R., and Johnston, R.A. (2004). Matching as an index of face familiarity. *Visual Cognition, 11*, 857-869.

Clutterbuck, R., and Johnston, R.A. (2005). Demonstrating how unfamiliar faces become familiar using a face matching task. *European Journal of Cognitive Psychology, 17*, 97-116.

Comish, S. E. (1987). Recognition of facial stimuli following an intervening task involving the Identi-kit. *Journal of Applied Psychology, 72*, 488-491.

Cook, S., and Wilding, J. (1997). Earwitness testimony 2: Voices, faces and context. *Applied Cognitive Psychology, 11*, 527-541.

Coolican, J., Eskes, G. A., McMullen, P. A. and Lecky, E. (2008). Perceptual biases in processing facial identity and emotion. *Brain and Cognition, 66*, 176-187.

Courtois, M. R. and Mueller, J. H. (1981). Target and distracter typicality in facial recognition. *Journal of Applied Psychology, 66*, 639-645.

Davies, G., Shepherd, J., and Ellis, H. (1979). Effects of interpolated Mugshot exposure on accuracy of eyewitness identification. *Journal of Applied Psychology, 64*, 232-237.

Davis, J.P., and Valentine, T. (2009). CCTV on trial: Matching video images with the defendant in the dock. *Applied Cognitive Psychology, 23*, 482-505.

de Gelder, B., and Rouw, R. (2000). Paradoxical configuration effects for faces and objects in prosopagnosia. *Neuropsychologia, 38*, 1271-1279.

Duchaine, B. and Nakayama, K. (2006). The Cambridge Face Memory Test: Results for neurologically intact individuals and an investigation of its validity using inverted face stimuli and prosopagnosic participants. *Neuropsychologia, 44*, 576–585.

Dysart, J. E., Lindsay, R. C. L., Hammond, R., and Dupuis, P. (2001). Mug shot exposure prior to lineup identification: Interference, transference, and commitment effects. *Journal of Applied Psychology, 86*, 1280-1284.

Dysart, J. E., Lindsay, R. C. L., MacDonald, T. K., and Wicke, C. (2002). The intoxicated witness: Effects of alcohol on identification accuracy. *Journal of Applied Psychology, 87,* 170-175.

Ellis, H.D., Shepherd, J.W., and Davies, G.M. (1979). Identification of familiar and unfamiliar faces from internal and external features: Some implications for theories of face recognition. *Perception, 8*, 431-439.

Fagan, J. F. (1984). Recognition memory and intelligence. *Intelligence, 8*, 31-36.

Failla, C. V., Sheppard, D. M. and Bradshaw, J. L. (2003). Age and responding-hand related changes in performance of neurologically normal subjects on the line-bisection and chimeric-faces tasks. *Brain and Cognition, 52*, 353-363.

Farah, M. J. (1996). Is face recognition 'special'? Evidence from neuropsychology. *Behavioural Brain Research, 76*, 181-189.

Farah, M. J., Drain, H. M., and Tanaka, J. W. (1995). What causes the face inversion effect? *Journal of Experimental Psychology: Human Perception and Performance, 21*, 628-634.

Farah, M. J., Wilson, K. D., Drain, H. M., and Tanaka, J. R. (1995). The inverted face inversion effect in prosopagnosia: Evidence for mandatory, face-specific perceptual mechanisms. *Vision Research, 35*, 2089-2093.

Flin, R., Boone, J., Knox, A., and Bull, R. (1992). The effect of a five-month delay on children's and adult's eyewitness memory. *British Journal of Psychology, 83,* 323-336.

Freire, A., Lee, K., and Symons, L. A. (2000). The face-inversion effect as a deficit in the encoding of configural information: Direct evidence. *Perception, 29*, 159-170.

Frowd, C., Bruce, V., McIntyre, A., and Hancock, P. (2007). The relative importance of external and internal features of facial composites. *British Journal of Psychology, 98*, 61-77.

Garrioch, L., and Brimacombe, E. (2001). Lineup administrators' expectations: Their impact on eyewitness confidence. *Law and Human Behavior, 25*, 299-315.

Gibling, F., and Davies, G. (1988). Reinstatement of context following exposure to post-event information. *British Journal of Psychology, 79*, 129-141.

Gobbini, M. I. and Haxby, J. V. (2007). Neural systems for recognition of familiar faces. *Neuropsychologia 45*, 32–41

Goldstein, A. G. (1983). Behavioral scientists' fascination with faces. *Journal of Nonverbal Behavior, 7*, 223-55.

Grimes, J. (1996). On the failure to detect changes in scenes across saccades. In K. Akins (Ed.), *Vancouver studies in cognitive science*: Vol. 5. Perception (pp. 89-110). New York: Oxford University Press.

Hancock, P.J.B., Bruce, V., and Burton, A.M. (2000). Recognition of unfamiliar faces. *Trends in Cognitive sciences, 4*, 330-337.

Haw, R. M., and Fisher, R. P. (2004). Effects of administrator-witness contact on eyewitness identification accuracy. *Journal of Applied Psychology, 89*, 1106-1112.

Haxby, J. V., Ungerleider, L. G., Clark, V. P., Schouten, J. L., Hoffman, E. A., and Martin, A. (1999). The effects of face inversion on activity in human neural system for face and object perception. *Neuron, 22*, 189-199.

Henderson, Z., Bruce, V., and Burton, A. M. (2001) Matching the faces of robbers captured on video. *Applied Cognitive Psychology, 15*, 445-464.

Hochberg, J. and Galper, R. E. (1967). Recognition of faces: 1. An exploratory study. *Psychonomic Science, 9*, 619-620.

Innocence Project (n.d.). Retrieved August 20, 2011, from Innocence Project Website: http://www.innocenceproject.org/.

Jenkins, F., and Davies, G. (1985). Contamination of facial memory through exposure to misleading composite pictures. *Journal of Applied Psychology, 70*, 164-176.

Johnson, M. H., Dziurawiec, S., Ellis, H., and Morton, J. (1991). Newborns preferential tracking of face-likes and its subsequent decline. *Cognition, 40*, 1-19.

Kanwisher, N. (2000). Domain specificity in face perception. *Nature Neuroscience, 3,* 759-763.

Kemp, R., Towell, N., and Pike, G. (1997). When seeing should not be believing: Photographs, credit cards and fraud. *Applied Cognitive Psychology, 11*, 211-222.

Kerstholt, J. H., Raaijmakers, J. G. W., and Valenton, M.J. (1992). The effect of expectation on the identification of known and unknown persons. *Applied Cognitive Psychology, 6,* 173-180.

Klatzky, R. L., and Forrest, F. H. (1984). Recognizing familiar and unfamiliar faces. *Memory and Cognition, 12*, 60-70.

Lavrakas, P. J., Buri, J. R. and Mayzner, M. S. (1976). A perspective on the recognition of other-race faces. *Perception and Psychophysics, 20*, 475-481.

Legge, G. E., Grosmann, C., and Pieper, C. M. (1984). Learning unfamiliar voices. *Journal of Experimental Psychology: Learning, memory and cognition, 10*, 298-303.

Leippe, M. R., wells, G. L., and Ostrom, T. M. (1978). Crime seriousness as a determinant of accuracy in eyewitness identification. *Journal of Applied Psychology, 63,* 345-351.

Leveroni, C. L., Seidenberg, M., Mayer, A. R., Mead, L. A., Binder, J. R., and Rao, S. M. (2000). Neural systems underlying the recognition of familiar and newly learned faces. *Journal of Neuroscience, 20*, 878 – 886.

Levin, D. T., and Simons, D. J. (1997). Failure to detect changes to attended objects in motion pictures. *Psychonomic Bulletin and Review, 4*, 501-506.

Levin, D. T., Simons D. J., Angelone B. L., and Chabris C. F. (2002). Memory for centrally attended changing objects in an incidental real-world change detection paradigm. *British Journal of Psychology, 93,* 289-302.

Li, J., Tian, M., Fang, H., Xu, M., Li, H., and Liu, J. (2010). Extraversion predicts individual differences in face recognition. *Communcation and Integrative Biology, 3*, 295-298.

Li, S. Z. and. Jain, A. K (2005). *Handbook of Face Recognition*. Springer. New York.

Lindsay, R. C. L., and Wells, G. L. (1985). Improving eyewitness identification from lineups: Simultaneous versus sequential lineup presentation. *Journal of Applied Psychology, 70,* 556-564.

Lindsay, R. C. L., Wallbridge, H., and Drennan, D. (1987). Do the clothes make the man? An exploration of the effect of lineup attire on eyewitness identification accuracy. *Canadian Journal of Behavioral Sciences, 19*, 463-477.

Liu, C. H., Seetzen, H., Burton, A. M., and Chaudhuri, A. (2003). Face recognition is robust with incongruent image resolution: Relationship to security video images. *Journal of Experimental Psychology: Applied, 9*, 33-41.

Luus, C. A. E., and Wells, G. L. (1991). Eyewitness identification and the selection of distracters for lineups. *Law and Human Behavior, 15*, 43-57.

Lyle, K. B., and Johnson, M. K. (2004). Effects of verbalization on lineup face recognition in an interpolated inspection paradigm. *Applied Cognitive Psychology, 18*, 393-403.

Maass, A., and Köhnken, G. (1989). Eyewitness identification: Simulating the "weapon effect". *Law and Human Behavior, 13*, 397-408.

Malone, D. R., Morris, H. H., Kay, M. C., and Levin, H. S. (1982). Prosopagnosia: a double dissociation between the recognition of familiar and unfamiliar faces. *Journal of neurology, Neurosurgery and Psychiatry, 45*, 820-822.

Malpass, R. S., and Devine, P. G. (1981). Eyewitness identification: Lineup instructions and the absence of the offender. *Journal of Applied Psychology, 66,* 482-489.

McAllister, H. A., Dale, R. H. I., Bregman, N. J., McCabe, A., and Cotton, C. R. (1993). When eyewitnesses are also earwitnesses: Effects on visual and voice identification. *Basic and Applied Social Psychology, 14*, 161-170.

McNeil, J. E., and Warrington, E. K. (1993). Prosopagnosia: A face-specific disorder. *Quarterly Journal of Experimental Psychology, 46A*, 1-10.

Megreya, A. M. and Burton, A. M. (2006a). Recognising faces seen alone or with others: When two heads are worse than one. *Applied Cognitive Psychology, 20*, 957-972.

Megreya, A. M., Bindemann, M. and Havard, C. (2011). Sex differences in unfamiliar face identification: Evidence from matching tasks. *Acta Psychologica, 137*, 83-89.

Megreya, A. M., White, D., and Burton, A. M (2011). The other race effect does not rely on memory: evidence from a matching task. *Quarterly Journal of Experimental Psychology, 64*, 1473-1483.

Megreya, A.M. and Bindemann, M. (2009). Revisiting the processing of internal and external features of unfamiliar faces: The headscarf effect. *Perception, 38*, 1831-1848.

Megreya, A.M. and Havard, C. (2011). Left face matching bias: Right hemisphere dominance or scanning habits? *Laterality: Asymmetries of Body, Brain and Cognition, 16*, 75-92.

Megreya, A.M., and Burton, A.M (2007). Hits and false positives in face matching: A familiarity based dissociation. *Perception and Psychophysics, 69,* 1175-1184.

Megreya, A.M., and Burton, A.M (2008). Matching faces to photographs: poor performance in eyewitness memory without the memory. *Journal of Experimental Psychology: Applied, 14*, 364-372.

Megreya, A.M., and Burton, A.M. (2006b). Unfamiliar faces are not faces: Evidence from a matching task. *Memory and Cognition, 34*, 865 – 876.

Megreya, A.M., Memon, A. and Havard, C. (in press). The headscarf effect: Direct evidence from eyewitness identification paradigm.

Meissner, C. A., and Brigham, J. C. (2001). Thirty years of investigating the own-race bias in memory for faces: A meta-analytic review. *Psychology, Public Policy, and Law, 7*, 3-35.

Memon, A., and Bartlett, J. (2002). The effects of verbalization on face recognition in young and older adults. *Applied Cognitive Psychology, 16,* 635-650.

Memon, A., and Bartlett, J. (2002). The effects of verbalization on face recognition in young and older adults. *Applied Cognitive Psychology, 16,* 635-650.

Memon, A., Hope, L. and Bull, R. (2003). Exposure duration: Effects on eyewitness accuracy and confidence. *British Journal of Psychology, 94*, 339-354.

Memon, A., Hope, L., Bartlett, J., and Bull, R. (2002). Eyewitness recognition errors: The effects of Mugshot viewing and choosing in young and old adults. *Memory and Cognition, 30*, 1219-1227.

Messick, S. and Damarin, F. (1964). Cognitive styles and memory for faces. *Journal of Abnormal and Social Psychology, 69,* 313-318.

Michel, C., Caldara, R., and Rossion, B. (2006). Same-race faces are perceived more holistically than other-race faces. *Visual Cognition, 14*, 55-73.

Michel, C., Rossion, B., Han, J., Chung, C., and Caldara, R. (2006). Holistic processing is finely tuned for faces of one's own race. *Psychological Science, 17*, 608-615.

Mograss, M. A., Guillem, F. and Stickgold, R. (2010). Individual differences in face recognition memory: Comparison among habitual short, average, and long sleepers. *Behavioural Brain Research 208*, 576-583.

Mohr, B., Landgrebe, A., and Schweinberger, S. R. (2002). Interhemispheric cooperation for familiar but not unfamiliar face processing. *Neuropsychologia, 40*, 1841-1848.

Moscovitch, M., Winocur, G., and Behrmann, M. (1997). What is special about face recognition? Nineteen experiments on a person with visual object agnosia and dyslexia but normal face recognition. *Journal of Cognitive Neuroscience, 9,* 555-604.

Mueller, J. H., Bailis, K. L., and Goldstein, A. G. (1979). Depth of processing and anxiety in facial recognition. *British Journal of Psychology, 70,* 511-515.

Münsterberg, H. (1908). *On the witness stand*. New York: Doubleday, Page and Company.

Nachson, I., and Shechory, M. (2002). Effect of inversion on the recognition of external and internal facial features. *Acta Psychologica, 109*, 227-238.

Neuner, F., and Schweinberger, S. R. (2000). Neuropsychological impairments in the recognition of faces, voices, and personal names. *Brain and Cognition, 44*, 342-366.

Nickerson, R. S. (1965). Short-term memory for complex meaningful visual configurations: A demonstration of capacity. *Canadian Journal of Psychology, 19*, 155-160.

Nowicki, S., Winograd, E., and Millard, B. A. (1979). Memory for faces: A social learning analysis. *Journal of Research in Personality, 13*, 460-468.

Osborne, C.D., and Stevenage, S.V. (2008). Internal feature saliency as marker of familiarity and configural processing. *Visual Cognition, 16*, 23-43.

Patterson, K. E. (1978). Person recognition: More than a pretty face. In M. M. Guneberg, P. E. Morris, and R. N. Sykes (Eds.). *Practical aspects of memory* (pp. 227-235). London: Academic press.

Phillips, M., McAuliff, B., Kovera, M., and Cutler, B. (1999). Double-blind photoarray administration as a safeguard against investigator bias. *Journal of Applied Psychology, 84,* 940-951.

Pozzulo, J. D., Crescini, C., Lemieux, J. M. T., and Tawfik, A. (2007). The effect of shyness on eyewitness memory and the susceptibility to misinformation. *Personality and Individual Differences, 43*, 1656–1666.

Pryke, S., Lindsay, R. C. L., Dysart, J. E., Dupuis, P. (2004). Multiple independent identification decisions: A method of calibrating eyewitness identification. *Journal of Applied Psychology, 89*, 73-84.

Read, J.D., Vokey, J. R., and Richard, H. (1990). Changing photos of faces: Effects of exposure duration and photo similarity on recognition and the accuracy-confidence relationship. *Journal of Experimental Psychology: Learning, Memory, and Cognition, 16*, 870-882.

Rensink, R. A. (2002). Change blindness. *Annual Review of Psychology, 53*, 245-277.

Rhodes, G., Brake, S., and Atkinson, A. P. (1993). What's lost in inverted faces? *Cognition, 47*, 25-57.

Rhodes, G., Brake, S., and Taylor, K. (1989). Expertise and configural coding in face recognition. *British Journal of Psychology, 80*, 313-331.

Rose, S. A. and Feldman, J. F. (1995). Prediction of IQ and specific cognitive abilities at 11 years from infancy measures. *Developmental Psychology, 31,* 685-696.

Rose, S. A., Feldman, J. F. and Jankowski, J. J. (2003). Infant visual recognition memory: Independent contributions of speed and attention. *Developmental Psychology, 39*, 563-571.

Rossion, B., Schiltz, C., Robaye, L., Pirenne, D., and Crommelinck, M. (2001). How does the brain discriminate familiar and unfamiliar faces? A PET study of face categorical perception. *Journal of Cognitive Neurosciences, 13,* 1019 – 1034.

Ryan, R. S. and Schooler, J. W. (1998). Whom do words hurt? Individual differences in susceptibility to verbal overshadowing. *Applied Cognitive Psychology, 12,* 105-125.

Saito, T., Nakamura, T. and Endo, T. (2005). Big five personality factors related to face recognition. *The Japanese journal of psychology, 75*, 517-522.

Schooler, J. W., and Engstler-Schooler, T. Y. (1990). Verbal overshadowing of visual memories: Some things are better left unsaid. *Cognitive Psychology, 22*, 36-71.

Schretlen, D. J., Pearlson, G. D., Anthony, J. C. and Yates, K. O. (2001). Determinants of Benton Facial Recognition Test performance in normal adults. *Neuropsychology, 15,* 405-410.

Searcy, J. H., and Bartlett, J. C. (1996). Inversion and processing of component and spatial-relational information in faces. *Journal of Experimental Psychology: human Perception and Performance, 22,* 904-915.

Simons, D. J. (2000). Current approaches to change blindness. *Visual Cognition, 7*, 1-15.

Simons, D. J., and Ambinder, M. S. (2005). Change blindness: Theory and consequences. *Current Directions in Psychological Science, 14*, 44-48.

Simons, D. J., and Levin, D. T. (1998). Failure to detect changes to people during a real-world interaction. *Psychonomic Bulletin and Review, 5*, 644-649.

Steblay, N., Dysart, J., Fulero, S. and Lindsay, R.C.L. (2003). Eyewitness accuracy rates in police showup and lineup presentation: A meta-analytic comparison. *Law and Human Behavior, 27*, 523-540.

Tanaka, J. W., and Farah, M. J. (1993). Parts and wholes in face recognition. *Quarterly Journal of Experimental Psychology, 46A,* 225-245.

Tanaka, J. W., and Sengco, J. A. (1997). Features and their configuration in face recognition. *Memory and Cognition, 25*, 583-592.

Tanaka, J., Kiefer, M., and Bukach, C. M. (2004). A holistic account of the own-race effect in face recognition: Evidence from a cross-cultural study. *Cognition, 93*, B1-B9.

Thompson, W. B. and Mueller, J. H. (1984). Face Memory and Hemispheric Preference: Emotionality and Extraversion. *Brain and Cognition, 3*, 239-248.

Tranel, D., Damasio, A. R., and Damasio, H. (1988). Intact recognition of facial expression, gender and age in patients with impaired recognition of face identity. *Neurology, 38,* 690-696.

Trouvé, R. J., and Libkuman, T. M. (1992). Eyewitness performance of personality types as a function of induced arousal. *American Journal of Psychology, 105*, 417-433.

Want, S.C., Pascalis, O., Coleman, M., and Blades M. (2003). Recognisizing people from the inner or outer parts of their faces: Developmental data concerning 'unfamiliar' faces. *British Journal of Psychology, 21*, 125.

Ward, R. A., and Loftus, E. F. (1985). Eyewitness performance in different psychological types. *The Journal of General Psychology, 112*, 191-200.

Warrington, E. K., and James, M. (1967). An experimental investigation of facial recognition in patients with unilateral cerebral lesions. *Cortex, 3,* 317-326.

Witkin, H. A., Dyk, R. B., Faterson, H. F., Goodenough, D. R., and Karp, S. A. (1974). *Psychological Differentiation: Studies of development.* Sec. Ed. New York. John Wiley and Sons.

Woodhead, M. M. and Baddeley, A. D. (1981). Individual differences and memory for faces, pictures, and words. *Memory and Cognition, 9*, 368-370.

Wright, D. B., and Stroud, J. N. (2002). Age differences in lineup identification accuracy: people are better with their own age. *Law and Human Behavior, 26*, 641–654.

Yarmey, A. D., Yarmey, A. L., and Yarmey, M. J. (1994). Face and voice identifications in showups and lineups. *Applied Cognitive Psychology, 8*, 453-464.

Yin, R. K. (1969). Looking at upside-down faces. *Journal of Experimental Psychology, 81*, 141-145.

Young, A. W., Hellawell, D., and Hay, D. C. (1987). Configurational information in face recognition. *Perception, 16,* 747-759.

Young, A. W., Newcombe, F., de Haan, E. H. F., Small, M., and Hay, D. C., (1993). Face perception after brain injury: selective impairments affecting identity and expression. *Brain, 116*, 941-959.

Young, A.W., Hay, D.C., McWeeny, K.H., Flude, B.M., and Ellis, A.W. (1985). Matching familiar and unfamiliar faces on internal and external features. *Perception, 14*, 737-746.

In: Face Recognition
Editors: Adamo Quaglia and Calogera M. Epifano
ISBN 978-1-61942-663-4

Chapter 2

EXTENDED 2-D PCA FOR FACE RECOGNITION: ANALYSIS, ALGORITHMS, AND PERFORMANCE ENHANCEMENT

Ana-Maria Sevcenco and Wu-Sheng Lu*
Department of Electrical and Computer Engineering,
University of Victoria, Victoria, Canada

ABSTRACT

Two-dimensional (2-D) principal component analysis (PCA) algorithms for face recognition are an attractive alternative to the traditional one-dimensional (1-D) PCA algorithms because they are able to provide higher accuracy in extracting facial features for human face identification with reduced computational complexity. The improved performance and efficiency are gained largely because the 2-D PCA algorithms treat facial images more naturally and effectively as matrices rather than vectors and, as a result, one can employ a covariance matrix of much reduced-size for analysis and algorithmic development.

This chapter presents an extended 2-D PCA algorithm for improving rate of face recognition. The new algorithm is deduced based on an analysis in which a pair of (rather than a single) covariance matrices are defined and utilized for extracting both row-related and column-related features of facial images. In addition, by incorporating a pre-processing procedure, which was recently developed by the authors based on perfect histogram matching, the performance of the proposed 2-D PCA algorithm can be considerably enhanced. Experimental results are presented to examine the performance of the proposed algorithms and their robustness to noise, face occlusion, and illumination conditions.

Keywords: Principal component analysis, Two-dimensional extension, Perfect histogram matching, Face recognition

* E-mail: wslu@ece.uvic.ca, tel: 250-721-8692, fax: 250-721-6052.

1. INTRODUCTION

Face recognition has been an active area of research in image processing and computer vision for more than two decades and is certainly one of the most successful applications of contemporary image analysis and understanding.

The face is a primary focus of attention in social activities and plays a critical role in conveying identity and emotions (Turk and Pentland 1991). One can recognize a great number of faces throughout his/her lifetime and, even after years of separation, just at a glance one can identify almost instantly familiar faces that have undergone considerable changes due to aging and distractions like glasses and changes in hairstyle and facial hair, demonstrating the amazing robustness of the human visual system (HVS) (Turk and Pentland 1991). It is therefore natural and desirable to develop computer-aided systems that mimics the HVS and can be used to automate the process of face recognition with satisfactory accuracy and improved speed. As a matter of fact, such development had started four decades ago, although the success of the system reported there was rather limited from today's standard.

Extensive research has been conducted by psychophysicists, neuroscientists, and engineers on various aspects of human and machine face recognition, such as whether face perception is a dedicated process (Gauthier and Logothetis 2000), and whether it is done by global or local feature analysis (Bruce et al. 1998). Studies have shown that distinctive faces are better retained in memory and faster recognized than typical faces (Bruce 1988; Bruce et al. 1994). The role of spatial frequency analysis was also examined. In Sergent (1986), it has been observed that gender classification can be successfully accomplished using low-frequency components only, while identification requires the use of high frequency components. Some experiments suggest that memory for faces is highly viewpoint-dependent (Hill et al. 1997), and various lighting conditions make harder to identity even familiar faces (Johnston et al. 1992). In addition, based on neurophysiological studies (Bruce 1988), it seems that analysis of facial expressions is not directly related to face recognition. On the other hand, from a machine recognition point of view, dramatic changes in facial expressions may affect face recognition performance.

Speaking automatic identification systems, we remark that although several other reliable methods of biometric personal identification exist, for example methods based on fingerprint analysis and retinal or iris scans, the success of these methods depends critically on cooperation of the participant. On the other hand, automatic face recognition is often effective independent of the participant's cooperation (Chellappa et al. 1995; Zhao and Yang 1999).

Primarily due to increasing security demands and potential commercial and law enforcement applications, automatic face recognition has been a subject of extensive study in the past several decades (Chellappa et al. 1995; Zhao et al. 2003), and remains to be an active filed of research as of today. As a result, numerous techniques and algorithms for face recognition have been developed, many of them proving effective in one way or another. Nevertheless, it has been realized that constructing satisfactory solutions to automatic face recognition remains to be a challenge. One of the main sources of difficulty has to do with variations in pose, illumination and expression that may occur across the images involved in a face recognition system.

The past two decades have witnessed sustained research endeavors that have led to new methods and algorithms with improved face recognition capability. These include principal component analysis (PCA) (Turk and Pentland 1991; Yang et al. 2004), independent component analysis (ICA) (Bartlett et al. 2002), linear discriminant analysis (LDA) (Etemad and Chellappa 1996), isomaps (Tenenbaum et al. 2000), locally linear embedding (LLE) (Roweis and Saul 2000; Saul and Roweis 2003), Laplacianfaces (He et al. 2005; Niu et al. 2008) based on Laplacian eigenmaps (Belkin and Niyogi 2002; Belkin and Niyogi 2008), and whitenedfaces (Liao et al. 2007).

Numerous PCA-based methods have been developed to improve PCA performance since the original work on PCA (Turk and Pentland 1991). As argued by Bartlett et al. (2002), a considerable amount of information that is useful for face recognition tasks may be contained in the higher-order relations among pixels. On the other hand, the PCA considers only second-order statistical information, taking into account the global structure of the image. In (Chen and Zhu 2004; Gottumukkal and Asari 2004; Hsieh and Tung 2009; Tan and Chen 2005), the original PCA is enhanced by taking into account local features by sub-pattern techniques, partitioning the original face images into several smaller sub-patterns. Moreover, the method of Hsieh and Tung (2009) combines an image partition technique with vertically centered PCA and whitened horizontally centered PCA to obtain a novel hybrid approach with recognition performance superior to the traditional methods.

A two-dimensional (2-D) approach was proposed by Yang et al. (2004). It consists of an image projection technique in which images are treated as matrices instead of vectors as in the original PCA (Turk and Pentland 1991). This method leads not only to better recognition rates, but also to improved computationally efficiency. In this chapter, we take a close look at the 2-D PCA algorithm (Yang et al. 2004) and propose an extended 2-D PCA (E-2DPCA) algorithm that utilizes a pair of covariance matrices to extract both row-related and column-related features of facial images. In conjunction with our extension are two new criteria for face classification. In addition, we describe several pre-processing techniques that can be incorporated into a PCA-based system for performance enhancement. These include perfect histogram matching (PHM), wavelet based image denoising, and a simple technique to deal with face occlusions. Experimental results are presented to demonstrate the performance of the proposed algorithms and their robustness to noise, face occlusion and various illumination conditions. The chapter is organized as follows. Section 2 introduces some background material related to the standard PCA algorithm (Turk and Pentland 1991) and its 2-D version (Yang et al. 2004). In Section 3, an extended 2-D PCA along with new classification criteria is proposed. Several pre-processing techniques are presented in Section 4 where a hybrid face recognition system which integrates some pre-processing techniques into the extended 2D-PCA is also proposed. Performance evaluations of the proposed E-2DPCA technique and comparisons with standard PCA and 2-D PCA methods are presented in Section 5, followed by evaluations of PHM E-2DPCA face recognition system's performance.

2. An Overview of PCA and 2-D PCA Methods

2.1. PCA

The PCA (Turk and Pentland 1991) is an eigenface-based approach for face recognition that seeks to capture the variation in a collection of face images and uses this information to encode and compare images of individual faces. Over the years, the conventional PCA has inspired a great deal of research interest in the field that in turn has led to a number of new PCA-based methods and algorithms with improved performance.

Given a data set $\mathcal{D}$, also called training set, of M face images of size $m \times n$ belonging to K individuals (classes), the PCA algorithm proposed by Turk and Pentland (1991) starts by transforming each image into a column vector Γ_i by concatenating the image rows. Next, an average face is computed as $\Psi = (\sum_{i=1}^{M} \Gamma_i)/M$, and subtracted from each column vector Γ_i to construct vector Φ_i as $\Phi_i = \Gamma_i - \Psi$. The resulting column vectors are employed to form data matrix A which is in turn used to construct the covariance matrix $C = AA^T$. It follows that

$$C = \frac{1}{M}\sum_{i=1}^{M}(\Gamma_i - \Psi)(\Gamma_i - \Psi)^T. \tag{1}$$

Note that C is a matrix of large size for typical image sizes. Instead of directly computing the eigenvectors u_i and eigenvalues λ_i of C, which usually is an intractable task for typical image sizes, the eigenvectors v_i and eigenvalues λ_i of a much reduced-size matrix $L = A^T A$ are computed first, and the normalized eigenvectors of matrix C are then found as

$$u_i = \lambda_i^{-1/2} A v_i \text{ for } i = 1, \dots, M. \tag{2}$$

These eigenvectors u_i are called eigenfaces of data set $\mathcal{D}$. Eigenfaces extract relevant facial information, which may or may not match human perception of face features such as eyes, nose, and lips, by capturing statistical variation between face images. Therefore, eigenfaces may be regarded as a set of features which offers a characterization of the global variation among the analyzed face images. Other advantages of using eigenfaces are efficient image representation using a small number of parameters and reduced computational and dimensional complexity (Turk and Pentland 1991; Zhao et al. 2003).

For face recognition purposes, eigenfaces are utilized to examine an input image Γ (in the form of a column vector) as whether or not it is a face image and, if it is, whether or not it is a member of a class or a stranger (non-member). The p most significant eigenfaces associated with the p largest eigenvalues of C form an orthogonal basis of a p-dimensional *face space* in $\mathbb{R}^{mn}$. The matrix composed of these p eigenfaces is denoted by $\widetilde{U}$. The value of p can be determined based on the distribution of eigenvalues λ_i, or as a certain percentage of the available number of eigenvectors u_i. The face images in the training set as well as the test image are projected onto the face space to yield the so-called pattern vectors of dimension p. A key point of PCA is that p is considerably smaller than the dimension of a face image, yet a pattern vector is able to catch global features of the associated facial image. The PCA carries out face recognition tasks by evaluation and comparison of the pattern vector of a test face image with those in the training set, as follows.

A p-dimensional pattern vector is obtained as $\Omega = \widetilde{U}^T \Phi$ where $\Phi = \Gamma - \Psi$, and is utilized to project the input image onto the face space as $\Phi_f = \widetilde{U}\widetilde{U}^T \Phi = \widetilde{U}\Omega$. The Euclidean distance d_0 between the input image Γ and the face space is computed as

$$d_0 = \|\Phi - \Phi_f\|_2. \tag{3}$$

If distance d_0 is below a chosen threshold δ_0, the input image Γ is classified as a face image, otherwise it is classified as a non-face image.

Furthermore, if Γ turns out to be a face image, it can be classified as a class member or non-member face. If Γ is a member, then the class it belongs is identified. These are achieved by (i) evaluating $d_k = \|\Omega - \Omega_k\|_2$ for $k = 1, \ldots, K$ where the class pattern vector Ω_k is calculated as $\Omega_k = (\sum_{i=1}^{L} \Omega_k{}^{(i)})/L$ with $\Omega_k{}^{(i)} = \widetilde{U}\Phi_k^{(i)}$ being the pattern vector of the ith image of the kth class; and (ii) comparing

$$d_{min} = \min_k d_k \tag{4}$$

with a prescribed threshold δ_1. If $d_{min} = \|\Omega - \Omega_{k^*}\|_2$ for some index k^*, and $d_{min} < \delta_1$, then the input image Γ is identified as a member of class k^*, else Γ is classified as a non-member.

2.2. Two-Dimensional PCA

Unlike the conventional PCA algorithm (Turk and Pentland 1991), the 2-D PCA (2DPCA) algorithm developed by Yang et al. (2004) treats an image of size $m \times n$ as an $m \times n$ matrix rather that a vector of length mn. This is obviously a more natural way to deal with digital images, and it leads to a covariance matrix of much reduced size compared to its 1-D PCA counterpart. Given a set of M training face images $\{A_i, i = 1, 2, \ldots, M\}$, a covariance matrix is constructed as

$$G = \frac{1}{M}\sum_{i=1}^{M}(A_i - \bar{A})^T(A_i - \bar{A}) \tag{5}$$

where $\bar{A}$ denotes the mean of the M training face images, i.e., $\bar{A} = (\sum_{k=1}^{M} A_k)/M$. On comparing (5) with (1), we see that matrix G is a natural 2-D extension of a covariance matrix.

Let $\{x_1, x_2, \ldots, x_p\}$ be the orthonormal eigenvectors of G associated with the first largest p eigenvalues. Each image A_i in the training set corresponds to a feature matrix $B_i = [y_1^{(i)}\ y_2^{(i)}\ \ldots\ y_p^{(i)}]$ with columns given by the linear transformation

$$y_k^{(i)} = A_i x_k \text{ for } k = 1, 2, \ldots, p. \tag{6}$$

Similarly, a test image A is associated with a feature matrix $B = [y_1\ y_2\ \ldots\ y_p]$ where $y_k = Ax_k$. In this way, a distance between a test image A and a training image A_i is induced in terms of the Euclidean distance between their feature matrices as

$$d(B, B_i) = \sum_{k=1}^{p} \left\| y_k - y_k^{(i)} \right\|_2. \tag{7}$$

Based on the evaluation of these distances (B, B_i) for $i = 1, 2, \ldots, M$, a test image can be identified as whether or not it is a face image and, if it is, to which class it belongs, in a way similar to the 1-D PCA method of Turk and Pentland (1991).

3. An Extended 2-D PCA Technique for Face Recognition

3.1. A Closer Look at 2-D PCA – a Row Oriented Processing Technique

Eqs. (5) and (6) describe two key components of 2DPCA algorithm (Yang et al. 2004): (5) constructs a covariance matrix G of the training facial images and (6) builds a feature matrix of a facial image by orthogonal projection of the image onto the p most significant eigenvectors $\{x_k, k = 1, \ldots, p\}$ of G.

We note that the projections performed in (6) are for the *rows* of A_i. Consequently, matrices B and B_i defined in (Yang et al. 2004) (see Sec. 2.2) may be regarded as row-related feature matrices. A question that naturally arises is what will happen if one applies a column-related processing for a given image? And what should one do to generate a column-related feature matrix for a given image? Given $\{x_k\}$, a simple solution would be to project the image columns onto the p eigenvectors by performing $z_k^{(i)} = A_i^T x_k$. Unfortunately, this fails to work when dealing with non-square images A_i of size $m \times n$, as G is of size $n \times n$, so its eigenvectors x_k are of size $n \times 1$, thus $A_i^T x_k$ can not be performed. Interpreting this issue from a different perspective, we see that the covariance matrix G in (5) is designed exclusively for row-related features and, for extracting column-related features, we need a different covariance matrix. In what follows, we present a column oriented 2-D PCA approach and, furthermore, an extended 2-D PCA technique in which one works with a pair of covariance matrices, associates them to respective feature matrices, and applies a new criterion for face classification.

3.2. A Column Oriented 2-D PCA

To address the column oriented processing of images A_i ($i = 1, 2, \ldots, M$) of size $m \times n$, following the approach given by (5) and (6), we construct a new covariance matrix H of the training facial images and build a new feature matrix C of a facial image A by orthogonal projection of the image onto the p most significant eigenvectors $\{ z_k, k = 1, \ldots, p\}$ of H as shown below

$$H = \frac{1}{M}\sum_{i=1}^{M}(A_i - \bar{A})(A_i - \bar{A})^T, \tag{8}$$

$$C = Z^T \cdot A = [c_1\, c_2\, \ldots\, c_p]^T. \tag{9}$$

From the way the image A is processed, one can note that the projection performed in (9) is for the *columns* of A. Experimental results included in Section 5 demonstrate that this is a meaningful and valuable approach for face recognition tasks.

3.3. An Extended 2-D PCA (E-2DPCA) Technique

Given a set of M training face images A_i of size $m \times n$, which contains K classes (individuals) $\{\Omega_j, j = 1, \ldots, K\}$ of data, with each class having $L = M/K$ images denoted by $\{A_k^{(j)}, k = 1, 2, \ldots, L\}$, we define a pair of covariance matrices $\{G, H\}$ of respective sizes $n \times n$ and $m \times m$ as

$$G = \frac{1}{M}\sum_{i=1}^{M}(A_i - \bar{A})^T(A_i - \bar{A})$$
$$H = \frac{1}{M}\sum_{i=1}^{M}(A_i - \bar{A})(A_i - \bar{A})^T \tag{10}$$

where $\bar{A} = (\sum_{k=1}^{M} A_k)/M$. Note that $G \in \mathbb{R}^{n\times n}$ is the same covariance matrix as defined in (2) which is employed in (Yang et al. 2004), while $H \in \mathbb{R}^{m\times m}$ is a new covariance matrix designed for extracting column-related features, see below for more details.

Let $\{x_k, k = 1, \ldots, p\}$ and $\{z_k, k = 1, \ldots, p\}$ be the p orthonormal eigenvectors of G and H that are associated with the largest p eigenvalues, respectively. Given a test (facial) image A, we construct two feature matrices, denoted by R and C, by orthogonal projection of the rows of A onto $\{x_k, k = 1, \ldots, p\}$ and columns of A onto $\{z_k, k = 1, \ldots, p\}$, respectively. Namely,

$$R = A \cdot X = [r_1\, r_2\, \ldots\, r_p]$$
$$C = Z^T \cdot A = [c_1\, c_2\, \ldots\, c_p]^T \tag{11}$$

where $X = [x_1\, x_2\, \ldots\, x_p]$ and $Z = [z_1\, z_2\, \ldots\, z_p]$. Note that $R \in \mathbb{R}^{m\times p}$ is the same feature matrix as that used in (Yang et al. 2004), while $C \in \mathbb{R}^{p\times n}$ gathers column-related features of the image.

Similarly, for each class Ω_j in the training set, a pair of class-average feature matrices $\{\bar{R}_j, \bar{C}_j\}$ are defined as the arithmetic means over the row-related and column-related feature matrices of the images in that class respectively, i.e.,

$$\bar{R}_j = \frac{1}{L}\sum_{k=1}^{L} R_k^{(j)} = \left[\frac{1}{L}\sum_{k=1}^{L} A_k^{(j)}\right] \cdot X = \bar{A}_j \cdot X$$
$$\bar{C}_j = \frac{1}{L}\sum_{k=1}^{L} C_k^{(j)} = Z^T \cdot \left[\frac{1}{L}\sum_{k=1}^{L} A_k^{(j)}\right] = Z^T \cdot \bar{A}_j \tag{12}$$

where $\bar{A}_j = (\sum_{k=1}^{L} A_k{}^{(j)})/L$ is the arithmetic mean of the images in class Ω_j.

3.4. Classification Measures

With the definitions and notation in (11) and (12), the Euclidean distances between a test facial image A and class Ω_j are defined as

$$\begin{cases} d_j^{(r)} = \sum_{k=1}^{p} \left\| r_k - r_k^{(j)} \right\|_2 \\ d_j^{(c)} = \sum_{k=1}^{p} \left\| c_k - c_k^{(j)} \right\|_2 \end{cases} \tag{13}$$

where $r_k^{(j)}$ and $c_k^{(j)}$ are the kth column and row of $\bar{R}_j$ and $\bar{C}_j$, respectively. Based on these, a first new criterion for facial image classification can be formulated as follows:

(i) Let $d_r^* = \min_{1 \le j \le K}(d_j^{(r)})$ that is reached at $j = j_r^*$.
(ii) Let $d_c^* = \min_{1 \le j \le K}(d_j^{(c)})$ that is reached at $j = j_c^*$.
(iii) The facial image A is classified to belong to class Ω_{j^*} where

$$j^* = \begin{cases} j_r^* \text{ if } d_r^* \le d_c^* \\ j_c^* \text{ if } d_r^* > d_c^* . \end{cases} \tag{14}$$

We remark that by regarding the pair of Euclidean distances $[d_j^{(r)}\ d_j^{(c)}]$ as a two-dimensional measure between a test image A and class Ω_j, the nearest neighbor-based classification criterion proposed above, which is found to offer satisfactory performance (see Section 5), is merely one of the many possibilities.

Another possible criterion is to use a weighted l_1-norm to combine the two distances $d_j^{(r)}$ and $d_j^{(c)}$ as follows:

(i) Let

$$d^* = \min_{1 \le j \le K} \left(w_1 \left| d_j^{(r)} \right| + w_2 \left| d_j^{(c)} \right| \right) \tag{15}$$

where w_1 and w_2 are two weights chosen as $w_1 \ge 0$, $w_2 \ge 0$ and $w_1 + w_2 = 1$.
(ii) The facial image A is classified to belong to class Ω_{j^*} if d^* is reached at $j = j^*$.

To summarize the proposed 2-D extension of existing 2DPCA method, the block diagram in Figure 1 illustrates the proposed E-2DPCA algorithm. It is expected that the dual processing (on rows and on columns) of a test face image will increase the likelihood of correct face identification.

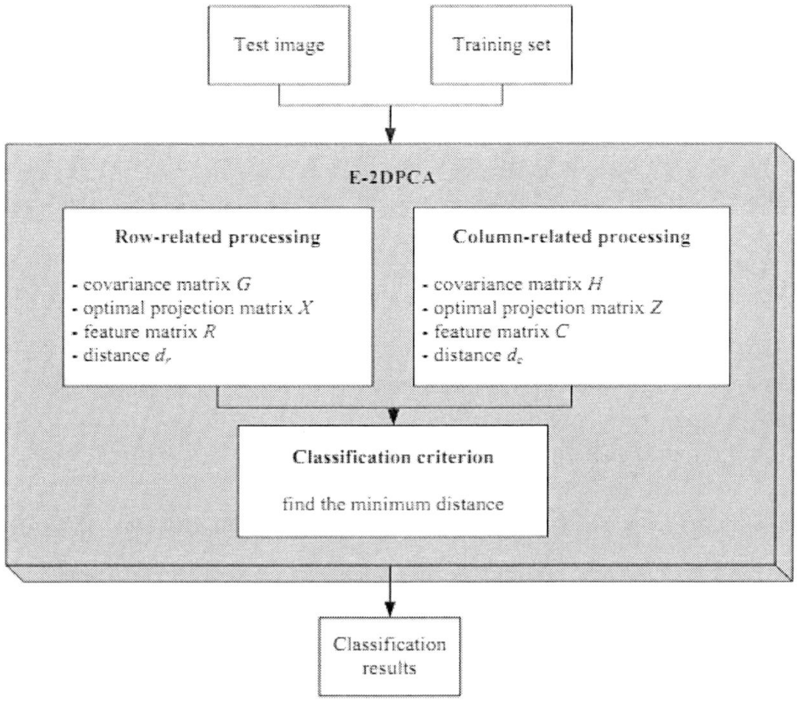

Figure 1. Block diagram of the proposed E-2DPCA algorithm.

4. Pre-Processing Techniques for Performance Enhancement

The performance of the conventional PCA is known to be sensitive to illumination variation in facial images, and the 2-D PCA is not an exception. In this section, we describe several pre-processing techniques that may be incorporated into PCA to ease the sensitivity hence enhance the performance.

4.1. Perfect Histogram Matching (PHM)

Pre-processing strategies based on histogram matching were recently proposed to deal with some of these problems (Sevcenco and Lu 2009; Sevcenco and Lu 2010). The technique in (Sevcenco and Lu 2010) modifies a given image of size $m \times n$ such that its histogram perfectly matches a desirable reference histogram while maintaining the global features as well as local details of the image. As a result, the perfect histogram matching (PHM) algorithm (Sevcenco and Lu 2010) helps generate a considerably more homogeneous tonal distribution in facial images and is found useful to improve recognition rate of the conventional PCA. Furthermore, in (Sevcenco and Lu 2010), PHM was shown to be more efficient in improving face recognition rates than several existing pre-processing techniques, e.g. *whitehedfaces* recognition technique employing PCA (Liao et al. 2007), Ramasubramanian and Venkatesh (2001) method that combines the discrete cosine transform and standard PCA, and histogram equalization pre-processing for PCA. In addition, it may be used in combination with other pre-processing steps, such as a wavelet-based illumination invariant technique (Goh et al. 2008).

For a natural, well-balanced and homogeneous appearance across the face images in the training set and test image, a discrete Gaussian histogram

$$h_d(r_j) = \text{round}\left[a e^{-\frac{(r_j - b)^2}{2c^2}} \right] \quad \text{for } j = 0, 1, \ldots, J-1 \tag{16}$$

is found suitable as a reference histogram, where r_j denotes the jth gray level, b is the center of the Gaussian function (b = 127.5 for 8-bit images), c controls the 'width' of the Gaussian curve, a is the height of the function, and J is the number of gray levels (J = 256 for 8-bit images).

Experimentally, it was found that c = 100 provides appropriate image contrast and increased recognition rates when PHM was applied in conjunction with PCA-based algorithms. For images of size $m \times n$, the value of parameter a is determined by imposing the constraint that the total number of pixels before and after the histogram equalization remains unchanged.

$$\sum_{k=0}^{G-1} \text{round}[a e^{-\frac{(r_k - b)^2}{2c^2}}] = mn \tag{17}$$

For example, for an 8-bit image with m = n = 128 and J = 256, the value of a so determined is found to be a = 99.4568.

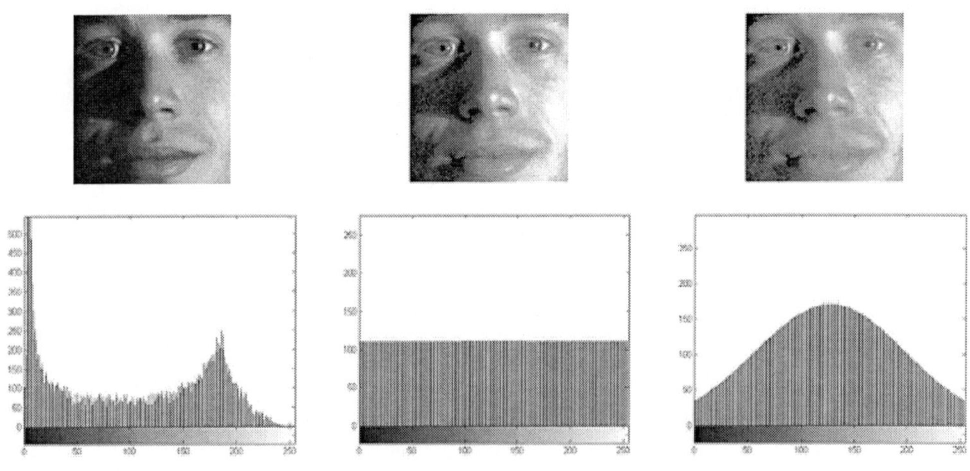

Figure 2. Effect of PHM pre-processing: original image and its processed counterparts using b = 127.5 and c = 2000 (for flat histogram) and 100, respectively, (top row) and their corresponding histograms (bottom row).

The PHM techniques ensures that (i) the histogram of the given image so modified matches perfectly the desired histogram (see Figure 2); and (ii) subject to perfect histogram matching, the changes made in the histogram of the given image are minimized in the sense that the average difference between the original and modified gray levels at any given pixel location remains the smallest.

4.2. De-Noising of Face Images by DWT and TV Minimization

Image de-noising has been a subject of extensive research in the last several decades, and promising de-noising results have been reported using methods such as discrete wavelet transform (DWT), custom filtering, or anisotropic diffusion (Perona and Malik 1990). A commonly used noise estimation method is based on Donoho's wavelet shrinkage technique, the mean absolute deviation (MAD) of wavelet coefficients at the highest resolution (Donoho 1995). Our approach to the de-noising problem (Sevcenco 2010) consists of two steps. First, an estimate of the noise variance (Donoho 1995) is obtained. Next, the noise estimation is employed for adjusting the weighting parameter λ for the de-noising algorithm based on total variation (TV) minimization problem (Rudin et al. 1992).

Tuning the input parameters (weight λ and number of iterations N) in Rudin et al. algorithm turns out to be of critical importance for achieving a satisfactory de-noising performance, the reader is referred to (Sevcenco 2010) for the technical details.

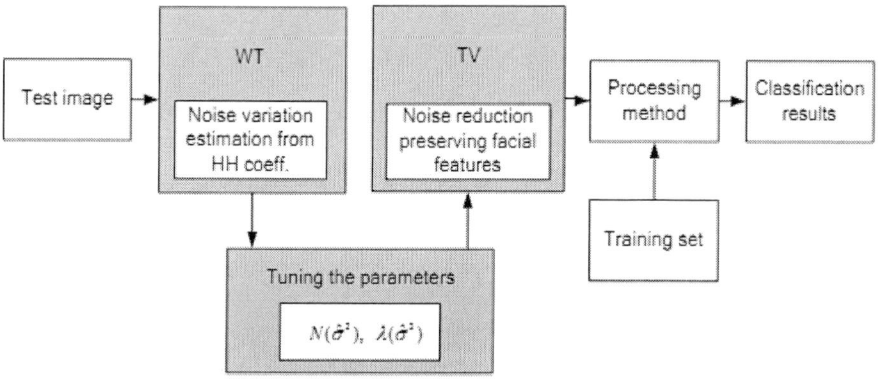

Figure 3. Block diagram of a WT – TV pre-processing module.

Figure 3 illustrates a block diagram of the WT – TV de-noising algorithm. As a first step, wavelet transform (WT) is applied to the testing set to estimate the noise variance of each test image. Based on this, the input parameters for TV algorithm are adjusted and the de-noising process is accomplished. Subsequently, a face recognition technique is applied to the training set and de-noised test image, and the classification results are acquired.

4.3. Dealing with Face Occlusions

Partial face occlusion introduces a challenging problem in face recognition. Face recognition systems often confront occluded faces in real world applications, as the systems need to deal with people wearing common accessories, such as scarves or sunglasses, covering their face with their hands, or carrying different objects which may obstruct their face. Face occlusion may also occur when external objects partially occlude the camera view.

Therefore, a face recognition system has to be robust to occlusion in order to guarantee reliable results.

Several studies have been conducted in order to address this problem. In (Martinez 2002), face images are analyzed locally in order to handle partial face occlusion, where the face image is divided into local regions and for each region an eigenspace is constructed. In this way, if a region is occluded, it will automatically be detected. Moreover, weighting of local regions are also proposed in order to provide robustness against expression variations. A similar approach is presented in (Tan et al. 2005), where a self-organizing map is used to model the subspace instead of Gaussians or mixtures of Gaussians as in (Martinez 2002).

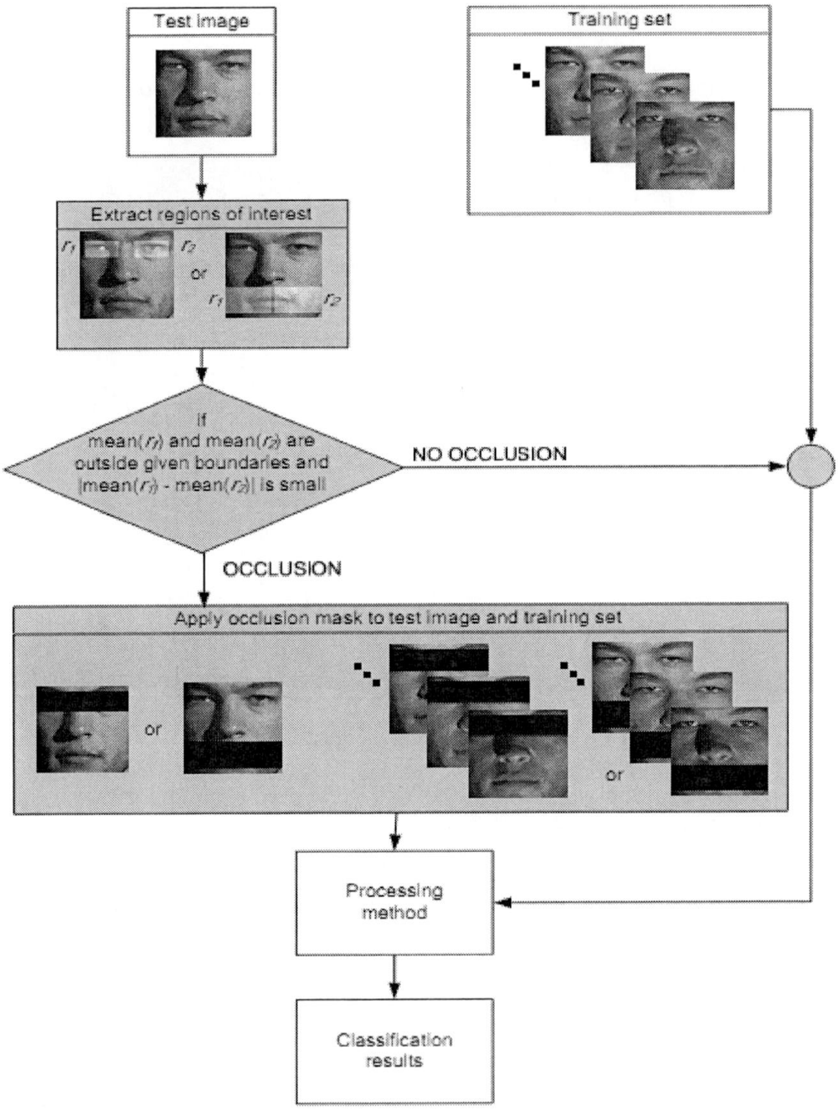

Figure 4. Block diagram of the OCCL algorithm.

In (Fidler et al. 2006), robustness against occlusion is provided by combining subspace methods that aim at best reconstruction (such as principal component analysis), with subspace methods that aim at discrimination (such as linear discriminant analysis). In (Fransens et al. 2006) a generative model based approach is proposed, where the model assumes that image pixels are generated by an inlier process which is responsible for producing the majority of the data, or an outlier process which generates pixels not adhering to the inlier model. Partitioning into inlier and outlier regions is made by employing a hidden binary map which is modeled as a Markov random field, and inference is made tractable by a mean field EM-algorithm.

A very recent approach, different from those mentioned above, consists of utilizing sparse signal representation to analyze partially occluded face images (Wright et al. 2009).

Below we present a simple yet effective approach to deal with two types of facial occlusions, namely the eyes occlusions and chin occlusions.

Given a test image, the potential occlusion problem is handled in a pre-processing step. First, the test image is examined to see if occlusion of eyes or chin (e.g., if the person wears sunglasses or has beard/scarf, respectively) exists. This is done by applying a binary mask to the original test image to select the regions of interest r_1 and r_2, as illustrated in Figure 4. Subsequently, a decision is made based on the mean values of regions of interest. If there is an eye or chin occlusion, then a binary occlusion mask is artificially created and applied to the test image and entire training set. In this way, negative effect of occlusion on recognition performance can be largely eliminated, and equal conditions are created among the training set and test image which are subsequently fed into a face recognition module and classification results are attained. For eye occlusion, an occlusion mask covers approximately one quarter of original image, while for chin occlusion it covers roughly one third of it. A block diagram of this occlusion-resolving (OCCL) algorithm is given in Figure 4.

4.4. An Enhanced Face Recognition System

Some of the pre-processing techniques described above can be incorporated into PCA to construct a hybrid system for face recognition. A representative of such systems is illustrated in Figure 5.

5. Experimental Results

5.1. The Databases

Two databases were employed to evaluate the performance of the face recognition algorithms. These are the Yale Face Database (Belhumeur et al. 1997) and extended Yale Face Database B (Georghiades et al. 2001; Lee et al. 2005). These bases were chosen as they include face images under slightly different poses and/or various illumination conditions.

The Yale Face Database contains a set of 165 grayscale images of 15 subjects, with 11 poses per subject, namely center-light, with glasses, happy, left-light, without glasses, normal, right-light, sad, sleepy, surprised, and wink, denoted as pose ‘a’, ‘b’, ..., and ‘k’, respectively. The Yale Face Database images employed in our simulations were cropped to 128×128 pixel size to minimize non-face areas such as hair and neck, with the image center approximately placed between the 2 nostrils of subject's nose.

The extended Yale Face Database B contains a total of 16128 images of 28 human subjects with 9 poses and 64 illumination conditions. In our experiments, we used the cropped version of this database which contains images of individuals taken under 64 different illumination conditions, with no pose variation, and each facial image was further manually aligned and cropped to size 168×168 pixels. To avoid working with some corrupted images from the cropped database, we selected only 20 individuals, with 64 images each.

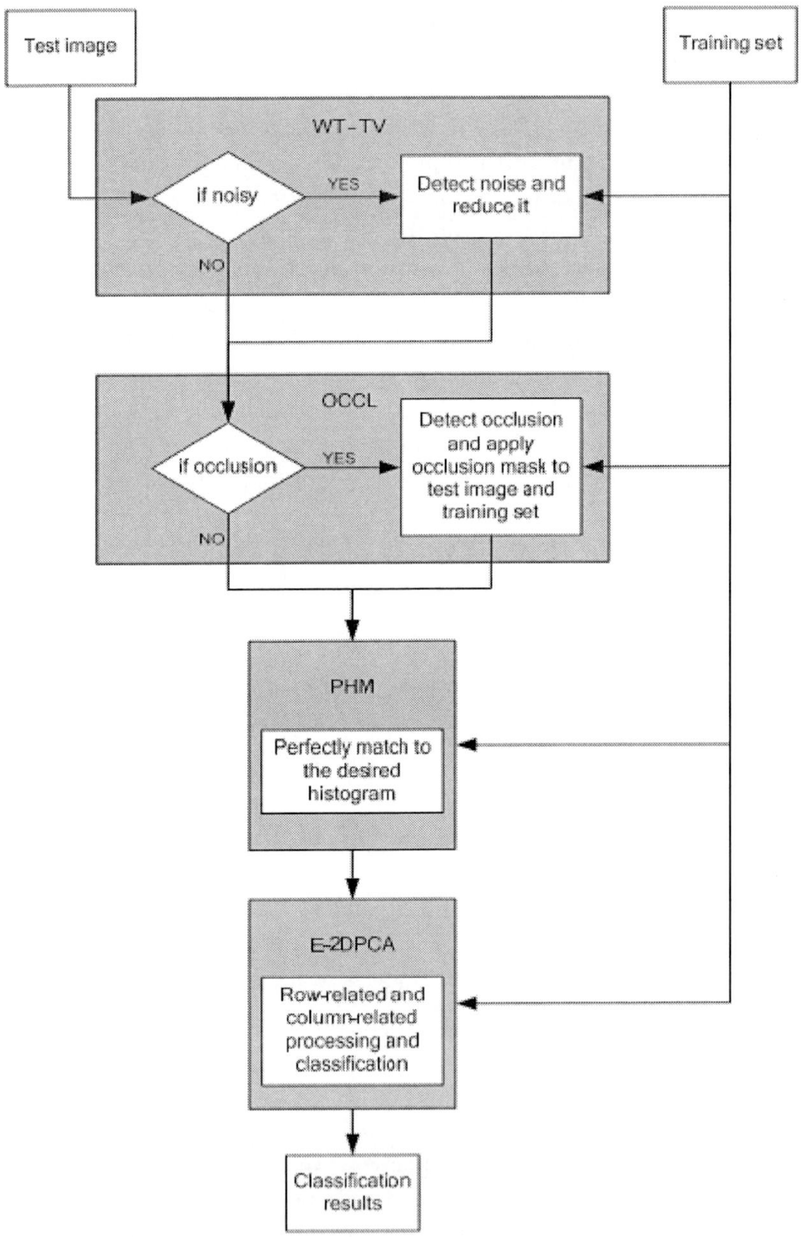

Figure 5. Block diagram of the proposed face recognition system.

5.2. Experimental Results of E-2DPCA – a Case Study

As addressed in Section 3, beside the original 2-D PCA algorithm which processes facial images on rows, one may consider the extended 2-D PCA method which takes into account also the column information. For E-2DPCA, we considered both classification measures proposed in Section 3.4, namely (i) the criterion given by (14), which does not require tuning of any additional parameters, and the algorithm in this case was denoted by E_{min}-2DPCA; and (ii) the criterion given by (15) with $w_1 = 0.2$ and $w_2 = 0.8$ and the algorithm was denoted by $E_{col0.8}$-2DPCA.

On comparing the three 2-D processing algorithm, namely 2DPCA, E_{min}-2DPCA and $E_{col0.8}$-2DPCA, with the standard PCA method, first we employed the Yale Face Database and constructed a training set containing poses 'a', 'd', 'e', 'g' of all 15 individuals, and a testing set with poses 'c', 'l', 'k', 'b' of the same individuals. Subsequently, based on the extended Yale Face Database B we defined a training set of 200 images with 20 poses per individual and a testing set of 80 images with 4 new poses with various angles of illumination per each individual.

Figure 6 illustrates the average recognition rates versus p, the number of eigenvectors employed for image representation. From Figure 6 it is observed that, the 2-D algorithms achieved higher recognition rates much faster than their 1-D counterpart.

When different facial expressions were considered as test images (Figure 6(a)), the proposed 2-D extended PCA-based algorithms demonstrate superior performance for $p \geq 3$ (with recognition rates higher than 85% for $p \geq 7$) in comparison with the two existing methods. The standard PCA method was able to provide satisfactory results for $p \geq 15$. However, this was not the case when different illumination conditions were considered in the testing set (Figure 6(b)), when the inferiority of the standard PCA was evident. When the Yale Face Database was employed, with $p = 1$, 2DPCA had a recognition rate of 48.4%, followed by E_{min}-2DPCA with 45%, $E_{col0.8}$-2DPCA with 38.3% and PCA with 15%. When at least 3 eigenvectors were employed, the E_{min}-2DPCA and $E_{col0.8}$-2DPCA algorithms outperformed 2DPCA and PCA, e.g. for $p = 5$, the recognition rates achieved were 83.3%, 81.7%, 75%, and 26.7%, respectively. Over the range 1 to 60 eigenvectors, $E_{col0.8}$-2DPCA attained a maximum performance of 90%, followed by E_{min}-2DPCA, 2DPCA and PCA with 88.3%, 83.4% and 80%, respectively.

In comparison with the above numerical results, for the extended Yale Face Database B, the E_{min}-2DPCA and $E_{col0.8}$-2DPCA algorithms outperformed 2DPCA and PCA even for small values of p. For example, with $p = 1$ the recognition rates achieved were 5%, 7.5%, 5%, and 5%, respectively, and with $p = 5$ the recognition rates achieved were 48.8%, 53.8%, 41.3%, and 10%, respectively. Satisfactory performance was obtained when E_{min}-2DPCA, $E_{col0.8}$-2DPCA and 2DPCA were employed with $p \geq 20$ (e.g. for $p = 25$, the recognition rates achieved were 96.3%, 96.3% and 87.5%, respectively). Over the range 1 to 60 eigenvectors, $E_{col0.8}$-2DPCA attained a maximum performance of 100%, closely followed by E_{min}-2DPCA and 2DPCA with 97.5% and 93.8%, respectively.

These results demonstrate the improvement that the extended 2-D approach, which utilizes the images information obtained by row *and* column processing, brings over the standard one.

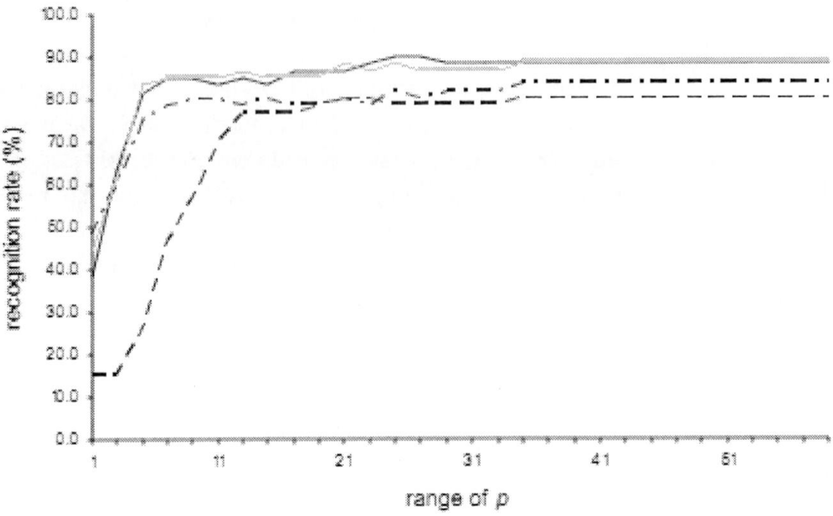

(a)

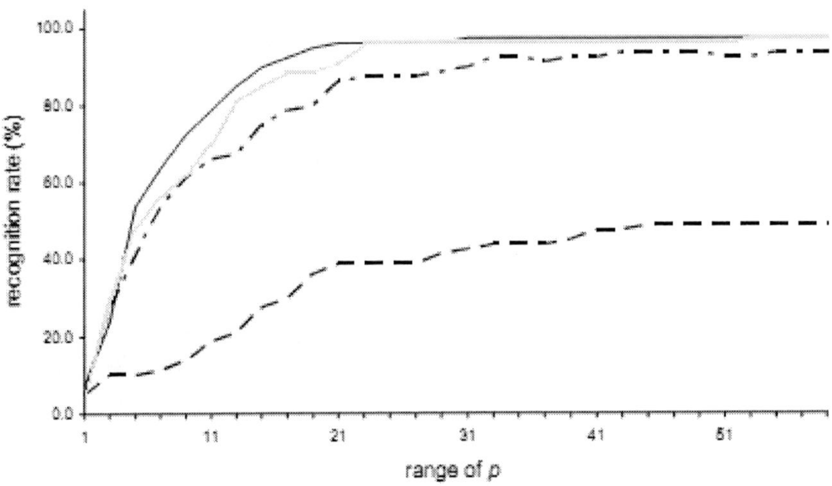

(b)

Figure 6. Performance comparison of PCA (dashed line), 2DPCA (dash-dotted line), E_{min}-2DPCA (gray line) and $E_{col0.8}$ -2DPCA (solid line) algorithms (a) using the Yale Face Database, and (b) the extended Yale Face Database B.

5.3. Additional Results for PCA, 2DPCA and E-2DPCA

By employing the Yale Face Database, a total of ten cases were designed and examined, each with specific training and testing sets. As shown in Table 1, these cases considered a variety of facial expressions (Cases 1 - 9) and face obstruction (Case 10).

Table 1. Ten cases from Yale Face Database

Case	Poses for training set (for all 15 members)	Poses for testing set (for all 15 members)
1	'a', 'c', 'd', 'e', 'g', 'h', 'i'	'f' – normal pose
2	'a', 'd', 'e', 'g'	'f' – normal pose
3	'a', 'e'	'f' – normal pose
4	'a'	'f' – normal pose
5	'a', 'd', 'e', 'g'	'c' – happy pose
6	'a', 'd', 'e', 'g'	'h' – sad pose
7	'a', 'd', 'e', 'g'	'i' – sleepy pose
8	'a', 'd', 'e', 'g'	'j' – surprised pose
9	'a', 'd', 'e', 'g'	'k' – wink pose
10	'a', 'd', 'e', 'g'	'b' – with glasses pose

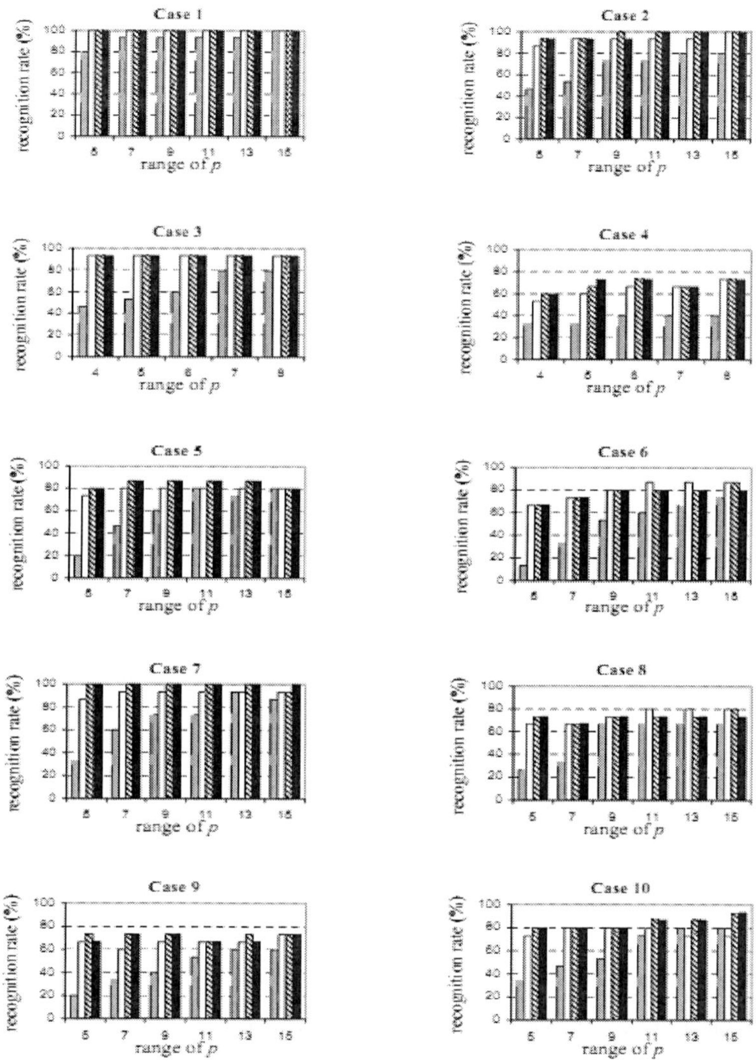

Figure 7. Comparison results for PCA (solid grey bar), 2DPCA (solid white bar), E_{min}-2DPCA (diagonal stripped bar) and $E_{col80\%}$-2DPCA (solid black bar), for all ten cases from the Yale Face Database.

Figure 7 illustrates the results obtained by applying PCA, 2DPCA and E-2DPCA approach (with E_{min}-2DPCA and $E_{col0.8}$-2DPCA versions of the algorithm) to these ten cases, in terms of recognition rate versus number of eigenfaces (p) employed. It is noticed that the recognition rate was improved for Cases 2, 4, 5, 7, 9 and 10 when E-2DPCA was utilized. For Cases 1 and 3, the E-2DPCA has identical performance as the 2DPCA algorithm. The only two exceptions when the proposed extended algorithm was slightly worse than 2DPCA were Cases 6 and 8, for $p = 11$, 13 and 15.

A separate set of experiments was conducted to examine the robustness of the proposed algorithm under illumination variations. The database employed was the extended Yale Face Database B with a selection of 520 images representing 20 persons with 26 poses per person. The training set contained 400 images representing 20 individuals, each with 20 poses. The testing set, representing the remaining 120 images, was divided into two groups. The first group contained 60 images representing 20 individuals, each having 3 images with mild illumination variations, as shown in the first row in Figure 8, while the second one contained 60 images representing the same 20 individuals, each having 3 images with severe illumination variations, see the second row in Figure 8.

The results of applying the same four algorithms to the above case study are depicted in Figure 9, where E-2DPCA was found to perform at least as good as 2DPCA, with higher recognition rate in Cases 2, 4, 5 and 6.

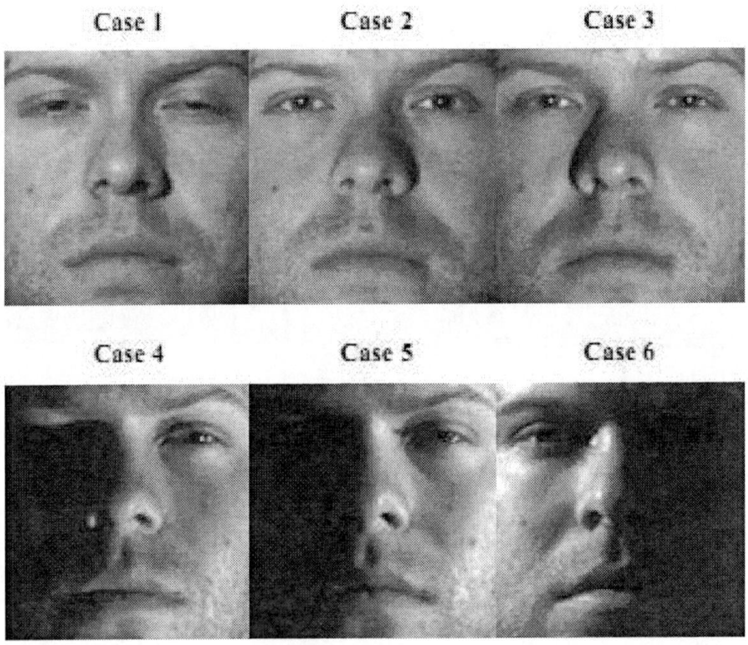

Figure 8. Six illumination conditions from the extended Yale Face Database B considered for six testing sets.

We note that the three algorithms evaluated did not work well for Case 6 because the test images in this case contained very large shadowed regions.

Concerning the complexity of the PCA, 2DPCA and E-2DPCA algorithms, face recognition process may be carried out using both offline and real time operations. The face identification task consists of finding the image representation, which is given by the pattern vector for PCA, feature matrix for 2DPCA, and pair of feature matrices for E-2DPCA, and classifying it based on evaluation of the minimum distance between the test image representation and the K classes representations. If the training set is promptly updated with newly identified test images, then the entire recognition process must be done in real time. In this case, the identification task includes also computing the covariance matrix/matrices, finding the eigenvectors, and obtaining the class pattern vectors (for PCA)/class average feature matrices (for 2DPCA)/pair of class average feature matrices (for E-2DPCA), which are typically offline operations.

The second column of Table 2 shows the number of multiplications required for computing all eigenvectors for a training set of M images of size $N \times N$ for the three algorithms being evaluated, while the third column of the table shows the number of multiplications required for finding the pattern vector (in the case of PCA), the feature matrix (in the case of 2DPCA) and the pair of feature matrices (in the case of E-2DPCA) for a test image using p eigenvectors. Note that if the number M of images from training set is much larger than size N, and if all the operations are done in real time, then the 2DPCA and E-2DPCA algorithms are more efficient than the standard PCA.

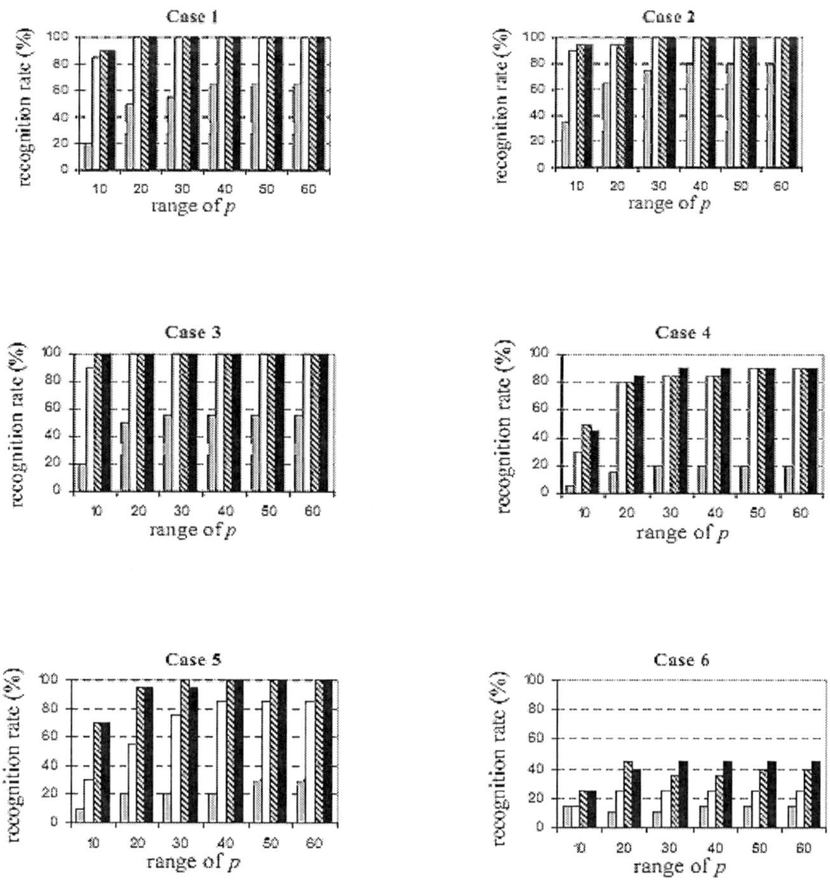

Figure 9. Comparison results for PCA (solid grey bar), 2DPCA (solid white bar), E_{min}-2DPCA (diagonal stripped bar) and $E_{col80\%}$-2DPCA (solid black bar), for the six cases from the extended Yale Face Database B.

An alternative and perhaps more realistic complexity measure is the normalized elapsed time. The elapsed time required by a given algorithm was normalized to the elapsed time taken by the conventional PCA to perform the entire face recognition process and also for only face identification task. Table 3 summarizes the average normalized elapsed time over 100 trials of the three algorithms, where the six cases from the extended Yale Face Database B were tested, i.e. $M = 400$ and $N = 168$. The original 2DPCA algorithm was found to be the fastest when entire process of face recognition was evaluated, followed by the E-2DPCA and PCA – both required comparable execution times.

We remark that with $M = 400$, $N = 168$ and $p = 20$ which represents 5% of the available number of eigenvectors, the numerical values obtained using the formulas in Table 2 (after normalization) were found to be [1 0.41 0.82] for the evaluation of eigenvectors and [1 1 2] for image representation. On comparing these values with those shown in Table 3, it is observed that the theoretical prediction of the computational complexity has a good match with the recorded time for the three algorithms.

Table 2. Computational complexity in terms of the number of multiplications for the three algorithms

Algorithm	Evaluation of eigenvectors	Image representation using p eigenvectors
PCA	$\frac{M(M+1)}{2}N^2 + M^3 + N^2M + N^2$	N^2p
2DPCA	$\frac{N^2(N+1)}{2}M + N^3$	N^2p
E-2DPCA	$2\left(\frac{N^2(N+1)}{2}M + N^3\right)$	$2N^2p$

Table 3. Normalized elapsed time for the three algorithms

Algorithm	Entire face recognition process	Face identification only
PCA	1	1
2DPCA	0.46	0.93
E-2DPCA	0.97	1.79

We conclude this subsection by commenting on two implementation issues:

- In E-2DPCA, the column-related and row-related processing operations were sequentially performed. To reduce the computational time, special-purpose hardware may be used to carry out these operations in parallel.
- Contrary to the 1-D PCA algorithm whose implementation may encounter memory limitations if the dataset contains many large images, the 2DPCA and E-2DPCA algorithms can handle considerably larger images. The 32-bit version of MATLAB, for example, can process matrices in double precision with about $155 \cdot 10^6$ elements. If the data set contains 1000 images of size 400×400, the data matrix A (see Section 2.1) in the 1-D PCA algorithm is of size 160000×1000 that exceeds the size limit

and the software will fail to work yielding the error message "out of memory". On the other hand, the covariance matrices encountered in the 2DPCA as well as E-2DPCA algorithms remain to be of size 400 $\times$ 400 (see Sections 2.2 and 3.3), a size far smaller than the limit.

5.4. Performance of an Enhanced Face Recognition System

The ten cases constructed from Yale Face Database (see Table 1) were used to examine the performance improvement due to the incorporation of a PHM pre-processing module (see (16)) into the E-2DPCA algorithm. Also, the six cases constructed from the extended Yale Face Database B (see Figure 8) were re-examined in view of PHM E-2DPCA. In addition, four large data sets of the extended Yale Face Database B were constructed to evaluate and compare PCA, 2DPCA and E-2DPCA algorithms and their counterparts when PHM-based pre-processing was incorporated.

For the Yale Face Database which includes images with different lighting conditions, a 100% recognition accuracy rate was achieved in Cases 1, 2, 3 and 7 for entire range of p (the number of eigenvectors employed) when PHM pre-processing module was applied to E-2DPCA algorithm for both classification measures (14) and (15). For cases 5 and 6, a constant value of 93.3% was achieved for all instances by both PHM E_{min}-2DPCA and PHM $E_{col0.8}$-2DPCA algorithms. For the remaining four cases, slightly different recognition rates were achieved by PHM E_{min}-2DPCA and PHM $E_{col0.8}$-2DPCA algorithms. For PHM E_{min}-2DPCA, there were two instances achieving a recognition rate of 86.7%, while for PHM $E_{col0.8}$-2DPCA there were three instances achieving a recognition rate of 86.7%. For the remaining instances recognition rates of 93.3% and 100% were attained. In comparison with PCA, 2DPCA and E-2DPCA methods, out of ten cases examined, there were seven cases (namely Cases 3, 4, 5, 6, 8, 9 and 10) where PHM E-2DPCA yielded improved performance with significant increase in recognition rate, while for the remaining three cases E-2DPCA and PHM E-2DPCA algorithms offered similar performance.

When applied to the six cases from extended Yale Face Database B, the PHM module in conjunction with E-2DPCA algorithm yielded recognition rates of 100% for Cases 1-5, for all instances of p with one exception (Case 4 with $p = 10$) where the rate was improved only to 85% for PHM E_{min}-2DPCA, and 80% for PHM $E_{col0.8}$-2DPCA. For Case 6 where other algorithms failed to perform face recognition adequately (see Figure 9), the PHM E-2DPCA algorithm offered substantial improvement in recognition rate, as is evidenced in Figure 10.

By employing the extended Yale Face Database B, four new data sets were constructed using 1280 facial images, representing 20 individuals, each with 64 images in various illuminations conditions. Table 4 describes these data sets.

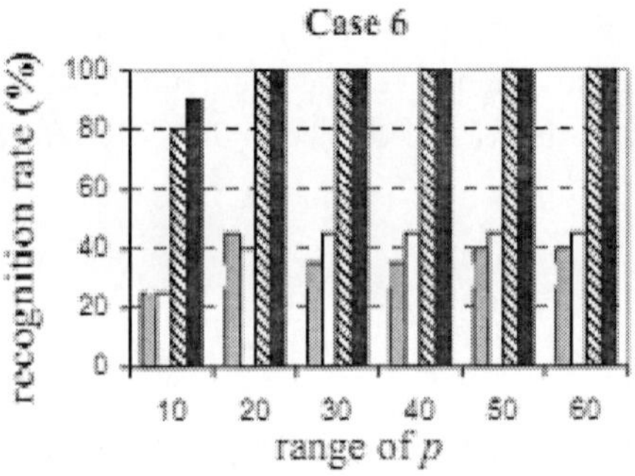

Figure 10. Comparison results for E_{min}-2DPCA (solid grey bar), $E_{col0.8}$ -2DPCA (solid white bar), PHM E_{min}-2DPCA (diagonal stripped bar) and PHM $E_{col0.8}$ -2DPCA (solid black bar), for Case 6 from the extended Yale Face Database B.

First, the four data sets of the extended Yale Face Database B were utilized to evaluate the performance of the PHM E-2DPCA algorithm. As a first step in our evaluation process, the question of what number of eigenvectors, *p*, should be employed in our simulations, was addressed. Table 5 shows the results obtained on Set 4, when 2.5%, 5%, 7.5% and 10% of the available eigenvectors were utilized. We see an increase of average recognition rate by 2.5% when the number of eigenvectors was increased from 2.5% to 5%. The use of 7.5% of the eigenvectors brings only a minor 0.5% improvement, while further increase of number of eigenvectors utilized does not lead to further performance improvement. As a result, in the subsequent simulations we have used 5% of the eigenvectors for the E-2DPCA algorithm, as it offered satisfactory performance with moderate computational complexity.

Table 4. Four sets from the extended Yale Face Database B

Set	Training set	Testing set	Remark
1	All 20 individuals with 54 poses.	All 20 individuals with remaining 10 poses.	A data set considered as *easy* to deal with as its testing set consists of images with small shadowed areas, while the training set contains most of poses.
2	All 20 individuals with 54 poses.	All 20 individuals with remaining 10 poses.	A data set with *medium* level of difficulty. The testing set contains images with large shadowed regions, while training set contains most of poses.
3	All 20 individuals with 32 poses.	All 20 individuals with remaining 32 poses.	A data set with *medium* level of difficulty as its training set contains relatively less number of poses.
4	All 20 individuals with 44 poses.	All 20 individuals with the remaining 20 poses.	A data set considered as *hard* to deal with as its training set contains only images with small or medium shadowed regions, while the testing set contains images with large shadowed regions.

Depending on the number of images from the training set involved, the number of eigenvectors used in the testing algorithms was set to 54, 54, 32 and 44 for Set 1, 2, 3 and 4, respectively, representing 5% of the total number of available eigenvectors. Utilizing the same four data sets described in Table 4, the performance of PCA, 2DPCA, E-2DPCA (with both versions, E_{min}-2DPCA and $E_{col0.8}$-2DPCA, respectively) and their PHM-enhanced versions was examined. As illustrated in Table 6, for Set 1 which represents the data set with the lowest level of difficulty, the 2-D PCA-based algorithms and their PHM-enhanced versions presented the highest performance, attaining average recognition rates of 84.5%, 87.5%, 91% and 100%, respectively. A recognition rate of 77.5% was achieved by PHM PCA, while PCA by itself fails to provide satisfactory results. However, for the remaining 3 data sets, neither 2DPCA algorithm nor E-2DPCA approach achieved satisfactory results, although E-2DPCA attained higher recognition rates than 2DPCA. When the PHM module was integrated into the system, significant performance improvement was obtained, especially for the more challenging Sets 2, 3, and 4, for which the other algorithms by themselves failed to work properly. Overall average recognition rates of 99.1% and 99.4% were attained by the PHM E_{min}-2DPCA and PHM $E_{col0.8}$-2DPCA based face recognition systems, respectively, as opposed to 97.1% for PHM 2DPCA.

Table 5. Choosing the appropriate number of eigenvectors for PHM E-2DPCA – results for Set 4 from the extended Yale Face Database B

PHM E-2DPCA				
Individual	$p = 22$ (2.5%)	$p = 44$ (5%)	$p = 66$ (7.5%)	$p = 88$ (10%)
1	95.0	100.0	100.0	100.0
2	85.0	90.0	90.0	90.0
3	100.0	100.0	100.0	100.0
4	100.0	100.0	100.0	100.0
5	90.0	95.0	100.0	100.0
6	80.0	95.0	100.0	100.0
7	90.0	90.0	90.0	90.0
8	100.0	100.0	100.0	100.0
9	100.0	100.0	100.0	100.0
10	100.0	100.0	100.0	100.0
11	95.0	95.0	95.0	95.0
12	95.0	100.0	100.0	100.0
13	100.0	100.0	100.0	100.0
14	90.0	95.0	95.0	95.0
15	95.0	100.0	100.0	100.0
16	100.0	100.0	100.0	100.0
17	100.0	100.0	100.0	100.0
18	100.0	100.0	100.0	100.0
19	90.0	95.0	95.0	95.0
20	100.0	100.0	100.0	100.0
Average	95.3	97.8	98.3	98.3

The performance of the PCA algorithm was found unsatisfactory for all four datasets. It was found that 5% of the total number of available eigenvectors did not suffice for PCA, but it provided satisfactory performance for 2-D PCA-based algorithms, when the image sets were PHM-pre-processed to achieve homogenous illumination conditions.

Table 6. Performance comparison of PCA, 2DPCA, E_{min}-2DPCA and $E_{col0.8}$-2DPCA, and their PHM-enhanced versions using the 4 data sets from Extended Yale Face Database B

Algorithm	Average rate (%)				**Overall rate (%)**
	Set 1	Set 2	Set 3	Set 4	
PCA	22.5	6.0	16.4	5.5	**12.6**
2DPCA	84.5	17.0	36.3	7.3	**36.3**
E_{min}-2DPCA	87.5	17.5	42.0	9.3	**39.1**
$E_{col0.8}$-2DPCA	91.0	18.5	43.0	9.0	**40.4**
PHM PCA	77.5	54.5	40.2	42.0	**53.5**
PHM 2DPCA	100	99.0	94.7	94.8	**97.1**
PHM E_{min}-2DPCA	100	100	98.8	97.8	**99.1**
PHM $E_{col0.8}$-2DPCA	100	100	98.9	98.8	**99.4**

Concerning the elapsed time for a typical face identification task, in average over the four data sets, the PHM E-2DPCA algorithm was found to be 12% more complex than the E-2DPCA algorithm.

5.5. Robustness of the Enhanced Face Recognition System to Noise and Face Occlusions

To evaluate the WT – TV de-noising procedure, the noise contaminated test images were constructed as follows. For each individual image, a specific seed was assigned to randomly generate additive zero-mean Gaussian white noise. The maximum amount of noise was varied from image to image up to a value of 10% of the maximum pixel light intensity. As a result, various variance values were obtained for each image, up to a maximum value of 0.0041, when a normalized range of pixel light intensities (i.e. [0, 1]) was considered.

Table 7 shows the performance of the PHM E-2DPCA (with classification measure given by (13) and no additional parameters) in two scenarios: (a) noise was applied to test images and no de-noising was performed, and (b) noise was applied to test images followed by WT – TV de-noising. As can be observed, for Set 1, which includes test images with “easy” illumination conditions, the algorithm was found to be robust against noise. Nevertheless, the algorithm did not handle the other three noise-corrupted data sets very well, where test images were with widely varying illumination conditions. On the other hand, the WT – TV de-noising algorithm applied as a pre-processing step to PHM E-2DPCA was able to offer a 19% overall performance improvement, with up to 33% recognition rate increase in average for Set 4. The robustness of the same PHM E-2DPCA algorithm against facial occlusions was examined for the four data sets of the extended Yale face database B. The OCCL occlusion-resolving module was employed as an initial pre-processing step in resolving the occlusion problem.

Table 7. Results for PHM E-2DPCA with noisy test images and no de-noising (left-hand side) and noisy test images and WT – TV de-noising (right-hand side) for four data sets from the extended Yale Face Database B

	PHM E-2DPCA : Noisy, no de-noising				PHM E-2DPCA : Noisy, WT-TV de-noising			
Average	95.5	58.0	77.5	47.8	99.5	84.5	90.2	80.8
Overall	69.7				88.7			

Table 8. Results for OCCL PHM E-2DPCA applied to eyes-occluded (left-hand side) and chin-occluded (right-hand side) images for four data sets from the extended Yale Face Database B

	OCCL PHM E-2DPCA : Eyes occlusion				OCCL PHM E-2DPCA : Chin occlusion			
Average	98.0	99.0	93.9	93.8	100	100	98.1	97.3
Overall	96.2				98.8			

Subsequently, the PHM algorithm was applied as a second pre-processing step. Table 8 shows the results obtained when eyes and chin occlusions occurred across the entire training sets. Similar results were obtained when the order of the two pre-processing modules was reversed. We remark that the OCCL PHM E-2DPCA algorithm was found to be quite efficient in dealing with eyes and chin occlusions, achieving overall recognition rates of 96.2% and 98.8%, respectively.

CONCLUSION

In this chapter, we have examined the 2-D PCA algorithm proposed by (Yang et al. 2004) and developed an extended 2-D PCA (E-2DPCA) algorithm for face classification. Experimental results are presented to demonstrate that together with pre-processing techniques such as perfect histogram matching and wavelet-based denoising, an E-2DPCA based face recognition system offers superior performance relative to several existing PCA-based systems.

REFERENCES

Bartlett, M.S.; Movellan, J.R.; Sejnowski, T.J. *IEEE Trans. Neural Netw.* 2002, 13(6), 1450–1464.

Belhumeur, P.N.; Hespanha, J.P.; Kriegman, D.J. *IEEE Trans. Pattern Anal. Mach. Intell.* 1997, 17(7), 711–720.

Belkin, M.; Niyogi, P. *Adv. Neural Inf. Process. Syst.* 2002, 14, 585–591.

Belkin, M.; Niyogi, P. J. *Comput. Syst. Sci.* 2008, 74(8), 1289–1308.

Bruce, V. *Recognizing faces*; Lawrence Erlbaum Associates; London, UK, 1988.

Bruce, V.; Burton, M.; Dench, N. *Quart. J. Exp. Psychol.* 1994, 47(A), 119–141.

Bruce, V.; Hancock, P.J.B.; Burton, A.M. F*ace recognition: from theory to applications;* Springer-Verlag; Berlin, DE, 1998; 51–72.

Chellappa, R.; Wilson, C.L.; Sirohey, S. *IEEE Proc.* 1995, 83(5), 705–741.

Chen, S.; Zhu, Y. *Pattern Recog*. 2004, 37, 1081–1083.

Donoho, D.L. *IEEE Trans. Inf. Theory*. 1995, 41(3), 613–627.

Du, B.; Shan, S.; Qing, L.; Gao, W. *IEEE Proc. ICASSP*. 2005, 2, 981–984.

Etemad, K.; Chellappa, R. *IEEE Proc. ICASSP*. 1996, 4, 2148–2151.

Fidler, S.; Skocaj, D.; Leonardis, A. *IEEE Trans. Pattern Anal. Mach. Intell.* 2006, 28(3), 337–350.

Fransens, R.; Strecha, C.; Van Gool, L. *Proc. Conf. CVPR Workshop*. 2006, 102–102.

Gauthier, I.; Logothetis, N.K. *J. Cog. Neuropsyc*. 2000, 17(1/2/3), 125–142.

Georghiades, A.S.; Belhumeur, P.N.; Kriegman, D.J. *IEEE Trans. Pattern Anal. Mach. Intell.* 2001, 23(6), 643–660.

Goh, Y.Z.; Teoh, A.B.J.; Goh, M.K.O. *Congr. Image Signal Process*. 2008, 3, 421–425.

Gonzales, R.C.; Woods, R.E. Digital Image Processing; Second Edition; Prentice-Hall, NJ, 2002.

Gottumukkal, R.; Asari, V.K. *Pattern Recog. Lett.* 2004, 25, 429–436.

Gross, R.; Brajovic, V. 4th Int. Conf. Audio Video-based Biometric Person *Authentication.* 2003, 10–18.

He, X.; Yan, S.; Hu, Y.; Niyogi, P.; Zhang, H.-J. *IEEE Trans. Pattern Anal. Mach. Intell.* 2005, 27(3), 328–340.

Hill, H.; Schyns, P.G.; Akamatsu, S. *Cognition.* 1997, 62, 201–222.

Hsieh, P.-C.; Tung, P.-C. *Pattern Recog*. 2009, 42(5), 978–984.

Jain, A.K. *Fundamentals of Digital Image Processing*; Prentice Hall, NY, 1989.

Johnston, A.; Hill, H.; Carman, N. *Cognition*. 1992, 40, 1–19.

Lee, K.C.; Ho, J.; Kriegman, D. *IEEE Trans. Pattern Anal. Mach. Intell*. 2005, 27(5), 684–698.

Liao, L.-Z.; Luo, S.-W.; Tian, M. *IEEE Signal Process. Lett*. 2007, 14(12), 1008–1011.

Martinez, A.M. *IEEE Trans. Pattern Anal. Mach. Intell.* 2002, 24(6), 748–763.

Niu, B.; Yang, Q.; Shiu, S.C.K.; Pal, S.K. *Pattern Recog*. 2008, 41(10), 3237–3243.

Perona, P.; Malik, J. *IEEE Trans. Pattern Anal. Mach. Intell*. 1990, 12(7), 629–639.

Ramasubramanian, D.; Venkatesh, Y.V. *Pattern Recog*. 2001, 34(12), 2447–2458.

Roweis, S.T.; Saul, L.K. *Sci.* 2000, 290(5500), 2323–2326.

Rudin, L.; Osher, S.; Fetami, E. *Physica D*. 1992, 60, 259–268.

Samaria, F.S.; Harter, A.C. *IEEE Proc. 2nd Workshop Appl. Comput. Vision*. 1994, 138–142.

Sergent, J. *Aspects of face processing*; Eds. Nijhoff, Dordrecht, NL, 1986.

Sevcenco, A.-M. Enhancement and extensions of principal component analysis for face recognition. *Ph.D. thesis*, 2010, 40–47.

Sevcenco, A.-M.; Lu, W.-S. *IEEE PacRim Conf. Commun. Comput. Signal Process.* 2009, 175–180.

Sevcenco, A.-M.; Lu, W.-S. J. *Multidim. Syst. Signal Process*. 2010, 21, 213–229.

Tan, K.; Chen, S. *Neurocomput.* 2005, 64, 505–511.

Tan, X.; Chen, S.; Zhou, Z.H.; Zhang, F. *IEEE Trans. Neural Netw*. 2005, 16(4), 875–886.

Tenenbaum, J.B.; Silva, V.; Langford, J.C. *Sci.* 2000, 290(5500), 2319–2323.

Turk, M.A.; Pentland, A.P. *IEEE Proc. Comput. Society Conf. CVPR*. 1991, 586–591.

Wright, J.; Yang, A.Y.; Ganesh, A.; Sastry, S.S.; Ma, Y. *IEEE Trans. Pattern Anal. Mach. Intell.* 2009, 31, 210–227.

Yang, J.; Zhang, D.; Frangi, A.F.; Yang, J.-Y. *IEEE Trans. Pattern Anal. Mach. Intell.* 2004, 26(1), 131–137.

Zhao L.; Yang, Y.-H. *Pattern Recog.* 1999, 34(4), 547–564.

Zhao, W.; Chellappa, R.; Rosenfeld, A.; Phillips, P.J. *ACM Comput. Surv.* 2003, 35(4), 399–458.

In: Face Recognition
Editors: Adamo Quaglia and Calogera M. Epifano
ISBN 978-1-61942-663-4

Chapter 3

FACE RECOGNITION BASED ON COMPOSITE CORRELATION FILTERS: ANALYSIS OF THEIR PERFORMANCES

***I. Leonard*[1], *A. Alfalou*[1,*] *and C. Brosseau*[2]**
[1]ISEN Brest, Département Optoélectronique,
Cuirassé Bretagne, France
[2]Université Européenne de Bretagne, Université de Brest,
Lab-STICC, France

ABSTRACT

This chapter complements our paper: "Spectral optimized asymmetric segmented phase-only correlation filter ASPOF filter" published in Applied Optics (2012).

1. INTRODUCTION

Intense interest in optical correlation techniques over a prolonged period has focused substantially on the filter designs for optical correlators and, in particular, on their important role in imaging systems using coherent light because of their unique and quite specific features. These techniques represent a powerful tool for target tracking and identification [1].

In particular, the field of face recognition has matured and enabled various technologically important applications including classification, access control, biometrics, and security systems. However, with security (e.g. fight terrorism) and privacy (e.g. home access) requirements, there is a need to improve on existing techniques in order to fully satisfy these requirements.

In parallel with experimental progress, the theory and simulation of face recognition techniques has advanced greatly, allowing, for example, for modeling of the attendant

* E-mail: ayman.al-falou@isen.fr.

variability in imaging parameters such as sensor noise, viewing distance, emotion recognition facial expressions, head tilt, scale and rotation of the face in the image plane, and illumination. An ideal real-time recognition system should handle all these problems.

It is within this perspective that we undertake this study. On one hand, we make use of a Vander Lugt correlator (VLC) [2]. On the other hand, we try to optimize correlation filters by considering two points. Firstly, the training base which serves to qualify these filters should contain a large number of reference images from different viewpoints. Secondly, it should correspond to the requirement for real-time functionality. For that specific purpose, our tests are based on composite filters.

The objectives of this chapter are first to give a basic description of the performances of standard composite filters for binary and grayscale images and introduce newly designed ASPOF (asymmetric segmented phase-only filter), and second to examine robustness to noise (especially background noise).

This paper deals with the effect of rotation and background noise problems on the correlation filtering performance. We shall not treat the deeper problem of lighting problems. Phong [3] described methods that are useful to overcome the lighting issue in terms of laboratory observables.

Adapted playgrounds for testing our numerical schemes are binary and grayscale image databases. Each binary image has black background with a white object (letter) on it with dimension 512 x 512 pixels. Without loss of generality, our first tests are based on the capital letters A and V because it is easy to rotate them with a given rotation angle (procedures for other letters are similar).

Next simulations were performed to illustrate how this algorithm can identify a face with grayscale images from the Pointing Head Pose Image Database (PHPID) [4] which is often used to test face recognition algorithms. In this study, we present comprehensive simulation tests using images of five individuals with 39 different images captured for each individual.

We pay special attention to adapting ROC curves for different phase only filters (POFs), for two reasons. Firstly, POFs based correlators and their implementations have been largely studied in the literature, see e.g. [1, 5].

In addition, optoelectronics devices, i.e. spatial light modulators (SLMs) allow implementing optically POFs in a simple manner. Secondly, numerical implementation of correlation have been considered as an alternative to all-optical methods because they show a good compromise between their performance and their simplicity.

High speed and low power numerical processors, e.g. field programmable gate array (FPGA) [6] provide a viable solution to the problem of optical implementation of POFs. Such numerical procedure allows one to reduce the memory size (by decreasing the number of reference images included in the composite filter) and does not consider the amplitude information which can be rapidly varying.

Face identification and underwater mine detection with background noise are two areas for which the FPGA has demonstrated significant performance improvement, such as image registration and feature tracking.

Following this brief introduction, we have divided the rest of the paper as follows: a general overview of the optical correlation methods is given in Sec. 2. Then, in Sec. 3, we review a series of correlation filters, which are next compared in Sec. 4.

2. Some Preliminary Considerations and Relation to Previous Work

The subject of correlation methods is long and quite a story. Here we will review various aspects of the problem discussed in the literature which relate to this paper. The modern study of optical correlation can be traced back to the pioneering research in the 1960s [2, 7]. In what became a classic paper, Vander Lugt presented a description of the coherent matched filter system, i.e. the VLC [2]. Basically, this method is based on the comparison between a target image and a reference image. This technique consists in multiplying an input signal (spectrum of image to be recognized) by a correlation filter, originating from a training base (i.e. reference base), in the Fourier domain. The result is a correlation peak (located at the center of the output plane i.e. correlation plane) more or less intense, depending on the degree of similarity between the target image and reference image. Correlation is perceived like a filtering which aims to extract the relevant information in order to recognize a pattern in a complex scene.

However, this approach requires considerable correlation data and is difficult to realize in real time. This led to the concept of POF (carried out from a single reference) whose purpose is to decide if a particular object is present or not, in the scene. To have a reliable decision about the presence, or not, of an object in a given scene, we must correlate the latter with several correlation filters taking into account the possible modifications of the target object, e.g. in-plane rotation and scale. Perhaps more problematic is the fact that a simple decision based on the presence, or not, of a correlation peak is insufficient. Thus, use of adequate performance criteria such as those developed in [8-9] is necessary.

During the 1970s and 1980s correlation techniques developed at a rapid pace. A plethora of advanced composite filters [10-12], and more general multi-correlation approaches [13] have been introduced. A good source for such results is the book of Yu [14]. However, experimental state of the art shows that optical correlation techniques almost found themselves in oblivion in the late 1990s for many reasons. While numerous schemes for realizing all-optical correlation methods have been proposed [13-15], up to now, they all face technical challenge to implement, notably those using spatial light modulators (SLMs) [16] because these methods are very sensitive to even small changes in the reference image. In addition, they usually require a lot of correlation data and are difficult to realize in real time.

Over the last decade, there has been a resurgence of interest, driven by recognition and identification applications [17-22], of the correlation methods. For example, Alam *et al.* [22] demonstrated the good performances of the correlation method compared to all numerical ones based on the independent component model. Another significant example in this area of research is the work by Romdhani *et al.* [23], which compared face recognition algorithms with respect to those based on correlation. Other recent efforts include the review by Sinha *et al.* [24] dealing with the current understanding regarding how humans recognize faces. Riedel *et al.* [25] have used the minimum average correlation energy (MACE) and unconstrained MACE filters in conjunction with two correlation plane performance measures to determine the effectiveness of correlation filtering in relation to facial recognition login access control.

Wavelets provide another efficient biometric approach for facial recognition with correlation filters [26]. A photorefractive Wiener-like correlation filter was also introduced by Khoury *et al.* [27] to increase the performance and robustness of the technique of correlation filtering. Their correlation results showed that for high levels of noise this filter has a peak-to-noise ratio that is larger than that of the POF while still preserving a correlation peak that is almost as high as that of the POF. Another optimization approach in the design of correlation filters was addressed to deal with the ability to suppress clutter and noise, an easy detection of the correlation peak, and distortion tolerance [28]. The resulting maximum average correlation height (MACH) filter exhibit superior distortion tolerance while retaining the attractive features of their predecessors such as the minimum average correlation energy filter and the minimum variance synthetic discriminant function filter.

A variant of the MACH filter was also developed in [29]. Pe'er and co-workers [30] presented a new apochromatic correlator, in which the scaling error has three zero crossings, thus leading to significant improvement in performance. These references are far from a complete list of important advances, but fortunately the interested reader can easily trace the historical evolution of these ideas with Vijaya Kumar's review paper, Yu's book, and the chapter of Alfalou and Brosseau containing an extensive bibliography [1, 14-15, 31]. As mentioned above, we have a dual goal which is first to introduce standard correlation filters, and second to compare their performances.

3. A Brief Overview of Correlation Filters

First we present the most common correlation filters. We turn attention to the general merits and drawbacks of composite filters. This discussion is simply a brief review and tabulation of the technical details for the basic composite filters. For that purpose we consider a scene s containing a single or several objects o with noise b. The input scene is written as $s(x,y)=o(x,y)+b(x,y)$. Let its two-dimensional FT be denoted by $S(\mu,\nu)=\rho(\mu,\nu)\exp[i\theta(\mu,\nu)]$. In the Fourier plane of the optical set-up, the scene spectrum is multiplied by a filter $H(\mu,\nu)$, where μ and ν denote the spatial frequencies coordinates.

Many approaches for designing filters to be used with optical correlators can be found in the literature according to the specific objects that need to be recognized. Some have been proposed to address hardware limitations; others were suggested to optimize a merit function. Attempts will be made throughout to use a consistent notation.

3.1. Adapted Filter (Ad)

The Ad filter [2] has for main purpose to optimize the SNR and reads

$$H_{Ad}(\mu,\nu)=\alpha\frac{R^{*}(\mu,\nu)}{\Gamma_{b}(\mu,\nu)} \quad (1)$$

where α denotes a constant, is the complex conjugate of the spectrum of the reference image ($R(\mu,\nu)=\rho_0(\mu,\nu)\exp(i\theta_0(\mu,\nu))$), and represents the spectral density of the input noise. If we assume that the noise is white and unit spectral density, we obtain $H_{Ad}(\mu,\nu)=\alpha R^{*}(\mu,\nu)$.

A main advantage of this filter is the increase of the SNR especially when white noise is present. The drawback of this filter is that it leads to broad correlation peaks in the correlation plane. Since the output plane is scanned for this peak, and its location indicates the position of the target in the input scene, we can conclude that the target is poorly localized. In addition, its discriminating ability is weak.

3.2. Phase-Only Filter (POF)

The phase is of paramount importance for optical processing with coherent light [32]. For example, Horner and Gianino [33] suggested a correlation filter which depends only on the phase of a reference image (with which the scene is compared). Without loss of generality, this POF is readily expressible as

$$H_{POF}(\mu,\nu)=\frac{R^{*}(\mu,\nu)}{\left|R(\mu,\nu)\right|}=\exp\left(-i\theta_{0}(\mu,\nu)\right) \tag{2}$$

The main feature of the POF is to increase the optical efficiency η. It is worthy to note that Eq. (2) depends only the phase of the reference. Besides the ability to get very narrow correlation peaks, POF have another feature that Ad filters lack: the capacity for discriminating objects. Because POF use only the reference's phase, they can be useful as edge detector. However, as is well known the POF is very sensitive to even small changes in rotation, scale and noise contained in the target image [34].

3.3. Binary Phase-Only Filter (BPOF)

We consider next the binarized version of the phase-only filter [35], or alternatively defined as a two-phase filter where the only allowed values are 1 and -1 such as

$$\begin{aligned} &H_{BPOF}=1 \quad \text{if the real part of POF filter} \geq 0 \\ &H_{BPOF}=-1 \quad \text{otherwise} \end{aligned} \tag{3}$$

Other definitions of BPOF were also considered by Vijaya Kumar [36]. Generally, BPOF have weaker performances than POF. It is helpful in certain applications for which the size of the filter should be small and also for optical implementation. Like POF, BPOF is very sensitive to rotation, scale, and noise in the target images.

3.4. Inverse Filter (IF)

IF [37-38] is defined as the ratio of POF by the magnitude of the reference image spectrum, and can be expressed as

$$H_{IF}(\mu,\nu)=\frac{R^*(\mu,\nu)}{\left|R(\mu,\nu)\right|^2}=\frac{\exp(-i\theta_0(\mu,\nu))}{\rho_0(\mu,\nu)} \tag{4}$$

The main advantage of this filter is to minimize the correlation peak width, or in other words, to maximize the PCE. It has the desirable property of being very discriminating. Despite this, an IF has a number of drawbacks. It is very sensitive to deformation and noise contained in the target image with respect to the reference image.

3.5. Compromise Optimal Filter (OT)

To realize a good correlation, the filter should be discriminating and robust. A filter showing a trade-off between these two properties was suggested in [39]. The OT filter is conveniently written out as

$$H_{OT}(\mu,\nu)=\frac{R^*(\mu,\nu)}{\alpha\Gamma_b(\mu,\nu)+(1-\alpha)\left|R(\mu,\nu)\right|^2}=\frac{\rho_0\exp(-i\theta_0)}{\alpha\left|\rho_b\right|^2+(1-\alpha)\left|\rho_0\right|^2} \tag{5}$$

where α denotes a discrimination and robustness degree. If α is set to zero, Eq. (5) yields the inverse filter, while the adapted filter is recovered when α is equal to one.

3.6. Classical Composite Filter (COMP)

In general, taking a decision based on a single correlation obtained by comparing the target image with only one filter, i.e. single reference, does not allow getting a reliable identification [31]. To alleviate the problems associated with this drawback, multi-correlation approaches have been suggested. One way to realize multi-correlation within the VLC configuration is by employed the classical composite filter (COMP). The basic idea consists in merging several references by linearly combining them such as

$$H_{Comp}(\mu,\nu)=\sum_{i=1}^{M}R_i(\mu,\nu) \tag{6}$$

where denotes each reference spectrum. Observe that a weighing factor can be used in some cases for specific purpose [13].

3.7. Segmented Composite Filter (SPOF)

For the purpose of reducing the number of correlation requested to take a reliable decision, the number of references in the filter should be increased. However, increasing the latter has for effect to induce a local saturation phenomenon in a classical composite filter [5].

This can be remedied by use of a recently proposed spectral multiplexing method [5]. This method consists in suppressing the high saturation regions of the reference images. Briefly stated, this is achieved through two steps [5]. First, a segmentation of the spectral plane of the correlation filter is realized into several independent regions. Second, each region is assigned to a single reference. This assignment is done according a specific energy criterion

$$\frac{E^{l}_{u,v}}{\sum_{i,j} E^{l}_{i,j}} \gtrless \frac{E^{k}_{u,v}}{\sum_{i,j} E^{k}_{i,j}} \quad (7)$$

This criterion compares the energy (normalized by the total energy of the spectrum) for each frequency of a given reference with the corresponding energies of another reference.

Assignment of a region to one of the two references is done according Eq. (7). Hence, the SPOF contains frequencies with the largest energy.

3.8. Minimum Average Correlation Energy (MACE)

For good location accuracy in the correlation plane and discrimination, we need to design filters capable of producing sharp correlation peaks. One method [12] to realize such filters is to minimize the average correlation plane energy that results from the training images, while constraining the value at the correlation origin to certain prespecified values.

This leads to the MACE filter which can be expressed in the following compact form:

$$H_{MACE} = D^{-1}S\left(S^{+}D^{-1}S\right)^{-1}c^{+} \quad (8)$$

where D is a diagonal matrix of size $d \times d$, (d is the number of pixels in the image) containing the average correlation energies of the training images across its diagonals; S is a matrix of size $N \times d$ where N is the number of training images and + is the notation for complex conjugate.

The columns of the matrix S represent the Discrete Fourier coefficients for a particular training image. The column vector c of size N contains the correlation peak constraint values for a series of training images. These values are normally set to 1 for images of the same class [14]. A MACE filter produces outputs that exhibit sharp correlation peaks and ease the peak detection process.

However, there is no noise tolerance built into these filters. In addition, it appears that these filters are more sensitive to intraclass variations than other composite filters [40].

3.9. Amplitude-Modulated Phase-Only Filter (AMPOF)

Awwal *et al.* [21, 28] suggested an optimization of the POF filter based on the following idea: if the correlation plane of the POF spreads large, it yields a correlation peak described by a Dirac function. One way to realize this has been put forward in Ref. [21, 28], where the authors suggested the amplitude-modulated phase-only filter (H_{AMPOF})

$$H_{AMPOF}(\mu,\nu)=\frac{D\exp(-j\phi(\mu,\nu))}{|F(\mu,\nu)|+a} \tag{9}$$

where is the reference image spectrum, μ and ν denote the spatial frequencies, D is a parameter within the range [0,1], and the factor a ($a \leq D$) appearing in the denominator is useful in overcoming the indeterminate condition and ensuring that the gain is less than unity. It can be a constant or a function of μ and ν, and thus can be used to either suppress noise or bandlimit the filter or both.

3.10. Optimal Trade-off MACH (OT MACH)

Another optimization approach in the design of correlation filters was addressed to deal with the ability to suppress clutter and noise, an easy detection of the correlation peak, and distortion tolerance [28].

The resulting maximum average correlation height (MACH) filter exhibit superior distortion tolerance while retaining the attractive features of their predecessors such as the minimum average correlation energy filter and the minimum variance synthetic discriminant function filter. A variant of the MACH filter was also developed in [29], i.e. the optimal trade-off MACH filter which can be written as

$$H_{OTMACH}=\frac{m_x^*}{\alpha C+\beta D_x+\gamma S_x} \tag{10}$$

where m_x is the average of the training image vectors, C is the diagonal power spectral density matrix of the additive input noise, D_x is the diagonal average power spectral density of the training images, S_x denotes the similarity matrix of the training images, and α, β, and γ are three numerical coefficients.

3.11. Asymmetric Segmented Phase Only Filter (ASPOF)

The last filter which is presented in this chapter is the ASPOF. See, e.g. [41], for its definition. The reference image database is divided in two sub-databases (with reference to Figure1).

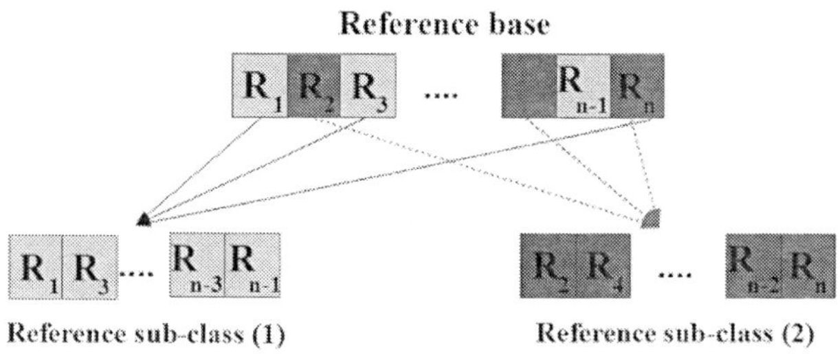

Figure 1. Technique used to separate the reference images into 2 sub-classes [41].

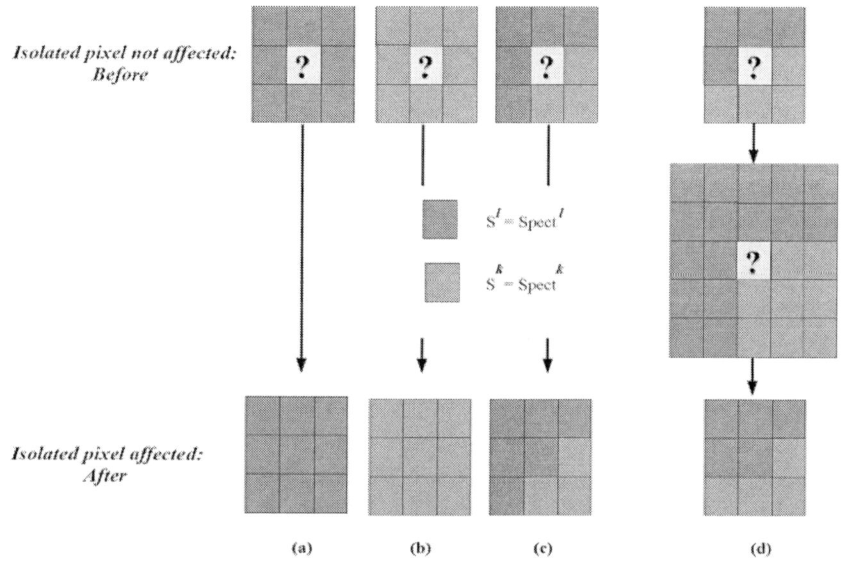

Figure 2. Illustrating the optimized assignment procedure for isolated pixels [41].

A SPOF is constructed from each of these databases according to the criterion defined by Eq.11.

$$\frac{E^{l}_{\mu,\theta}}{\sum_{i,j} E^{l}_{\mu,\theta}} \gtrless \alpha \frac{E^{k}_{\mu,\theta}}{\sum_{i,j} E^{k}_{\mu,\theta}} \quad (11)$$

Pixels which are not assigned using Eq.(11) are further assigned to the majority reference in the pixel's neighborhood (see Figure2).

4. Comparative Study of Composite Correlations Filters with Binary Images

Much research has been devoted to discovering new composite filters with higher efficiencies. An extensive review of composite filters has been found to be given by, where much can be found about distortion-invariant optical pattern recognition.

Table 1. Illustrating the Different Composite Filters Used

Composite filter	Notation	Equation
Adapted filter	$H_{comp_{Ad}}$	(1)
Phase-only filter	$H^1_{comp_{POF}}$, $H^2_{comp_{POF}}$	(2)
Binary phase-only filter	$H^1_{comp_{BPOF}}$, $H^2_{comp_{BPOF}}$	(3)
Inverse filter	$H_{comp_{IF}}$	(4)
Compromise optimal filter	$H_{comp_{OT}}$	(5)
Segmented filter	H^1_{SPOF}, H^2_{SPOF}	(7)
Segmented binary filter	H^1_{BSPOF}, H^2_{BSPOF}	(7)
Minimum average correlation energy filter	$H_{comp_{MACE}}$	(8)
Amplitude modulated phase-only filter	$H_{comp_{AMPOF}}$	(9)
Optimal trade off MACH	$H_{comp_{OTMACH}}$	(10)
Asymmetric segmented phase only filter	$H_{comp_{ASPOF}}$	(11)

$H_{comp_{Ad}}$ denotes the Adapted composite filter. This later is realized by considering a linear combination of reference images, and then using the adapted filter definition (Eq. (1)). $H_{Comp\text{-}POF}$ is the POF composite filter. We tested two different schemes for realizing the Composite POF filter. In the first scheme ($H^1_{comp_{POF}}$) we used a linear combination of reference images to create the POF; i.e. Eq. (2). The second scheme ($H^2_{comp_{POF}}$) involves performing the POF, via Eq. (2), for each reference, and then using the linear combination of these POFs. $H^1_{comp_{BPOF}}$ and $H^2_{comp_{BPOF}}$ are the binarized versions of the filters $H^1_{comp_{POF}}$ and $H^2_{comp_{POF}}$ obtained from Eq. (3), respectively. The composite inverse filter $H_{comp_{IF}}$ is the inverse filter (Eq. (4)) of the linear combination of reference images. The optimal composite filter $H_{comp_{OT}}$ is realized by linearly combining reference images (Eq. (5)). $H^1_{comp_{SPOF}}$ denotes the segmented filter realized by doing segmentation and assignment with the energy criterion (Eq. (7)). The calculation of filter $H^2_{comp_{SPOF}}$ is done by replacing the energy in Eq. (7) with the square of the real part of the different references spectra to be merged. $H_{comp_{MACE}}$ is the composite filter of the MACE filter developed in Eq. (8). $H_{comp_{AMPOF}}$ is the composite version of AMPOF (Eq. (9)). $H_{comp_{OTMACH}}$ is the composite version of OTMACH (Eq.(10)). $H_{comp_{ASPOF}}$ is the ASPOF (Eq.(11)). [41].

In particular, there are many other facets of composite filters not mentioned in section (3). In a general context, it is instructive to compare the performance of a selection of composite filters described in section (3). To aid the reader of this section, we briefly recap the filters characteristics and some of our terminology in Table 1. The main goal of this section is to identify the parameters which introduce limitations in the performances of these composites filters with and without noise in the input plane.

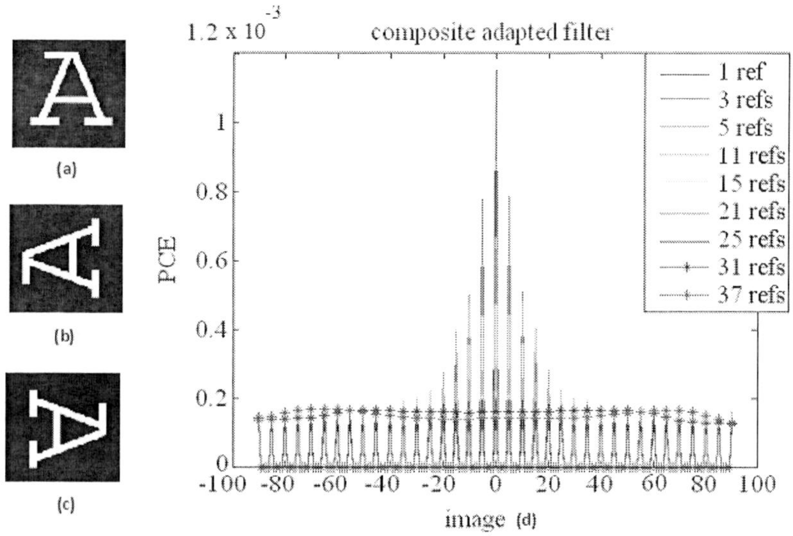

Figure 3. (Color online) Binary image for the uppercase letter A in the English alphabet: (a) standard, (b) 90° counterclockwise rotation, (c) the same as a 90° clockwise rotation, (d) PCEs obtained with the composite adapted filter. The colors shown in the inset denote the different composite adapted filters depending on the number of references used.

The binary (black and white) images from Figure 3 (a)-(c) were chosen for testing the composite filters because they are easier to process and analyze than gray level images, and the letter base can be digitized under controlled conditions, i.e. easy to process morphological operation and addition of input noise. Each image has black background with a white object (letter) on it with dimension 512×512 pixels. Here, we will limit ourselves to a data-base by rotating the A image (Figure 3(a)) in increments of 1° counter clockwise to get 181 images.

We now compare in a systematic way the performances of the composite filters of Table I for the data-base displayed in Figure 1(a)-(c). In performing this comparison a normalization of the correlation planes was realized. An illustration of the effects of the number of reference images (typically ranging from 1 to 37) employed to realize the composite filter on rotation of the input image will also be given.

4.1. Adapted Composite Filter

We start our discussion by considering the adapted composite filter in the Fourier plane of the VLC. Figure 3 (d) shows PCE by introducing every image of the data-base of 181 images, one by one, in the entrance plane. Each curve of Figure 1 (d) has a specific color which depends on the number of references used to realize the adapted filter, e.g. the red one considers a 3-reference filter (-5°, 0°, and 5°).

As expected the adapted composite filter is robust against rotation. It is also worthy to observe that the energy contained in the correlation peak decreases as the number of references chosen to realize the filter is raised. This decrease is detrimental to the usefulness of this type of composite filter. Its low discriminating character is more and more visible as the number of references is increased. This is consistent with previous studies [13].

4.2. Composite POF

Figure 4 (a) shows the PCE results for the composite POF $H^{1}_{comp_{POF}}$. As described previously, $H^{1}_{comp_{POF}}$ is realized by considering a linear combination of reference images (ranging from 1 to 37) to create a composite image.

The input images are then correlated with this filter. We find that the energy contained in the correlation peak decreases significantly, i.e. the PCE is decreased by a factor of 3 when using a POF containing 3 references by contrast with a POF realized with a single reference. For a 11-reference POF, the PCE is decreased by an order of magnitude which renders unreliable the decision on the letter identification. For 3 references only the images forming the filter are recognized.

However, beyond 11 references, the weakness of the magnitude of the PCE makes the recognition of the images forming the filter very difficult. Figure 4 (b) shows the correlation obtained with filter which is obtained by linearly combining the different POFs of different reference images.

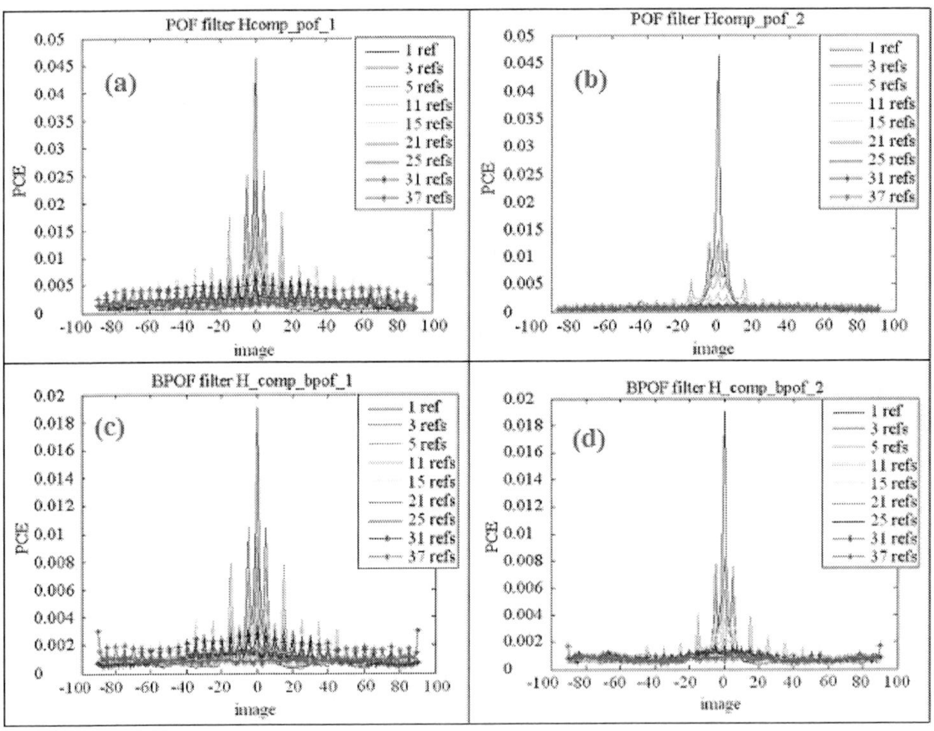

Figure 4. (Color online) (a) PCEs obtained with the POF composite filter. The colors shown in the inset denote the different filters depending on the number of references used. (b) Same as in (a) for filter Hcomp_pof_2 . (c) and (d) Same as in (a) and (b) for Binary filter.

The magnitude of the PCE decreases with raising the number of reference images of the filter. From the point of view of recognition application it appears that the saturation problem is more serious than that obtained with filter $H^{1}_{comp_{POF}}$, i.e. it is difficult to recognize a letter with a filter composed of more than 5 reference images even if the letter to be recognized belongs to the set of reference images. Thus, the overall performance for letter identification using this correlation technique decrease by employing filter $H^2_{comp_{POF}}$.

From the combined observations above, an especially meaningful feature emerges: to get a reliable decision, a 3-reference POF should be used. One of the distinctive features shown in Figure 4 (a) is that this filter allows one to recognize the letter A only taking a range for angle of rotation from -7° to 7°. Recognition of the full base requires fabricating at least 12 POFs, each having 3 references. Hence, this procedure cannot permit significant reduction in the time of decision since other phenomena can also affect the target image, e.g. scale.

4.3. Composite Binary POF

Binarized POF in the Fourier domain (Eq. (3)) is an alternative to POF. Figure 4 (c) (resp. Figure 4 (d)) shows PCE results obtained by binarization of $H^1_{comp_{POF}}$ (resp. $H^2_{comp_{POF}}$). Our calculations shown in these two graphs can be discussed in the same way as was done for Figs. 2 (a) and (b). At the same time, a comparison between Figs. 4 (a) and (b) and Figs. 4 (c) and (d) indicates a decrease of the PCE values. This is reminiscent of the noise induced by the binarization protocol.

4.4. Inverse Composite Filter

It has been known for a while that the inverse filter shows a strong discriminating ability and a low robustness against small changes of the target image with respect to the reference image. In practice, is realized by defining the inverse filter of the linear combination of different references.

In Figure 5 we plot the corresponding PCE values for the letter base A correlated with filter and different numbers of references. These results are consistent with our previous observation of the PCE decrease as the number of references is raised. We also check that these simulations are consistent with the above mentioned characteristics of the inverse filter. Indeed, correlation vanishes even when the target image is identical to one of the reference images used to realize the filter.

Up to now, our results show that filter has the best performance among the selected composite filters studied so far. To orient the subsequent discussion, we show the good discriminating ability of the composite POF, with parameters chosen for comparison with the above-described data. Our previous calculations suggest that the more discriminating efficiency of the filter is associated with the weaker false alarm rate. For that specific purpose, the letter V base (Figure6 (a)), i.e. constituted by 19 images obtained by rotating the V every 10°, was correlated with filter realized with reference images of letter A. Although the letter V has a great similarity with the letter A with a 18*0*° *rotation*, it is easily seen that the different composite POFs do not recognize V as being an A since no false alarm can be detected (Figure6 (b)). Nominal values of PCE are less than 0.002, ca. over 20 times less than the maximum value seen in Figure 4 (c). This is a clear indication of the good discriminating ability of the POF.

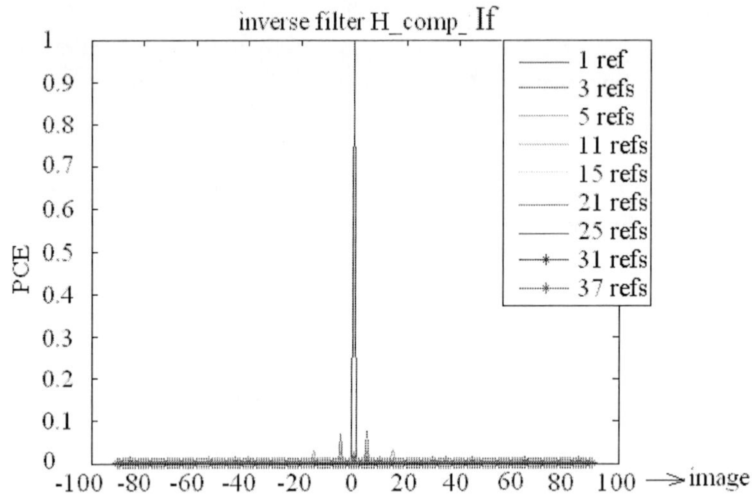

Figure 5. (Color online) PCEs obtained with the inverse composite filter. The colors shown in the inset denote the different adapted filters depending on the number of references used [41].

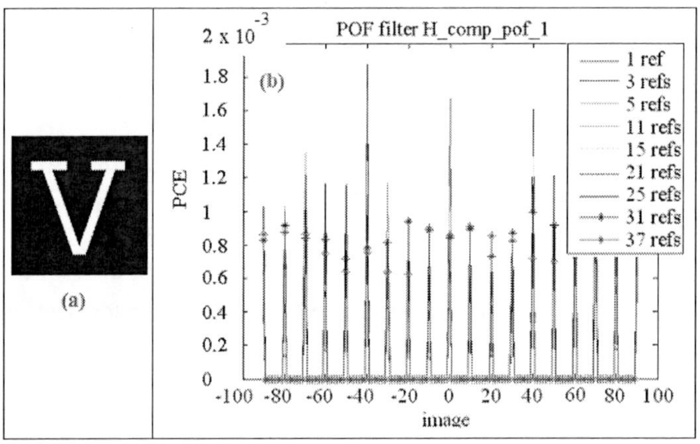

Figure 6. (Color online) Discrimination tests: (a) The target image considered is the letter V. (b) PCEs obtained with a filter realized with reference images of letter A. The colors shown in the inset denote the different adapted filters depending on the number of references used [41].

4.5. Robustness against Noise

In realistic object recognition situations, some degree of noise is unavoidable. A second series of calculations was conducted in which standard noise types were added to the target image. In this section, we shall mainly consider the compromise optimal filter (OT) $H_{comp_{OT}}$ since it represents a useful trade-off between adapted and inverse filters. Its tolerance to noise is also remarkable. Throughout this section, our calculations will be compared with results obtained with filter $H^1_{comp_{POF}}$. At a first look at the performance of the OT filter with noise, we consider the special case of background noise, i.e. the black background is replaced by the gray texture shown in Figure 7 (a). Figure 7 (b) shows the uppercase letter A with rotation (-45°).

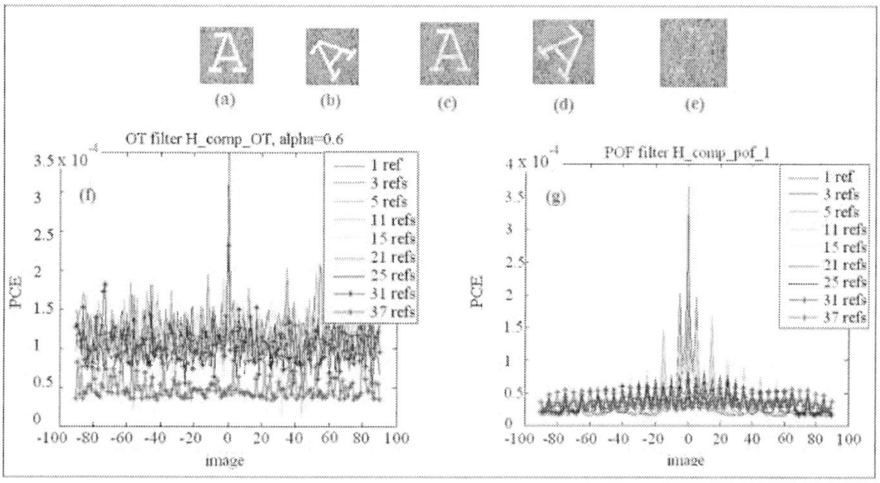

Figure 7. (Color online) (a) Illustrating the letter A with additive background structured noise. (b) Same as in (a) with a rotation angle of -50°. (c) Illustrating the letter with structured noise. (d) Same as in (c) with a rotation angle of 50°. (e) Illustrating the letter A for a weak contrast. (f) PCEs obtained with the OT composite filter taking α=0.6. The colors shown in the inset denote the different adapted filters depending on the number of references used. (g) Corresponding PCEs for a POF. The colors shown in the inset denote the different adapted filters depending on the number of references used.

Figure 7 (f) shows that the filter OT can recognize this letter only for a noisy image oriented at 0°. The results indicate that PCE decreases as α is increased. If α is set to zero, this filter cannot recognize any letter.

We also observe that the filter OT is not robust to image rotation when the images are noisy, especially if the noise cannot be explicitly evaluated.

One of the reasons we will not pursue the characterization of this filter stems from the fact that the input noise cannot be always determined in a real scene. We now exemplify the effect of background noise (applying an analysis similar to that above) by evaluating the performance of the POF ($H^1_{comp_{POF}}$). A noise was also added in the white part of the letter (with reference to Figs. 7 (c) and (d)). As illustrated in Figure 7 (g), POF is more robust to background noise than filter OT. As mentioned previously, this is consistent with the good discrimination ability of the composite POF filters. One interesting result is that the performances of composite filters decrease when the input image is weakly contrasted with respect to background, as evidenced in Figure 7 (e).

In another set of calculations, we considered the case of a Gaussian white noise on the composite POF for which the expectation value can be 0 or 1, and its variance can be set to 0, 0.1 and 1 (Table 2).

Examples of noisy images are shown in the second row of Table II. Insight is gained by observing in the third row of Table 2 how the correlation results vary for different composite

POFs realized with noise free reference images. As was evidenced for the standard POF, composite POFs show robustness to noise, i.e. we were able to identify noisy images using filter $H^1_{comp_{POF}}$. However, it is apparent that only noisy images which have been rotated with similar angles to the reference images have been identified.

Table 2. Calculated correlation results (third row) obtained with different composite POFs. The first row considers the numerical characteristics of the white Gaussian noise used. The second row shows a typical realization of the noisy images

White centered Gaussian noise, with variance set to 0.1		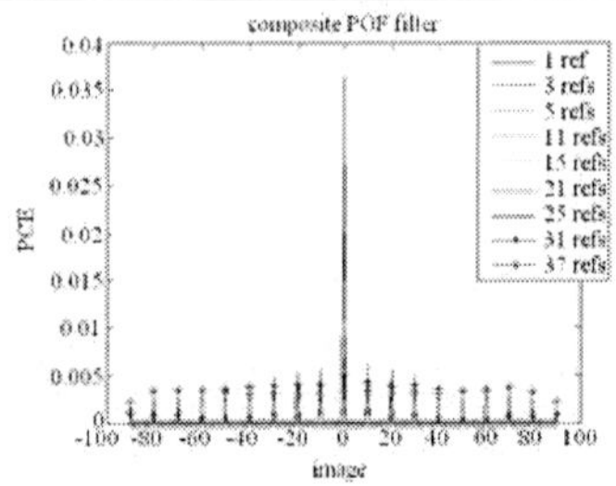
White centered Gaussian noise, with variance set to 1		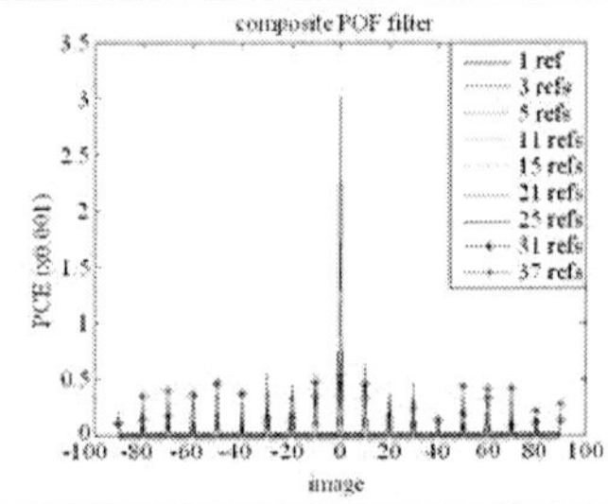
White centered Gaussian noise, with expectation value set to 1 and variance equal to 0.1		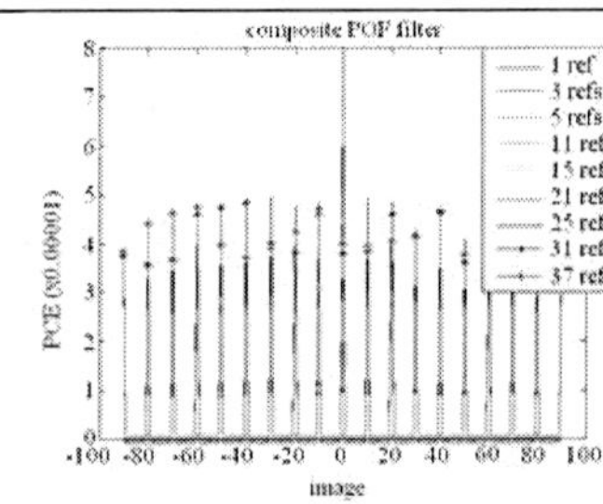

As we have seen so far, the compromise optimal filter is robust to noise when the latter is clearly identified. However, the performance of POF is better when the characteristics of noise are unknown. It is also important to point out that the performance of both composite filters decrease when the number of reference images forming the filter is increased. It should be emphasized once more that this effect is more likely when the images are noisy.

4.6. Optimized Composite Filters

Next, we are interested in the design of an asymmetric segmented composite phase-only filter whose performance against rotation will be compared to the MACE filter, POF, SPOF and AMPOF. To illustrate the basic idea, let us consider composite filters which are constructed by using 10 reference images obtained by rotating the target image by 0°, -5°, +5°, -10°, +10°, -20°, +20°, +25°, respectively.

To begin our analysis, we consider the composite filter MACE. Figure 8 presents correlation results of the letter base A (data-base obtained by rotating the A image in increments of 1° within the range (-90°,+90°)) with a composite MACE filter containing 10 reference images (0°, -5°, +5°, -10°, +10°, -20°, +20°, +25°). Here, the basic purpose is to recognize the letter A even when it is rotated with an angle ranging from -20° to 25°. In the angular dependence of the PCE value shown in Figure 8, we can distinguish three regions exhibiting distinct correlation characteristics (referred to as A, B and C, respectively). One notices in Figure 8 that if we restrict ourselves to region B only, correlation appears when the target image is similar to one of the reference images (Figure 8). No correlation is observed in regions A and C of Figure 8. The MACE composite filter is weakly robust to structured noise. Another example is shown in Figure 9 (a) when a centered Gaussian noise of variance 0.1 is added to the input image. This figure shows the sensitivity of the MACE composite filter against this type of noise. In fact, it gives lower PCE values even with a low noise level.

Figure 9 (b) shows the results for the filter MACE with a structured background noise. With reference again to Figure 9 (b) no correlation were observed even in the angular region ranging from –20° to 25° suggesting the poor correlation performances of filter MACE. We have also confirmed that the MACE composite filter is very sensitive to noise, and especially to structured noise. For this reason, we will not pursue the study of this filter in the remainder of this paper. The preceding analysis prompted us to study the composite filter performances based on different optimized versions of the POF, i.e. filters H_{SPOF} , $H_{comp_{AMPOF}}$ and $H_{comp_{ASPOF}}$. Here we reinvestigate the identification problem of letter A in the angular region ranging from -20° to 25° by considering a 10-reference composite filter. Furthermore, we shall compare these results with those obtained using the classic composite filter $H^1_{comp_{POF}}$. Parenthetically, there are similarities between the PCE calculations obtained for filters and $H^2_{comp_{POF}}$ with those based on filters and $H^1_{comp_{POF}}$.

Our illustrative correlation calculations for filter and the letter base A (data-base obtained by rotating the A image in increments of 1° within the range (-90°,+90°)) are given in Figure 10 (a) and (b). Shown in this figure are the PCEs for the composite POF (blue curve), the segmented composite POF (red curve), the composite AMPOF (black curve) and the composite ASPOF (green curve). We first note, in Figure 10 (a) that the PCE values for the composite ASPOF are larger than the corresponding values when the optimization stage (see Figure 2) has been applied to the filter. When the optimization stage has not been applied, the ASPOF PCE values are similar to the SPOF PCE values, see Figure 10 (b) [41]. Otherwise, even if the PCEs for the composite AMPOF are larger than those for the two other filters, there is a range of rotation angle, i.e. region A, for which the segmented filter shows correlation. Also apparent is that the PCE values calculated for the segmented filter H^1_{SPOF} are larger than the corresponding values of the classical composite POF in the correlation region A.

In this region A, we observe large variations of the PCE values, but all the correlation values are larger than the PCE values obtained in the no-correlation regions B and C. Maximal PCE values correspond to auto-correlation of the 10 reference images. Outside the A region correlation deteriorates rapidly. From these simulations, we concluded that it is difficult to identify the letter for the three filters considered. The PCE results show significant dependence on the rotation of the target image with respect to the reference images for composite AMPOF.

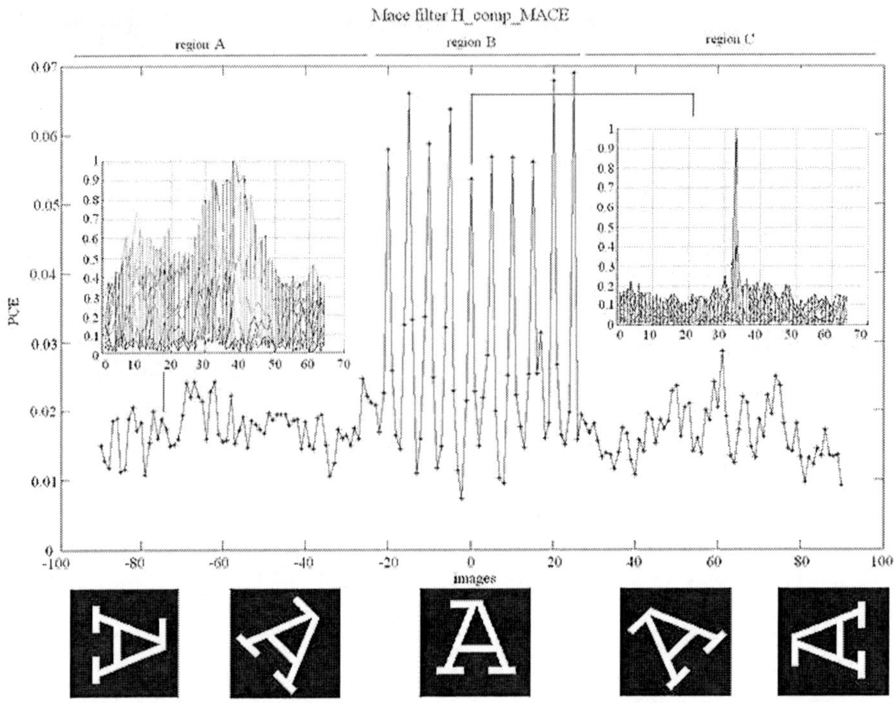

Figure 8. (Color online) PCEs obtained with a 10-reference MACE when the target images are noise free. Several examples of the rotated letter A are illustrated at the bottom of the figure. The insets show two correlation planes: (right) autocorrelation obtained without rotation, (left) inter-correlation obtained with the letter A oriented at -75° [41].

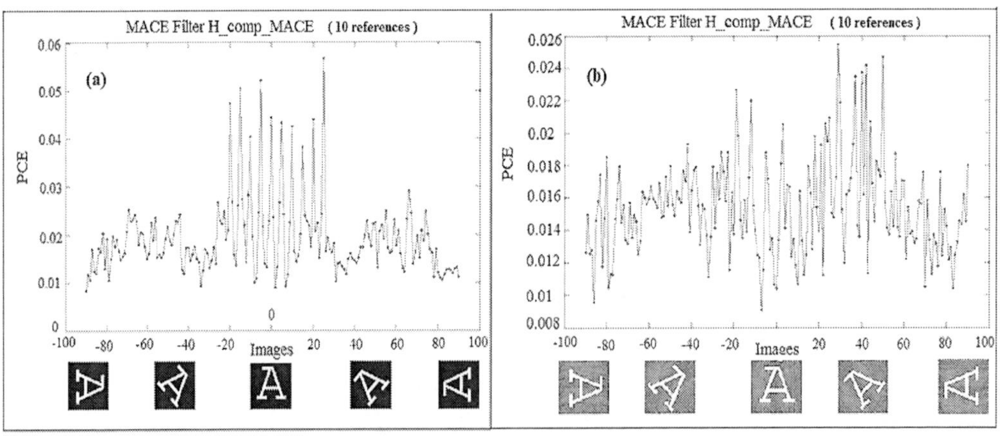

Figure 9. (Color online) (a) PCEs obtained with Mac composite filter and additive Gaussian centered noise of variance 0.1. (b) Same as in (a) with additive background structured noise.

Having discussed image rotation dependence without noise of the composite filters response we now determine the impact of noise. For this purpose, we applied two types of noise to the target image, either background structured noise (Figure 7 (a)), or a centered white noise with variance set to 0.01. Interestingly, one can see in Figs. 10 (c) and (d) the results of the PCE calculations which show the good performance of asymmetric segmented filter H_{comp_aspof} . Even when noise is present, the ASPOF yields correlation in region A. By contrast, there is no correlation in the A region with the AMPOF composite filter.

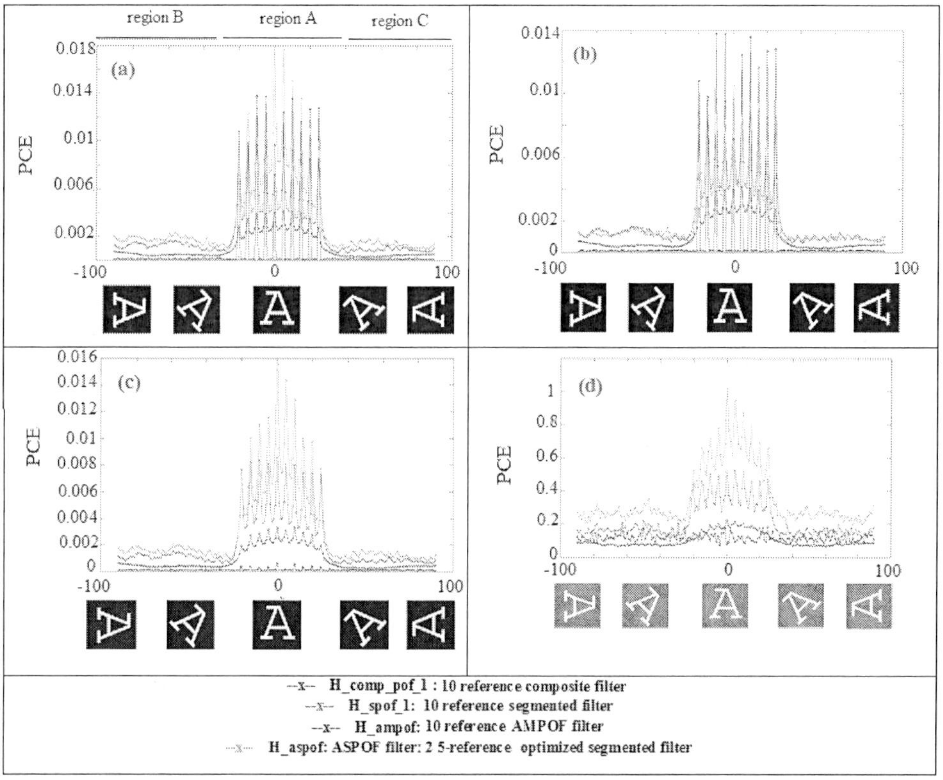

Figure 10. (Color online) Comparison between the different correlations of letter A (we consider rotation angles ranging between -90° and 90°) with the 10-reference composite filters: POF (blue line), Segmented (red line), AMPOF (black line), and ASPOF (green line). (a) PCEs obtained using the optimization stage concerning the isolated pixels, (b) PCEs obtained without the optimization stage concerning the isolated pixels. (c) and (d) represent the PCEs obtained with noised target images.

However, identification of the full letter data-base requires an increase of the reference images. This leads to the decay of the segmented filter's performance. Interestingly, Figure 11 indicates that the segmented filter's performance is very sensitive to the number of references forming the filter. We also studied the effect of binarization on the performances of the segmented composite filter. In fact, this binarization can be an effective solution to reduce the memory size to store theses filters without altering the efficiency of the decision.

To further show the interest in using a segmented filter with respect to the saturation problem which affects the classical composite filter, we show in Figure 12 (b) the 8-bit image of the sum (without segmentation) of the three spectra corresponding to the reference images.

Figure 12 (c) shows the corresponding sum with segmentation. Our calculations clearly indicate that the image with segmentation shows significantly less saturation than that obtained without segmentation.

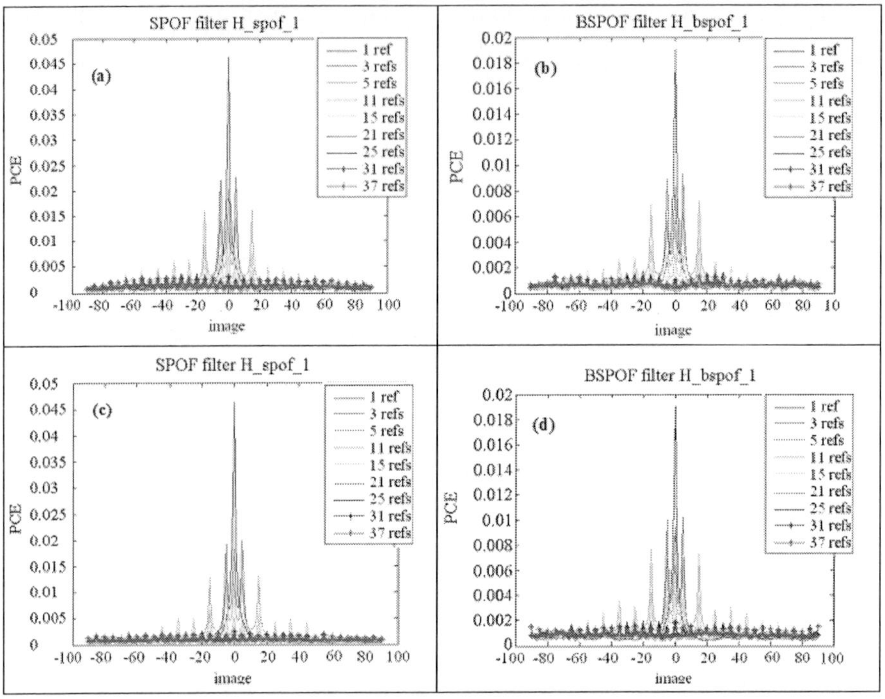

Figure 11. (Color online) PCEs obtained with a segmented composite filter : (a) using the energy criterion, (b) using the segmented binarized filter, (c) using filter the real part criterion, (d) corresponding binarized filter to (c).

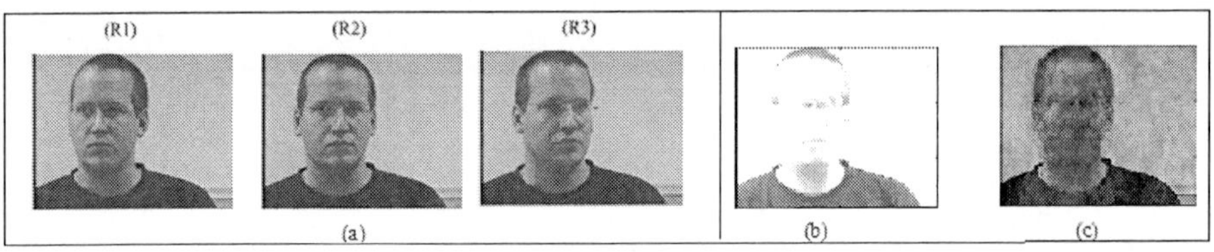

Figure 12. Illustrating the saturation effect: (a) three 8-bit grey scale images. (b) Image obtained by a classical linear combination of the three images shown in (a). (c) Image obtained using an optimized merging (spectral segmentation).

CONCLUSION

We now conclude with a brief discussion of the robustness of the ASPOF. In Figure 13, we have represented the ROC curves obtained with filters (Composite-POF, SPOF, AMPOf and ASPOF) containing each 10 references (from -60° to +60°).

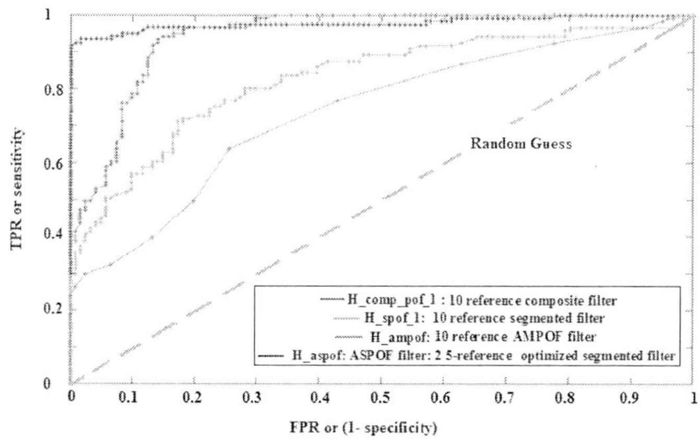

Figure 13. (Color online) ROC curves obtained with 10-reference composite filters: POF (red), SPOF (green), AMPOF (purple) and ASPOF (navy blue). The sky-blue line shows the random guess [41].

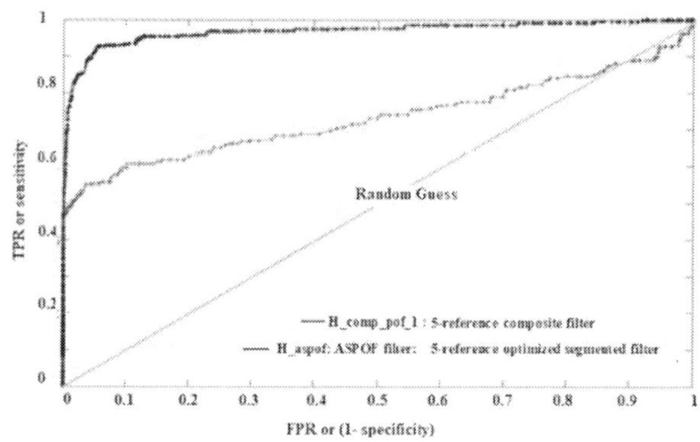

(a)

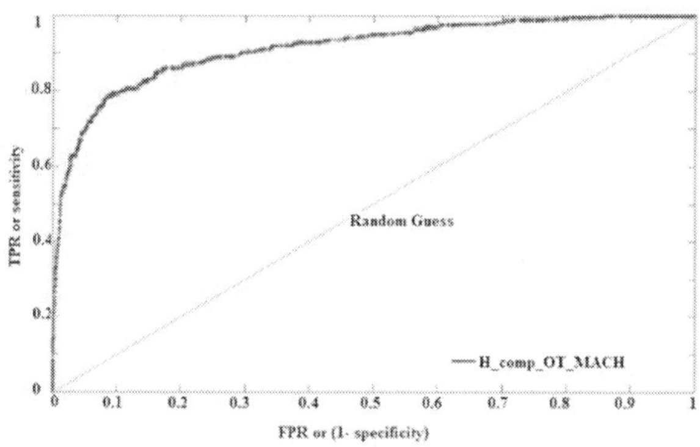

(b)

Figure 14. (Color online) (a) ROC curves obtained by correlating faces of a given subject, e. g. Figure 12 (a), with 6 other individuals with 5-reference ASPOF (navy blue) and POF (red) composite filters. The sky-blue line shows the random guess. (b) ROC curve obtained with an OT MACH.

We can see that the ASPOF filter is effective for image recognition. The ttrue recognition rate is equal to 92% when the false alarm rate is set to 0% .

We also compared the ROC curves obtained with the ASPOF, POF, and OT MACH filters for the face recognition application (with reference to Figure 14). We fabricated 5-reference composite filters. For the ASPOF, we used a 2-reference SPOF and a 3-reference

SPOF to compute the ASPOF. The reference images correspond to -45°, -30°, -15°, +15° and +45° rotation angles. The ASPOF produces better correlation performances than the POF filter (Figure 14 (a)). We also compared these results with the ROC curve of the OT MACH (Figure 14 (b)). The distance between the two curves is shorter than the distance between the ROC curves of the ASPOF and POF filters but the ASPOF still indicates better performances.

Acknowledgments

The authors acknowledge the partial support of the Conseil Régional de Bretagne and thank A. Arnold-Bos (Thales Underwater Systems) for helpful discussions. They also acknowledge S. Quasmi for her help with the simulations. Lab-STICC is Unité Mixte de Recherche CNRS 6285.

References

[1] Alfalou and C. Brosseau "Understanding Correlation Techniques for Face Recognition: From Basics to Applications," in Face Recognition, Milos Oravec (Ed.), ISBN: 978-953-307-060-5, In-Tech (2010).

[2] VanderLugt, "Signal detection by complex spatial filtering," *IEEE Trans. Inf. Theor.* 10, 139-145 (1964).

[3] B.T. Phong, "Illumination for computer generated pictures", *Communications of the ACM*, 18, no.6, (1975).

[4] Pointing Head Pose Image (PHPID), http://www.ecse.rpi.edu/~cvrl/database/other_Face_Databases.htm.

[5] Alfalou, G. Keryer, and J. L. de Bougrenet de la Tocnaye, "Optical implementation of segmented composite filtering," *Appl. Opt.* 38, 6129-6135 (1999).

[6] Y. Ouerhani, M. Jridi, and A. Alfalou, "Implementation techniques of high-order FFT into low-cost FPGA," presented at the Fifty Fourth IEEE International Midwest Symposium on Circuits and Systems, Yonsei University, Seoul, Korea, 7-10 Aug. 2011.

[7] S. Weaver and J. W. Goodman, "A technique for optically convolving two functions," *Appl. Opt.* 5, 1248–1249 (1966).

[8] V. K. Vijaya Kumar and L. Hassebrook, "Performance measures for correlation filters," *Appl. Opt.* 29, 2997-3006 (1990).

[9] J. L. Horner, "Metrics for assessing pattern-recognition performance," *Appl. Opt.* 31, 165-166 (1992).

[10] H. J. Caufield and W. T. Maloney, "Improved discrimination in optical character recognition," *Appl. Opt.* 8, 2354-2356 (1969).

[11] F. Hester and D. Casasent, "Multivariant technique for multiclass pattern recognition," *Appl. Opt.* 19, 1758-1761 (1980).

[12] Mahalanobis, B. V. K. Vijaya Kumar, and D. Casassent, "Minimum average correlation energy filters," *Appl. Opt.* 26, 3633-3640 (1987).

[13] Alfalou, "Implementation of Optical Multichannel Correlators: Application to Pattern Recognition," *PhD Thesis*, Université de Rennes 1–ENST Bretagne, Rennes-France (1999).

[14] T. S. Yu, S. Jutamulia "*Optical Pattern Recognition*," Cambridge University Press (1998).

[15] J. L. Tribillon, "*Corrélation Optique*," Edition Teknéa, Toulouse, (1999).

[16] Keryer, J. L. de Bougrenet de la Tocnaye, and A. Alfalou, "Performance comparison of ferroelectric liquid-crystal-technology-based coherent optical multichannel correlators," *Appl. Opt.* 36, 3043-3055 (1997).

[17] Alfalou and C. Brosseau, "Robust and discriminating method for face recognition based on correlation technique and independent component analysis model," *Opt. Lett.* 36, 645-647 (2011).

[18] M. Elbouz, A. Alfalou, and C. Brosseau, "Fuzzy logic and optical correlation-based face recognition method for patient monitoring application in home video surveillance," *Opt. Eng.* 50, 067003(1)-067003(13) (2011).

[19] Leonard, A. Arnold-Bos, and A. Alfalou, "Interest of correlation-based automatic target recognition in underwater optical images: theoretical justification and first results," *Proc. SPIE* 7678, 76780O (2010).

[20] V. H. Diaz-Ramirez, "Constrained composite filter for intraclass distortion invariant object recognition, "*Opt. Lasers Eng.* 48, 1153 (2010).

[21] A. S. Awwal, "What can we learn from the shape of a correlation peak for position estimation?," *Appl. Opt.* 49, B40-B50 (2010).

[22] Alsamman and M. S. Alam, "Comparative study of face recognition techniques that use joint transform correlation and principal component analysis," *Appl. Opt.* 44, 688-692 (2005).

[23] S. Romdhani, J. Ho, T. Vetter, and D. J. Kriegman, "Face recognition using 3-D models: pose and illumination," in *Proceedings of the IEEE* 94, 1977-1999 (2006).

[24] P. Sinha, B. Balas, Y. Ostrovsky, and R. Russel, "Face recognition by humans: nineteen results all computer vision researchers should know about", in *Proceedings of the IEEE* 94, 1948-1962 (2006).

[25] D. E. Riedel, W. Liu, and R. Tjahyadi "Correlation filters for facial recognition login access control", in *Advances in Multimedia Information Processing*, 3331/2005, 385-393 (2005).

[26] P. Hennings, J. Thorton, J. Kovacevic, and B. V. K. Vijaya Kumar, "Wavelet packet correlation methods in biometrics," *Appl. Opt.* 44, 637-646 (2005).

[27] J. Khoury, P. D. Gianino, and C. L.Woods, "Wiener like correlation filters," *Appl. Opt.* 39, 231-237, 2000.

[28] Mahalanobis, B. K. V. Vijaya Kumar, S. Song, S. R. F. Sims, and J. F. Epperson, "Unconstrained correlation filters," *Appl. Opt.* 33, 3751–3759 (1994).

[29] Zhou and T.- H. Chao, "MACH filter synthesizing for detecting targets in cluttered environment for grayscale optical correlator," *Proc. SPIE* 3715, 394 (1999).

[30] Pe'er, D. Wang, A. W. Lohmann, and A. A. Friesem, "Apochromatic optical correlation," *Opt. Lett.* 25, 776-778 (2000).

[31] V. K. Vijaya Kumar, "Tutorial survey of composite filter designs for optical correlators," *Appl. Opt.* 31, 4773-4801 (1992).

[32] V. Oppenheim and J.S. Lim, “The importance of phase in signals,” *Proc. of IEEE* 69, 529–541 (1981).

[33] J. L. Horner and P. D. Gianino, “Phase-only matched filtering,” *Appl. Opt.* 23, 812-816 (1984).

[34] J. Ding, M. Itoh, and T. Yatagai, “Design of optimal phase-only filters by direct iterative search” *Opt. Comm.* 118, 90-101 (1995).

[35] J.L. Horner, B. Javidi, and J. Wang, “Analysis of the binary phase-only filter,” *Opt. Comm.* 91, 189–192 (1992).

[36] V. K. Vijaya Kumar, “Partial information filters,” *Digital signal processing* 4, 147–153 (1994).

[37] R. C. Gonzalez and P. Wintz, “*Digital Image Processing*,” Addison-Wesley (1987).

[38] Inbar and E. Marom, "Matched, phase-only, or inverse filtering with joint-transform correlators," *Opt. Lett.* 18, 1657-1659 (1993).

[39] P. Refrégier, "Optimal trade-off filters for noise robustness, sharpness of the correlation peak, and Horner efficiency," *Opt. Lett.* 16, 829-831 (1991).

[40] Casasent and G. Ravichandran, “Advanced distorsion-invariant MACE filters,” *Appl. Opt.* 31, 1109-1116 (1992).

[41] Leonard, A. Alfalou and C. Brosseau, "Spectral optimized asymmetric segmented phase only correlation filter", *Appl. Opt.* (2012)

In: Face Recognition
Editors: Adamo Quaglia and Calogera M. Epifano
ISBN 978-1-61942-663-4

Chapter 4

FACE RECOGNITION EMPLOYING PCA BASED ARTIFICIAL IMMUNE NETWORKS

Guan-Chu Luh
Department of Mechanical Engineering, Tatung University, Taipei, Taiwan, ROC

ABSTRACT

This study proposes a face recognition method based on Principal Component Analysis (PCA) and artificial immune networks. The PCA extracts principal eigenvectors of the face image to get best feature description, consequently to reduce the size of feature vectors of the artificial immune networks. Hereafter these reduced-dimension image data are input into immune network classifiers to be trained. Subsequently the antibodies of the artificial immune networks are optimized using genetic algorithms. The performance of the proposed method was evaluated employing the ORL (ATandT Laboratories Cambridge) face database. The results show that this method gains higher recognition rate in contrast with most of the developed methods even for single training sample problem.

INTRODUCTION

Face recognition has received considerable interest and attention from various researchers in the pattern recognition field over the last two decades. Face recognition is nowadays a significant issue due to its extensive range of prospective applications related to biometrics, information security, video surveillance, law enforcement, identity authentication, smart cards, access control systems and so forth [1-4]. The purpose of face recognition is to identify or verify a person from a set of digital images or video frames from a video source. It is typically used in security systems and can be compared to other biometrics such as fingerprint or eye iris recognition systems. Face recognition has numerous advantages over the other biometric technologies since it is natural, non-intrusive, and easy to use. People can access it in comfortable without direct contact. Furthermore, it can be used ubiquitously and employed in diverse applications. Recent surveys of face recognition techniques can be found in literatures [4-7].

Face recognition is an image pattern recognition problem. A face recognition system usually contains four modules: detection, alignment, feature extraction, and matching. Its performance depends highly on the extracted features to characterize the face pattern and the classification methods utilized to make a distinction between faces. Essentially, the face representation was achieved by means of two categories, appearance-based and feature-based approaches. The first one applies holistic texture features and is used to the face or specific region of it while the second category employs the geometric relationship between the facial features such as eyes, nose, and mouth. Amongst the appearance-based approach, principal components analysis (PCA) [8] is a distinguished dimension reduction and feature extraction technique that has been effectively and extensively implemented in the field of pattern recognition, computer vision and signal processing. Based on Karhunen–Lòeve transform [9], PCA algorithm finds an optimal linear transformation to reduce the dimensionality of a vector by approximating it with most major eigenvectors. Sirovich and Kirby [10, 11] first applied PCA for efficient representation of a face image. Afterward Turk and Pentland [12] developed the well-known Eigenface for face recognition in 1991. Since then, PCA relative face recognition schemes have been comprehensively investigated [13-18]. PCA based face recognition typically contain two stages: training and classification. In the training phase, an eigenspace is established from the training samples and then mapped to the eigenspace for classification. As to the classification phase, an input face is projected to the same eigenspace and subsequently classified by appropriate classifiers.

In visual classification, it has been verified [19-21] that the combination of an ensemble of classifiers can achieve superior performance in respect of a single classifier in that the deficiencies of every classifier may be reimbursed each other. Different structures for combining classifier systems may be clustered into three types: cascade, parallel and hybrid [20, 21]. In the field of pattern recognition, the neural networks are among the most successful classification systems that can be trained to perform complex functions. Plenty of theoretic literature dissertates the applications of neural networks in face recognition [22-25] due to its rapid classification capability. However, relative less work has applied the artificial immune networks to face recognition. Both immunity-based systems and neural networks are bio-inspired techniques with the capability of identifying patterns of interest [26, 27]. They use learning, memory, and associate retrieval to solve recognition and classification tasks. Robustness is the common feature as basic cognitive mechanism for immune and neural systems [26] as well. There has been an increasing interest in the field of artificial immune systems (AIS) and their applications over the last few years [27-29].

In this study, a novel face recognition architecture based on PCA followed by artificial immune networks called PCA-IN was developed. The recognition mechanism consists of two phases: the PCA feature extraction phase and the immune network classification phase. The artificial immune networks are utilized as a collection of individual classifiers. Figure 1 shows the schematic diagram for the proposed method. In PCA-IN, each person has his/her corresponding immune classifier containing a number of antibodies. PCA-IN is trained (optimized) employing genetic algorithms (GAs) before face recognition implementation. GAs is based on the mechanism of natural selection and evolution and has been utilized in searching for the global optimum for many applications. It combines survival of the fittest individual among population with a structured and randomized information exchange to form a search algorithm with some of the innovative flair of human search.

GAs starts from a set of random strings to represent the individuals of population and proceed repetitively from generation to generation using three basic genetic operators: reproduction, crossover, and mutation. In each generation, the number of clones of each individual is duplicated proportional to its fitness value for next generation. Because the fitness value represents the survival probability, the selection procedure keeps strong individuals and eliminates the weak ones to emulate the evolution of nature. Obviously, the result and performance of search employing GAs depend on the definition of fitness function considerably. The reproduction operator is the source of exploitation and several reproduction techniques have been studied for improving the selection process. The main purpose of crossover is to exchange genetic information between parent pairs without losing any important schemata. Crossover operator recombines genetic information of two individuals to produce the offspring for the next generation. In short, crossover operator can be viewed as a two-step process. In the first step, the individuals of mating pairs are chosen from the mating pool of population. Subsequently transaction of chromosome segments between mating pairs is performed. Different crossover operators have been proposed to decrease the probability of disruption of strongly fitted schemata during the search process. The purpose of mutation is to introduce genetic diversity into the population. A random number is generated and it is checked with the probability of mutation. If the random number is less than the defined threshold, the selected chromosome has to undergo mutation. Typically the mutation rate lies in 0.001 to 0.01.

Both the crossover and mutation operators are the sources of genetic exploration. They will disrupt some of the schemata on which they operate. In the process of genetic search, there is a tradeoff between exploitation (*i.e.* reproduction) and exploration (*i.e.* crossover and mutation). The difficulty of GAs is seeking the balance between exploitation and exploration that determine the convergence and diversity of the optimal search.

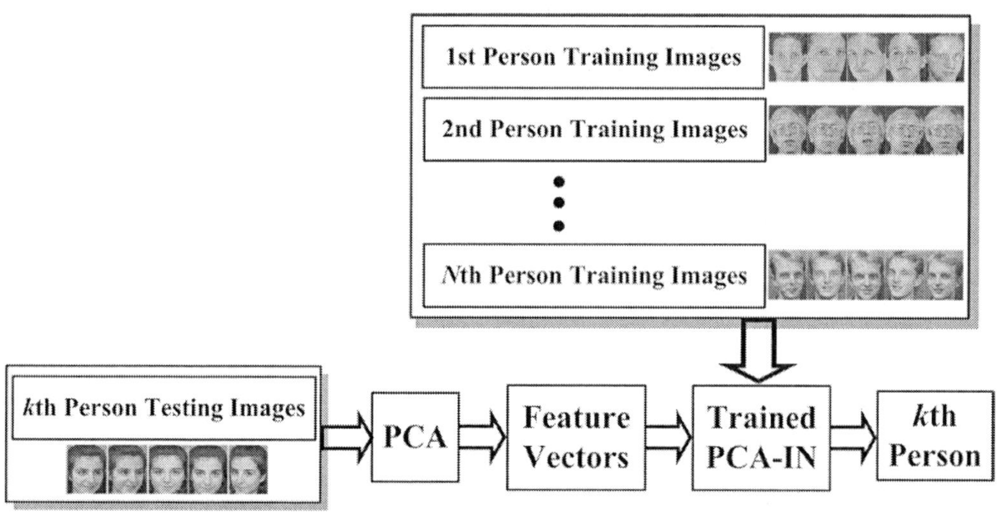

Figure 1. Architecture of the proposed face recognition system.

To evaluate the performance of the developed PCA-IN, two experimental studies (five training samples and one training sample per person) are carried out on the ORL laboratories database. Face recognition is a difficult problem due to several image variations in real-life including illumination, lighting, facial expression, partial occlusion and imprecise localization of face area. The typical approach to handle these variations is using large and representative training sample sets. Nevertheless, there is frequently only one training sample per person in many applications such as law enforcement, identity card or passport verification. This kind of realistic "one sample per person problem" severely challenges existing face recognition techniques, particularly their robustness performances under possible variations and has rapidly emerged as an active research sub-area in recent years. Although several methods [30-39] have been proposed dealing with the one sample problem, the variation issue is far from solved. Recent surveys of face recognition techniques employing one training image can be found in literatures [40].

The rest of this paper is organized as follows. Feature extraction using PCA is introduced in Section 2. Artificial immune system is described in Section 3. Section 4 presents the PCA-IN technique. Finally, Sections 5 and 6 present the experimental results, discussions and conclusions.

Feature Extraction Using PCA

As mentioned previously, PCA is a generally utilized dimension reduction method employing in face recognition to transform several possibly interrelated variables into a smaller number of uncorrelated principal components. The main process for feature extraction employing PCA can be stated as follows [12, 40]. A face image in two-dimension with size $N \times N$ can be considered as a vector of dimension N^2. Images of faces, being similar in overall configuration, will not be randomly distributed in this huge image space and therefore can be described by a comparatively low dimensional subspace. The key idea of the principle component is to find the vectors that best comprise the distribution of face images within the whole image space. These vectors characterize the subspace of face images called "face space". Each of these vectors is a linear combination of the original face images. They are defined as "eigenfaces" since these vectors are the eigenvectors of the covariance matrix respective to the original face images.

Let the training set of face images be $\mathbf{\Gamma}_1, \mathbf{\Gamma}_2, \ldots, \mathbf{\Gamma}_M$, then the average of the set is given as follows,

$$\mathbf{\Psi} = \frac{1}{M}\sum_{i=1}^{M}\mathbf{\Gamma}_i$$

Consequently, each face differs from the average by the vector $\mathbf{\Phi}_i = \mathbf{\Gamma}_i - \mathbf{\Psi}$. This set of very large vectors is then subject to PCA to seek a set of orthonormal vectors best describing the distribution of the data. The kth orthonormal vector, $\boldsymbol{u}_k$, is chosen such that,

$$\lambda_k = \frac{1}{M}\sum_{i=1}^{M}\left(\boldsymbol{u}_k^T \mathbf{\Phi}_i\right)^2$$

is a maximum, subject to

$$u_\ell^T u_k = \begin{cases} 1, & \text{if } \ell = k \\ 0, & \text{otherwise} \end{cases}$$

The vectors u_k and the corresponding scalars λ_k are the eigenvectors and eigenvalues of the covariance matrix

$$C = \frac{1}{M}\sum_{i=1}^{M}\left(\Phi_i \Phi_i^T\right)^2 = AA^T$$

where the matrix $A=[\Phi_1, \Phi_2, \ldots., \Phi_M]$. Since the covariance matrix C is an $N^2 \times N^2$ real symmetric matrix, it will be a difficult task to calculate the N^2 eigenvectors and eigenvalues for typical image sizes. As a result a computationally feasible method to find these eigenvectors is required. Consider the eigenvectors v_i of A^TA such that $A^TAv_i=\mu_i v_i$. Pre-multiplying both sides by matrix A, we have

$$A^T AAv_i = \mu_i Av_i$$

Obviously, Av_i are the eigenvectors and μ_i are the associated eigenvalues of covariance matrix C. We can then construct the $M \times M$ matrix $L=A^TA$, where $L_{ij} = \Phi_i^T \Phi_j$, and derive the M eigenvectors of L. These vectors determine linear combinations of the M training set face images to form the eigenfaces u_ℓ

$$u_\ell = \sum_{k=1}^{M} v_{\ell k}\Phi_k, \qquad \ell = 1, 2, \cdots, M$$

The computations will be thus significantly reduced from the order of the number of pixels in the images (N^2) to the order of the number of images in the training set (M). The calculations become quite manageable since the training set of face images is fairly small ($M \ll N^2$) in realistic applications. Besides, the corresponding eigenvalues allow us to rank the eigenvectors according to their usefulness in characterizing the variation among the images. The eigenface images derived from the eigenvectors of L span a basis set that can be used to illustrate face images.

In real life applications, lesser number of eigenfaces is satisfactory for face recognition since exact reconstruction of the image is not necessary. Sirovich and Kirby [41] have shown that 40 eigenfaces were adequate for a very good description of the set of 115 face images. In the task of face recognition, the eigenfaces span an n ($n < M$) dimensional subspace from the original N^2 image space are satisfactory for consistent representation of the faces and the n significant eigenvectors of the L matrix are selected as those with the largest associated eigenvalues. After that, any new input face image (Γ_{new}) can be transformed into its eigenface components as follows,

$$\omega_k = \boldsymbol{u}_k^T(\boldsymbol{\Gamma}_{new} - \boldsymbol{\Psi}), \qquad k = 1, 2, \ldots, n$$

The weights form a projection vector $\boldsymbol{\Omega}^T = [\omega_1\ \omega_2 \ldots\ \omega_n]$ which describes the contribution of each eigenface in representing the input face image and treats the eigenfaces as a basis set for face images. Accordingly classification can be accomplished by comparing the projection vectors of the training face images with that of the input face image using the Euclidean Distance between the face classes and the input face image shown below,

$$\varepsilon_k = \left\| \boldsymbol{\Omega} - \boldsymbol{\Omega}_k \right\|$$

Artificial Immune System

The natural immune system protects living bodies from the invading of foreign substances, called antigens, including viruses, bacteria, and other parasites. There are primarily two types of lymphocytes, namely B-cells and T-cells, playing an essential role in immunities. The former takes part in the humoral immunity that secretes antibodies (Abs) by clonal proliferation, while the latter takes part in cell mediated immunity. One class of T-cells, called Killer T-cell, destroys the infected cell whenever they recognize the virus. The other one which activates clonal expansion and stimulate/suppress antibody formation is called Helper T-cell. Lymphocytes drift freely in blood and lymph nodes, and patrol everywhere for antigens, then gradually float back to the lymphatic system, to begin the sequence all over again [42]. Figure 2 depicts the model describing the relationship between the major components in the immune system.

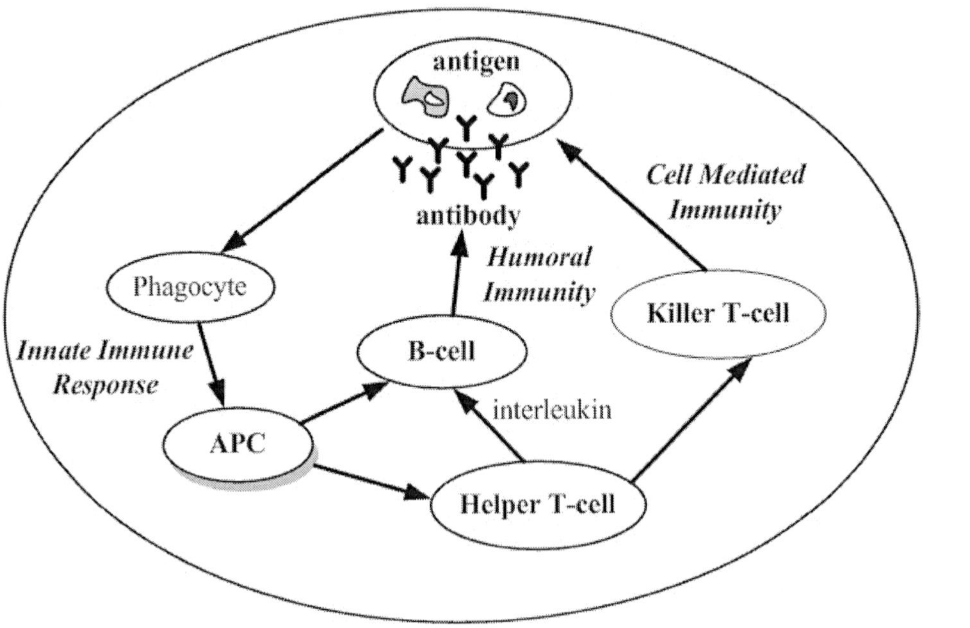

Figure 2. Illustration of the biological immune system.

Once an infectious foreign pathogen assaults the human body, the macrophage has surface receptors to detect and destroy the invader. Then the macrophage turns into an Antigen Presenting Cell (APC). The APC interprets the antigen appendage and extracts the associated features, by processing and presenting antigenic peptides on its surface to T-cell and B-cell. These antigenic peptides are kinds of molecules called MHC (Major Histocompatibility Complex) used to differentiate a "self" from other "non-self" (antigen). These lymphocytes will be able to sensitize this antigen and be triggered. Afterward the Helper T-cell releases the interleukines, the stimulation or suppression signals, and acting on the cells. In the other hand, B-cell becomes stimulated when an antibody binds to an antigen. In addition, B-cells are as well affected by the Helper T-cells during the immune responses. The Helper T-cell plays a extraordinary key role for deciding the immune system to the cell mediated immunity or the humoral immunity, and connects the non-specific immune response to make a more efficiency specific immune response.

Affinity maturation arises when the maturation rate of a B-cell clone increases in response to a match between the clone's antibody and an antigen. Then those mutant cells are bound more firmly and stimulated to divide more quickly. Affinity maturation dynamically balances exploration versus exploitation in adaptive immunity. It has been depicted that the immune system has the capability to recognize foreign pathogens, learn and memorize, process information, and discriminate between self and non-self [42]. Inspired by self-nonself discrimination of natural immune system, Forrest *et al.* [43] proposed a negative-selection algorithm to detect any novelty. Moreover the immunity can be preserved even faced with a dynamically changing environment. The biological immune system is generally viewed as a mechanism of a highly adaptive, learning, distributed, and detection system [26]. Furthermore it can identify different pathogen patterns and cause discriminating immune responses. Identification is achieved by inter-cellular binding, which is determined by molecule shape and electrostatic charge. Hence, B-cell becomes stimulated when an antibody binds to an antigen. Antibodies have the capability of binding pathogens that they have never learned to recognize. This kind of anticipatory capability is due to a broad coverage of pathogen space realized by the antibody produced by the immune system.

The concepts of the artificial immune system are inspired by ideas, processes, and components, which extracted from the biological immune system. There are abundance source of theories in immune system, which can play an important role in giving insights for engineering or computer based methods. It has been demonstrated that the learning and adaptive capabilities of AIS have a great potential in the fields of machine learning, computer science and engineering. Jerne [44] has proposed an idiotypic network hypothesis (immune network hypothesis) based on mutual stimulus and suppression among antibodies shown in Figure 3. This hypothesis is modeled as a differential equation simulating/suppressing the concentration of a set of lymphocytes. The concept of immune networks states that the network dynamically maintains the memory using a feedback mechanism within the network. Jerne concluded that the immune system is similar to the nervous system when viewed as a functional network. Based on Jerne's immune network hypothesis, several theories and mathematical models for immune system have been developed [45-47].

The following equations proposed by Farmer *et al.* [46] calculate the variation on the concentration of antibodies in immune networks.

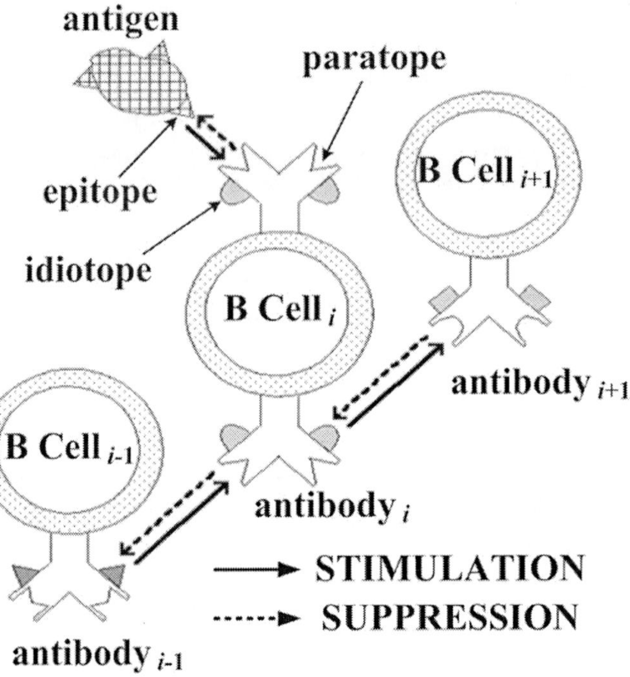

Figure 3. Idiotypic network hypothesis.

$$\frac{dA_i(t)}{dt} = \left(\sum_{j=1}^{N_{Ab}} m_{ij}^{st} a_j(t) - \sum_{k=1}^{N_{Ab}} m_{ki}^{su} a_k(t) + m_i - k_i \right) a_i(t) \tag{1}$$

$$a_i(t) = \frac{1}{1+\exp(0.5 - A_i(t))} \tag{2}$$

where $i, j = 0, 1, \cdots, N_{Ab}$ are the subscripts to distinguish the antibody types and N_{Ab} is the number of antibodies. A_i and are the stimulus and concentration of the ith antibody. m_{ij}^{st}, indicate the stimulative and suppressive affinity between the ith and the jth, kth Abs, respectively. m_i denotes the affinity among antigen and the ith antibody, and k_i represents the natural death coefficient. Equation (1) is composed of four terms. The first term shows the stimulation, while the second term indicates the suppressive interaction between the antibodies. The third term illustrates the stimulus from the antigen, and the final term is the natural extinction term, which depicts the dissipation tendency in the absence of any interaction. Equation (2) is a squashing function to ensure the stability of the concentration.

Different from the Jerne's idiotypic network hypothesis, Hightower *et al.* [48] suggested that all antigens could be declared as a collection of set points in an "antigen space" and antigen molecules with similar shapes occupy neighboring points in that space. It indicates that an antibody molecule can recognize some set of antigens and consequently covers some portion of antigen space as Figure 4 illustrated.

The collective immune response of the immune networks is thus represented as

$$\sum_{i=1}^{N_{Ab}} f(Ab_i) \tag{3}$$

where $f(Ab_i)$ is the immune response function between antigen and the ith antibody. Note that any antigen in the overlapping converge could be recognized by several different antibodies simultaneously.

Table 1. Pseudo-code of the proposed PCA-IN

```
procedure PCA-IN_face recognition
  N_Ag = Number of antigens/training face images;
  N_Ab = Number of antibodies in each immune network classifiers;
  n = Number of eigenfaces;
  N_pop = Number of population size;
  N_iter = Stopped iteration of PCA-IN;
  P_c = Crossover rate;
  P_m = Mutation rate;

procedure training/optimizing PCA-IN employing genetic algorithms
Set k = 0;
    Randomly selected training face images;
    Randomly initialize immune network classifiers;
    Randomly initialize distribution coefficient;
 Generate the initial individual/chromosome;
      Calculate the affinity value;
      Calculate the fitness value;

      while ( k < N_iter )
      Selection;
      Crossover;
      Mutation;
      Calculate the fitness value of offspring population;
      Update and save the best individual;
      end while
  end procedure
```

Afterward, Timmis *et al.* [49] introduced similar concept named Artificial Recognition Ball (ARB). Each ARB represents a certain number of B-cells or resources, and total number of resources of system is limited. Additionally each ARB describes a multi-dimensional data item that could be matched to an antigen or to another ARB in the network according to the Euclidean distance. Those ARBs located in the other's influence regions would either be merged to limit the population growth or pulled away to explore new area. ARBs are essentially a compression mechanism that takes the B-cells to a higher granularity level.

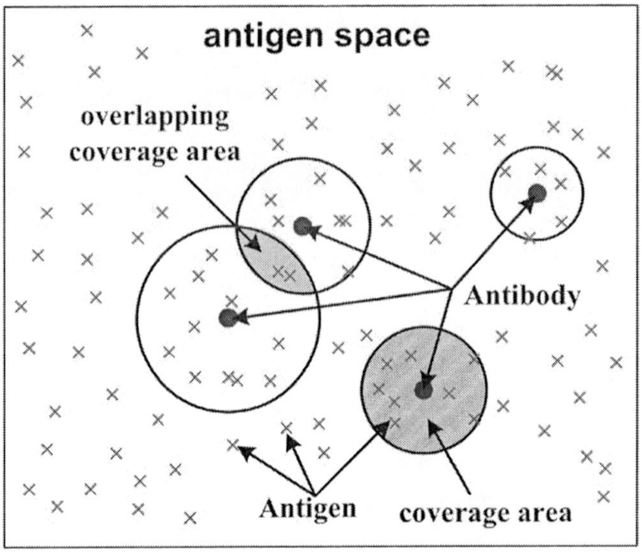

Figure 4. The antigen space.

PCA Based Artificial Immune Networks

In the proposed PCA-IN scheme, the antigen space is defined as the real data set of n-dimensional eigenvectors $\{\boldsymbol{v}_i|\ i=1,\ 2,\ \ldots,\ N_{Ag},\ \boldsymbol{v}_i \in \Re^n\}$; N_{Ag} indicates the number of antigens/training face images. For the purpose of efficiently neutralizing the antigen, different antigens require qualitatively different immune responses. The antigenic context has become correlated with the associated appropriate types of immune response. Here the antibody is defined as $\{\boldsymbol{p}_j|\ j=1,\ 2,\ \ldots,\ N_{Ab},\ \boldsymbol{p}_j \in \Re^n\}$; N_{Ab} indicates the number of antibodies in each immune network classifier. The pseudo-code for the proposed PCA-IN algorithm is listed in Table 1 and described in the following steps.

(1) *Random selection of the training face images/antigens*

Training face image for the ith person is randomly selected and then converted into an $N_{Ag}\times n$ dimensional eigenface

$$\boldsymbol{v}_i = \begin{bmatrix} v_{i,11} & v_{i,21} & \cdots & v_{i,N_{Ag}1} \\ v_{i,12} & v_{i,22} & \cdots & v_{i,N_{Ag}2} \\ \cdots & \cdots & \cdots & \cdots \\ v_{i,1n} & v_{i,2n} & \cdots & v_{i,N_{Ag}n} \end{bmatrix}$$

where N_{Ag} is the number of antigen/training face images and n is the number of eigenvector.

(2) *Random initialization of immune network classifiers*

Antibodies of the artificial immune network classifier for the jth person are initialized randomly. Immune classifier for each person is characterized by a $N_{Ab}\times n$ matrix shown below,

$$\boldsymbol{p}_j = \begin{bmatrix} p_{j,11} & p_{j,21} & \cdots & p_{j,N_{Ab}1} \\ p_{j,12} & p_{j,22} & \cdots & p_{j,N_{Ab}2} \\ \cdots & \cdots & \cdots & \cdots \\ p_{j,1n} & p_{j,2n} & \cdots & p_{j,N_{Ab}n} \end{bmatrix}$$

where N_{Ab} is the number of antibodies in each immune classifier.

(3) *Chromosome representation of genetic algorithms*

GAs is utilized to optimize the PCA-IN and the corresponding individual/chromosome for the jth immune network classifier is defined as the following $N_{Ab}\times(n+1)$ matrix,

$$\boldsymbol{IN}_j = \begin{bmatrix} \beta_{j,1} & \beta_{j,2} & \cdots & \beta_{j,N_{Ab}} \\ p_{j,11} & p_{j,21} & \cdots & p_{j,N_{Ab}1} \\ p_{j,12} & p_{j,22} & \cdots & p_{j,N_{Ab}2} \\ \cdots & \cdots & \cdots & \cdots \\ p_{j,1n} & p_{j,2n} & \cdots & p_{j,N_{Ab}n} \end{bmatrix}$$

where β_j is a vector of distribution factors of antibodies including in the jth immune network classifier.

(4) *Calculate the affinity value between antigens and antibodies*

The affinity $m_{k\ell}$, defined as the matching ratio between the kth antigen epitope and the ℓth antibody paratope for each immune classifier, is characterized as a Boltzmann-Gibbs distribution function [50, 51],

$$m_{k\ell} = \frac{e^{-\beta_\ell d_{k\ell}}}{Z} \tag{4}$$

Where β_ℓ is a parameter controlling the distribution shape, and $d_{k\ell}=\| \boldsymbol{v}_k - \boldsymbol{p}_\ell \|$ is the Euclidean distance between the kth antigen epitope vector and ℓth antibody paratope vector. The normalizing factor $Z = \sum_{k=1}^{N_{Ab}} e^{-\beta_k d_{k\ell}}$ is called the partition function. Obviously the coverage range provided by an antibody is determined by the distribution factor β_ℓ. The larger the value of β_ℓ, the smaller the cover area occupied. In other word, the immune response becomes more specific with respect to large β_ℓ value. Note that the distribution factor β_ℓ is initialized randomly. The distance $d_{k\ell}$ represents the structural similarity between the antigen epitope and antibody paratope. Smaller distance anticipates that the antigen is more matched to antibody. It should be noted that each antibody receptor gives a significant affinity only in a neighborhood near the center. The affinity decreases monotonically with distance from the center. This phenomenon allows the immune system to recognize similarity between antigens in terms of overlapping sets of epitopes, and hence use previous memory clones for induction of the appropriate types of immune response against correlated antigen.

(5) *Calculate the fitness value of the immune classifiers*

The response of the overall immune networks is derived by determining the set of affinities associated with the receptors and the structural similarity between antigen and antibody defined by quantification of the distance in antigen space. The collective immune response function for the ith antigen/training image of the immune networks is represented by the following equation,

$$f(v_i) = \sum_{j=1}^{N_{Ab}} m_{ij} \tag{5}$$

For the PCA-IN, the *i*th immune classifier tries to maximize the immune response of the self antigens (training images of the *i*th person) while minimize the responses to non-self antigens (the remaining training images of the other persons). Subsequently the fitness function of the *i*th immune classifier can be defined as following,

$$fit_i = w_1 \cdot \frac{\sum_{j=1}^{N_{self}} m_{ij}}{N_{self}} + w_2 \cdot \frac{1}{\sum_{k=1}^{N_{non-self}} m_{ik} / N_{non-self}} \tag{6}$$

where N_{self} and $N_{non\text{-}self}$ represent the number of self/training images of the *i*th person and that of the non-self/images of the remaining persons, respectively. Parameters w_1 and w_2 are the respecting weighting values, $w_1+w_2=1$. Each *i*th immune network tries to maximize its immune response with the associate *i*th personal training images and minimize its immune response with the remaining training images of the other persons.

(6) *Optimizing PCA-IN employing genetic algorithms*

The genetic operators adopted are roulette wheel selection, arithmetic crossover and Gaussian mutation with crossover and mutation rate of 0.8 and 0.05, respectively. In roulette wheel selection, individuals are given a probability of being selected that is directly proportionate to their fitness. Two individuals are then chosen randomly based on these probabilities and produce offspring. The fittest individuals have a greater chance of survival than weaker ones. This replicates nature in that fitter individuals will tend to have a better probability of survival and will go forward to form the matting pool for the next generation. However, weaker individuals are not without a chance since such individuals may have genetic coding that may prove useful to future generations in nature.

Arithmetical crossover is defined as a linear combination of two parent individuals/immune network classifiers. If IN_i and IN_j are two individuals to be crossed, the resulting offspring are

$IN_{i,offspring} = w \cdot IN_i + (1-w) \cdot IN_j$

$IN_{j,offspring} = w \cdot IN_j + (1-w) \cdot IN_i$

where w is a random number uniformly distributed in [0.0, 1.0]. *Gaussian mutation* consists in adding a random value from a Gaussian distribution to each element of an individual's matrix to create a new offspring as following,

$IN_{offspring} = (1+N(-1,1)) \cdot IN$

where N(-1,1) is a random number distributed in [-1, 1].

(7) *Stopping criteria*

The training of PCA-IN stops optimizing once a predefined number of iterations, N_{iter}, is reached. Otherwise, the procedure will be repeated from steps 4 to step 6.

EXPERIMENT RESULTS AND DISCUSSIONS

To evaluate the performance of the developed PCA-IN, two experimental studies (five training samples and single training sample per person) are carried out on the ATandT laboratories database (formerly also referred to as "The ORL database") of faces images of Cambridge University. The ORL database contains 400 face images from 40 individuals (4 female and 36 male) captured over the span of a 2-year period from subjects aged between 18 and 81. The total number of images for each person is 10. None of the 10 samples is identical to any other. They vary in position, rotation, scale and expression. The changes in orientation have been accomplished by rotating the person a maximum of 20° in the same plane; each person has changed his/her facial expression in each of 10 samples (open/closed eye, smiling/not smiling) as well. The changes in scale have been achieved by changing the distance between the person and the video camera. For some persons, the images were taken at different time, varying facial details (glasses/no glasses). Moreover the images have been manually cropped and re-scaled to a resolution of 112 × 92, 8-bit grey levels. Thumbnails of all of the images are shown in Figure 5.

The first experiment was executed with randomly selected 5 training images and 5 test images per person for a total of 200 training and 200 test images. It should be noted that there is no overlap between the training and test images. Each case was repeated 30 times by randomly choosing different training and testing sets and the average recognition rate is used to evaluate the classification performance. The face recognition simulations were implemented in C++ programming language on an Intel Core 2 2.34 GHz computer with 2G RAM running on Window Vista. It takes nearly 40 seconds (N_{Ab}=1) to 54 seconds (N_{Ab}=40) to train/optimize the PCA-IN, respectively. However, once the whole PCA-IN (consisting 40 immune network classifiers) is determined, it takes less than 20 *ms* to recognize a face. A simulation window of face recognition, its setting parameters, and the results are shown in Figure 6. This figure indicates that five randomly selected images (red block) are employed for training, while the rest ones (yellow block) are used for testing. It demonstrates that the PCA-IN correctly recognizes the image as the 32nd person. Moreover, the information indicated in the top right side block shows that the recognition rate of the trained/optimized immune networks is 100%.

First of all, PCA is employed to obtain eigenvalues and the associated eigenvectors of the face images. In order to reduce the amount of arithmetic operation without losing any important recognition information, eigenvectors that accord with the first 20 maximal eigenvalues are chosen. Afterward the randomly selected 5 training samples are input into the immune networks which are optimized using GAs. The population size of GAs is 200 while the stopping criterion is 1000 generations. The operators utilized are Roulette Wheel selection, arithmetic crossover and *Gaussian* mutation with crossover and mutation rate of 0.8 and 0.05, respectively. The performances of the proposed method are evaluated by varying the number of antibodies of each immune classifier (N_{Ab}) in addition to the weighting values (w_1 and w_2). Each experiment was repeated for 30 times and the "average recognition rate" (ARR) and the corresponding standard deviation (SD) and "ratio of one hundred percent recognition" (RHPR) are illustrated in Table 2. In addition, Figure 7 indicates the average recognition rates with respect to N_{Ab} and the weighting values. Apparently ARR is nearly increased proportional to the number of antibodies set in the immune network classifiers.

Additionally it seems that ARR increases exponentially when N_{Ab} is between 1 and 10. On the contrary, it seems that there is no much improvement of ARR if N_{Ab} is above 25. Moreover, it shows that the larger the weighting value w_1 the higher the recognition rate. The proposed PCA-IN achieves maximum ARR when w_1 equals to 1.0. In such situation, each immune classifier can be trained simply utilizing its corresponding person images and thus the training of the 40 immune classifiers can be decoupled. In other words, immune network classifier for any new person image can be trained separately and involved in the immune networks without affect the existing immune network classifiers.

Table 2. ARR+SD (%) and RHPR varies with N_{Ab} and w_1

20 eigenfaces		w_1=0.5 w_2=0.5	w_1=0.7 w_2=0.3	w_1=0.9 w_2=0.1	w_1=1.0 w_2=0.
N_{Ab} =1	ARR+SD (%)	78.07±2.543	81.47±2.144	84.15±3.121	85.84±2.641
	RHPR	0/30	0/30	0/30	0/30
N_{Ab} =3	ARR+SD (%)	93.25±2.314	94.43±2.019	95.55±1.700	96.18±1.336
	RHPR	0/30	0/30	0/30	0/30
N_{Ab} =5	ARR+SD (%)	95.58±1.421	96.51±1.495	97.40±1.264	98.23±1.105
	RHPR	0/30	0/30	0/30	0/30
N_{Ab} =10	ARR (%)	97.9±0.684	98.48±0.680	99.28±0.523	99.16±0.795
	RHPR	0/30	0/30	2/30	1/30
N_{Ab} =15	ARR+SD (%)	98.29±0.771	99.21±0.421	99.53±0.385	99.58±0.421
	RHPR	0/30	2/30	4/30	5/30
N_{Ab} =20	ARR+SD (%)	98.90±0.721	99.19±0.381	99.63±0.299	99.75±0.227
	RHPR	1/30	1/30	6/30	10/30
N_{Ab} =25	ARR+SD (%)	98.99±0.519	99.48±0.334	99.72±0.243	99.80±0.152
	RHPR	0/30	4/30	9/30	8/30
N_{Ab} =30	ARR+SD (%)	98.97±0.579	99.56±0.299	99.74±0.391	99.80±0.249
	RHPR	1/30	5/30	12/30	14/30
N_{Ab} =35	ARR+SD (%)	99.18±0.521	99.53±0.331	99.74±0.213	99.86±0.194
	RHPR	1/30	2/30	9/30	16/30
N_{Ab} =40	ARR+SD (%)	99.23±0.347	99.62±0.234	99.78±0.205	99.85±0.181
	RHPR	1/30	4/30	11/30	15/30

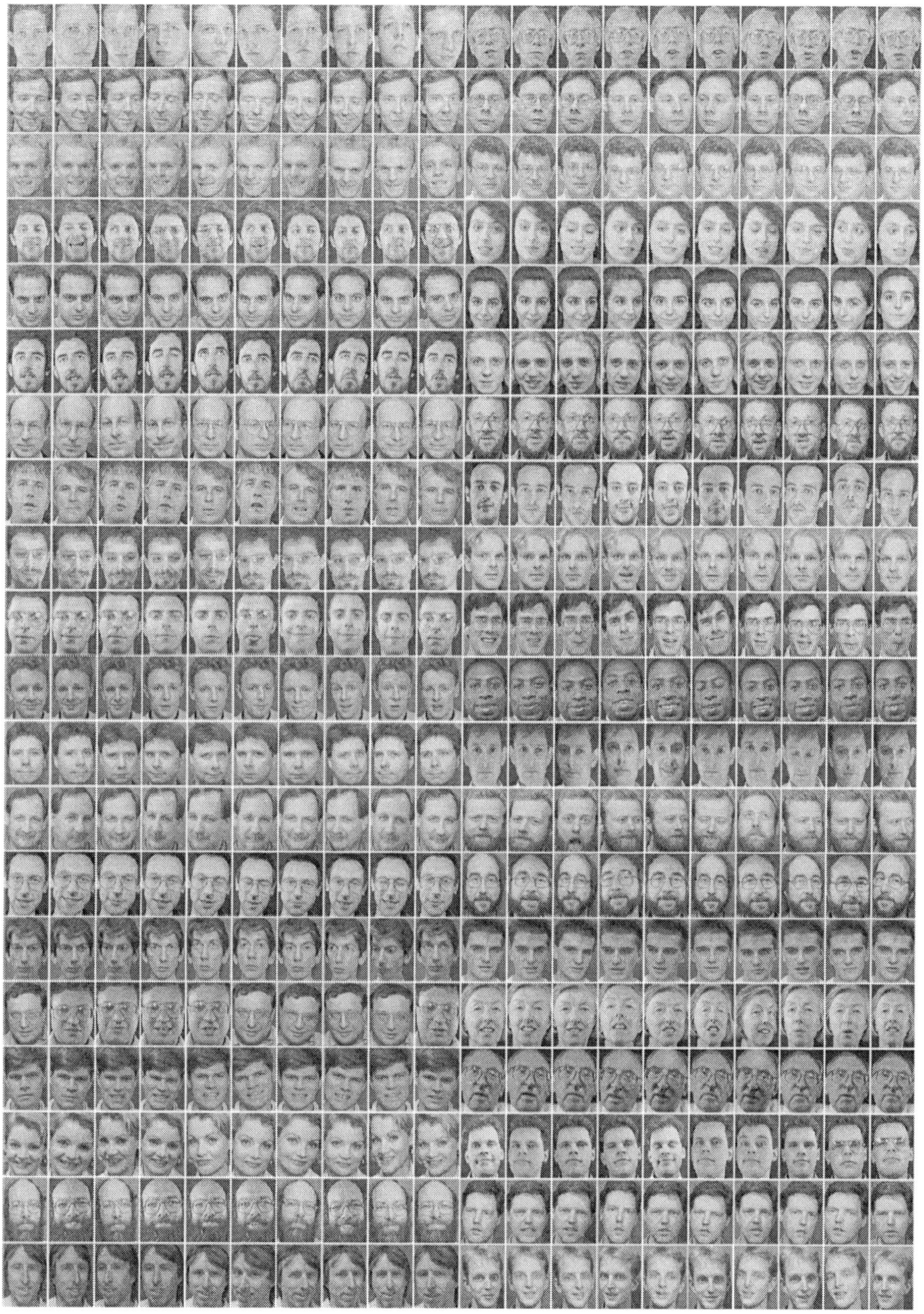

Figure 5. The ORL face database.

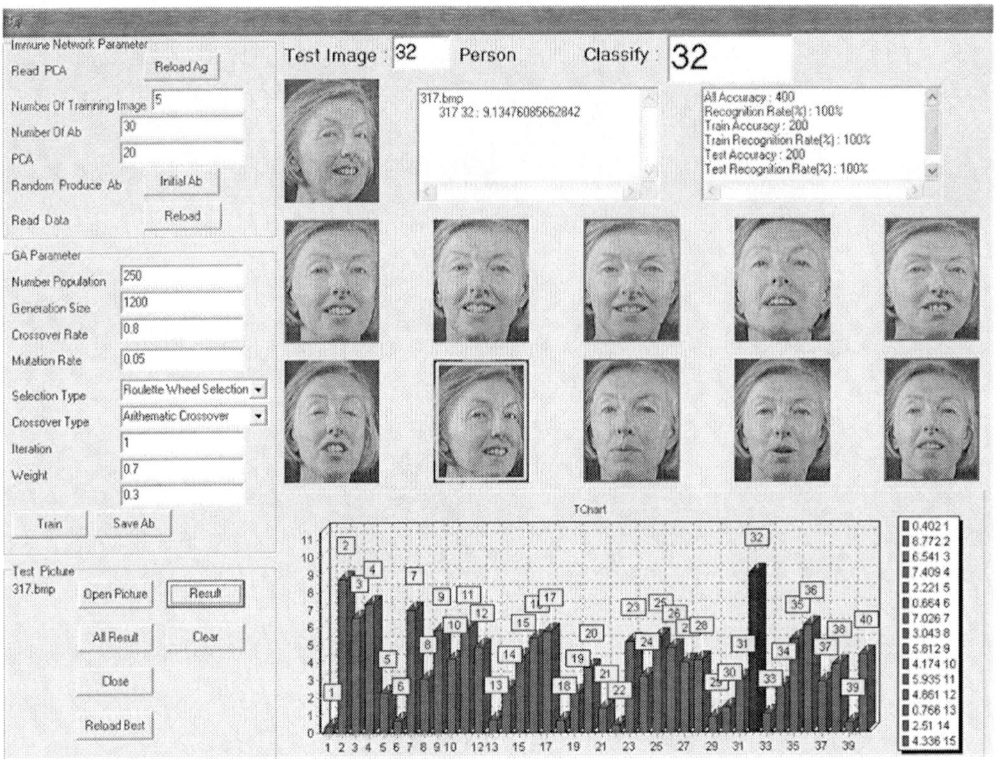

Figure 6. Simulation window for face recognition.

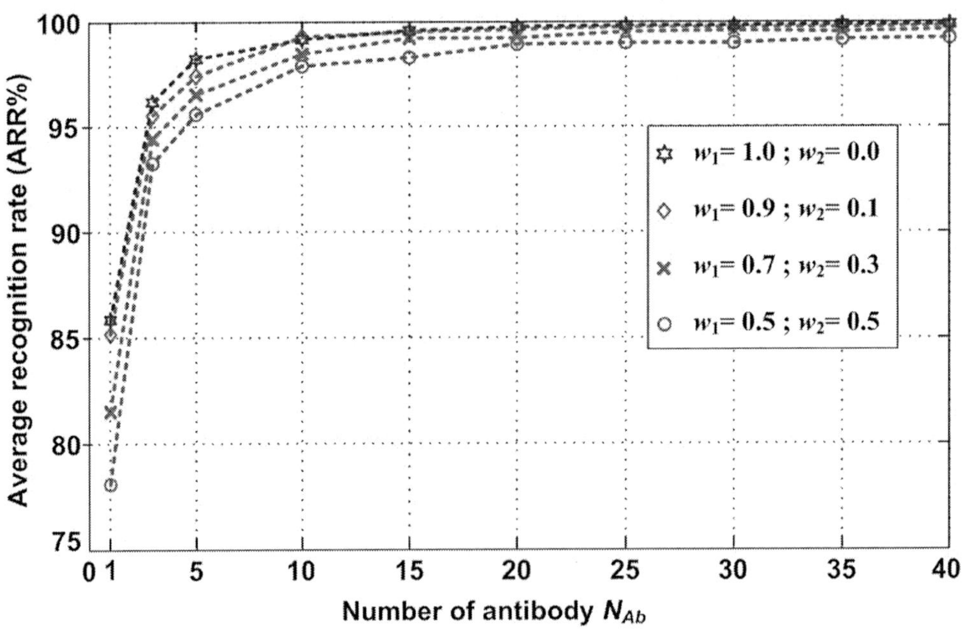

Figure 7. Average recognition rate varies with the number of antibodies and weighting values.

A two-way ANOVA (analysis of variance) without replication for ARR values is further performed to the experimental results in Table 2 employing Microsoft Office Excel. The results shown in Table 3 indicate that both the parameters N_{Ab} and w_1 are important because the associated P-Values are much less than 0.05.

Table 4 indicates how ARR+SD (%) and RHPR vary with the number of antibodies N_{Ab} and eigenfaces N_{eig} adopted on the ORL face image database when the weighting value w_1 equal to 1. Again, the larger the number of antibodies (N_{Ab}) the higher the ARR value derived. It shows that PCA-IN can achieve maximum 99.88% ARR when the immune classifiers contain 40 Abs with 40 eigenfaces utilized. In addition, PCA-IN attains nearly 98% minimum ARR even though there are only 5 antibodies (N_{Ab}=5) in each immune classifier with 5 eigenfaces (N_{eig}=5) employed. However, it seems that the number of eigenfaces has inconsistent influence on the performance of PCA-IN. In other words, larger number of eigenfaces does not assure better recognition performance. Furthermore, Tale 4 shows that PCA-IN has 100% recognition rate if $N_{Ab} \geq 10$ according the value of RHPR.

Table 3. Results of a two-way ANOVA without replication

source of variance	SS	df	MS	F	P-Value	F-crit
Rows (N_{Ab})	1030.003	9	114.4448	124.2437	1.31×10^{-19}	2.250131
Columns (w_1, w_2)	22.64409	3	7.548029	8.194306	0.000488	2.960351
Error	24.87054	27	0.921131			
Total	1077.517	39				

Table 4. ARR+SD (%) and RHPR varies with N_{Ab} and N_{eig}

w_1=1.0; w_2=0.0		N_{Ab}=5	N_{Ab}=10	N_{Ab}=20	N_{Ab}=30	N_{Ab}=40
N_{eig} =5	ARR+SD (%)	97.93±0.97	99.09±0.58	99.68±0.31	99.78±0.24	99.81±0.23
	RHPR	0/30	0/30	10/30	12/30	15/30
N_{eig} =10	ARR+SD (%)	98.04±0.99	99.29±0.47	99.72±0.27	99.82±0.22	99.82±0.17
	RHPR	0/30	3/30	10/30	13/30	11/30
N_{eig} =20	ARR+SD (%)	98.23±1.11	99.16±0.79	99.75±0.23	99.80±0.25	99.85±0.18
	RHPR	0/30	1/30	10/30	14/30	15/30
N_{eig} =30	ARR+SD (%)	98.45±0.63	99.25±0.55	99.69±0.25	99.81±0.20	99.82±0.15
	RHPR	0/30	2/30	8/30	13/30	10/30
N_{eig} =40	ARR+SD (%)	98.16±0.84	99.33±0.48	99.73±0.24	99.76±0.23	99.88±0.23
	RHPR	0/30	1/30	9/30	10/30	21/30
N_{eig} =50	ARR+SD (%)	98.18±0.89	99.24±0.53	99.68±0.29	99.78±0.24	99.85±0.16
	RHPR	0/30	3/30	7/30	12/30	14/30

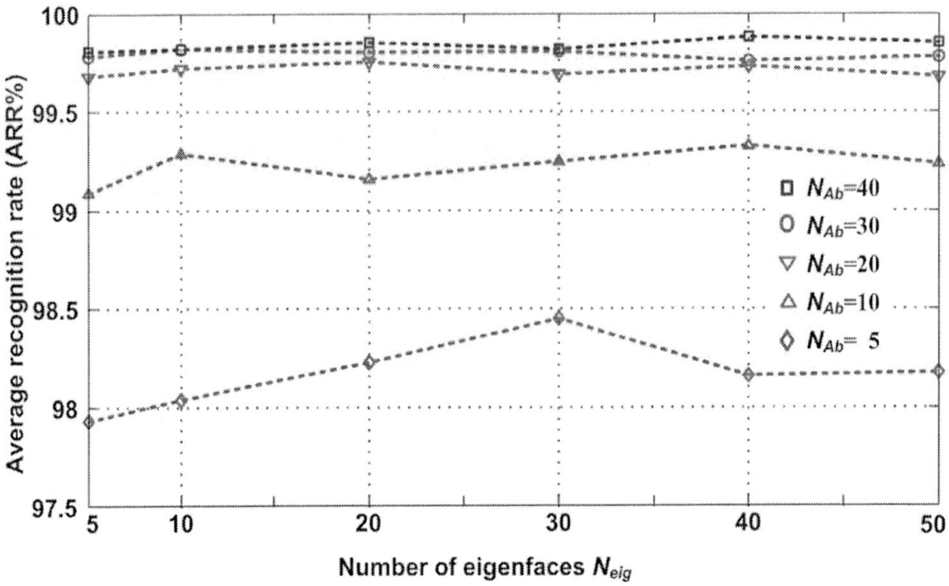

Figure 8. Average recognition rate varies with the numbers of antibodies and eigenfaces.

Figure 8 illustrates that the larger the number of antibodies the less the variations of ARR due to the number of eigenfaces. The deviation is a little bigger when N_{Ab} is equals to five. However, it may due to the randomly selecting training images and the randomized characteristics of GAs. Again, a two-way ANOVA without replication for ARR values is further performed to the experimental results in Table 5. The results indicate that N_{Ab} is an important factor since its P-Value is much less than 0.05. However, parameter N_{eig} may not have much influence because its P-Value is larger than 0.05. Table 6 lists the mean computational CPU time required for PCA-IN training/optimization for these experiments. Obviously, the larger the N_{Ab} is, the longer the time required.

Table 5. Results of a two-way ANOVA without replication

source of variance	SS	df	MS	F	P-Value	F-crit
Rows (N_{Ab})	11.88779	4	2.971946	375.8785	1.65×10^{-18}	2.866081
Columns (w_1, w_2)	0.047199	5	0.009439	1.193929	0.347474	2.710889
Error	0.158133	20	0.007906			
Total	12.09311	29				

Table 6. Mean computational CPU time for PCA-IN training

	Number of antibodies N_{Ab}									
	1	3	5	10	15	20	25	30	35	40
CPU time (sec)	40	41.5	43.2	44.6	46.1	47.6	48.9	50.6	52.1	53.5

The performance (in terms of the average recognition rates associated with standard deviation) of the proposed method was compared with the approaches reported in [52-56] as shown in Table 7. It should be noted that the average recognition rates for these methods are based on 10 and 20 runs of experiments, respectively. It may be observed from the table that the proposed PCA-IN is superior to the other methods containing simply 10 antibodies and 10 eigenfaces. In addition, the maximum ARR derived by the proposed PCA-IN was compared with those reported in [57-63] as shown in Table 8. In this table, the proposed PCA-IN method outperformed all other methods in addition to the point symmetry distance-based RBFNN (with 128 features, 120 hidden layer units) [25]. The difference of the average recognition rates is about 0.05%. However, it should be noted that RBFNN took 14 min to determine the required parameters while our proposed method took much less time to train PCA-IN.

Table 7. Comparison of ARR+SD (%) of different approaches

Method	ARR+SD (%)
Fuzzy fisherface [52]	98.37±0.89
2DMSD [53]	96.45±1.8
NDLPP [54]	96.3±1.42
NLDA [54]	96.8±1.2
FKFD (Polynomial) [55]	93.35±0.88
2DPCA-AMD [56]	96.3±1.25
proposed PCA-IN (10 antibodies, 10 eigenfaces) proposed PCA-IN (40 antibodies, 40 eigenfaces)	99.29±0.47 99.88±0.23

Table 8. Comparison of ARR (%) of PCA-IN with some other methods using the ORL database

Method	ARR (%)
N-feature neural network [57]	99.52%
UDT [58]	97.5%
KCLPP+LDA (ORL_C) [59]	98.5%
point symmetry distance-based RBFNN [25]	99.93%
Multiple classifier (ordered layers) [60]	97.1%
FND [61]	98.9%
IO+PCA+KFLD 4*4 Block [62]	97.7%
Combined LDA framework [63]	97.65%
proposed PCA-IN (40 antibodies, 40 eigenfaces)	99.88%

Numerous methods could deal well with frontal view face recognition if there were sufficient number of representative training samples. Nevertheless, few of them work well when only a single training sample per person is available. To evaluate the performance of the proposed PCA-IN, the simulation was executed with randomly selected 1 training images and 9 test images per person for a total of 40 training and 360 test images. There is no overlap between the training and test images.

Table 9. ARR(%) vs N_{Ab} and N_{eig} (w_1=0.5; w_2=0.5)

N_{Ab}	N_{eig}=5	N_{eig}=10	N_{eig}=20	N_{eig}=30	N_{eig}=40
1	78.18	77.55	77.78	78.24	78.13
2	88.48	88.14	88.46	88.19	88.50
3	92.57	92.64	93.01	92.29	92.31
4	94.17	94.09	94.51	94.60	94.67
5	95.77	95.80	95.62	95.56	95.84
6	96.41	96.64	96.34	96.19	96.58
7	96.96	97.16	96.59	96.90	96.81
8	97.44	97.41	97.00	97.20	97.25
9	97.64	97.72	97.44	97.52	97.33
10	97.90	97.80	97.75	97.82	97.61
15	98.53	98.07	98.55	98.30	98.49
20	98.61	98.75	98.70	98.80	98.77

Table 10. ARR(%) vs N_{Ab} and N_{eig} (w_1=1.0; w_2=0.0)

N_{Ab}	N_{eig}=5	N_{eig}=10	N_{eig}=20	N_{eig}=30	N_{eig}=40
1	85.48	86.67	85.91	85.87	86.67
2	93.34	94.13	94.14	93.49	93.59
3	96.61	96.58	96.69	96.53	95.86
4	97.66	97.78	97.63	97.67	97.57
5	98.01	98.41	98.13	97.95	98.41
6	98.79	98.82	98.51	98.46	98.61
7	98.96	98.84	98.73	98.72	98.91
8	98.98	99.14	98.96	98.93	99.12
9	99.02	99.15	99.09	99.18	99.16
10	99.26	99.33	99.12	99.35	99.31
15	99.44	99.47	99.59	99.50	99.61
20	99.64	99.68	99.69	99.78	99.72

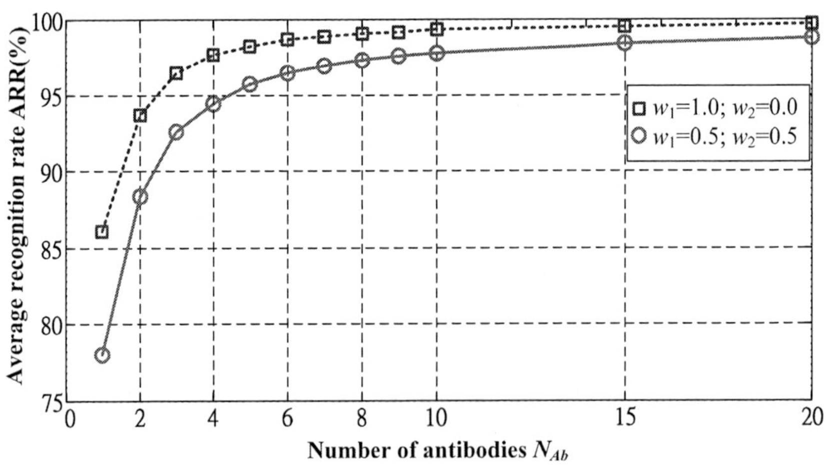

Figure 9. Average recognition rate vs. number of antibodies.

It takes nearly 32 seconds (N_{Ab}=1) to 40 seconds (N_{Ab}=20) training the PCA-IN, respectively and less than 20 *ms* to recognize a face once the whole PCA-IN (consisting 40 immune network classifiers) is determined. The performances of the proposed method are evaluated by varying the number of Abs of each immune classifier (N_{Ab}), eigenfaces (N_{eig}) and the weighting values (w_1 and w_2). Each experiment was repeated for 30 times and the "average recognition rate" (ARR) is illustrated in Table 9 and Table 10 for w_1=0.5 and w_1=1.0, respectively. In addition, Figure 9 indicates the average recognition rates with respect to N_{Ab} and the weighting values. Clearly ARR is nearly increased proportional to the number of antibodies adopted in the immune network classifiers. Additionally it seems that ARR increases exponentially when N_{Ab} is between 1 and 10. However, there is little improvement of ARR when N_{Ab} is above 10. Again, the number of eigenfaces N_{eig} has not consistent effect on the ARR values. Identical to the results derived in the first experiment, it shows that PCA-IN achieves better ARR when w_1 equals to 1.0. Compared with part of the results obtained in Table 4 and Table 8, it seems that the performance of the optimized PCA-IN is almost independent on the number of training sample per person.

Finally, the best performance (99.78%) of the proposed immune network classifiers was compared with the results reported in [1-9] as shown in Table 11. Obviously, the proposed PCA-IN method outperformed all other methods.

Table 11. Comparison of ARR of PCA-IN with some other method

Methods	ARR
SFLDA [30]	74.28%
S2DLDA [31]	76.17%
SVD [32]	69.56%
enhancement method based on WT [33]	89.72%
projection map and SVD [34]	88.61%
2DPCA [35]	76.70%
RBF SVM [36]	84.50%
DDCT and 2PCA [37]	76.25%
Modular Weighted $(2D)^2$PCA [38]	72.22%
Proposed PCA-IN	99.78%

CONCLUSION

This study presented PCA-IN architecture for face recognition problem. The PCA abstracts principal eigenvectors of the image in order to get best feature description, hence to reduce the number of inputs of artificial immune networks. After this, these image data of reduced dimensions are input into immune network classifiers whose structures are optimized using genetic algorithms. The performance of the proposed PCA-IN was evaluated using the ORL face database. The results show that the proposed method gains good recognition rate if only the corresponding person trained images are considered in the immune classifier (i.e. w_1=1.0). This result greatly increases the practical application of the developed PCA-IN in real life. Besides, the average recognition rate is almost irrelative to the number of eigenfaces. Finally the performance of the PCA-IN was compared with other reported methods. The proposed PCA based immune networks learn faster and provides better recognition rate than most of the developed technologies.

ACKNOWLEDGMENTS

The author would like to acknowledge the National Science Council, Taiwan, ROC, for making this work possible with grants NSC93-2213-E-036-016 and NSC94-2213-E-036-002.

REFERENCES

[1] W. A. Barrett, *Syst. and Comp.* 1, 301 (1998).
[2] J. L. Center Jr., Proceedings of the NATO Advanced Study Institute on Face Recognition: From Theory to Applications, 23, June 1997 (Stirling, UK) pp 402-408.
[3] A. Pentland and T. Choudhury, *IEEE Computer* 33, 50 (2000).
[4] W. Zhao, R. Chellappa, P.J. Phillips, and A. Rosenfeld, *ACM Comp. Surv.* 35, 399 (2003).
[5] A. F. Abate, M. Nappi, D. Riccio, and G. Sabatino, *Pattern Recognition Letters* 28, 1885 (2007).
[6] S.G. Kong, J. Heo, B.R. Abidi, J. Paik, and M.A. Abidi, *Comp. Vis. Image Understanding* 97, 103 (2005).
[7] A. Samal and P. A. Iyengar, *Patt. Recog.* 25, 65 (1992).
[8] I.T. Jolliffe, *Principal Component Analysis*, Springer, New York (1986).
[9] M. Lòeve, *Probability Theory*, Van Nostrand, Princeton (1955).
[10] M. Kirby, L. Sirovich, *IEEE Trans Patt. Anal. Mach. Intel.* 12, 103 (1990).
[11] L. Sirovich and M. Kirby, *J. of Opt. Soc. of Amer* 4, 519 (1987).
[12] M. Turk and A. Pentland, *J. Cogn. Neuro.* 3, 71 (1991).
[13] S. Bartlettm, J. R. Movellan, and T. J. Sejnowski, *IEEE Trans. Neu. Net.* 13, 1450 (2002).
[14] R. Gottumukkal and V.K. Asari, *Patt. Recog. Lett.* 25, 429 (2004).
[15] H. Kong, X. Li, L. Wang, E.K. Teoh, J.-G.Wang, and R. Venkateswarlu, Proceedings IEEE International Joint Conference on Neural Networks, 31, July 2005, (Montreal, Canada) pp 108-113.
[16] G. L. Marcialis and F. Roli, *Patt. Anal. Appl.* 7, 151 (2004).
[17] A. M. Martinez and A. C. Kak, *IEEE Trans Patt. Anal. Mach. Intel.* 23, 228 (2001).
[18] A. Pentland, B. Moghaddam, and T. Starner, Proceedings of Computer Vision and Pattern Recognition, 21, June 1994 (Seattle, USA) pp84-91.
[19] G. Giacinto, F. Roli, and G. Fumera, IEEE International Joint Conference on Neural Network, 24, July 2000 (Como, Italy), pp155-159.
[20] T.K. Ho, J.J. Hull, and S.N. Srihari, *IEEE Trans Patt. Anal. Mach. Intell.* 16, 66 (1994).
[21] J. Kittler, M. Hatef, R.P.W. Duin, and J. Matas, *IEEE Trans Patt. Anal. Mach. Intel.* 20, 226 (1998).
[22] M. J. Aitkenheada and A. J. S. Mcdonald, *Eng. Appl. Artif. Intel.* 16, 167 (2003).

[23] S. Lawrence, C. L. Giles, A. C. Tsoi, and A. D. Back, *IEEE Trans. Neu. Net.* 8, 98 (1997).

[24] B. J. Oh, Proceedings on IEEE International Conference on Systems, Man and Cybernetics, 10, Oct. 2005, (Hawaii, USA) pp1699-1703.

[25] J. K. Sing, D. K. Basu, M. Nasipuri, and M. Kundu, *Appl. Soft Comp.* 7, 58 (2007).

[26] D. Dasgupta, Proceedings of the IEEE System, Man, and Cybernetics Conference, 12, Oct. 1997 (Orlando, USA) pp873-878.

[27] L. N. de Castro and T. Jonathan, *Artificial immune systems: a new computational intelligence approach*. Springer-Verlag, Berlin Heidelberg (2002).

[28] D. Dasgupta, *Artificial Immune Systems and Their Applications*, Springer-Verlag, Berlin Heidelberg (1999).

[29] E. Hart, J. Timmis, *Appl. Soft Comp.* 8, 191 (2008).

[30] H. Yin, P. Fu, and S. Meng, *Neurocomputing* 69, 2443 (2006).

[31] H. Yin, P. Fu, and S. Meng, First International Conference on Innovative Computing, Information and Control, 30, Aug. 2006, (Beijing, China) pp113-116.

[32] D. Zhang, S. Chen, and Z.-H. Zhou, *Appl. Math. Comput.* 163, 895 (2005).

[33] J. He, and D. Zhang, IEEE Congress on Image and Signal Processing, 27, May 2008, (Sanya, China) pp 216-219.

[34] J. He and M. Du, International Conference on computational Intelligence for Modelling, Control and Automation, 28, Nov. 2005, (Vienna,) pp20-24.

[35] J. Yang, D. Zhang, A. Frangi, and J.-y. Yang, *IEEE Trans. Patt. Anal. Mach. Intell.* 26, 131 (2004).

[36] Jerry Yokono and Tomaso Poggio, "Boosting a biologically inspired local descriptor for geometry-free face and full multi-view 3D object recognition", MIT-CSAIL-TR-2005-046.

[37] Jun-ying Gan, Jian-hu Gao, and Chun-zhi Li, "Face recognition based on diagonal discrete cosine transform and two-dimensional principal component analysis", Computer Engineering and Applications, Vol. 43, No. 31, pp. 210-213, 2007.

[38] Dashun Que, Bi Chen and Jin Hu, "A Novel Single Training Sample Face Recognition Algorithm Based on Modular Weighted $(2D)^2$PCA", Proceedings of ICSP Conference, Beijing, pp. 1552-1555, Oct. 2008.

[39] Xiaoyang Tan, Songcan Chen, Zhi-Hua Zhou, and Fuyan Zhang, "Face recognition from a single image per person: A survey", Pattern Recognition, Vol. 39, No. 9, pp. 1725-1745, Sept. 2006.

[40] M. Turk, *Interactive-Time Vision: Face Recognition as a Visual Behavior*, PhD Thesis, Massachusetts Institute of Technology, USA (1991).

[41] L. Sirovich and M. Kirby, *J. of Opt. Soc. of Amer* 4, 519 (1987).

[42] I. Roitt, J. Brostoff, and D. K. Male, *Immunology*, 5th ed. Mosby International Limited (1998).

[43] S. Forrest, A. S. Perelson, L. Allen, and R. Cherukuri, Proceedings of IEEE Symposium on Research in Security and Privacy, 16, May 1994 (Oakland, USA) pp202-212.

[44] N.K. Jerne, *Scientific American* 229, 52 (1973).

[45] J. Carneiro, A. Coutinho, J. Faro, and J. Stewar, *J. theor. Boil.* 182, 513 (1996)

[46] J. D. Farmer, N. H. Packard, and A. S. Perelson, *Physica D* 2, 187 (1986).

[47] G.W. Hoffmann, IEEE International Symposium on Circuits and Systems, 8, May 1989 (Portland, USA) pp1620-1623.
[48] R. Hightower, S. Forrest, and A.S. Perelson, Proceedings of Sixth International Conference on Genetic Algorithms, 15, July 1995 (Pittsburgh, USA) pp344-350.
[49] J. Timmis, M. Neal, and J. Hunt, IEEE International Conference on Systems, Man, and Cybernetics, 12, Oct. 1999, (Tokyo, Japan) pp922-927.
[50] P. F. Baldi and B. Soren, *Bioinformatics: The machine Learning approach*, The MIT Press (1999).
[51] J. H. Lin and C. Isik, Proceedings of the Fifth IEEE International Conference on Fuzzy Systems, 8, Sept. 1996, (New Orleans, USA) pp156-161.
[52] K.-C. Kwak and W. Pedrycz, *Patt. Recog.* 38, 1717 (2005).
[53] J. Wang, W. Yang, Y. Lin, and J. Yang, *Neurocomputing* 72, 352 (2008).
[54] L. Yang, W. Gong, X. Gu, W. Li, and Y. Liang, *Neurocomputing* 71, 3644 (2008).
[55] Y.-J. Zheng, J. Yang, J.-Y. Yang, and X.-J. Wu, *Neurocomputing* 69, 1806 (2006).
[56] W. Zuo, D. Zhang, and K. Wang, *Patt. Recogn. Lett.* 27, 210 (2006).
[57] J. Haddadnia and M. Ahmadi, *Im. Vis. Comp*. 22, 1071 (2004).
[58] Z. Jin, J.-Y. Yang, Z.-S. Hu, and Z. Lou, *Patt. Recog.* 34, 1405 (2001).
[59] J.-B. Li, J.-S. Pan, and S.-C. Chu, *Inform. Sci.* 178, 1825 (2008).
[60] K. Sirlantzis, S. Hoque, and M. C. Fairhurst, *Appl. Soft Comp.* 8, 437 (2008).
[61] T. Tan and H. Yan, Proceedings of the 15th International Conference on Pattern Recognition, 9, Sept. 2000, (Barcelona, Spain) pp781–784.
[62] Z.-Q. Zhao, D.-S. Huang, and B.-Y. Sun, *Patt. Recogn. Lett.* 25, 1351 (2004).
[63] W. Zuo, K. Wang, D. Zhang, and H. Zhang, *Neurocomputing* 70, 735 (2007).

In: Face Recognition
Editors: Adamo Quaglia and Calogera M. Epifano
ISBN 978-1-61942-663-4

Chapter 5

DISTRIBUTED FACE RECOGNITION

Angshul Majumdar,* Rabab K. Ward and Panos Nasiopoulos
Department of Electrical and Computer Engineering,
University of British Columbia, Canada

ABSTRACT

This work addresses the problem of distributed face recognition. In this problem, the training data does not reside on a single computer; it resides in multiple computers which are distributed geographically. The challenge is to develop a face recognition system where the dimensionality reduction and classification modules have access to only a small portion (few classes) of the entire training data. Such problems will arise when face recognition are employed at a large scale such as automatic client authentication in bank ATMs or automatic employee authentication in offices. Popular dimensionality reduction methods such as Principal Component Analysis (PCA), Linear Discriminant Analysis (LDA) etc. are data-dependent and so are classification algorithms like Neural Networks and Support Vector Machines. Therefore these methods are not suitable for this problem. This paper proposes a novel solution of the problem based on recognizing faces from video sequences.

For dimensionality reduction, we employ random projections as a data-independent alternative to PCA or LDA. The classification is carried out in parallel by the Hidden Markov Model (HMM) and our newly proposed Nearest Subspace Classifier (NSC). The classifiers are designed in such a way that they can be applied to each class separately; therefore they can operate on the smaller portions (few classes) of the data that reside on individual computers. The results from the two classifiers are finally fused to arrive at the final classification decision.

We have identified a new problem in face recognition. Therefore there are no previous studies that can address this problem. However, in order to see how our proposed method works with previous ones we have compared our results with a few previous works in video based face recognition. Our method shows better results than the ones we have compared with.

* E-mail: angshulm@ece.ubc.ca.

Keywords: Face Recognition, Random Projection, Hidden Markov Model

I. INTRODUCTION

Face recognition has been an active area of research for the past two decades [1]. Research in this area has mostly concentrated on problems arising due to i) changes in head pose [2], ii) changes in illumination [2], iii) changes in expression [3] and iv) occlusion [4]. Although these are still pertinent problems, we investigate another practical problem that will arise while deploying a large-scale face recognition system, namely the problem of distributed face recognition. For the traditional face recognition problem, the training data reside in one central computer and the training and testing are carried on these data. For the distributed recognition problem, the data can reside in multiple sites so does the computational process.

Face recognition involves two aspects of machine learning – dimensionality reduction and classification. As face images have a very high dimensional representation when expressed in the pixel domain and as the computational complexity of classification is dependent on the dimensionality of the input features, the direct use of pixel values as feature sets for classification becomes computationally prohibitive. This is especially the case since traditional dimensionality reduction techniques (Principal Component Analysis, Linear Discriminant Analysis) and classification methods (Support Vector Machine, Artificial Neural Network) are data-dependent, i.e., they require access to all the training data for their operation. Distributed face recognition systems do not satisfy this criterion, and hence require new dimensionality reduction and classification methods to address it.

As the name suggests, distributed face recognition precludes the necessity of having one central computer for training and testing purposes. In this scenario all the training data are not accessible simultaneously, therefore machine learning algorithms are required that can operate piecemeal, i.e., on individual samples or classes. Moreover, the results of the training should be de-coupled as well. The trained modules cannot be stored in a central server either; rather they are stored at different individual sites. Most standard machine learning methods as mentioned above are not equipped to handle this problem; this work proposes a novel solution to this problem.

We propose a fusion scheme to address this problem, taking video-based face recognition. A video sequence is recorded during training, and machine learning algorithms are deployed on it. During testing, another video sequence of the person is recorded and this is compared with the trained modules to determine whether it has a match amongst the stored modules. Classification is carried out with the Hidden Markov Model (HMM) in a suitable modular fashion, and also by a newly proposed classifier (Nearest Subspace Classifier) designed specifically for this problem. The scores from the two classifiers are then merged to arrive at the final decision. Our proposed solution precludes the use of a large scale central computer (which is an expensive solution) and depends on the network infrastructure (which is obviously in place nowadays and does not involve any extra cost).

The problem of distributed face recognition may arise in banks, for example for authenticating clients at ATMs based on face recognition or authenticating persons entering a certain country at different cities or borders. The A more detailed analysis of the banking scenario is shown in the next section. The problem of biometric authentication can be carried out with other biometric traits as well, such as fingerprint, iris, signature etc. Face is the premier biometric trait [5] owing to its high universality, permanence, distinctiveness, collectability, acceptability, circumvention, and is by far the most challenging. Owing to these reasons we have chosen to work on the problem of face recognition. However the techniques developed in this paper are applicable to any other biometric authentication as well.

The rest of the paper will be organized into several sections. Section 2 discusses the problem. The dimensionality reduction and classification approaches are described in Sections 3 and 4 respectively. Section 5 describes the details of the implementation. The experimental results are presented in Section 6, and the conclusions of the work can be found in Section 7.

II. THE PROBLEM

The following figure shows a simple banking scenario consisting of 3 branches of a bank and 5 ATMS. The three branches are distributed in different regions as are the ATMs. They are all connected to each other.

We focus only on the problem of client authentication for such a bank system. When a new customer opens an account with the bank at any of its branches, a video sequence of that person is recorded as the training sequence. The ATMs are also equipped with video cameras, and they take a video sequence of a client trying to operate the ATM. This new video sequence (test sequence) is compared with the stored training sequence to authenticate that person.

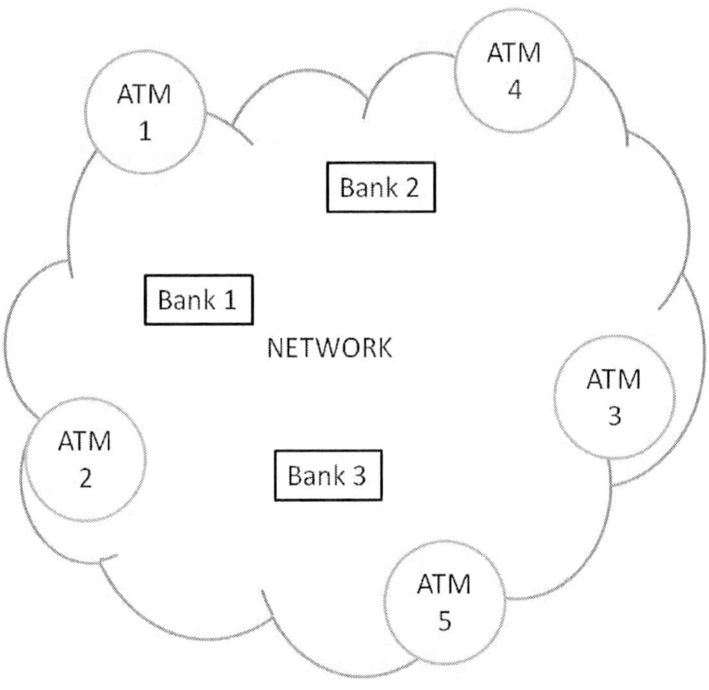

Figure 1. Simple banking scenario.

It is clear that this is a multi-class problem. It is not enough to verify whether the person at the ATM is a client of the bank or not (this would be a binary classification problem); the client should also be identified to be the person he/she claims to be. This can be easily double-checked from the bank (debit) card the person uses at the ATM machine.

Now we analyze the problem from the perspective of face recognition. First the training sequences for the different clients are distributed (in our case in the three bank branches). Standard dimensionality reduction and classification methods demand that all the training data be available at one place. Such is not the case in the given scenario. If traditional methods are to be applied, a huge computer having very large storage and computational resources needs to installed at a central data processing center. Such infrastructure obviously will be expensive for large banks and constitutes a brute-force solution to the problem at hand. In this work, we propose elegant new methods to address this problem.

The brute-force solution has some technical problems as well. Traditional dimensionality reduction techniques (Principal Component Analysis (PCA), Linear Discriminant Analysis (LDA) etc.) or their more sophisticated versions (2DPCA [6], class specific LDA [7]) and classification methods (Support Vector Machine (SVM) [8], Artificial Neural Network (ANN) [9] etc.) are data-dependent (also referred to as adaptive). Whenever new data are added, the dimensionality reductioon have to be computed anew using the stored and new data. In banks, new clients are added constantly. If a traditional face recognition system is in place, it will be required to carry out a new set of computations from scratch whenever a new client is added. Generally the computational load is dependent on the amount of training data. As the training data are increased whenever a new client is added, the brute-force face recognition system based on traditional machine learning methods will have to solve a more and more computationally demanding problem each time. The hardware requirements of such a computer system would have no upper bound!

In this paper, we propose new training methods that proceed in a class-wise fashion, i.e., the training is carried out on each person's sequence separately. The class-wise training modules are stored at the same branch where the client opened his/her account. There is no need to accumulate all the training samples or the trained modules at a central processor. Moreover, new data can be added any time. As the training proceeds separately for each person's sequence, whenever there is a new client, only his/her data are required for training without any reference to other people's data. Such a training approach addresses two problems that arise in the brute-force traditional face recognition system – 1) the need for a central processor with magnificent storage and processing power, and 2) the ability to update the training module with the new person's sequence without any reference to other people's data.

Now we will describe how the actual classification is performed. The dimensionality reduction method proposed in this paper is completely data-independent; i.e., unlike methods such as PCA or LDA, where the entire training data must be present before the dimensionality reduction matrix can be computed, we propose a dimensionality reduction method that is fixed and is data-independent. Since the dimensionality reduction can be performed on-the-fly (without reference to any data), it is implemented inside the ATM. Therefore dimensionality reduced data are generated by the ATM, these data are then sent to all the branches, where they are used by the class-wise trained modules to generate certain scores. The maximum score from each branch is returned to the ATM. Based on these returned scores, the person is authenticated.

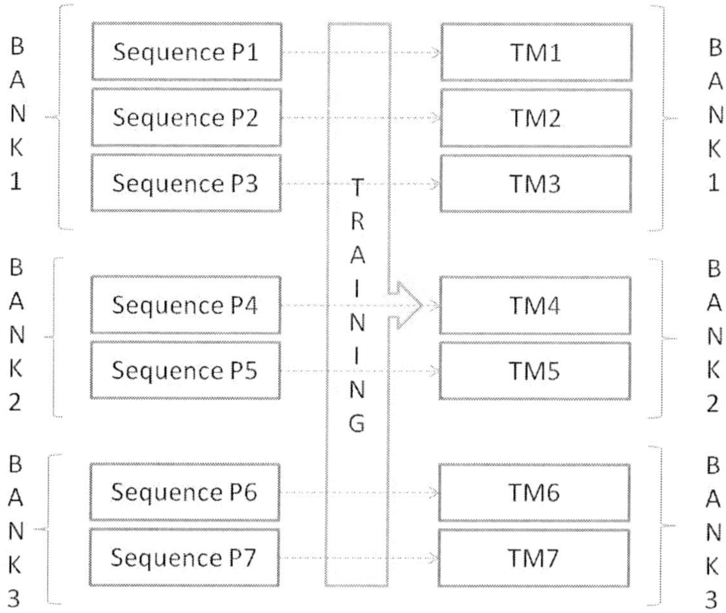

Figure 2. Training.

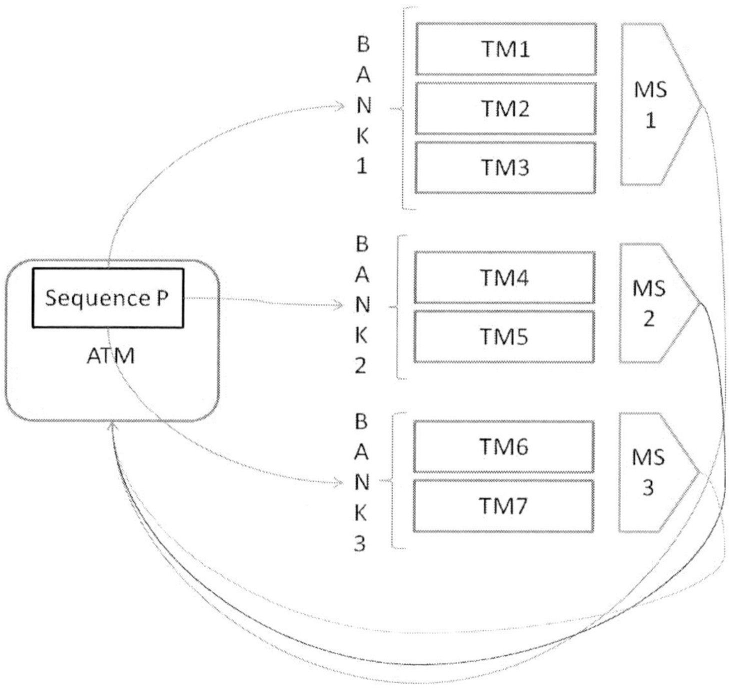

Figure 3. Testing.

The proposed architecture for training and testing are schematically shown in figures 2 and 3 respectively. We consider a toy bank, where there are seven customers in all. The first branch has three customers and the other two have two customers each. In the training phase, a trained module (TM) is generated for each person's (P) sequence. The trained module is stored in the same bank where the customer had opened the account. During testing, the test data are generated at the ATM. These data are sent to all the banks. The training module of each bank produces a matching score and the maximum score from each bank is transmitted back to the ATM. Based on these scores the customer is authenticated at the ATM.

III. Dimensionality Reduction

As mentioned above, adaptive dimensionality reduction methods such as PCA), LDA which have traditionally been widely used in face recognition. These techniques preserve the structure of the original data required for classification but are data-dependent i.e. require access to all the training data for operation. Such methods thus cannot be employed in distributed face recognition. We are seeking a dimensionality reduction method that is non-adaptive, i.e., independent of previous training data, but at the same time preserves the structure of the data that is necessary for classification.

A survey of dimensionality reduction methods [10] provides detailed information pertaining to adaptive linear methods like PCA, Factor Analysis, Projection Pursuit and their non-linear counterparts, but it cursorily mentions Random Projection (RP). We are interested in RP as it is a non-adaptive method. Since RP has not been extensively explored in dimensionality reduction, we briefly review a few theoretical and applied studies that use RP for dimensionality reduction.

Almost all theoretical studies on RP dimensionality reduction are extensions of the Johnson-Lindenstrauss lemma. It is shown in [11] that by setting each column of the projection matrix to be i.i.d (independently and identically distributed) Gaussian and orthonormalizing the columns by Gram-Schmidt lead to an RP projection matrix that is well suited for dimensionality reduction of Gaussian mixtures. Another method in [11] proposes a novel method to create an RP matrix from a Bernoulli type distribution. A related work [12] shows that by creating a simple RP matrix with its column drawn from i.i.d Gaussian distribution and projecting it to a suitable number of dimensions, it is possible to preserve some important structure in the data, like pairwise distances, distances from a line, areas of triangles, etc. Another property that is approximately preserved under RP is similarity (cosine distances) [13].

Theoretical studies in RP [11] compare RP with PCA as a dimensionality reduction scheme for machine learning problems. These studies find that PCA is better than RP that employs a moderate number of lower dimensional projections. However, for a very low number of projections, PCA cannot preserve the structure of the data and the results are drastically worse. The results from RP degrade smoothly as the number of projections is decreased. As the number of projections increase the recognition results obtained from RP become comparable to those obtained from PCA. These theoretical findings are corroborated by practical studies [14-16]. However, while applying RP for practical problems [14-16], it was found that a single RP is unstable and that multiple RP matrices are required for stabilizing the results. Experimental results show that about 5 separate RP matrices are sufficient to stabilize the results.

IV. CLASSIFICATION

There are two approaches to recognize faces from video sequences – i) video-to-video (V2V) and ii) image-to-image (I2I). In V2V, the video is treated as a time varying sequence and various dynamic modeling tools [17, 18] are used to learn the model parameters from the observed sequence. When a new (test) video becomes available , it is compared with the learnt models to find the best match, and based on this result the test video is classified. In I2I methods [19], each frame of the video is separated out as a different image. The frames from the training video are used to train a classifier. Similarly the individual frames from the test video are separately classified by the trained classifier, and the results from the test frames are fused by some voting scheme to arrive at the final classification result.

In this work we employ both the V2V and the I2I methods. The results from the V2V and I2I are fused to arrive at the final classification decision. Owing to the operational requirements of distributed face recognition, we employ two non-standard classifiers to tackle the face recognition problem. We intend to fuse the two classification algorithms in order to boost the recognition accuracy. The Hidden Markov Model (HMM) is employed as the V2V classifier and a new classifier called the Nearest Subspace Classifier is proposed here as the I2I classifier. Fusing results from the two classifiers will be discussed later on.

A. Hidden Markov Model

Hidden Markov Model (HMM) is parameterized by a triplet, and has a finite number of states (N) - $\{S_1, S_{2,..} S_N\}$ which are hidden from the observer. At each instant of time, the chain occupies one of the states given by q_t , $1 \le t \le T$, where T is the total length (number of frames) of the sequence.

The initial state distribution is given by π, where $\pi_i = P(q_1 = S_i)$, $i = 1$ to N .

From one instance to the next, the transition occurs according to a Markov state transition matrix A. $A = \{a_{i,j}\}$, where

$$a_{i,j} = P(q_t = S_j \mid q_{t-1} = S_i),\ 1 \le i, j \le N$$

$$\text{and } \sum_{j=1}^{N} a_{i,j} = 1$$

These state vectors (S) are not observable; only the observation vectors O is measurable. In [3] the observation vector 'O' is comprised of Principal Components of a frame. In our case 'O' is the RP of a frame.

B ($= b_i(O)$) is the observation probability density function where

$$b_i(O_t) = p(O_t \mid q_t = S_i)$$

Generally, $b_i(O)$ is modeled as a Gaussian Mixture Model (GMM).

The problem now is to estimate the triplet (A,B,π), given a sequence of observations O_t, $t=1$ to T. This can be done by the Expectation Maximization algorithm, which is the standard method for HMM parameter estimation.

Suppose there are video sequences of C people. During training, one video sequence for each person is available (if we consider the bank ATM scenario, this video sequence is acquired when a customer opens a new bank account). Each frame is projected to a lower dimensional subspace by an RP projection matrix. We fit an HMM for each video sequence and obtain a triplet (A_k, B_k, π_k), where $k=1$ to C.

During testing, the video sequence of the person is recorded (e.g., by a camera at the ATM) and the frames are projected to a lower dimensional subspace by the same RP matrix. Then, the likelihood score of the observation vectors (O), given each HMM, is computed as $P(O|(A_k, B_k, \pi_k))$. The video sequence is assigned to a person having the maximum likelihood score.

It should be noted that an HMM when used in this fashion gets trained on the classes (persons) separately and generates a model specific to the class. During testing, the test sequence can thus be tested in parallel for all the trained models. Thus we see, that the HMM satisfies the requirement imposed by distributed face recognition.

B. Nearest Subspace Classifier

The Nearest Subspace Classifier (NSC) is based upon a novel classification assumption. It assumes that the samples of a particular class lie on a subspace. Additionally, it is assumed that the training samples of each class are sufficient to span this subspace. Therefore any new test sample belonging to that class can be represented as a linear combination of the training samples of that class, i.e.,

$$v_{test} = \sum_{i=1}^{n_k} \alpha_{k,i} \cdot v_{k,i} + \varepsilon_k \tag{1}$$

where v_{test} is the test sample represented by a vector of features, $v_{k,i}$ is the ith training sample for the kth class, and ε_k is the approximation error for the kth class.

To find the class 'k', the test sample belongs to, we need to compute the error $\varepsilon_k = v_{test} - \sum_{i=1}^{n_k} \alpha_{k,i} v_{k,i}$ for each of the classes k=1:C. The correct class is assumed to be the class having the minimum error.

To find the class that has the minimum error for every class 'k', the coefficients $\alpha_{k,i}$ k=1:C must be estimated first. This can be performed by rewriting (1) in matrix-vector notation

$$v_{test} = V_k \alpha_k + \varepsilon_k \tag{2}$$

where and $\alpha_k = [\alpha_{k,1}, \alpha_{k,2} ... \alpha_{k,n_k}]^T$.

If the number of training samples in the class is less than the dimensionality of each sample, a closed form solution to (2) can be obtained by,

$$\hat{\alpha}_k = \arg\min_{\alpha} \| v_{k,test} - V_k \alpha \|_2^2 \tag{3}$$

But if the number of training samples is larger than the dimensionality it is desirable to regularize the solution and solve the Tikhonov regularized version instead:

$$\hat{\alpha}_k = \arg\min_{\alpha} \| v_{test} - V_k \alpha \|_2^2 + \lambda \| \alpha \|_2^2 \tag{4}$$

The analytical solution of (4) is

$$\hat{\alpha}_k = (V_k^T V_k + \lambda I)^{-1} V_k^T v_{test} \tag{5}$$

Plugging this expression in (2), and solving for the error term, we obtain

$$\varepsilon_k = (V_k (V_k^T V_k + \lambda I)^{-1} V_k^T - I) v_{test} \tag{6}$$

The advantage of (6) is that $(V_k (V_k^T V_k + \lambda I)^{-1} V_k^T - I)$ which is the orthoprojector, can be computed piecemeal for different classes. Therefore the NSC can be trained separately for each class. There is no need for the classifier to have access to all the training data, it can operate piecemeal. Consequently, the testing also proceeds in parallel. During testing, the orthoprojector is multiplied with the test sample and the norm of the resulting vector is calculated. This gives the distance of the sample from the class (subspace). The sample is assigned to the class (subspace) having minimum error.

Based on these simple derivations (6), we devise a very efficient algorithm for classification

Training

1. For each class 'k', compute the orthoprojector (the term in brackets in Equation (6)).

Testing

2. Calculate the error for each class 'k' by computing matrix vector product between the orthoprojector and vtest, equation (6).
3. Classify the test sample as the class having the minimum error ($\|\varepsilon_k\|$).

V. PROPOSED METHOD

A. Pre-Processing

The first step is to detect the face image in each frame. There are several face detection algorithms, but the most widely used is the Viola-Jones detector [20]. This algorithm has good detection rate and is extremely fast; it can process 30 frames per second – which is the frame rate for most video standards. The algorithm detects only that part of the face from the forehead to the chin, consequently, the recognition system becomes invariant to changes in hairstyle. Once the face is detected in a frame, it is normalized to a 48X48 pixel square.

For the video-to-video method, i.e., the HMM, face detection is the only necessary pre-processing step. For image-to-image based methods, it was found that the subsequent frames carry a lot of redundant information, therefore using all the frames as samples only adds to the processing cost without adding much extra information. In [21], two methods were proposed for choosing video frames from the video sequence. The first method was based on audio-visual synchronization (A-V sync) and the second method was by random selection of frames. [21] showed that there is only a slight improvement in recognition accuracy when A-V sync is used instead of random selection. Therefore we chose to employ random selection over A-V sync for two reasons – i) Audio data are not always available (as in the database used in our work); and ii) A-V sync is computationally more expensive than random selection. Other methods [22] propose statistical methods based on Robust PCA to select frames from the video sequence, but such methods are computationally even more expensive, and cannot be updated real time. We aim to reduce the computational cost wherever possible, and therefore prefer the simple random selection of frames method over others.

The random selection of frames is carried out only for the image-to-image based method; it is carried out for both the training and the test sequences. For the image-to-image approach, as mentioned earlier we need one more step so that only a few frames from the entire sequence are selected. We randomly select the frames from the video sequence. We use random jitter sampling [23] in place of ordinary random sampling to guarantee that the chosen frames are not temporally very close to each other.

B. Dimensionality Reduction

The first step towards classification is dimensionality reduction. For this step, we use RP dimensionality reduction. Five sets of random projections were used for stabilizing the classification results as suggested in [15, 16].

Five random projection matrices are created by normalizing the columns of an i.i.d. Gaussian matrix. After pre-processing, each 48X48 frame is concatenated to form a vector of length 2304. The original vector is projected to a lower dimensional vector by the RP projection matrices. Thus, 5 sets of lower dimension vectors are obtained for each frame.

C. Classification

The first step towards classification is dimensionality reduction. For this step, we use RP dimensionality reduction. Five sets of random projections were used for stabilizing the classification results as suggested in [15, 16].

HMM Classification

Most Let each training video sequence S be the resulting sequence after pre-processing and concatenation to a vector. Therefore, S is a matrix with 2304 rows (the dimensionality of the input vector) and columns equal to the number of frames in the video sequence. Let $R_i,\ i = 1 \text{ to } 5$ be the RP matrices.

1. Images in each sequence are projected to a lower dimension by a random projection matrix. As mentioned earlier, each random projection do not give stable result, therefore multiple (in our case 5) lower dimensional projections are made of each sequence. If S be the original sequence, then each of its lower dimensional projection is denoted by $l_i = R_i S,\ \text{i=1 to 5}$.
2. For each projection, create a Hidden Markov Model for the person whose video sequence is S. The model is parameterized by $(A_{c,i}, B_{c,i}, \pi_{c,i})$, where i=1:5 and c denotes the person (class).
3. During testing, the pre-processing and dimensionality reduction steps of the test sequence are the same as during training. There are 5 sets of lower dimensional test sequences $l_{test,i}$ i=1:5.

For each lower dimensional projection of the test sequence, compute the likelihood of $l_{test,i}$ for each of the 5 sets of HMM parameters for each person, $L(c,i) = P(l_{test,i} \mid A_{c,i}, B_{c,i}, \pi_{c,i})$, i=1:5 and c=1:C.

NSC Classification

Let P be the number of frames randomly selected in the pre-processing step. As mentioned earlier, this selection is done only for I2I classification. Let $R_i,\ i = 1 \text{ to } 5$ be the RP matrices.

1. For each frame $I_p,\ \text{p = 1 to P}$, repeat the following steps.
2. Project I_p to lower dimension $l_p(i) = R_i I_p$.
3. For each projection i, find the error for each class $e_p(c,i)$ (error for the ith projection of the pth frame with respect to the cth class) for all the classes $c = 1 \text{ to } C$.

For each projection i and class c, find the aggregate error for all the frames $error(c,i) = \sum_{p=1}^{P} e_p(c,i)$. This gives an estimate of the error between the test sequence and each training class for a particular lower dimensional projection.

Hybrid Classification: Mixing Outputs of HMM with NSC

Previous studies in classification reported that instead of using a single classifier, score based matching boosts the classification accuracy. Such improvements in accuracy were reported for face [23, 24] and character recognition [25] experiments. The proposed approach is in no way similar to the previous works, but is motivated by the improvement in results there in.

Finally we combine the results from HMM and NSC. There are several ways to combine the results. Performance evaluations have shown that the following combination gave the best recognition results.

1. Find the score for each projection for each person $score(c,i) = L(c,i) \times 1/error(c,i)$.
2. Find aggregate the score for each projection $AggScore(c) = \sum_{i=1}^{5} score(c,i)$
3. The test sequence is assigned to the class having the maximum aggregate score.

Note that the entire classification proceeds in class-wise modules, therefore both the training and the testing can occur in parallel. In this work, the scores from all the classes are obtained and the final decision is made based on the highest score. However in a distributed scenario, it is only necessary to send the highest score from each bank/computer.

VI. Performance Evaluation and Discussion

We tested our hybrid recognition approach on the CMU Faces in Action (FIA) database [27]. This database has both indoor and outdoor shots of each person. We envisage the application of our work in indoor environments, such as client authentication in ATMs. Therefore, we tested our method with the indoor video sequences from the FIA database. The indoor database consists of 20-second videos of face data from 153 participants mimicking a passport checking scenario. Such indoor sequences have only slight variations in illumination but considerable variations in head pose. None of the sequences contain marked changes in facial expression; they are all neutral. There are three video sequences for each person. The gap between video sequences was around 3 months to emulate realistic conditions.

The images were normalized to 48 by 48 pixels. Two issues need to be addressed in our method – i) the number of random projections in lower dimension, and ii) the number of hidden states in the HMM. Unfortunately for none of the problems, there is a fixed criterion for decision. Therefore we chose both these numbers through trials. Even in previous studies [15, 16], the number of lower dimensional random projections were obtained through trial and error.

First, we looked at the problem of deciding the number of lower dimensional projections. In our image-to-image method, instead of using all the frames in the video sequences, we use jitter sampling to randomly choose the frames. The following graph shows the recognition accuracy of the image-to-image approach for different numbers of randomly selected frames.

The X-axis shows the number of selected frames and the Y-axis shows the recognition accuracy.

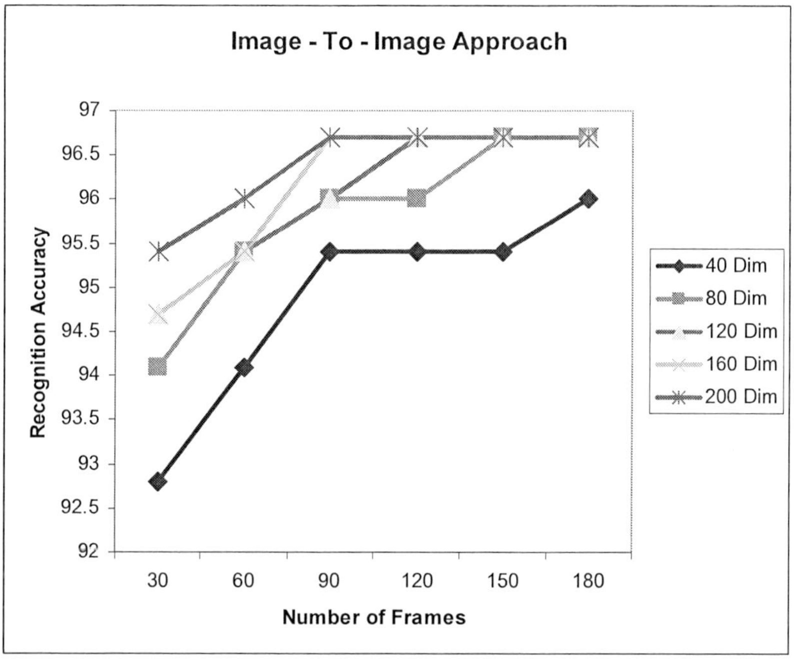

Figure 4. Recognition accuracy vs Number of selected frames.

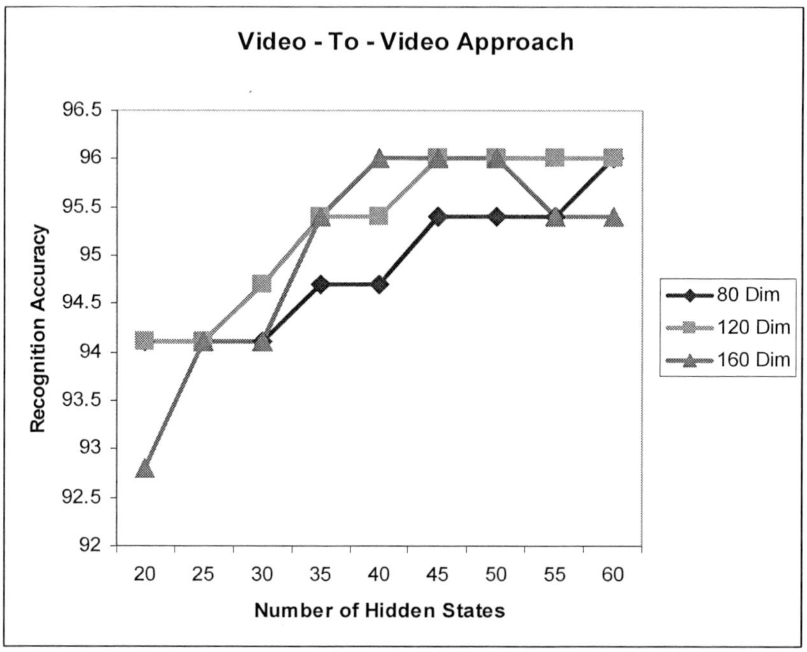

Figure 5. Recognition accuracy vs Number of Hidden States.

Table 1. Recognition accuracy from different methods

Method	Recognition Accuracy (%)
Liu and Chen	98.0
Aggarwal et al.	96.0
Majumdar and Nasiopoulos	96.7
Price and Gee	92.8
Proposed	99.3

From Figure 4, we observe that keeping the dimensionality (number of projections) fixed and increasing the number of frames results in an initial increase in recognition accuracy, but saturates after a while. This is because with too many frames, some frames look very similar to others and do not add value to the training set in terms of variability.

For the video-to-video approach, the number of hidden states in the HMM must be decided. The number of hidden states is varied to study the effect on the overall recognition accuracy keeping the number of observations fixed. From Figure 4, we observe that the recognition accuracy increases to a certain extent after which it either stops increasing or begins to fall. This is because, the greater the number of hidden states the better is the modeling, but at the same time the number of HMM parameters to be estimated is greater. Since the length of the video sequence is fixed, as the number of parameters to be estimated increases, the model begins to overfit, and consequently its recognition accuracy decreases.

For our hybrid approach, we combine the results from Figures 4 and 5. For the image-to-image approach, the best results are obtained at 120 frames or more. To keep the computational cost minimal we use 120 dimensions and 120 frames. For the video-to-video approach, the best results are obtained for 120 dimensions with 45 hidden states. These are the setting used in our proposed approach.

In Table 1, our hybrid recognition methods are compared with 2 video-to-video [28, 29] based methods and 2 image-to-image [30, 31] based methods.

The results in Table 1 show that our method outperforms other comparable methods. However, it is important to remember that the other methods are not suitable for the distributed face recognition scenario.

CONCLUSION

This paper studies the problem of distributed face recognition. This practical problem will arise at immigration checking centers at airports or borders of a certain country or when large organizations such as banks deploy face recognition based client authentication at ATMs. In such situations, the database of the training samples of all persons or clients will not be available at one site. Each module of the training algorithm will have access to data from a fraction of all the classes. In such a scenario, traditional dimensionality reduction and classification methods are not directly applicable. In this paper, we address this problem of distributed face recognition.

We use a lesser-used dimensionality reduction technique, random projection, and devise a classifier that work well with such dimensionality reduction. The advantage of such dimensionality reduction is that it is data independent, i.e., the projection from higher to lower dimension does not depend on previously stored data as in the case of traditional methods like Principal Component Analysis. Our classification algorithm is a fusion of Hidden Markov Model (HMM) and a newly developed classifier called the Nearest Subspace Classifier (NSC). Both, HMM and NSC can act on classes separately and are appropriate for the aforementioned problem.

In this work, the face recognition system is based on video sequences. We have compared our method with other video-based face recognition algorithms [28-31], and shown that our method performs better. It should be remembered that our method should not be judged only by its recognition accuracy but also by the complexity of the scenario it can handle. None of the other algorithms [28-31] are capable of addressing the problem of distributed face recognition.

References

[1] W. Zhao, R. Chellappa, A. Rosenfeld, and P.J. Phillips, "Face Recognition: A Literature Survey", *ACM Computing Surveys*, pp. 399-458, 2003.

[2] R. Gross, S. Baker, I. Matthews and T. Kanade, "Face Recognition Across Pose and Illumination", Handbook of Face Recognition, Stan Z. Li and Anil K. Jain, ed., Springer-Verlag, 2004.

[3] S. Chen, Brian C. Lovell, "Illumination and Expression Invariant Face Recognition with One Sample Image", icpr, vol. 1, pp.300-303, *17th International Conference on Pattern Recognition* (ICPR'04) - Volume 1, 2004.

[4] A. Lanitis, "Person identification from heavily occluded face images", *Proceedings of the 2004 ACM symposium on Applied computing*, pp. 5-9, 2004.

[5] A. K. Jain, A. Ross and S. Pankanti, "Biometrics: A Tool for Information Security", *IEEE Trans. Information Forensics and Security*, Vol. 1 (2), pp.125-143, 2006.

[6] J. Yang and C. Liu, "Horizontal and Vertical 2DPCA-Based Discriminant Analysis for Face Verification on a Large-Scale Database", *IEEE Trans. Information Forensics and Security*, Vol. 2 (4), pp.781-792, 2007.

[7] G. Goudelis, S. Zafeiriou, A. Tefas, and I. Pitas, "Class-Specific Kernel-Discriminant Analysis for Face Verification", *IEEE Trans. Information Forensics and Security*, Vol. 2 (3), pp.570-587, 2007.

[8] Z. Li, and X. Tang, "Using Support Vector Machines to Enhance the Performance of Bayesian Face Recognition", *IEEE Trans. Information Forensics and Security*, Vol. 2 (2), pp.174-180, 2007.

[9] J. Lu, X. Yuan, and T. Yahagi, "A Method of Face Recognition Based on Fuzzy c-Means Clustering and Associated Sub-NNs" *IEEE Trans. Neural networks*, Vol. 18 (1), pp.150-160, 2007.

[10] I. K. Fodor, "A survey of dimension reduction techniques", *Technical Report*, UCRL-ID-148494, 2002.

[11] D. Achlioptas, "Database-friendly random projections", *ACM Symposium on the Principles of Database Systems*, pp. 274–281, 2001

[12] A. Magen, "Dimensionality reductions that preserve volumes and distance to affine spaces, and their algorithmic applications", *International Workshop on Randomization and Approximation Techniques in Computer Science*, pp. 239-253, 2002.
[13] S. Kaski, "Dimensionality reduction by random mapping: Fast similarity computation for clustering". *IEEE Joint Conference on Neural Networks*, 413-418, 1998.
[14] X. Z. Fern and C. E. Brodley, "Random projection for high dimensional data clustering: A cluster ensemble approach", *International Conference on Machine Learning*, pp. 186-193, 2003.
[15] N. Goel, G. M. Bebis and A. V. Nefian, "Face recognition experiments with random projections", *SPIE Conference on Biometric Technology for Human Identification*, pp. 426-437, 2005.
[16] Y. Yang, J. Wright, Y. Ma and S. S. Sastry, "Feature Selection in Face Recognition: A Sparse Representation Perspective", *IEEE Transactions on Pattern Analysis and Machine Intelligence*, Vol. 31 (2), pp. 210-227, 2009.
[17] X. Liu, and T. Chen, "Video-based face recognition using adaptive hidden Markov models", *IEEE Conference on Computer Vision and Pattern Recognition*, pp. 340-345, 2003.
[18] G. Aggarwal, A. K. Roy-Chowdhury, and R. Chellappa, "A System Identification Approach for Video-based Face Recognition", *IEEE International Conference on Pattern Recognition*, Vol. 4, pp. 175-178, 2004.
[19] X. Tang, and Z. Li, "Video based face recognition using multiple classifiers". *IEEE International Conference on Automatic Face and Gesture Recognition*, pp. 345-349, 2004.
[20] P. Viola and M. Jones, "Rapid object detection using a boosted cascade of simple features", *IEEE Conference on Computer Vision and Pattern Recognition*, pp. 511-518., 2001.
[21] X. Tang, and Z. Li, "Video based face recognition using multiple classifiers". *IEEE International Conference on Automatic Face and Gesture Recognition*, pp. 345-349, 2004.
[22] S. A. Berrani, and C. Garcia, „Enhancing face recognition from video sequences using robust statistics", *IEEE Conference on Advanced Video and Signal Based Surveillance*, pp. 324-329, 2005.
[23] G. Hennenfent and F. J. Herrmann, Simply denoise: wavefield reconstruction via jittered undersampling", *Geophysics*, Vol. 73(3), pp. V19-V28, 2008.
[24] Md. H. Mahoor and Md. Abdel-Mottaleb, "A Multimodal Approach for Face Modeling and Recognition", *IEEE Trans. Information Forensics and Security*, Vol. 3 (3), pp.431-440, 2008.
[25] S. Gundimada and V. K. Asari, "Facial Recognition Using Multisensor Images Based on Localized Kernel Eigen Spaces", *IEEE Trans. Image Processing*, Vol. 18 (6), pp.1314-1325, 2009.
[26] U. Bhattacharya and B. B. Chaudhuri, "Fusion of Combination Rules of an Ensemble of MLP Classifiers for Improved Recognition Accuracy of Handprinted Bangla Numerals", *IEEE Conference on Document Analysis and Research*, pp. 322-326, 2005.
[27] R. Goh, L. Liu, X. Liu and T. Chen, „The CMU Face In Action (FIA) Database", *IEEE International Conference of Computer Vision*, pp. 225-263, 2005.

[28] X. Liu, and T. Chen, "Video-based face recognition using adaptive hidden Markov models", *IEEE Conference on Computer Vision and Pattern Recognition*, pp. 340-345, 2003.

[29] G. Aggarwal, A. K. Roy-Chowdhury, and R. Chellappa, "A System Identification Approach for Video-based Face Recognition", *IEEE International Conference on Pattern Recognition*, Vol. 4, pp. 175-178, 2004.

[30] A. Majumdar, and P. Nasiopoulos, P., 2008. Frontal Face Recognition from Video, *International Symposium on Visual Computing*, pp. 297-306, 2008.

[31] J. R. Price and T. E. Gee, "Towards robust face recognition from video", *Applied Imagery Pattern Recognition Workshop*, pp. 94-100, 2001.

In: Face Recognition
Editors: Adamo Quaglia and Calogera M. Epifano
ISBN 978-1-61942-663-4

Chapter 6

FACIAL IDENTITY, FACIAL EMOTION RECOGNITION AND COGNITION IN REMITTED VS. NON-REMITTED PATIENTS WITH SCHIZOPHRENIA

Filomena Castagna, Cristiana Montemagni, Monica Sigaudo, Cinzia Mingrone and Paola Rocca*
Department of Neuroscience, Psychiatric Section, University of Turin, Via Cherasco, Turin, Italy

ABSTRACT

Aim. A growing interest has been directed to evaluate whether a symptom-based remitted state, based on standardized criteria for schizophrenia, also corresponds to an overall good functioning. This study aimed to examine the relationships between remission status and two outcome parameters in a group of schizophrenic patients: face processing (facial identity and facial emotion recognition) and basic cognitive abilities.

Methods. Ninety patients in stable phase were enrolled, of whom 28 patients attained "cross-sectional" remission, and 62 patients failed to. Facial emotion perception performances were assessed with the Comprehensive Affect Testing System, a standardized measure of emotion processing. Cognitive functions were evaluated by a wide battery of tests for attention, verbal memory/learning, perceptual-motor speed and executive functions.

Results. The two groups of patients were homogeneous in demographic and clinical variables (age of onset, length of illness, previous relapses, dose equivalent to 100 mg/day of chlorpromazine, type of antipsychotics). Emotion perception was not different between the two groups, nevertheless the ability to discriminate facial identity was better in patients with symptomatic remission. Compared to non-remitted patients, remitted ones obtained higher scores in the executive functions task. No differences were detected in attentive functions, verbal memory/learning, and perceptual-motor speed. Among the

* Corresponding Author: Paola Rocca, M.D. Department of Neuroscience, Psychiatric Section, University of Turin Via Cherasco 11, 10126 Turin, Italy, Tel. 0039-011-6336780; Fax: 0039-011-673473, Email: paola.rocca@unito.it

significant variables of the groups comparison, only facial identity discrimination was a contributing factor to the remission status.

Conclusion. These data suggest that remission criteria for schizophrenia can only partially be considered an index of "functional" remission and that other aspects of social functioning, such as cognitive impairments, must be considered in order to focus on recovery from the illness.

Keywords: Schizophrenia and psychosis; cognition; emotion perception; remission criteria

INTRODUCTION

Despite the remarkable successes of antipsychotic medications that have contributed to reducing morbidity and relapse rate in patients with schizophrenia, outcome in these subjects still remain unsatisfactory (Altamura et al., 2007). To evaluate long-term outcomes, it is important to have an operational definition signalling that a new phase of the treatment work should begin and that helps clinical decision-making (Dunayevich et al., 2006). In order to standardize a definition for outcome in schizophrenia a "Remission in Schizophrenia Working Group" (Andreasen et al., 2005) proposed operationally criteria based predominantly on establishing a clinical severity threshold during a period of 6 months, using assessment tools currently available for evaluation of symptoms, such the Positive and Negative Syndrome Scale, PANSS (Kay et al., 1987), the Scale for the Assessment of Positive Symptoms, SAPS, and the Scale for the Assessment of Negative Symptoms, SANS (Andreasen and Olsen, 1982), or the Brief Psychiatric Rating Scale, BPRS (Overall and Gorham, 1962). The items were selected to represent the three major symptom domains identified in factor analyses (reality distortion, disorganization, psychomotor poverty) (Bilder et al., 1985; Andreasen et al., 1986; Liddle, 1987; Andreasen et al., 1995; Gur et al., 1991; Liddle et al.,1989) and the five criteria specified in DSM IV for a diagnosis of schizophrenia (delusions, hallucinations, disorganized speech, grossly disorganized or catatonic behaviour, negative symptoms). Limiting the criteria to these core symptoms provides both specificity and sensitivity. In naturalistic populations, the rate of remission status is about 30-40% of patients receiving antipsychotic medications, without introducing specific approaches in medical or cognitive and behavioural therapies explicitly proposed in order to achieve remission (Lasser et al., 2005; Emsley et al., 2007; San et al., 2007).

A growing interest in literature has been directed to verify how this symptom-based remitted state also corresponds to an overall good functioning. Different studies reported that symptomatic remission is significantly associated with better social and daily functioning, but not necessarily accompanied with functional remission in all domains. Compared with non-remitted patients, those who achieved remission had significantly improved activity of daily life, social functioning in society (Helldin et al., 2007; Eberhard et al., 2009), satisfaction with treatment/adherence to treatment (Malla et al., 2006; Docherty et al., 2007), healthy status (Docherty et al., 2007), insight (De Hert et al., 2007; Eberhard et al., 2009; Yen et al., 2009) and quality of life (Dunayevich et al., 2006; van Os et al., 2006; Emsley et al., 2007). However, in a multi-centre study comprising more than 1000 patients, only a small proportion of remitted patients had an adequate social/ vocational functioning (San et al., 2007).

Despite a general consensus about their role as important determinant of outcome in schizophrenia (Couture et al., 2006; Juckel and Morosini, 2008), social cognitive abilities and cognitive abilities have been scarcely investigated in relation to remission status.

Currently, few authors have investigated whether social cognitive abilities (including theory of mind abilities, emotion processing, social perception and knowledge, attributional bias) (Green et al., 2008) are implied in the remission process. Preliminary data showed that a better global social cognitive function was a predicting factor of the symptomatic remission in patients with schizophrenia (San et al., 2007; Ciudad et al., 2009), and that a deficit in theory of mind was related to residual symptoms of schizophrenia in a group of remitted patients (Bora et al., 2008; Mo et al., 2008). No study has previously focussed on the relationship between remission and other social cognitive abilities (particularly facial emotion perception).

As for cognitive abilities, it has been shown that impairments in cognitive abilities could significantly limit the ability to acquire, retain, or relearn skills necessary for real-word functioning (Lasser et al., 2007). Moreover, in patients with schizophrenia cognitive dysfunctions to be more important for the prognosis than positive and negative symptoms (Velligan et al., 1997; Evans et al., 2004). In remitted vs. non-remitted patients superior performances in different areas of cognitive functioning were observed in two studies (Helldin et al., 2006; Haro et al., 2006), but this result was not confirmed in other reports (Buckley et al., 2007; Emsley et al., 2007; Eberhard et al., 2009). Further research would be useful to confirm these data.

The current analysis aimed to verify whether face processing (facial identity and facial emotion recognition) and cognitive functions differed in remitted vs. non-remitted patients with schizophrenia, and whether these abilities could be contributing factors for achieving remission.

Methods

Subjects

Patients (N=92) included in the study were recruited from a population of consecutive out-patients who were referred to the Department of Neuroscience, Psychiatric Section and the Department of Mental Health Department ASL 1 Molinette-Turin, Italy, in the period between 1st February 2008 and 28 February 2009. Patients were initially evaluated by a clinician-psychiatrist, and if they met DSM-IV-TR criteria for schizophrenia, they were subsequently seen by our research team (C.M, M.S., C.M.).

Subjects were excluded if they had a current disorder other than schizophrenia on Axis I of the DSM IV-TR, a current or past codiagnosis of autistic disorder or another pervasive developmental disorder, a history of severe head injury (coma $\geq$ 48hours) and a diagnosis of mental disorder due to a general medical condition. At the time of study entry, patients had been clinically stable for at least 6 months as judged by the treating psychiatrist, i.e. during this period all patients had to be treated as outpatients, treatment regimens had not been modified, and there was no essential change in psychopathology. In addition to medical records, patients were considered to be in a stable phase as assessed from reports from patients themselves, and observations of the psychiatric staff, personnel in the community psychiatry and relatives. All the patients were receiving antipsychotic medication at the time of assessment.

Applying the severity criterion proposed by Andreasen et al. (2005), we divided patients in two groups if they had or had not a mild or lower level (<3) on 8 key PANSS items, which are: delusions, conceptual disorganization, hallucination behaviour, blunted affect, social withdrawal, lack of spontaneity, mannerisms/posturing and unusual thought content. The full remission criteria require maintaining this threshold of symptom severity continuously for six months. In this study, time criterion had to rely on reports from the patients themselves, relatives and caregivers, in combination with information from the medical records. As underlined by Helldin et al. (2009), some confusion has arisen surrounding the concept of remission as many studies are only based on cross-sectional severity. In cases where only symptom control is taken into account, the authors recommend using the term "cross-sectional remission", while "remission" should be reserved for studies that fulfil the criteria on both symptom control and duration. Based on these recommendations, the subjects were divided in two groups: twenty-eight "cross sectional" remitted patients and sixty-two non-remitted patients.

The study was carried out in accordance with the Declaration of Helsinki 1995 (as revised in Edinburgh 2000) and Good Clinical Practice. The protocol was approved by a Local Research Ethics Committee and written informed consent was obtained from all subjects after a complete description of the study.

Psychiatric Assessment

The diagnosis of schizophrenia was confirmed, using the Structured Clinical Interview for DSM-IV disorders (SCID) (First et al., 1987). A semi-structured interview was used to assess demographic and clinical features: sex, age, education, age at onset of schizophrenia (report of first contact with a psychiatric service), length of illness, number of previous relapses, type and dosage of antipsychotic medication. For each patient the dose equivalent to 100 mg/day of chlorpromazine was calculated (Woods, 2003). All data were confirmed by clinical chart review. Current levels of psychopathological symptoms were assessed using the Positive and Negative Syndrome Scale (Kay et al., 1987). All psychiatric assessments were performed by experienced psychiatrists (C.M., M.S.,C.M.). In an attempt to reduce inter-rater reliability, all raters were trained to administer the psychometric tools according to common standards. Also prior to the commencement of the present study, they participated in a pilot study in order to reach a consensus on ratings that were obtained using psychometric scales. We conducted rater training under rather naturalistic clinical conditions using videotaped, semi-structured PANSS interviews of schizophrenic patients until all participants were trained during five standardized sessions. The inter-rater reliability was 0.87-0.91 for the positive, 0.83-0.87 for the negative and 0.88-0.92 for the general psychopathology subscales.

Face Processing Assessment

In order to study the ability to infer emotional information from facial expressions, we used the Comprehensive Affect Testing System, CATS (Froming et al., 2000-2006), an ensemble of computerized tests that enables to assess the ability to recognize emotions expressed by human faces. The faces, based on the standardized Ekman collection (Ekman and Friesen, 1976), have been digitally modified to remove elements that might facilitate identification or discrimination of affect expressed by facial muscles. The instructions for the recognition of facial emotion tasks were translated by our group into Italian language and used for the present research (http://www.psychologysoftware.com/testing_instruments.htm). CATS represents an instrument able to discriminate patients with schizophrenia from healthy subjects in facial emotion recognition abilities (Rocca et al., 2009).

Testing session was about 40 min. and was conducted in a quiet room free from auditory and visual distractions. The computer monitor was placed directly in front of the participant, at a distance of about 90 cm. Emotional stimuli included the following emotions: happiness, sadness, anger, surprise, disgust, fear, or neutral mood.

One trained psychologist (F.C.) administered these tasks, pressing the button on the computer after the subject's answer, without time limits.

A complete description of each selected subtest follows, and an example of each task is illustrated in Figure 1:

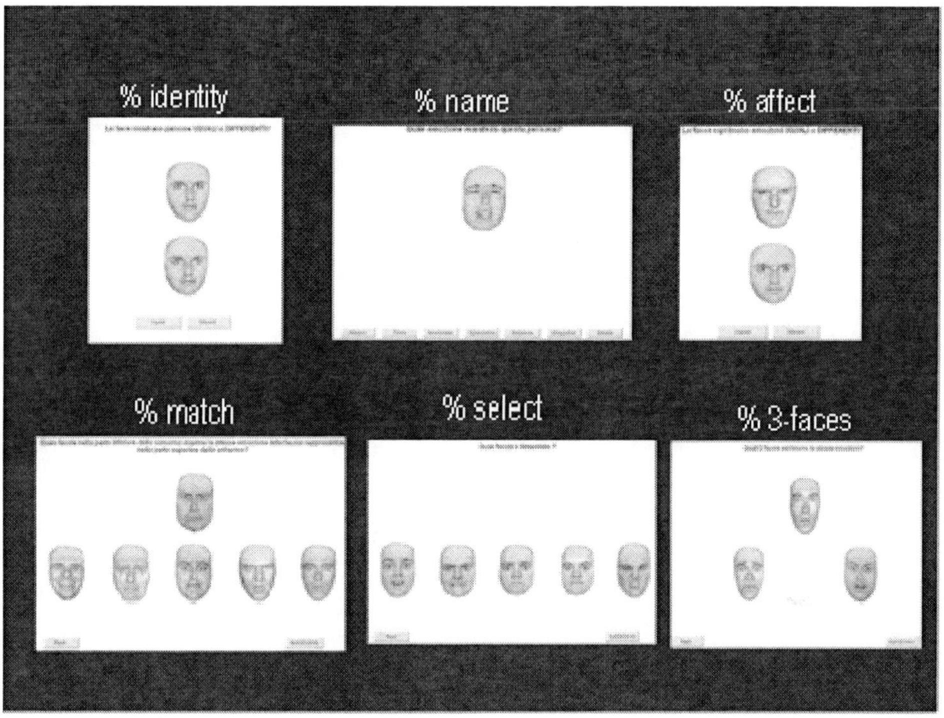

Abbreviations: % identity= Identity Discrimination; % affect= Affect Discrimination; % name= Affect Naming; % select= Select Affect; % match= Affect Matching; % 3-face= Three Faces Task.

Figure 1. Examples of Comprehensive Affect Testing System tasks (CATS).

- Identity Discrimination: two faces of individuals expressing a neutral mood are shown at a time. The subject indicates whether these faces display the same or a different person.

- Affect Discrimination: two portraits of the same person are presented at a time. The subject indicates whether the pictures exhibit the same or different affects.
- Affect Naming: a single portrait is shown. The subject identifies the emotion expressed by the person in the picture, choosing between the words written on the bottom of the screen. They can be happy, sad, angry, surprised, disgusted, frightened, or neutral.
- Affect Matching: one face is shown at the top of the screen and five others on the bottom row. The subject indicates which of the five faces displays the same affect shown by the portrait on the top.
- Select Affect: five faces are shown simultaneously. A sentence appears on the screen asking to select the face showing a specified emotion, such as "happy", or "sad".
- Three Faces Task: three faces are shown at a time. The subject identifies the two faces expressing the same emotion.

Cognitive Assessment

Patients were also assessed with a neuropsychological test battery by one trained psychologist (F.C.), who was unaware of clinical characteristics and results of psychiatric rating scales. The battery was administered and scored according to the established procedures for each test the day after the psychiatric assessment. The testing time was fixed in one session of one hour per patient. No subject was familiarized with the tests.

The neuropsychological battery evaluated attentive functions using the Stroop Test (Stroop, 1935) and the part B of Trial Making Test (Reitan, 1958), verbal memory-learning using the California Verbal Learning Test, CVLT (Delis et al., 1987), executive functions using the Wisconsin Card Sorting Test, WCST (Heaton et al., 1993), perceptual-motor speed using the Part A of Trial Making Test, TMT A, and pre-morbid intelligence using Test di Intelligenza Breve, TIB (Sartori et al., 1997), an equivalent version of the National Adult Reading Test, NART) (Nelson, 1982) for Italian people.

Statistical Analysis

Statistical analyses were performed using the software Statistical Package for the Social Sciences, SPSS, version 17 (SPSS Inc., 2008).

The comparison between remitted vs. non-remitted patients on demographic features (sex, age, education), clinical variables (age of onset, length of illness, number of previous relapses), PANSS scores (PANSS positive, PANSS negative, PANSS general psychopathology, PANSS total), type of treatment (first generation antipsychotics, FGAs vs. second generation antipsychotics, SGAs), chlorpromazine-equivalent daily dosage (CPZ-equivalent), facial identity and facial emotion recognition (% of errors on CATS subtests), and cognitive functions (Stroop test, CVLT, TMT, WCST) was performed, using one-way ANOVA for continuous measures and Chi square for categorical variables.

One binary logistic regression using remission state (0=remission, 1=no remission) as the dependent variable was applied to test the relation with the significant variables identified by the univariate comparisons of the two groups of patients, with a significance level$\leq$0.05.

Results

Ninety patients were enrolled, of whom 28 patients attained "cross-sectional" remission (31%), and 62 patients failed to (69%).

Table 1. Demographic and clinical variables of the study population

Variables	Non-remitted patients (N=62)	Remitted patients (N=28)	Statistics[a]	
			F/χ^2	P level
Sex, Males/Females	38/24	15/13	0.606	0.291
Age, M±SD	42.1±9.67	42.1±11.8	0.000	0.990
Education, M±SD	11.5±3,23	10.5±3.54	1.563	0.215
Age of onset, M±SD	26.4±9.13	25.1±9.68	0.363	0.548
Length of illness, M±SD	15.7±9.58	16.9±11	0.316	0.575
Previous relapses, N	3.96±5.75	3.64±3.90	0.098	0.755
FGAs/SGAs, N	16/46	5/23	0.746	0.280
CPZ-equivalent, mg	301.67±215.62	257.19±146.73	0.921	0.340

Abbreviations: M=mean; SD=standard deviation; N=number; CPZ-equivalent=dose equivalent to 100 mg/day of chlorpromazine; FGAs=first generation antipsychotics; SGAs=second generation antipsychotics.

[a] For continuous measures the statistic is the one-way ANOVA, for categorical variables is the Chi square test.

Table 2. Facial emotion processing of the study population (% errors)

Variables	Non-remitted patients (N=62)	Remitted patients (N=28)	One-way ANOVA	
			F	P level
Identity Discrimination[a]	9.69±12	4.35±7,29	4.375	0.040
Affect Discrimination[a]	8.80±8,65	7.02±8.53	0.760	0.386
Affect Naming[a]	30.5±19.2	32.6±24	0.187	0.667
Select Affect[a]	18.4±17.8	12.9±16	1.790	0.18
Affect Matching[a]	30.4±16.7	31.3±9.24	0.076	0.783
Three Faces Task[a]	45.6±12.7	43.2±10.5	0.708	0.403

[a]Values are expressed in mean±standard deviation.

No statistically significant differences were found between remitted vs. non-remitted patients in demographic and clinical variables (Table 1). No differences were found in facial emotion recognition abilities between the two groups, while performances at the Identity discrimination task were better in remitted patients (Table 2). Executive functions (WCST total errors) were significantly less impaired in remitted patients than non-remitted ones. No differences were found in attentive functions, verbal memory/learning, perceptual-motor speed, and pre-morbid intelligence (Table 3). When the variables - that showed significant differences between patients with and without remission - were included in a logistic regression model, independent significant relations were only found between remission status and Identity discrimination (standardized β=-0.06; S.E.=0.03; p=0.04).

Table 3. Cognitive performances of the study population

Variables	Non-remitted patients (N=62)	Remitted patients (N=28)	One-way ANOVA	
			F	P level
Stroop Color[a]	38.2±7.97	38±8.81	0.015	0.904
Stroop Color Word[a]	19.2±5.43	20.6±6.88	1.260	0.285
CVLT trial 1_5[a]	38.1±10.8	42.2±12	2.727	0.102
CVLT intrusions during immediate recall[a]	1.69±2.67	1.07±1,72	1.276	0.262
CVLT intrusions during delayed recall[a]	0.74±2.02	0.64±0.83	0.057	0.811
CVLT delayed recall[a]	8.3±3.22	9.39±3.51	2.110	0.150
CVLT recognitions[a]	14.2±2.10	14.8±1.98	1.591	0.211
CVLT false recognitions[a]	3.18±3.44	2.07±2.2	2.354	0.129
TMT A[a]	56.2±22.7	48±30.2	2.057	0.155
TMT B[a]	143.61±75.97 1	112.70±67.1 54	3.331	0.071
TMT B-A[a]	87.5±72.3	66.8±61.1	1.678	0.199
WCST total errors[a]	23.1±11.1	18±8.52	4.388	0.039
TIB[a]	107.17±6.95	106.48±8.38	0.165	0.685

Abbreviation: Stroop=Stroop Test; CVLT=California Verbal Learning Test; TMT=Trail Making Test; WCST=Wisconsin Card Sorting Test; TIB=Test di Intelligenza Breve.

[a]Values are expressed in mean±standard deviation.

DISCUSSION

This study aimed to explored face processing and cognitive functions in remitted vs. non-remitted patients. Approximately one-third of our schizophrenic patients fulfilled the criteria for remission, in accordance to the percentages reported in other studies (De Hert et al., 2007; Helldin et al., 2006; Lasser et al., 2005). The two groups of schizophrenic patients were homogeneous in demographic characteristics (sex, age, education), and in several clinical variables (age of onset, length of illness, number of previous relapses, type of antipsychotic medication, CPZ-equivalent daily dosage of antipsychotics).

To the best of our knowledge, this is the first study exploring the role of face processing in achieving a remission status in schizophrenia. We have analysed separately facial identity recognition and facial emotion recognition because an unresolved question is whether deficit in facial emotion perception is specific for facial emotion, or it is secondary to an impairment in face perception (Chapman and Chapman, 1978; Kosmidis et al., 2007; Bediou et al., 2005; Martin et al., 2005).

In our research, remitted patients vs. non-remitted performed better in facial identity recognition, while no differences were found in facial emotion perception tasks (Affect Discrimination, Affect Naming, Affect Matching, Select Affect, Three Faces Task). These results support the idea that, even if related, facial identity and facial emotion recognition represent two different components of face processing with different impact on remission status. Our suggestion is that emotion perception deficit was not associated to the remission status, as it represents a stable characteristic of illness, only marginally related to symptoms. Previous studies concluded that deficits in emotion perception in schizophrenia appear to be stable, they occur across different phases of the disorder (Gaebel and Wölwer, 1992; Penn and Combs, 2000; Penn et al., 2000), and they are not related to symptoms' status (Marwick and Hall, 2008). Contrary, the ability to recognize facial identity was better in patients who were in remission than those who did not meet the remission status.

Facial identity recognition resulted to be a significant contributor of remission status, suggesting a link between this component of face processing and symptoms of schizophrenia. To interpret this link, it has been proposed that non-specific cognitive factors may contribute to this deficit. Cognitive contribution on face perception deficit has been observed in tasks with high mnemonic and attentional demands (Marwick and Hall, 2008). The cognitive demands of the Facial Identity discrimination task we used, were minimized, as two faces of individuals expressing a neutral mood were shown at a time and the subject had to indicate whether these faces display the same or a different person, without limits time. Besides, results by cognitive functions and remission status permit to exclude that the contribution of face perception to remission status was due to a general cognitive dysfunctions. In fact, the group comparison between remitted vs. non-remitted patients showed no differences in attentive functions, verbal memory/learning, perceptual-motor speed, and pre-morbid intelligence. Remitted subjects had only a lower number of total errors at WCST than non-remitted ones. However, WCST total error did not reach the significance level to be a significant contributor of remission status in the logistic regression.

Previous research on the relationship between cognitive functions and remission status produced mixed results. Our results are consistent with a part of these studies that did not find differences in the most of cognitive functions between remitted and non-remitted patients (Buckley et al., 2007; Emsley et al., 2007; Eberhard et al., 2009). In one of these studies (Buckley et al., 2007), it has been underlined that not only the development of remission was not predicted by baseline cognitive functioning (cognitive composite score), but also the development of remission and cognitive improvements in follow-up analysis were not inter-related. Nevertheless, other authors found contrary evidences (Haro et al., 2006; Helldin et al., 2006). Helldin et al. (2006), for example, revealed marked differences in attention, memory, and visuomotor speed between remitted and non-remitted patients, but this difference could be due to the fact that the patients with remission had a higher pre-morbid functioning level. Our patients, instead, had a homogeneous pre-morbid intelligence (TIB value for non-remitted patients= 107.17± 6.95; remitted patients=106.48± 8.38, p=0.685). Finally, Haro et al. (2006) found that a higher clinical severity (included cognitive symptoms) was associated with a significantly lower likelihood of achieving remission, but they did not apply specific tools of neuropsychological assessment.

A final consideration is about a possible relation between antipsychotic treatment, facial identity recognition, executive functions and remission status. Our patients were homogeneous respect to type of antipsychotics and chlorpromazine-equivalent daily dosage. No pharmacological or treatment intervention have been explicitly provided for the purpose of patients' attainment of remission. These observations allow to exclude that the relationship between facial identity recognition/executive functioning and remission status was due to treatment. In addition, no substantial improvements in facial affect recognition were found after treatment with either typical or atypical antipsychotic drugs (see review by Hempel et al., 2010), and previous studies focussing specifically on the impact of antipsychotics on executive functions have shown that deficits in executive functions remain relatively resistant to amelioration by antipsychotic medication in comparison to symptoms (O'Grada and Dinan, 2007).

Some limitations of this report have to be considered. The first one concerns the cross-sectional design of the study. Applying the remission criteria proposed by Andreasen et al. (2005), we only used the symptom-severity component, reconstructing the time criterion retrospectively with indirect data on symptomatologic stability over time. In literature other authors based their research on remission solely on symptom control and relatively brief, if any, follow up (Sethuraman et al., 2005; Helldin et al., 2006; Eberhard et al., 2009; Jäger et al., 2009). As stated by Helldin et al. (2009), the time criterion of remission would ideally require one weekly follow-up examination for 6 months using the PANSS scale (that is based on symptoms present during the previous week), but it is unlikely in routine clinical practice. The assessment should be based on reports from the patients themselves, relatives and caregivers, in combination with information from the medical records about the requirements for changes in medications, symptom exacerbation, relapse or hospitalization. A second limitation concerns the small sample size of patients. Further studies would be needed using a larger sample to elucidate the relationship between remission status and outcome parameters we considered in this research.

Despite these limitations, there are some strengths of our work that should be noted. The focus of this study has been previously scarcely addressed. It is the first study to explore emotion perception and face perception in remitted and non-remitted patients with schizophrenia. Secondly, we administered a standardized cross-culturally valid neuropsychological measure of emotion processing, which evaluates a large group of domains of emotion processing (i.e. discrimination, selection, labeling and matching facial emotions) and a wide neuropsychological battery consisted of tests evaluating several cognitive functional domains.

In conclusion, these results suggest that remission criteria for schizophrenia (Andreasen et al., 2005) can only partially be considered an index of "functional" remission. Other aspects of social functioning should be considered in order to focus on recovery from the illness, and a more comprehensive approach to treatment in schizophrenia - possibly including psychological interventions addressed to the remediation of social and basic cognitive deficits - should be recommended as an important component of functional recovery.

Acknowledgments

This study was supported by a research grant from Ministero dell'Università e della Ricerca, Programmi di Ricerca Scientifica di rilevante interesse nazionale (Bando 2006), and from Regione Piemonte, Bando Regionale per il finanziamento di Progetti di Ricerca Scientifica Applicata (Bando 2004).

References

Altamura AC, Bobo WV, Meltzer HY. 2007. Factors affecting outcome in schizophrenia and their relevance for psychopharmacological treatment. *Int. Clin. Psychopharmacol.* 2007; 22: 249-67.

Andreasen NC, Arndt S, Alliger R, Miller D, Flaum M. 1995. Symptoms of schizophrenia: methods, meanings, and mechanisms. *Arch. Gen. Psychiatry.* 1995; 52: 341–351.

Andreasen NC, Carpenter WT Jr, Kane JM, Lasser RA, Marder SR, Weinberger DR. Remission in schizophrenia: proposed criteria and rationale for consensus. *Am. J. Psychiatry* 2005; 162: 441-9.

Andreasen NC, Grove WM. Evaluation of positive and negative symptoms in schizophrenia. *Psychiatrie et Psychobiologie* 1986.

Andreasen NC, Olsen S. Negative v positive schizophrenia. Definition and validation. Arch. Gen. Psychiatry 1982; 39(7): 789-94.

Bediou B, Franck N, Saoud M, Baudouin JY, Tiberghien G, Daléry J, d'Amato T. Effects of emotion and identity on facial affect processing in schizophrenia. *Psychiatry Res.* 2005;133:149-157.

Bilder RM, Mukherjee S, Rieder RO, Pandurang AK. Symptomatic and neuropsychological components of defect states. *Schizophr. Bull.* 1985; 11: 409–419.

Bora E, Gökçen S, Kayahan B, Veznedaroglu B. Deficits of social-cognitive and social-perceptual aspects of theory of mind in remitted patients with schizophrenia: effect of residual symptoms. *J. Nerv. Ment. Dis.* 2008; 196: 95-9.

Buckley PF, Harvey PD, Bowie CR, Loebel A. The relationship between symptomatic remission and neuropsychological improvement in schizophrenia patients switched to treatment with ziprasidone. *Schizophr. Res.* 2007; 94: 99-106.

Chapman LJ, Chapman JP. The measurement of differential deficit. *J. Psychiatr. Res.* 1978;14:303-311.

Ciudad A, Alvarez E, Bobes J, San L, Polavieja P, Gilaberte I. Remission in schizophrenia: results from a 1-year follow-up observational study. *Schizophr. Res.* 2009; 108: 214-22.

Couture SM, Penn DL, Roberts DL. The functional significance of social cognition in schizophrenia: a review. *Schizophr. Bull* 2006; 32 Suppl 1: S44-63.

De Hert M., van Winkel R, Wampers M, Kane J, van Os J, Peuskens J. Remission criteria for schizophrenia: evaluation in a large naturalistic cohort. *Schizophr. Res.* 2007; 92: 68-73.

Delis DC, Kramer JH, Kaplin E, Ober B. California Verbal Learning Test Adult Version Research Edition Manual. New York, NY, *The Psychological Corporation.* 1987.

Docherty JP, Bossie CA, Lachaux B, Bouhours P, Zhu Y, Lasser R, Gharabawi GM. Patient-based and clinician-based support for the remission criteria in schizophrenia. *Int. Clin. Psychopharmacol.* 2007; 22: 51-5.

Dunayevich E, Sethuraman G, Enerson M, Taylor CC, Lin D. Characteristics of two alternative schizophrenia remission definitions: relationship to clinical and quality of life outcomes. *Schizophr. Res.* 2006; 86: 300-8.

Eberhard J, Levander S, Lindström E. Remission in schizophrenia: analysis in a naturalistic setting. *Compr. Psychiatry* 2009; 50: 200-8.

Ekman P, Friesen WV. Pictures of Facial Affect. Palo Alto, CA, *Consulting Psychologist's Press* 1976.

Emsley R, Rabinowitz J, Medori R. Early Psychosis Global Working Group. Remission in early psychosis: Rates, predictors, and clinical and functional outcome correlates. *Schizophr. Res.* 2007; 89: 129-39.

Evans JD, Bond GR, Meyer PS, Kim HW, Lysaker PH, Gibson PJ, Tunis S. Cognitive and clinical predictors of success in vocational rehabilitation in schizophrenia. *Schizophr. Res.* 2004; 70: 331-42.

First MB, Gibbon M, Spitzer RL, Williams JBW, Benjamin LS. Structured Clinical Interview for DSM-IV Disorders (SCID). Washington DC, *American Psychiatric Press* 1987.

Froming KB, Levy CM, Shaffer SG, Ekman P. *Comprehensive Affect Testing System* (CATS). © 2000-2006; http://www.psychologysoftware.com/testing_instruments.htm.

Gaebel W, Wolwer W. Facial expression and emotional face recognition in schizophrenia and depression. *Eur. Arch. Psychiatry Clin. Neurosci.* 1992;242:46–52.

Green MF, Penn DL, Bentall R, Carpenter WT, Gaebel W, Gur RC, Kring AM, Park S, Silverstein SM, Heinssen R. Social cognition in schizophrenia: an NIMH workshop on definitions, assessment, and research opportunities. *Schizophr. Bull.* 2008; 34: 1211-20.

Gur RE, Mozley PD, Resnick SM, Levick S, Erwin R, Saykin AJ, Gur RC. Relations among clinical scales in schizophrenia. *Am. J. Psychiatry.* 1991; 148: 472–478.

Haro JM, Novick D, Suarez D, Alonso J, Lépine JP, Ratcliffe M. SOHO Study Group. Remission and relapse in the outpatient care of schizophrenia: three-year results from the Schizophrenia Outpatient Health Outcomes study. *J. Clin. Psychopharmacol.* 2006; 26: 571-8.

Heaton RK, Chelune GJ, Kay KK, Curtiss G. Wisconsin Card Sorting Test Manual. Revised and expanded. Los Angeles, CA, *Western Psychological Services* 1993.

Helldin L, Kane JM, Hjärthag F, Norlander T. The importance of cross-sectional remission in schizophrenia for long-term outcome: A clinical prospective study. *Schizophr. Res.* 2009;115: 67-73.

Helldin L, Kane JM, Karilampi U, Norlander T, Archer TJ. Remission and cognitive ability in a cohort of patients with schizophrenia. *Psychiatry Res.* 2006; 40: 738-45.

Helldin L, Kane JM, Karilampi U, Norlander T, Archer T. Remission in prognosis of functional outcome: a new dimension in the treatment of patients with psychotic disorders. *Schizophr. Res.* 2007; 93: 160-8.

Hempel RJ, Dekker JA, van Beveren NJ, Tulen JH, Hengeveld MW. The effect of antipsychotic medication on facial affect recognition in schizophrenia: a review. *Psychiatry Res.* 2010; 178(1):1-9.

Jäger M, Schmauß M, Laux G, Pfeiffer H, Naber DG, Schmidt L, Gaebel W, Klosterkötter J, Heuser I, Maier W, Lemke MR, Degner D, Buchkremer G, Gastpar M, Möller HJ, Riedel M. Early improvement as a predictor of remission and response in schizophrenia: Results from a naturalistic study. *Eur. Psychiatry* 2009;24: 501-6.

Juckel G, Morosini PL. The new approach: psychosocial functioning as a necessary outcome criterion for therapeutic success in schizophrenia. *Curr. Opin. Psychiatry* 2008; 21: 630-9.

Kay SR, Fiszbein A, Opler LA. The positive and negative syndrome scale (PANSS) for schizophrenia. *Schizophr. Bull.* 1987; 13: 261-276.

Kosmidis MH, Bozikas VP, Giannakou M, Anezoulaki D, Fantie BD, Karavatos A. Impaired emotion perception in schizophrenia: a differential deficit. *Psychiatry Res.* 2007;149:279-284.

Lasser RA, Bossie CA, Gharabawi GM, Kane JM. Remission in schizophrenia: Results from a 1-year study of long-acting risperidone injection. *Schizophr. Res.* 2005; 77: 215-27.

Lasser RA, Nasrallah H, Helldin L, Peuskens J, Kane J, Docherty J, Tronco AT. Remission in schizophrenia: applying recent consensus criteria to refine the concept. *Schizophr. Res.* 2007; 96: 223-31.

Liddle PF, Barnes TRE, Morris D, Haque S. 1989. Three syndromes in chronic schizophrenia. *Br. J. Psychiatry* 1989; 155(suppl 7):119 122.

Liddle PF. The symptoms of chronic schizophrenia: a re-examination of the positive-negative dichotomy. *Br. J. Psychiatry.* 1987; 151: 145–151.

Malla A, Norman R, Schmitz N, Manchanda R, Béchard-Evans L, Takhar J, Haricharan. Predictors of rate and time to remission in first-episode psychosis: a two-year outcome study. *Psychol. Med.* 2006; 36: 649-58.

Martin F, Baudouin JY, Tiberghien G, Franck N. Processing emotional expression and facial identity in schizophrenia. *Psychiatry. Res.* 2005;134:43-53.

Marwick K, Hall J. Social cognition in schizophrenia: a review of face processing. *Br. Med. Bull.* 2008; 88: 43-58.

Mo S, Su Y, Chan RC, Liu J. Comprehension of metaphor and irony in schizophrenia during remission: the role of theory of mind and IQ. *Psychiatry Res.* 2008; 157: 21-9.

Nelson HE. The National Adult Reading Test (NART): test manual. In: Nelson HE (ed). NFER-Nelson Publishing 1982.

O'Grada and Dinan, 2007. "Executive functions in schizophrenia: what impact do antipsychotics have?" Hum. *Psychopharmacol. Clin. Exp.* 2007; 22: 397–406.

Overall JE, Gorham DR. The Brief Psychiatric Rating Scale. *Psychol. Rep.* 1962; 10: 799–812.

Penn DL, Combs DR, Ritchie M, Francis J, Cassisi J, Morris S, Townsend M. Emotion recognition in schizophrenia: further investigation of generalized versusspecific deficit models. *J. Abnorm. Psychol.* 2000;109:512-516.

Penn DL, Combs DR, Ritchie M, Francis J, Cassisi J, Morris S, Townsend M. Emotion recognition in schizophrenia: further investigation of generalized versus specific deficit models. *J. Abnorm. Psychol.* 2000;109(3):512-6.

Reitan R. Validity of the Trial Making Test as an indicator of organic brain disease. *Percept. Mot. Skills* 1958; 8: 271-276.

Rocca P, Castagna F, Mongini T, Montemagni T, Rasetti R, Rocca G, Bogetto F. Exploring the role of face processing in facial emotion recognition in schizophrenia. *Acta. Neuropsychiatr.* 2009; 21: 292–300.

San L, Ciudad A, Alvarez E, Bobes J, Gilaberte I. Symptomatic remission and social/vocational functioning in outpatients with schizophrenia: prevalence and associations in a cross-sectional study. *Eur. Psychiatry.* 2007; 22: 490-8.

Sartori G, Colombo L, Vallar G, Rusconi ML, Pinarello A. T.I.B. test di intelligenza breve per la valutazione del quoziente intellettivo attuale e premorboso. *Q. J. Exp. Psychol.* A 1997; 4: 1-6.

Sethuraman G, Taylor CC, Enerson M, Dunayevich E. A retrospective comparison of cumulative time spent in remission during treatment with olanzapine or risperidone among patients with schizophrenia. *Schizophr. Res.* 2005; 79: 337-40.

Stroop J. Studies of interference in serial verbal reactions. Q. J. Exp. Psychol. A 1935; 18: 643-662.

van Os J, Drukker M, Campo J, Meijer J, Bak M, Delespaul P. Validation of remission criteria for schizophrenia. *Am. J. Psychiatry.* 2006; 163: 2000-2.

Velligan DI, Mahurin RK, Diamond PL, Hazleton BC, Eckert SL, Miller AL. The functional significance of symptomatology and cognitive function in schizophrenia. *Schizophr. Res.* 1997; 25: 21-31.

Woods SW. Chlorpromazine equivalent doses for the newer atypical antipsychotics. *J. Clin. Psychiatry.* 2003; 64: 663-7.

Yen CF, Cheng CP, Huang CF, Ko CH, Yen JY, Chang YP, Chen CS. Relationship between psychosocial adjustment and executive function in patients with bipolar disorder and schizophrenia in remission: the mediating and moderating effects of insight. *Bipolar Disord.* 2009; 11: 190-7.

In: Face Recognition
Editors: Adamo Quaglia and Calogera M. Epifano
ISBN 978-1-61942-663-4

Chapter 7

FACE RECOGNITION: DIFFERENT ENCODING METHODS ON NEWBORN INFANT RESEARCH

***Cecchini Marco*[1]*, Iannoni Maria Elena*[1]*, Di Florio Eugenio*[1]*, Altavilla Daniela*[1]*, Piccolo Federica*[1]*, Aceto Paola*[2] *and Lai Carlo*[1]**

[1] Dynamic and Clinical Psychology
University of Rome Sapienza Rome, Italy
[2]Anaesthesiology Institute Catholic University
of Sacred Heart Rome, Italy

ABSTRACT

Many studies have investigated cognitive and social competences of newborn infants as face recognition, ability to imitate facial gestures and communicative skills.

The preferential looking paradigm showed that newborns prefer to look at a human face-like stimulus compared to any other non human face-like stimulus.

Furthermore, it is highlighted a newborn preference to look at a new face compared to a face previously seen from the habituation procedure (novelty effect); to explain this effect, it is assumed that the newborns are able to build a *perceptive representation* of the face that they looked at, *like an expression of a motivation for novelty.* This effect disappeared if the known face is the mother's face which is looked at more when it is compared to a new face (familiarity effect); it is assumed that the newborns are able to build a *dynamic "social" representation* of the face through few communicative interactions with their mother in the first hours of life.

The studies about the novelty effect and the familiarity effect are based on a preference-task, where a new face is compared with a known face. These studies show a large heterogeneity of the encoding methods related to the gazing behaviour of the newborns. The most widely used methods in literature are summarized in three big classes: live encoding, frame by frame video encoding, real time video encoding.

This chapter will focus on the differences among encoding methods of the gazing behaviour of the newborns. Moreover the findings of an empirical study on the comparisons among different encoding methods will be reported.

CURRENT FINDINGS ON FACE PREFERENCE IN NEWBORNS

In the last two decades, many studies have been performed on cognitive and social competences of newborns (Farroni, Mansfield, Lai, and Johnson, 2003; Cecchini et al., 2007; 2010; 2011b). Some studies showed the communicative competencies of newborns as their ability to imitate facial gestures like “tongue protrusion” or “mouth opening” (Meltzoff, 1999; Meltzoff andMoore, 1977). A neuro- biological study on four-month infants showed that the cerebral areas activated during communicative face to face interactions are the same as in adults (temporal and prefrontal areas) (Grossmann, Johnson, Farroni, and Csibra, 2008). In the last forty years, the preferential looking paradigm (Bushnell, 2001; Horowitz, Paden, and Self, 1972; Morton and Johnson, 1991; Pascalis, de Schonen, andMorton, 1995) demonstrated that newborns prefer to look at a human face-like stimulus compared to any other non human face-like stimulus (Morton and Johnson, 1991). Moreover, it is clearly demonstrated that newborns prefer to look at a new face compared to a face previously showed during a habituation paradigm (Bushnell, 2001; Horowitz et al., 1972; Pascalis et al., 1995). Some authors (Horowitz et al., 1972) speculated that newborns have an innate motivation to look at new faces (novelty effect) when these faces are compared to faces previously seen and known from the habituation procedure. This interpretation assumes that the newborns are able to build a perceptive representation of the face that they looked at and that their preference for the new face is an expression of a motivation for novelty (Horowitz et al., 1972). Other studies showed that this effect is absent when the known face is the mother’s face which is looked at more when it is compared to a new face (Bushnell, 2001; Pascalis and de Schonen, 1994; Pascalis et al., 1995). It is unclear why newborns have this preference for the mother’s face, which shows a familiarity effect that overrides the novelty effect (Scott and Nelson, 2004). Some authors (Pascalis et al., 1995) hypothesized an “operating conditioning” according to which the mother’s face is preferred because it gives positive reinforcements. The novelty effect and the familiarity effect alone are insufficient to explain the two demonstrated preferences of newborns to look at new faces and to look at the mother’s face. It is interesting that when newborns were engaged in the habituation paradigm with the mother’s face, in a successive preference task they preferred the new face (Pascalis et al., 1995; Scott and Nelson, 2004). Another interpretation (Cecchini et al., 2011a) consider the hypothesis that few communicative interactions with the mother in the first hours of life could motivate newborns to look more at the mother’s face instead of a new one. This interpretation implicates that newborns are able to build a dynamic social representation of the face that they were looking at in a communicative context.

This dynamic social representation generates a communicative expectation (Meltzoff, 1999) which could orient the preference to look at or to avoid the known face. The preference for the new face after the habituation paradigm could be not only an expression of a motivation for novelty but also an avoidance for the known face during a still face condition. Recent studies demonstrated that, in three-month infants (Bertin and Striano, 2006) and also newborns (Nagy, 2008), the time spent looking at a face was decreased when it became a freeze face (still-face situation). This also occurred for the mother’s face (Yato et al., 2008). It is possible that newborns are likely attracted by their mother’s face (Bushnell, Sai, and Mullin, 1989; Field, Cohen, Garcia, and Greenberg, 1984; Sai, 2005; Walton, Bower, and Bower, 1992) because, unlike the still face, the mother’s face confirms an expectation of communication; therefore, the newborns would be able to build a dynamic "social" representation of the face through few communicative interactions with their mother in the first hours of life (Cecchini et al., 2011a). For many years some studies focused on the issue of novelty preference (Horowitz et al., 1972) and other studies on familiar preference (Field, Cohen, Garcia, and Greenberg, 1984; Bushnell, Sai, and Mullin, 1989; Walton, Bower, and Bower, 1992; Sai, 2005) assuming two different innate motivations of the newborns: to prefer new faces (Horowitz, Paden, and Self, 1972) and to prefer her/him mother face (Sai, 2005). A recent study (Cecchini et al., 2011a) suggests to consider the variable "precedent communication with the face" in order to understand the relation between the newborn's familiar vs novelty preference: during a preference task between a known and a new face, the newborns prefer to look at the new only when the known face was known in an immobility condition. More visual-imitative interactions the newborns had with the known face more they prefer to look at it compared with the new face, using different looking strategies. This suggests that newborns prefer to look at a communicative face and that they actively avoid previously known face in an immobility condition.

The cause of the attraction could not be the face movements and vocalizations, but the contingency of those movements and vocalizations with the movements and vocalizations of the newborns. These findings suggest that, during interactions with a specific human face, the newborns are able to build a dynamic representation with expectations that orient their looking behaviour at this face.

Newborn Infant Recruitment Criteria

It is very difficult to recruit newborns for face preference tasks. As for other behavioural tasks on newborns, there are some inclusion (healthy full-term; apgar index at first [6-10] and fifth minutes [8-10]; alert with open eyes condition; weight) and exclusion (fussing, crying, sleeping) a-priori criteria. A-posteriori inclusion criteria are: insufficient eyes opening necessary to codify gazing at the faces; side bias in their looking (insufficient gazing at the least preferred side during the face preference task) and in their facing behaviours (insufficient changing their facing orientation during the face preference task).

Procedures

The newborn can stay lying supine in their cradles, in a quite room (as shown in Figure 1), where all the experimental sessions are recorded using an audio-video apparatus (Figure 1). During a 3-minute baseline registration, the newborns have to be in an alert state, not fussing or crying. At the end of the baseline period, the newborns are randomly assigned to two groups.

The experimental procedures used in many studies were as follows:

- Brief Baseline;
- habituation to a face following an objective or subjective criteria (Horowitz, Paden, and Self, 1972);

- Preference Task I Trial (Figure 2): the previous face (Known Face) was presented with a New Face (Horowitz, et al., 1972; Field, et al., 1984; Walton, Bower, and Bower, 1992; Pascalis and de Schonen, 1994; Sai, 2005). Preference Task I Trial began with the newborn's fixation of either face and terminated after 20 seconds of fixation to either or both faces (Known and New Face) have been elapsed (20 seconds looking duration criteria).
- Preference Task II Trial (Figure 2): after the I Trial, the newborns were picked up from the apparatus and the two faces changed side to counteract the influence of side bias. The II trial ended following the same 20 seconds looking duration criteria as the I Trial.

The independent variable was the face stimuli (Known Face vs New Face) during the two Preference Tasks (I and II Trials).

During the preference task (Figure 2) two voluntary stranger females were asked to come out by a large white screen (2 x 2,5 m) into which at head height were cut out two openings (30 x 25 cm), one each side of mid-line and separated by 12 cm. The distance between the face of the newborn and the strangers' face was 20 cm. These conditions allowed a good view of the air and face of the stimuli from the point of view of the newborn, who remained in the cradle. In order to prevent any contamination of the data due to differences in the clothes of the stimulus faces, they each wear a white gown. The visible background was the same for both stimulus faces.

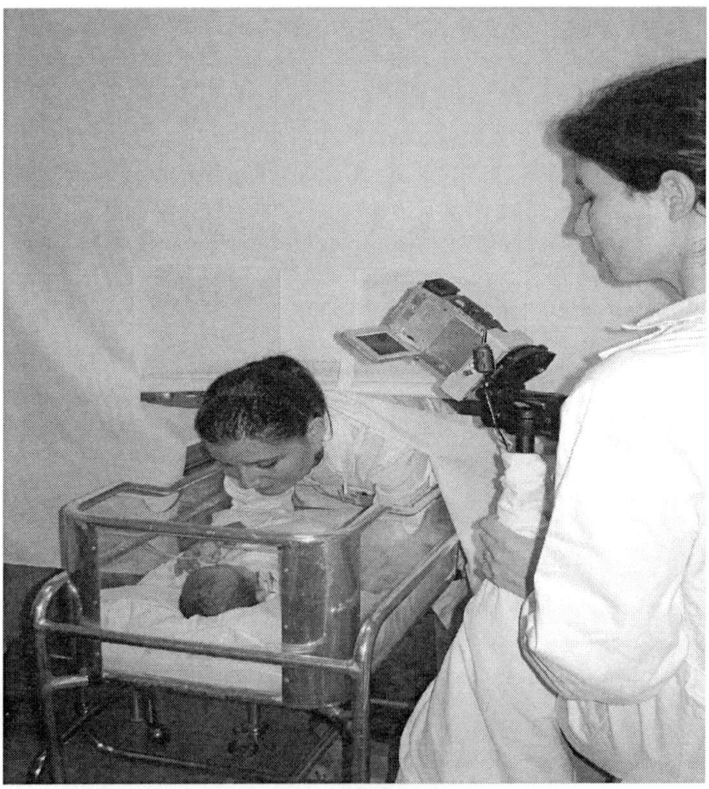

Figure 1. Experimental apparatus during the presentation of the face.

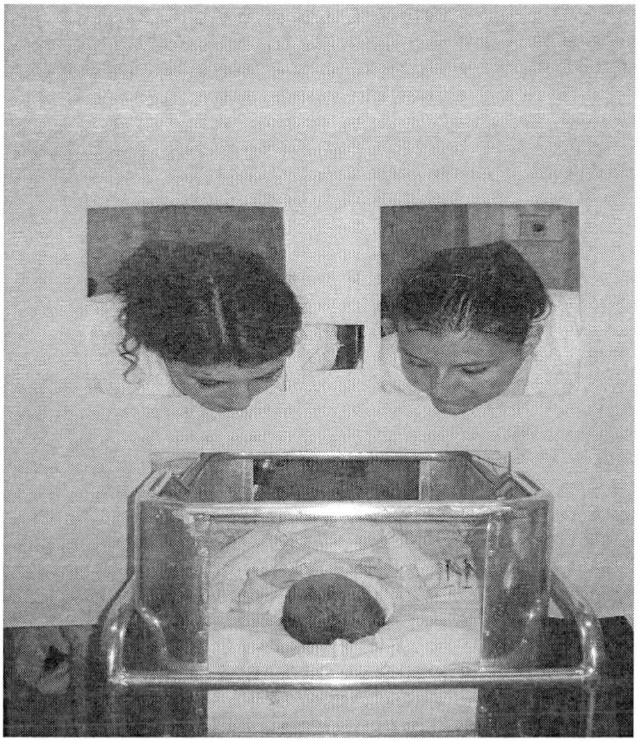

Figure 2. Preference task apparatus.

The face stimuli were real tri-dimensional woman's faces (22 cm×15 cm) with brown hair and broadly comparable. The stimuli were posed at a 20 cm distance from the newborn's face. In some studies the face stimuli were pictures of faces.

During the preference task the right and left order has to be balanced for the two faces (Known and New).

The dependent variables during the Preference Tasks were amount, and mean duration of the occurrences for looking (time spent in gazing at each face) and facing (time spent in directing newborn's face to each face) behaviour for each newborn.

The audio-video recorded looking and facing behaviour was coded following operative definitions of gazing at the known and the new face.

An independent observer coded the newborn's facing and gazing behaviour on video data.

STATISTICAL ANALYSIS

Amount and mean duration of the occurrences for looking and facing behaviours has to be analysed. In this type of experimental design it is necessary to use single sample t test on the mean and standard deviation of looking at known or new face timing vs. 10 seconds (equal-distribution control condition) considering that the sum of the looking at the known and the new faces time is 20 seconds. Inter-raters reliability (Cohen k or Pearson r) on a sample of 30% of the number of newborns have to be performed for looking behaviour and for facing behaviour.

Looking at Encoding Methods

The studies about the novelty and familiarity effects are based on a preference-task (Cecchini et al., 2011a), where a new face is compared with a known face; these studies show a large heterogeneity of the encoding methods related to the gazing behaviour of the newborns: the methods most widely used in literature are summarized in three modality: live encoding, frame by frame video encoding, real time video encoding. Recent advances in corneal reflection (CR) eye tracking techniques have provided investigators of human development with a new tool that holds much promise. Corneal reflection methods for evaluating gaze movements were originally developed by Salapatek, Kessen, and Haith (Haith, 1969; Salapatek, and Kessen, 1966). The method relies on the fact that a light source reflected from the cornea will remain relatively stationary when the eye moves because of spherical properties of the eyeball. Therefore, if the positions of these light reflections are related to the center of the pupil it is possible to make an estimate of gaze direction. With this technique it becomes possible to measure how infants perceive the world with a high spatial and temporal accuracy. A recent special issue of the journal Infancy illustrates the broad applicability of state of the art eye tracking, reporting on infants' ability to categorize visual and auditory events (McMurray and Aslin, 2004), perceive object unity (Johnson, Slemmer, and Amso, 2004), represent temporarily occluded objects (Gredebäck and von Hofsten, 2004), and scan dynamic human faces (Hunnis and Geuze, 2004); no systematic attempts (besides the Infancy special issue) have been made to describe the use of eye tracking on infant populations, special attention is required in order to enhance the availability and ease of use of eye tracking technology in this pre-verbal population.

The overview of the literature on face preference task on newborns revealed that several studies on face recognition are often compared even if they used different encoding data methods.

In order to comprehend if different encoding methods showed the same findings different encoding methods are compared.

The behaviors considered were the face preference (looking at new face time vs. looking at known face time) during a preference-task; and the preference-task's duration (the time necessary to newborns to complete the task).

For the coding of gaze direction of the newborns, four encoding methods has been proposed: frame by frame video encoding; live encoding; real time video encoding looking at the new and the known faces; real time video encoding facing at the right and left sides.

The four encoding methods differed in terms of:

- Encoding setting (live vs. video);
- Speed of visualization (real time vs. frame by frame);
- Encoding object (gaze direction of the newborns towards the face vs. towards the side where the face is oriented);
- Encoding criteria (as referred to an operational definition vs. intuitive encoding).

In literature, the studies on face preference task conducted on newborns use many different encoding methods. In the Sai's study (Sai et al, 2005), the authors described a live encoding of gaze direction and a video encoding performed in the lab and the encoding of gaze direction was addressed to the mother's or to the stranger's face. However, the author used the expression "sides". So it is not clear if the experimenter encoded the gaze direction toward the side (right or left) or towards the faces (new or known). It seems important to define this aspect taking into consideration that a newborn could look towards a side but not towards the face.

In another relevant study (Kelly, Quinn, Slater, Lee, Ge, and Pascalis, 2007), the video was analyzed frame by frame on a computer by two independent observers, using a specialized software. For each frame, observers coded whether the newborn was looking at the image (photo of the face on the monitor). It is still unclear if the observer coded when newborns looked at the faces or at the side of faces. Also in this case it is not specified the difference between looking at the face or looking out of the face but in the same side.

In order to test possible differences between encoding toward the faces, and towards the sides, four encoding methods were performed:

- Encoding setting (live vs. video);
- Speed of visualization (real time vs. frame by frame);
- Encoding object (gaze direction of the newborns towards the Face vs. towards the Side where the face is present);
- Encoding criteria (as referred to an Operational Definition vs. Intuitive Encoding).

Each of these modes is based on specific encoding criteria that are narrower for the Frame by Fame video encoding, and wider for real time video encoding towards the sides.

1. Frame by Frame Video Encoding

For the Frame by Frame video encoding, it was used the Noldus software "The Observer 5.0.31" that allows researchers view the video at different speeds. The coding of the parameter "Gaze Direction" was realized at frame by frame speed because of the need to accurately measure the gaze direction towards the one and / or the other face. The video was analyzed frame by frame to determine the beginning and end of each occurrence of behavior; the encoding was performed by two observers blind to the position of the two faces in the preference-task and it was defined by a specific operational definition, which provided very precise rules for the gaze direction encoding. This encoding method required more stringent criteria and was based on rigid rules because it required the assignment of a code for each frame of the video.

2. Live Encoding

The live encoding was the first to be carried out. The observer, during the preference-task, was placed centrally and behind the two faces; he / she observed the newborn and his /

her fixations towards the faces through the hole in the cloth for the camera. To avoid possible sources of disturbance in the visual field of the newborn, the experimenter did wear a white mask with two holes for eyes, she did wear a white coat, her hair were tied.

The device for live encoding was called Bip and Bop for the emission of two different sounds: the experimenter pressed the button that was in his right hand (Bip) whenever the newborn looked towards the face to the right side and pressed the button that is in his left hand (Bop) if conversely, and released the button when the newborn looked out of the two faces. Furthermore, the device had a timer that signals the achievement of the 20" of newborn fixation with an acoustic signal. These sounds (Bip and Bop) was acquired directly from the camera and recorded on the hard disk of the computer. Subsequently, the video impressed with the audio track of Bip and Bop was further encoded in the laboratory by assigning each sound (bip or bop) the relative code "Look to the right", "Look to the left" or "Look Out" with Observer software.

3. Real Time Video Encoding Towards the Faces

This type of encoding was performed in the laboratory, looking the video at normal speed (real time) and using the same device used for the Live Encoding (Bip and Bop). This encoding method was performed by two observers blind to the research hypothesis and to the position of the two faces in the preference-task; also, they did not know the operational definition used for the Frame By Frame Video Encoding, but they observed a simulation of the preference-task the laboratory through a reconstruction of the experimental setting; coders must determine, by pressing the corresponding buttons (Bip or Bop), if the newborn is looking towards the one and / or the other face. This type of encoding is also called "intuitive encoding" because it is founded on the idea that the two observers must assign codes the newborns gaze direction basing simply on personal impressions; it was assumed that any adult was reliably able to attribute the gaze direction of another person, even though in the case a newborn, it was more difficult, due to the excessive dilation of the pupils and the lack of a good control of eye muscles by the newborn.

4. Real Time Video Encoding Towards the Sides

The Video Encoding Towards The Sides was the method with the wider criteria because it was not based on rigid rules, as in the case of Frame By Frame Video; it was based simply on the attribution of the newborns gaze direction towards the side to the right or the left, unlike the previous encoding methods that established if the newborn was looking towards the face to the right or to the left side. This type of encoding was based on the idea (not necessarily correct) that it is sufficient that the newborn looks to the side where the face is present in order to establish that he is watching exactly that face; in fact, the two faces are very close to that one of the newborn (20-25 cm) and are so "large", compared to his face, so that take up the whole visual field of the newborn. In this encoding method, the possibility that the newborn could look towards the side but not necessarily into the face is not considered. Even this method is carried out in the laboratory, looking at the video at normal speed (real time) and using the same device (Bip and Bop) used for the Live Encoding. It is performed by two observers blind to the position of the two strangers in the preference-task; they know the Operational Definition for the gaze direction coding but they don't use it, because they had to identify the newborn's behavior only according to an "intuitive encoding", as in the case described above.

All the encoding methods are performed since the fixations towards one and / or the other face reach up to 20".

AGREEMENT BETWEEN ENCODERS

In the literature, the correlation between two independent coders is measured using the Pearson r to assess the reliability of coding.

The studies examined shown a agreement very high: for example, in the Sai's study the agreement calculated between the live encoding and the video encoding at normal speed is 0.86 for the first experiment and 0.87 for the other three experiments; in the Kelly's study the agreement between observers using the same type of encoding (frame by frame) is 0.97.

Both for "Sai" and "Kelly" studies, inter-observer reliability is calculated on the total duration of fixations to the one or the other face / side / image, for both trials taken into account together. In our study, we tried to evaluate, in the same way, the reliability of various encoding methods measuring the degree of agreement between two independent coders on the Gaze Direction parameter (expressed as total seconds of fixation towards one or the other face), using Pearson r (Cecchini et al., 2011a).

For each encoding method two different encoders were used except for live encoding which is performed by a single encoder during the experiment; the encoders are seven in total.

The encodings of two independent observers were compared to each other both between the same encoding method (e.g.: Encoder 1 – Frame by Frame Encoding vs. Encoder 2 - Frame by Frame Encoding), and between two different encoding methods (e.g., Encoder 1 - Frame by Frame Encoding vs. Encoder 3 - Live Encoding).

This procedure was repeated for all encoding methods.

The encodings have been performed on the same newborns and for the same performance.

Agreements were calculated on:

- the total duration of fixations towards the known face coded by another coder because the total duration of fixations are complementary to the New Face (total: 20" of fixation);
- for both trials (together) of the preference-task.

The results of the comparison, between two independent coders who have used the same encoding method, show a high agreement coefficient in all three cases.

The Frame By Frame Video encoding, Real Time Video Encoding Towards The Faces and that Towards The Sides would be so reliable.

Also from the comparison of coders who have used different coding method is came out a high correlation.

This finding showed: a low correlation between the encoding methods in terms of: Encoding Setting (live vs. video); Speed of visualization (normal vs. limited); Encoding object (gaze direction toward the Side vs. the Face); Encoding Criteria (Intuitive vs. Operational Definition).

Moreover the analysis of video-recording's time necessary for the observer to encode the 20" of fixation toward one and/or the other face in relation to each encoding method.

From a theoretical point of view, it is possible distinguish between:

- encoding method used;
- time required to the experimenter to reach the encoding of 20" of fixation toward one and/or the other face according to the specific encoding method used;
- time required to the newborn to finish the task, reaching thereby the 20" of fixation, according to the presented stimulus.

Each author uses different encoding method to analyze the same behavior, and this can lead to substantial differences both in terms of results in the preference-task and in terms of time necessary to reach the newborn's 20" of fixation (this time can vary greatly with respect to the encoding method used). Researchers interested to study the face preference tasks in newborns have to consider these problematic aspects.

Results showed the following:

Regarding to the Encoding Method used, the most important finding is that the Frame by Frame Encoding decreased the differences on fixation time between the two faces in both trials, while the differences, however, emerge for other three encoding methods.

Although Frame by Frame Encoding method analyze newborn behavior in detail, it seems to ignore the context within which the behavior is located, eliminating any difference in terms of time to reach 20" of fixation. It is unable to observe the movement, and therefore this method does not allow a natural evaluation of the behavior studied. It is based on strict criteria and rules, previously determined, that might make missed the many facets in the facial of the newborns, visible instead with live encoding or with an encoding at normal speed.

The Encoding Method Towards The Sides, despite it takes less time to reach the 20" of fixation compared to Encoding Method Towards The Faces, unlike the Frame by Frame Encoding Method, brings out a significant preference for the New Face; it shows results similar to those of Encoding Method Towards The Faces.

Regarding to the Encoding Type used by the experimenter, the time to reach the 20" of fixation is lower for Frame by Frame Video Encoding than Real Time Video Encoding Towards The Faces and that Towards The Sides. In fact, Frame by Frame Video Encoding is based on depth study of the Operational Definition which has very strict criteria for the gaze direction encoding; also the video is looked at a limited speed (each frame is encoded by the experimenter) and so every detail of newborn's behavior is considered ; for these reasons, the Frame By Frame Video Encoding reaches the 20" of fixation before than other methods. Evidently, however, the gaze direction encoding in less time than the other methods may not be sufficient to achieve the preference towards either of the two faces.

Regarding to the interaction between Stimulus Type and Encoding Type, reaching quickly the 20" of fixation, neglects a lot of aspects on the newborn's behavior that instead can be seen with the other three encoding methods.

Furthermore, the differences in 1nd Trial, regard to the time needed to complete the test, both in relation to the Stimulus Type, both in relation to the Encoding Type used, are attenuated in the 2nd Trial.

Overall, the results of our research suggest that it is important to consider that there are differences between the various encoding methods used and therefore it is essential to properly evaluate the encoding method to be used as this may not provide an adequate analysis of the newborns behavior; these encoding methods may lead to different results and therefore it is not appropriate to compare results of studies that are based on different encoding methods.

The studies on face recognition show a large heterogeneity of the encoding methods related to the gazing behaviour of the newborns; different and not standardized encoding methods may not highlight the complexity of the newborn's behaviour.

Encoding and analysis methods more accurate and valid, may be the ones recently discovered, who use a device that records eye movements through the pupil and corneal reflection: the Eye Tracking.

Eye Tracking allows an objective and qualitative analysis, overcomes the lack of objectivity of other approaches based on the opinions and impressions of the investigators; its use is particularly useful because it allows to record with absolute precision and in a scientifically valid, areas and components of the greatest attentional importance, well as to record the times for each one.

Recent advances in these techniques have provided important clues about human development; with this device can be measured, with high spatial and temporal precision, as infants perceive the world.

A recent special issue of the journal Infancy showed the broad applicability of Eye Tracking, in relation to children's ability to classify visual and auditory events (McMurray and Aslin, 2004), to perceive the unity of an object (Johnson, Slemmer, e Amso, 2004), to represent objects temporarily hidden (Gredeback and von Hofsten 2004), and finally to scan human faces (Hunnis and Geuze, 2004).

Although there are some descriptions of the Eye Tracking use with adults and children, in both normal and clinical populations (Karatekin, 2007; Luna, Velanova, Geier, 2008; Trillenberg, Lencer, Heide, 2004), until a few years ago were not made systematic attempts to describe the use with newborns; to overcome this deficiency, in 2009, Gredeback, Johnson e von Hofsten have published a review of the Eye Tracking for an introduction to the use in newborns, the authors provide a detailed description of how to calibrate and analyze the gaze of newborns in a variety of experimental paradigms, many data are lost because of head movements of subjects, however the use of Eye Tracking with newborns is still developing.

This methodology review, which we refer for further details, it is proposed to describe the above mentioned problems, choose solutions, discuss the pros and cons of using the Eye Tracking to investigate the development of perception and cognition in very young children.

At today eye trucker systems used in order to record looking at stimuli in newborn infants are unsatisfactory. Probably the new systems with multiple cameras could open the possibility to use an objective encoding system of looking at behavior in order to comprehend the underlying process of analyses that newborns operate when they look at a human face.

References

Bertin, E., and Striano, T. (2006). The still-face response in newborn, 1.5-, and 3-month-old infants. *Infant Behavior and Development, 29,* 294-297.

Bushnell, I.W.R. (2001). Mother's face recognition in newborn infants: learning and memory. *Infant and Child Development, 10,* 67-74.

Bushnell, I.W.R., Sai, F., and Mullin, J.T. (1989). Neonatal recognition of the mother's face. *British Journal of Developmental Psychology, 7,* 3-15.

Cecchini, M., Baroni, E., Di Vito, C., Piccolo, F. and Lai, C. (2011a). Newborn preference for a new face vs. a previously seen communicative or motionless face. *Infant Behavior and Development*, 34, 424-433.

Cecchini, M., Baroni, E., Di Vito, C. and Lai, C. (2011b). Smiling in newborns during communicative wake and active sleep. *Infant Behavior and Development*, 34, 417-423.

Cecchini, M., Lai, C., and Langher, V. (2010). Dysphonic newborn cries allow prediction of their perceived meaning. *Infant Behavior and Development*, 33, 314-320.

Cecchini, M., Lai, C., and Langher, V. (2007). Communication and crying in newborns. *Infant Behavior and Development, 30,* 655-665.

Farroni, T., Mansfield, E., Lai, C., and Johnson, M.H. (2003). Infants perceiving and acting on the eyes: tests of an evolutionary hypothesis. *Journal of Experimental Child Psychology, 85,* 199-212.

Field, T.M., Cohen, D., Garcia, R., and Greenberg, R. (1984). Mother-stranger face discrimination by the newborn. *Infant Behavior and Development, 7,* 19-25.

Gredebäck, G., Johnson, S., and von Hofsten, C. (2009): Eye Tracking in Infancy Research, *Developmental Neuropsychology*, 35 (1), 1-19.

Gredebäck, G., and von Hofsten, C. (2004). Infants' evolving representation of moving objects between 6 and 12 months of age. *Infancy*, 6(2), 165-184.

Grossmann, T., Johnson, M.H., Farroni, T., and Csibra, G. (2008). Social perception in the infant brain: gamma oscillatory activity in response to eye gaze. *Social Cognitive and Affective Neuroscience, 2,* 284-291.

Haith, M. M. (1969). Infrared television recording and measurement of ocular behavior in the human infant. *Americal Psychologist*, 24 (3), 279-283.

Horowitz, F.D., Paden, L., Bhana, K., and Self, P. (1972). An infant control procedure for studying infant visual fixations. *Developmental Psychology, 7,* 90.

Hunnis, S., and Geuze, R. H. (2004). Developmental changes in visual scanning of dynamic faces and abstract stimuli in infants: A longitudinal study. *Infancy, 6*(2), 231-255.

Johnson, S. P., Slemmer, J. A., and Amso, D. (2004). Where infants look determines how they see: Eye movements and object perception performance in 3-month-olds. *Infancy*, 6, 185-201.

Karatekin, C. (2007). Eye tracking studies of normative and atypical development. *Developmental Review*, 27, 283-348.

Kelly, D.J., Quinn, P.C., Slater, A.M., Lee, K., Ge, L., and Pascalis, O. (2007). The other-race effect develops during infancy: Evidence of perceptual narrowing. *Psychological Science, 18*, 1084-1089.

Luna, B., Velanova, K., and Geier, C. F. (2008). Development of eye-movement control. *Brain and Cognition*, 68, 293-308.

McMurray, B., and Aslin, R. N. (2004). Anticipatory eye movements reveal infants' auditory and visual categories. *Infancy*, *6*(2), 203-229.

Meltzoff, A.N. (1999). Origins of theory of mind, cognition and communication. *Journal of Communication Disorders, 32,* 251-269.

Meltzoff, A.N., and Moore, M.K. (1977). Imitation of facial and manual gestures by human neonates. *Science, 198,* 75-78.

Morton, J., and Johnson, M.H. (1991). CONSPEC and CONLERN: A Two-Process Theory of Infant Face Recognition. *Psychological Review, 98,* 164-181.

Nagy, E. (2008). Innate Intersubjectivity: Newborns' Sensitivity to Communication Disturbance. *Developmental Psychology, 44,* 1779-1784.

Pascalis, O., and de Schonen, S. (1994). Recognition memory in 3- to 4-day-old human neonates. *Neuro Report, 14,* 1721-1724.

Pascalis, O., de Schonen, S., and Morton, J. (1995). Mother's Face Recognition by Neonates: A replication and an extension. *Infant Behavior and Development, 18,* 79-85.

Sai, F.Z. (2005). The Role of the Mother's Voice in Developing Mother's Face Preference: Evidence for Intermodal Perception at Birth. *Infant and Child Development, 14,* 29-50.

Salapatek, P., and Kessen, W. (1966). Visual scanning of triangles by the human newborn. *Journal of Experimental Child Psychology, 3*, 155-167.

Scott, L.S., and Nelson, C.A. (2004). The developmental neurobiology of face perception. Chapter in J. M. Oldman, and M.B. Riba (Series Editors) *Review of Psychiatry Series*, Volume 23. American Psychiatric Publishing, Inc.

Trillenberg, P., Lencer, R., and Heide, W. (2004). Eye movements and psychiatric disease. *Current Opinion in Neurology*, 17, 43-47.

Walton, G.E., Bower, N.J.A., and Bower, T.G.R. (1992). Recognition of familiar faces by newborns. *Infant Behavior and Development, 15,* 265-269.

Yato, Y., Kawai, M., Negayama, K., Sogon, S., Tomiwa, K., Yamamoto, H. (2008). Infant responses to maternal still-face at 4 and 9 months. *Infant Behavior and Development, 31,* 570-577.

In: Face Recognition
Editors: Adamo Quaglia and Calogera M. Epifano
ISBN 978-1-61942-663-4

Chapter 8

MULTI-CLASS LEARNING FACIAL AGE ESTIMATION WITH FUSED GABOR AND LBP FEATURES

Jian-Gang Wang*
Institute for Infocomm Research
Connexis, Singapore

ABSTRACT

Face image-based age estimation is an approach to classify a face image into one of several pre-defined age-groups. It is a challenging problem because the aging variation is specific to a given individual and is determined by not only the person's gene, but also by many external factors, such as exposure, weather conditions (e.g. ambient humidity), health, gender, living style and living location. Age estimation is a multiclass problem. One of the Adaptive Boosting (AdaBoost) or Support Vector Machine (SVM) extensions for solving the multiclass problem is the combination of the method of Error-Correcting Output Codes (ECOC) with boosting using a decision tree based classifier or binary SVM classifier. In this paper, we apply this extension to solve the age estimation problem. Gabor and LBP aging features are combined at the feature level to represent the face images. Experimental results on FG-NET and Morph database are reported to demonstrate its effectiveness and robustness. The ECOC can achieve nearly similar results when it was combined with AdaBoost or SVM. However, ECOC plus AdaBoost is much faster than ECOC plus SVM. The results obtained using the fused LBP and Gabor features are better than the one when using either LBP or Gabor alone.

Keywords: Facial age estimation, Multi-class learning, ECOC, feature fusion, Gabor, LBP

1. INTRODUCTION

A human face conveys much information that we can easily decipher in our day-to-day communication. This includes the identity of a person, as well as gender, look direction,

* Email: jgwang@i2r.a-star.edu.sg

emotion and age. Among them, automatic facial age estimation *has attracted* much *attention* recently for its wide potential *applications. For instance,* vending machine can prevent the dispensing of alcoholic drinks or cigarette to an underage customer by finding out the estimated age range of the customer using a computer vision system. Facial aging effects display some unique characteristics: the age progression displayed on faces is uncontrollable, is individual and time dependent. Such special characteristics of aging variation cannot be captured accurately due to the prolific and diversified information conveyed by the human faces. There have been many face recognition algorithms as well as algorithms to detect the gender of a person [1] and the head pose [2]. However, age estimation algorithm is still lacking. Therefore, developing an automated way to estimate the age of a person from the face image is crucial. This is a key motivation for our work. Such capability, when developed successfully, will enable many applications including automated vending, gaming and customization of digital signage.

There are several studies on automated age estimation. A recent survey can be found in [3]. Kwon and Lobo [4] first worked on the age classification problem. They referred to cranio-facial research, theatrical makeup, plastic surgery, and perception to find out the features that change with age. A probe gray-scale facial image can be classified into three age-groups: babies, young adults, and senior adults. The proposed algorithm is computationally expensive and thus the system might not be suitable for real-time applications. Adopting the Active Appearance Model (AAM) [5] approach, Lanitis et al. [6] devised a combined shape and intensity model to represent face images. Age is modeled as a function of the vector of the face model parameters. The aging function is defined as linear, quadratic and cubic functions. Later, they [7] reported a quantitative evaluation of the three classifiers (quadratic function, shortest distance, artificial neural network) using a 400 images database. Gen et al. [8] proposed an AGing pattErn Subspace (AGES) for estimating age from appearance. In order to handle incomplete data such as missing ages in the training sequence, the AGES method models a sequence of individual aging face images by learning a subspace representation. The age of a test face is determined by the projection in the subspace that can best reconstruct the face image. Fu et al. [9] construct a low-dimensional manifold from a set of age-separated face images and use linear and quadratic regression functions on the low dimensional feature vectors from the respective manifolds to estimate the age of a face. Adopting similarly approach, Guo et al. [10] proposed an age manifold learning scheme for extracting face aging features and design a locally adjusted robust regressor for learning and prediction of human age. Ramanathan et al. [11] proposed a craniofacial growth model that takes into account both psychophysical evidences on how humans perceive age progression in faces and anthropometric evidences on facial growth. The proposed model is used to predict a person's appearance across age and to improve face recognition results across age. Yan et al. also dealt with the age uncertainty by formulating a semi-definite programming problem [12] or an EM-based algorithm [13]. Wang et al. [14] solved the incomplete data problem (missing labels) in age estimation via active learning with a furthest nearest-neighbour (FNN) criterion. By boosting Local Binary Pattern (LBP) [15] features, Yang et al. [16] identified a sequence of local features which when combined into a strong classifier performs the task of age classification successfully.

Most of the conventional methods for age estimation are intended for accurate estimation of the actual age. However, it is difficult to accurately estimate an actual age from a face image because age progression is specific-dependent and the aging subspace is obtained based on a largely incomplete database. Fortunately, for some applications, it is not necessary to obtain the precise estimates of the actual age. Therefore, in this paper, we pay attention to the mechanism of human age perception, i.e. we limit the estimation to a few age ranges. Subspace approaches mentioned-above [8] concentrated on designing a set of optimal features and then applying standard machine-learning algorithms. In fact, some recent advances in machine learning can be applied to improve the estimation performance. Multiclass learning with error-correcting output codes (ECOC) [17, 18, 19] is an example. ECOC is initially developed for channel coding. The basic idea is to allocate additional bits over and above the bits required to code the source message in order to provide error correcting capability. ECOC is a robust method to convert a multi-class learning problem to a sequence of two-class problems. Kittler et al. [20] proposed a two-stage solution to apply the ECOC to face verification which is a two-class problem. Boosting is a general method of deriving a strong classifier from a set of weak classifiers. The combination of AdaBoost and ECOC has been verified to be a fast and robust face recognition method with high accuracy [21]. This motivated us to investigate the boosting ECOC for age categorization. Multi-class boosting algorithms based on error correcting codes [19, 18, 17] tackle the error correlation among the base classifiers by deliberately re-weighting the training examples. They usually start off with an empty coding matrix and all classes indistinguishable from others, then iteratively append columns to the matrix and train the base classifiers so that the confusion between classes can be gradually reduced. The examples are re-weighted in a fashion similar to the weighting scheme in the binary AdaBoost [22], aiming at uncorrelated errors. Support Vector Machine (SVM) is an alternative binary classifier which can be combined with ECOC to do age categorization.

1.1. Proposed Method

This paper presents an innovative method for visual age classification from facial images by combining ECOC with boosting or SVM. In order to improve the accuracy, Gabor and Local Binary Pattern (LBP) features of a face image are fused at the feature level to represent the face image. The proposed age classification is then used to classify input images into one of four age-groups: child (0-11), teen age (12-21), adult (22-60) and senior adult (61 and above).

Although pattern subspace methods have been proposed for age estimation, our proposed method is significantly faster and requires less programming effort to create the base learning algorithm. Our method has advantages of both boosting/SVM and ECOC. Similar to ECOC, it only requires that the base learning algorithm work on binary-labeled data. Similar to boosting, our method comes with strong theoretical guarantees on the training and generalization error of the final combined hypothesis assuming only that each of the base classifiers perform slightly better than random guess.

2. ECOC and Binary Classifier

The majority of work in the supervised learning literature up to now has been devoted to the binary classification problem, such as face detection [23]. A straightforward solution to a multi-class classification problem, e.g. age classification, with more than two different class labels, is to reformulate it as a collection of binary problems. Error-Correcting Output Coding (ECOC) [17] is one of the methods for decomposing a multi-class problem into many two-class problems, and then combining the results of the subtask into a hypothesized solution to the original problem. The original motivation for encoding multiple classifiers using an error-correcting code is based on the idea of modelling the prediction task as a communication problem, in which class information is transmitted over a channel. Errors introduced into the process arise from various aspects of the learning algorithm, including features selected and finite training sample. The error-correcting theory [18] has shown that a matrix designed to have d bits error-correcting capability implies that there is a minimum Hamming Distance $2d+1$ between any pair of code words. Assuming each bit is transmitted independently, it is then possible to correct a received pattern having fewer than d bits in error, by assigning the pattern to the codeword closest in Hamming distance. Design of optimal codes has been discussed by Windeatt and Ghaderi in [24]. We will briefly explain the mathematical details of the original ECOC algorithm in the following section.

2.1. ECOC Algorithm

In the ECOC algorithm, a binary codeword matrix $\mathbf{M}_{k\times T}$ has one row (codeword) for each of k classes, where T is the length of the codeword. Each column defines a binary partition of k classes over data from which a binary classifier is trained. After T training steps, it produces T classifiers h_1, h_2, …, h_T. A given sample is classified by choosing the class whose associated codeword is the closest in $L1$-norm or Minkowski distance to the sequence of the predictions generated by h_1, h_2, …, h_T. T classifiers are applied to a test pattern arrive at

$$y = [y_1, y_2, \dots, y_T]' \tag{1}$$

In which y_j is the real-valued output of jth base classifier.

The distance ($L1$-norm) between output vector and codeword for each class is given by

$$L_i^1 = \sum_{j=1}^{T} |M_{ij} - y_j| \tag{2}$$

and the decoding rule is to assign a test pattern to the class corresponding codeword

$$arg\ min_i L_i^1$$

2.2. AdaBoost

AdaBoost was first introduced by Freund and Schapire [22]. It is a popular algorithm that has been shown to work very well for two-class problems. In each round t, a training set with a new distribution D, that depends on the performance of the base classifiers derived at the (t - 1)th round, is provided. The error of each classifier is measured with respect to D and is used to calculate the weight for each training example in D. In round t, if the example is correctly classified by the base classifier, its weight is decreased. These weights are used either in re-sampling or in re-weighting. Consequently, those repeatedly misclassified patterns have their weights increased, and the sequentially generated classifiers are forced to concentrate on these difficult patterns.

2.3. Multi-Class AdaBoost via ECOC

AdaBoost has been extended to solve the multi-class problem, e.g. AdaBoost.M1, AdaBoost.M2 and AdaBoost.MH [22] and AdaBoost.OC [19]. In this paper, we present an extension in which AdaBoost is merged with ECOC to solve multi-class problems, called AdaBoost.ECC in [18]. The method is given in Algorithm 1. Some variants of the AdaBoost.ECC can be found in [25, 26].

Algorithm 1: AdaBoost.ECC

Input: A training set $\{(x_i, y_i)\}_{i=1}^{N} : x_i \in X, y_i \in Y$, $[\![Y]\!] = k$; T: length of codeword

Output: the final hypothesis

Initialize: $\widetilde{D}_1(i,l) = 1/N(k-1)\ if\ l \neq y_i, \widetilde{D}_1(i,l) = 0\ if\ l = y_i$

For $t = 1,2,\ldots,T$

Choose the t-th column M, $\mathbf{M}(\cdot,t) \in \{-1,+1\}^k$

$$U_t = \sum_{i=1}^{N}\sum_{l \in Y} \widetilde{D}_t(i,l) I(\mathbf{M}(l,t) \neq \mathbf{M}(y_i,t))$$

$$D_t(i) = U_t^{-1} \sum_{l \in Y} \widetilde{D}_t(i,l) I(\mathbf{M}(l,t) \neq \mathbf{M}(y_i,t))$$

Train a decision stump h_t with distribution D_t

$$\widetilde{D}_{t+1}(i,l) = \widetilde{Z}_t^{-1} \widetilde{D}_t(i,l) \exp^{-h_t(x_i)(\mathbf{M}(y_i,t)-\mathbf{M}(l,t))/2}$$

where $\widetilde{Z}_t$ is a normalization factor.

End

Output: the final hypothesis

$$H(x) = \arg\max_{l \in Y} \sum_{t=1}^{T} h_t(x)\mathbf{M}(l,t)$$

Let M be the coding matrix. Given an unseen data x, an ECOC classifier will generate an ensemble output $H(x) = (h_1(x), \ldots, h_T(x))$ from T binary classifiers. Hamming distance instead of L1-norm is used in this paper. The Hamming distance between $H(x)$ and $\mathrm{M}(l, \cdot)$, the l-th row of M, is defined as

$$\Delta(\mathbf{M}(l), H(x)) = \sum_{i=1}^{T}(1 - \mathbf{M}(l,i)h_i(x))/2 \quad (3)$$

Then the predicted class $\hat{y}$ of x is obtained by

$$\hat{y} = \arg\min_{l} \Delta(\mathbf{M}(l), H(x)) \quad (4)$$

i.e. if x is classified as y, $\Delta(M(y),H(x))$ must be smaller than $\Delta(M(l),H(x))$ for any $l \neq y$.

A *margin* is defined to measure an example (x, y) for class l,

$$\rho_l(x, y) = \Delta(\mathbf{M}(l), H(x)) - \Delta(\mathbf{M}(y), H(x)) \quad (5)$$

The goal of using a machine learning method here is to maximize the class margin of the training examples. Assuming we have N training samples, AdaBoost.ECC tries to optimize the exponential objective function

$$O_M(H) = \sum_{i=1}^{N} \sum_{l \neq y_i} e^{-\rho_l(x_i, y_i)} \quad (6)$$

Given a coding matrix M, AdaBoost.ECC minimizes the objective function using the negative gradient method. The negative gradient method can be reduced to

$$U_t \sum_{i=1}^{N} D_t(i) M(y_i, t) h_t(x_i) = U_t(1 - 2\varepsilon_t) \quad (7)$$

where U_t and $D_t(i)$ are defined in Algorithm 1 and is the error rate of classifier h_t. AdaBoost.ECC tries to maximize the negative gradient. Then objective function $O_M(H)$ can be minimized along the negative gradient.

2.4. Multi-Class SVM via ECOC

SVM is originally designed for binary classification, and its target is to find an optimal separating hyperplane w, which can minimize the number of errors made on the training set while simultaneously maximizing the margin between the individual classes. When ECOC is combined with support vector machine, called SVM.ECC in this paper, each column of ECOC is corresponding to a SVM, that is, a SVM is constructed for each column via the training data of classes labeled "0" against the training data of classes labeled "1" during training. The training algorithm of the proposed method is given in Algorithm 2.

Algorithm 2: SVM.ECC

Input: A training set $X=[X_1, X_2,\ldots X_n]^T$, $Y=[Y_1,Y_2,\ldots Y_n]^T$, where X_i is the ith train sample, one example per row in X, and Y_i is the class label for X_i, Y_i is a number in the range $1\ldots k$. T: length of codeword

Output: A learner set L; $L(i)$ is the classifier of the i-th bit of the codeword

Initialize: Create a Support Vector Machine classifier with rbf kernel
For t =1:T
the tth bit learner is trained given training data X with class labels Y.
End
Output: A learner set L (T SVM classifiers); L(i) is the classifier of the i-th bit of the codeword

To classify a new example X, the T classifier are evaluated on X to obtain a binary sequence $X_b \in \{x_{b1}, x_{b2}, ..., x_{bT}\}$. The distance of X_b to codeword for each class are computed the class of X corresponding to the class of the nearest codeword.

3. Face Feature Extraction

Gabor and Local Binary Pattern (LBP) are two local feature representations which separately have been proved to have outstanding performance in facial image analysis. They are complementary in the sense that LBP captures small appearance details while Gabor features encode facial shape over a wider range of scales. Aiming to achieve a robust age estimation system, a facial age estimation algorithm, based on fusion of Gabor and LBP Features at the feature-level with adaboost, is presented in this paper.

3.1. Gabor Feature

The Gabor feature is an effective representation for face image analysis. Several works [27] have also shown that the Gabor wavelet representation of face images is robust against variations due to illumination and facial expression changes. In this paper, Gabor wavelet features at five scales and eight orientations are extracted to represent the faces. The complete set of Gabor wavelet representations of the image $I(z)$ is

$$G(I) = \{ O_{u,v}(z) : u \in \{0...7\}, v \in \{0...4\}, z=(x, y)\} \quad (8)$$

where

$$O_{u,v}(z) = I(z) * \varphi_{u,v}(z) \quad (9)$$

is the Gabor feature, is Gabor kernel, u and v define the orientation and scale of the Gabor kernel and "*" represent the convolution operation. The resulting features for each orientation, scale and position are concatenated pixel by pixel to form the aging feature vector of the image.

3.2. Local Binary Pattern

The original Local Binary Pattern (LBP) operator [15] labels the pixels of an image by thresholding the 3×3 neighborhood of each pixel i_n, $n = 0, 1, .., 7$ with the center value i_c and considering the result as a binary number

$$LBP = \sum_{n=0}^{7} S(i_n - i_c)2^n \tag{10}$$

which characterizes the spatial structure of the local image texture. $S(x)$ is 1 if $x \geq 0$ and 0 otherwise.

A local binary pattern is called uniform if it contains at most two bitwise transitions from 0 to 1 or vice versa when the binary string is considered circular. Recently, Ahonen et al. [28] proposed a Local Binary Pattern Histogram Fourier Features (LBP-HF) which is a rotation-invariant image descriptor based on uniform Local Binary Patterns [15]. Unlike the earlier local rotation-invariant features, the LBP-HF descriptor is formed by first computing a non-invariant LBP histogram over the whole region and then constructing rotationally invariant features from the histogram. This means that rotation invariance is attained globally, and the features are thus invariant to rotations of the whole input signal but they still retain information about relative distribution of different orientations of uniform local binary patterns. In this paper, we adopt the LBP-HF to extract facial features. Let us denote a specific uniform LBP pattern by $U_P(n, r)$. The pair (n, r) specifies a uniform pattern so that n is the number of 1-bits in the pattern and r is the rotation of the pattern.

The rotation invariant LBP is defined as

$$LBP^{u2} - HF(n_1, n_2, u) = H(n_1, u)\overline{H}(n_2, u) \tag{11}$$

where $H(n, \cdot)$ be the DFT of nth row of the histogram $h_I(U_P(n, r))$, i.e.

$$H(n,u) = \sum_{r=0}^{P-1} h_I(U_P(n,r))e^{-2\pi ur/P} \tag{12}$$

and $\overline{H}(n_2, u)$ denotes the complex conjugate of $H(n_2, u)$.

A face image is divided into small regions from which LBP histograms are extracted and concatenated into a single, spatially enhanced feature histogram. The histogram provides an effective description of the face on two different levels of localisation: the labels for the histogram contain information about the patterns at the pixel level while the labels summed over a small region provide information at the regional level.

3.3. Feature Fusion

The research in multimodal biometrics fusion has revealed that a robust recognition system requires fusion of different kind of appearance information. The fusion can be done at the feature level, matching score level or decision level with different fusion models. In general, the performance by feature-level fusion can give better results than the other two schemes. Most of the existing studies on multi-modal fusion focused on combining the outputs of multiple classifiers at the decision level. In this paper, the Gabor and LBP features are fused at the feature level. This can be done by concatenating the normalized Gabor and LBP features to represent the face image. The Gabor and LBP features are normalized by the standard deviations of the two features, respectively. LBP encodes the fine details of facial appearance and texture while the Gabor features encode facial shape and appearance information over a range of coarser scales. Both representations are rich in information and computationally efficient. Their complementary nature makes them good candidates for fusion [29].

We face the memory problem when we apply proposed ECOC_SVM to the fused LBP and Gabor features (high-demensional). This is a common problem when applying SVM to the feature-level fused features [29]. Hence, a dimension reduction process is necessary. In this paper, Pincipal Component Analysis (PCA) is adopted to reduce the dimension of the LBP and Gabor features respectively before concatenating them into a single vector. However, no such problem is encountered in the ECOC_AdaBoost because the feature is selected from fused Gabor and LBP feature by AdaBoost. In that case, the features are concatenated into a vector directly and then ECOC_AdaBoost is applied to the fused feature directly.

4. Experimental Results

For our study, we define four age groups: children, teen age, adult and senior adult. The age ranges of the four groups are 0-11, 12-21, 22-60 and 61 and above respectively. The age groups defined in this paper is a rough partition. Our focus is only to investigate the performance of our proposed method and the partitioning adopted is only for proof of principle. Nevertheless, this partitioning is not without basis. In general, a person's appearance will undergo noticeable changes due to physiological and social factors. The first is at puberty, when for girls it is around the age of twelve. The average graduation age of the undergraduate study and finding the first job is about 21. The retirement age of the male people in the world is about 60.

We used a database which includes the face images from both the FG-NET and Morph aging databases since we need a database which has enough face images for each age range mentioned-above. The FG-NET [30] and Morph [31] databases have been made available for research in areas related to age-progression. The FG-NET database contains 1,002 face images from 82 subjects, with approximately 10 images per subject. In the MORPH database, there are 1,724 face images from 515 subjects. Each subject has around 3 aging images. We manually group the face images into four classes defined above according to their ground truth. In doing so, we have a total of 2726 images. We adopt the Viola-Jone's face detector

[23] to detect the face and all faces are then geometrically normalized to 88×88 image. Some samples in the four age ranges are shown in Figure 3 to Figure 6, respectively.

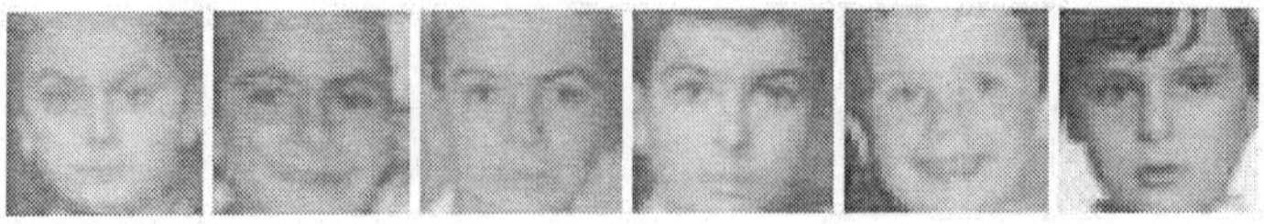

Figure 3. Samples of child class.

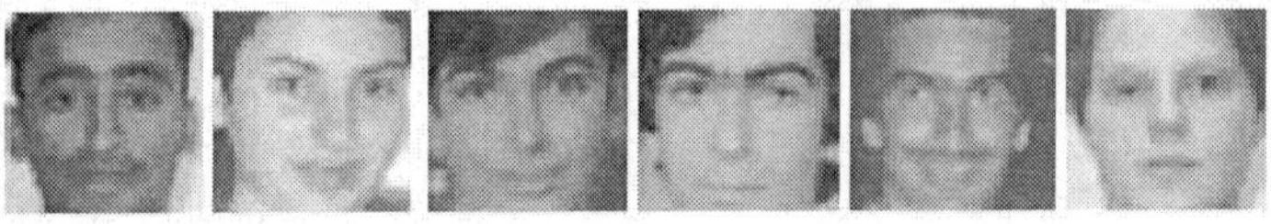

Figure 4. Sample of teen age class.

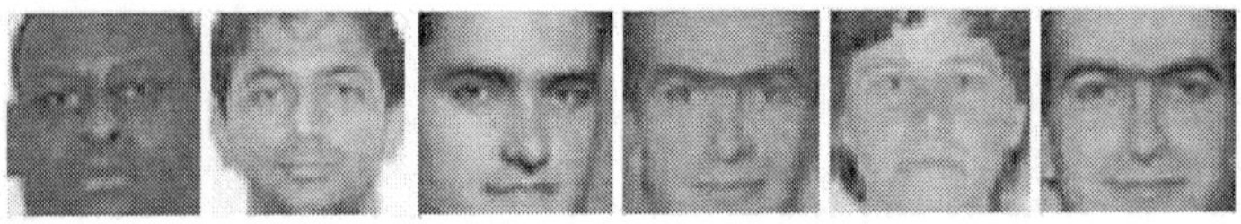

Figure 5. Sample of adult class.

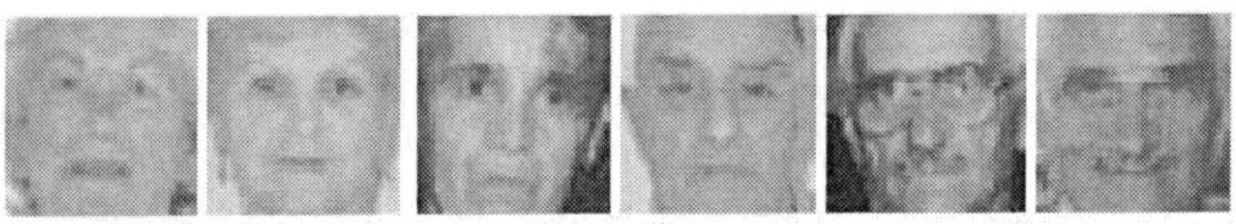

Figure 6. Sample of senior adult class.

Hence, the dimension of the Gabor representation is 309,760 (88×88×40). In order to reduce the dimension of the feature vector, 16 times down sampling of the Gabor features is adopted, so the reduced dimension is 19360. Like the Gabor feature, the LBP descriptor is usually high dimensional. In this paper, the 88×88 image is divided into 8×8 blocks and the histograms of these 121 histograms are concatenated into a vector to represent the image. Hence the dimension is 7139 (121 patches with 59 entries/patch).

In our experiments, the base classifiers in GML AdaBoost Matlab Toolbox and OSU SVM Toolbox for MATLAB are used. The evaluation framework for the combined aging database is the Leave-One-Person-Out (LOPO) mode, i.e., in each fold, the images of one person are used as the test set and those of the others are used as the training set. After 597 folds, each subject has been used as test set once, and the final results are calculated based on all the estimations. In this way, the algorithms are tested in the case similar to real applications, *i.e.*, the subject for whom the algorithms attempt to estimate his/her age is not seen in the training set. The average classification rates of SVM with ECOC and AdaBoost with ECOC and using various features are listed in Table 1.

As we have four age groups, the ECOC coding matrix used in our experiment is as follows [17]:

$$\begin{bmatrix} 1 & 1 & 1 & 1 & 1 & 1 & 1 \\ -1 & -1 & -1 & -1 & 1 & 1 & 1 \\ -1 & -1 & 1 & 1 & -1 & -1 & 1 \\ -1 & 1 & -1 & 1 & -1 & 1 & -1 \end{bmatrix}$$

Table 1. The age classification accuracy (%) on FG-NET + MORPH database

Method	E +S	E+S	E+S	E+A	E+A	E+A
Feature	L	G	L+G	L	G	L+G
Child	88.3	93.1	96.4	90.6	91.4	95.0
Teen age	87.4	91.6	92.1	87.2	89.3	91.9
Adult	83.8	87.1	89.5	83.1	86.5	87.5
Senior adult	79.6	81.5	83.8	77.5	79.1	81.8

Notations: L: LBP; G: Gabor; L+G: LBP + Gabor; E+S: ECOC + SVM; E+A: ECOC + AdaBoost.

We can see from Table 1 that the combination of ECOC with SVM can achieve slightly better results than the combination of ECOC with AdaBoost. However, the computational load of the ECOC+SVM is much larger than the ECOC+AdaBoost. In our implementation, Acer VerVeriton 7900 C2D 2.66Ghz 4GB/320GB is used and average processing time for testing one image using ECOC+AdaBoost is about 0.1s. However, it takes about 4s for testing one image using ECOC+SVM. We can see also that the results based on the fused features of Gabor and LBP are better than the one based on Gabor alone or LBP alone.

Based on the proposed ECOC+AdaBoost approach, an age estimation prototype has been developed. The age ranges of the subjects can be simultaneously estimated automatically. We used the Logitech Webcam Pro 9000 to capture face images while face detection and tracking are done using the face detector of the OpenCV library [32] and the kernel-based mean shift algorithm [33] respectively. Future research includes the robustness to expression, pose and lighting variation.

CONCLUSION

In this paper, we have proposed a fast facial age estimation approach. The Gabor and LBP features of a face image are fused at the feature level to represent the face because these two kinds of features could compensate each other efficiently in the face age classification. Multi-class AdaBoost or Multi-class SVM is applied to the fused Gabor and LBP features to categorize a face image into one of four possible age groups (child, teenage, adult and senior adult). The contributions of this paper are: (1) Solved age categorization using the combination of ECOC with AdaBoost or SVM and (2) Proposed an efficient method to fuse the LBP and Gabor features. Experimental results on the FG-NET and Morph databases have demonstrated the effectiveness and robustness of the proposed age categorization approach.

The results show that the fused features are better than the one based on Gabor alone or LBP alone.

REFERENCES

[1] J.-G. Wang, J. Li, W.-Y. Yau and E. Sung. Boosting dense SIFT descriptors and shape contexts of face images for gender recognition. 2010. *IEEE Conference on Computer Vision and Pattern Recognition Workshops* (CVPRW). 96-102.

[2] J.-G. Wang and E. Sung. EM enhancement of 3D head pose estimated by point at infinity, *Image and Vision Computing*, 25(12): 1864-1874, 2007.

[3] N. Ramanathan, R. Chellappa and S. Biswas. Age progression in Human Faces : A Survey. Visual Languages and Computing (*Special Issue on Advances in Multimodal Biometric Systems*), 2009.

[4] Y. H. Kwon, N. D V. Lobo. Age Classification from Facial Images. *Computer Vision and Image Understanding* 74(1): 1-21, 1999.

[5] T.F. Cootes, G.J. Edwards, and C.J. Taylor. Active appearance model. 5th European Conference on Computer Vision, Freiburg, Germany, 1998.

[6] A Lanitis, C. J. Taylor and T. F. Coots. Toward automatic simulation of age effects on face images, *PAMI*, 24(4), 442-455, 2002.

[7] A. Lanitis, C. Draganova and C. Christodoulou. Comparing Different Classifiers for Automatic Age Estimation. *IEEE Transactions on SMC-Part B, Cybernetics*, 34(1), 621-628, 2004.

[8] X. Geng, Z.-H. Zhou, Y. Zhang, G. Li, and H. Dai. Learning from facial aging patterns for automatic age estimation. 2006. *ACM Conf. Multimedia*, 307–316.

[9] Y. Fu and T. S. Huang. Human age estimation with regression on discriminative aging manifold, *IEEE Trans. Multimedia*, 10(4): 578-584, 2008.

[10] G. Guo, Y. Fu, C. R. Dyer, T. S. Huang. Image-Based Human Age Estimation by Manifold Learning and Locally Adjusted Robust Regression, *IEEE Transactions on Image Processing*, Volume 17(7): 1178 – 1188, 2008.

[11] N. Ramanathan and R. Chellappa. Modeling age progression in young faces. 2006. *IEEE Conference on Computer Vision and Pattern Recognition* (CVPR), 387–394.

[12] S. Yan., H. Wang, X. Tang and T. S. Huang. *Learning auto-structured regressor from uncertain nonnegative labels*. 2007. *IEEE International Conference on Computer Vision* (ICCV).

[13] S. Yan, H. Wang, T. S. Huang and X. Tang. Ranking with uncertain labels. 2007. *IEEE Conf. Multimedia and Expo*, 96–99.

[14] J.-G. Wang, E. Sung, W.-Y. Yau. Active learning for solving the incomplete data problem in facial age classification by the furthest nearest-neighbor criterion, *IEEE Transactions on Image Processing*. 20(7): 2049-2062, 2011.

[15] T. Ojala, M. Pietikainen and T. Maenpaa. Multiresolution gray-scale and rotation invariant texture classification with Local Binary Patterns. *PAMI* 24(7): 971-987, 2002.

[16] Z. Yang and H. Ai. Demographic classification with local binary patterns. 2007. *International Conference on Biometrics* (ICB), 464–473.

[17] T. G. Dietterich and G. Bakiri. Solving multiclass learning problems via error-correcting output codes. *J. Artif. Intell. Res*, 2 : 263–286, 1995.

[18] V. Guruswami and A. Sahai. Multiclass learning, boosting, and error-correcting codes, 1999. *12th Annual Conference on Computational Learning Theory*. ACM Press. 145–155.

[19] R. E. Schapire. Using output codes to boost multiclass learning problems. 1997. *14th International Conference on Machine Learning. USA*, 313–321.

[20] J. Kittler, R. Ghaderi, T. Windeatt and J Matas. Face verification via ECOC, 2001. *British Machine Vision Conference* (BMVC).

[21] T. Windeatt and G. Ardeshir. Boosting ensemble ECOC for face recognition. 2003. *IEE Conf Visual Information Engineering*, Univ. of Surrey, 165-168.

[22] Y. Freund and R. Schapire. A decision-theoretic generation of on-line learning and an application to boosting. *Journal of Computer and System Science,* 55(1): 119–139, 1997.

[23] P. Viola and M. J. Jones. Robust Real-Time Face Detection. *International Journal of Computer Vision* 57(2), 137–154, 2004.

[24] T. Windeatt and T. Ghaderi. Coding and decoding strategies for multi-class learning problems. *Inf. Fusion*. 4(1): 11-21, 2003.

[25] Y.-S. Lin and C.-N. Hsu. Boosting multiclass learning with repeating codes. Technical report TR-IIS-07-014, 2007, Institute of Information Science, Acedemia Sinica.

[26] L. Li. Multiclass boosting with repartitioning. 2006. *23rd International Conference on Machine Learning.*

[27] C. J. Liu. Capitalize on Dimensionality Increasing Techniques for Improving Face Recognition Grand Challenge Performance. *PAMI* 28(5), 725-737, 2006.

[28] T. Ahonen, J. Matas, C. He and M. Pietikainen. Rotation invariant image description with local binary pattern histogram Fourier features. 2009. *16th Scandinavian Conference on Image Analysis* (SCIA), Oslo, Norway.

[29] X. Tan and B. Triggs. Fusing Gabor and LBP Feature Sets for Kernel-based Face Recognition. 2007. *Analysis and Modelling of Faces and Gestures*, 2007, 235-249.

[30] The FG-NET Aging Database, November 2007, http://webmail.cycollege.ac.cy/~alanitis/fgnetaging/.

[31] K. Ricanek, Jr. and T. Tesafaye. MORPH: a longitudinal image database of normal adult age-progression. 2006. *7th International Conference on Automatic Face and Gesture Recognition* (FGR '06), 341–345, Southampton, UK.

[32] Face Detection using OpenCV. http://opencv.willowgarage.com/ wiki/FaceDetection.

[33] D. Comaniciu, V. Ramesh, P. Meer. Kernel-based object tracking, *PAMI,* 25(5): 564-577, 2003.

In: Face Recognition ISBN: 978-1-61942-663-4
Editors: Adamo Quaglia and Calogera M. Epifano © 2012 Nova Science Publishers, Inc.

Chapter 9

Techniques of Frequency Domain Correlation for Face Recognition and its Photonic Implementation

***Pradipta K. Banerjee*[1*] *and Asit K. Datta*[2†]**
[1] Department of Electrical Engineering
Future Institute of Engineering and Management,
Sonarpur, India
[2] Department of Applied Optics and Photonics
University of Calcutta,
Acharya Prafulla Chandra Road, India

Abstract

Majority of systems whose primary interest is face recognition emphasizes on the analysis of the spatial representation of the images i.e. the intensity value of images, however the use of frequency domain approach sometimes achieves better performance with respect to speed and robustness. Frequency domain techniques are executed by cross-correlating the Fourier transform of test face image with a synthesized template or filter,generated from Fourier transform of training images and processing the resulting correlation output via inverse fast Fourier transforms. The correlation output is searched for peaks and the relative heights of these peaks are analysed to determine whether the test face is recognized or not. Correlation filters offer several advantages. Correlation filters are shift-invariant and are based on integration operation and thus offer graceful degradation in any impairment to the test image. Correlation filters can be designed to exhibit noise tolerance and high discrimination ability.

The main purpose of the chapter is to review the status of the several general purpose correlation filters and compare their performance for face recognition task under various facial expressions and varying lighting conditions. Correlation filters like maximum average correlation height (MACH), unconstrained minimum average correlation energy (UMACE), Optimal Trade-off MACH (OTMACH), quad phase UMACE (QPUMACE), phase only UMACE (POUMACE) and distance classifier

*E-mail address: pradiptak.banerjee@gmail.com
†E-mail address: asitdatta@gmail.com

correlation filter (DCCF) are synthesized and tested over several databases including AMP, Cropped YaleB, PIE and AR.

The photonics instrumentation technique offers advantages of parallel non-interactive high speed processing in optical domain and therefore is a better candidate for hardware implementation of frequency domain algorithms. However, the need of optics to electronics conversion and vice-versa limits the achievable speed of operations. Hardware implementation of the frequency domain systems for face recognition using photonic architectures along with the device constraints which limit the speed are also discussed in this chapter.

Keywords: Face recognition, Correlation filter, Photonics implementation

1. Brief survey of face recognition in frequency domain correlation filters

In the last twenty years, the techniques of face recognition have become an active area of research for its potential biometric interest. Majority of systems whose primary interest is face recognition and understanding of face images emphasize on the analysis of the spatial representation of the images i.e. the intensity values of the images. While there has been varying and significant levels of performance achieved through the use of spatial 2-D image data, the use of a frequency domain representation sometimes achieves better performance for the face recognition tasks. The use of the Fourier and other frequency domain transforms allow to quickly and easily obtain raw frequency data which are significantly more discriminative (after appropriate data manipulation) than the raw spatial data, from which it is derived. One can further increase the discrimination ability through additional and specific feature extraction algorithms intended for use in the frequency domain. In majority cases, correlation filters are used to achieve desired performances.

There are many contributions in the field of frequency domain face recognition techniques using correlation filters. Different constrains on the face images such as illumination variations, occlusion, pose variations yielded many types of correlation filters [26, 28, 25, 29, 21, 14]. In [22] Kumar et.al applied the constrained correlation filter e.g. minimum average correlation energy (MACE) filter over AMP facial expression database [1] of population $13 \times 75 = 975$ and have shown promising results with overall 0.1% equal error rate (EER). Savvides et al in [27] has presented a comparative performance of MACE and individual eigenface subspace method (IESM) for face recognition in terms of margin of separations where peak-to-side lobe ratio (PSR) is used for MACE and residual reconstruction error is used for IESM as performance metric. In [24] an efficient method of designing the MACE filter is proposed and the same verification accuracy has been achieved with a reduced complexity filters having very little memory requirements in frequency domain by introducing the idea of four level correlation. The memory storage requirement of MACE filters is reduced by retaining only the phase of the filter and quantizing it 4 levels such as $\pi/4, 3\pi/4, 5\pi/4, 7\pi/4$.

High identification accuracy has been achieved in [30] by the unconstrained MACE (UMACE) filter for PIE-NL dataset of population $65 \times 21 = 1365$. In this study, a fixed global threshold has been selected for maintaining the separation between authentic and impostors. An idea of incrementally updating the unconstrained filters for limited memory devices is also successfully proposed in [30]. An on line training algorithm is implemented on a face verification system for synthesizing correlation filters to handle pose/scale variations as well a way to perform efficient face localization in [24]. A hybrid correlation filter is proposed and is termed as coreface technique by exploiting the principal component analysis (PCA) in frequency domain, where only the phase information of face images are considered for illumination invariant face recognition [35]. Face class code based approach using correlation filter and support vector machine (SVM) is proposed in [15]. A successful implementation of SVM [37] is also used in optimizing the margin between the true peak and false peak in the correlation plane for improving accuracy in face recognition. A different approach of using correlation filter is suggested in [39], where a quaternion array is developed from wavelet decomposition and used in synthesizing the correlation filter. In spite of template matching method by correlation filter in [38, 40] those are used for feature extraction purpose where the cosine distance is measured from a similarity score. This method is successfully experimented over FRGC2.0 dataset. In [3], it has been shown that kernel correlation feature analysis (KCFA) has good representation and discrimination ability for unseen datasets and produces better verification and identification rates on PIE [36],FERET [31] and AR dataset [23].

In general, the two dimensional(2D) correlation feature analysis (2D-CFA) cannot be used for vectors and $N^{th}(N \geq 3)$ order tensors. This limitation is overcome by Yan et.al. in [42], where a generalized method of analysis is proposed by using the image data as tensors. The improved recognition rate is obtained by tensor based method in comparison to traditional 2D-CFA for PIE, FERET, FRGC and AR face databases. Yan et. al. also proposed an 1D-CFA [41] in low dimensional subspace (PCA) instead of 2D-CFA, peak height is minimized subject to linear constraint by developing a new correlation filter.

1.1. Correlation filtering technique in frequency domain

Correlation is a robust and general technique for pattern recognition and is used in many applications, particularly in biometric and optical character recognition. The frequency domain correlation for face recognition can be obtained by correlating the Fourier transform version of reference and test face images. Mathematically, the operation can be represented as,

$$c(x, y) = FFT^{-1}\{\mathbf{R}(u, v) \otimes \mathbf{T}(u, v)\} \tag{1}$$

where $c(x, y)$ is the correlation plane in spatial domain. **R** and **T** are the Fourier transformed version of spatial 2D array $r(x, y)$ (reference face image) and $t(x, y)$ (test face image) and the symbol $\otimes$ represents the correlation process.

Correlation can be thought of as the output from a *matched filter* (MF) or a linear, shift-invariant (LSI) filter whose impulse response is the reflected version of the reference signal or image. Such filters are collectively referred to as correlation filters since they are designed for implementation in frequency plane correlators. An ideal correlation filter for face recognition would yield sharp correlation peak for a perfect match of test face image with a face image present in the database. High discrimination against unwanted objects, excellent suppression of noise in the input scene and high tolerance to distortions in the test face image give high degree of robustness. Fig(1) shows schematically how the cross-correlation is obtained using fast Fourier transforms (FFTs) and recognition of face is performed using a correlation filter (CF). The correlation filter is generated from the Fourier transformed data of the training face image(s) and is multiplied with the Fourier transformed data of the test face image. The correlation peak is obtained in spatial domain after inverse Fourier transform of the result of multiplication. A test metric can then be used for recognition.

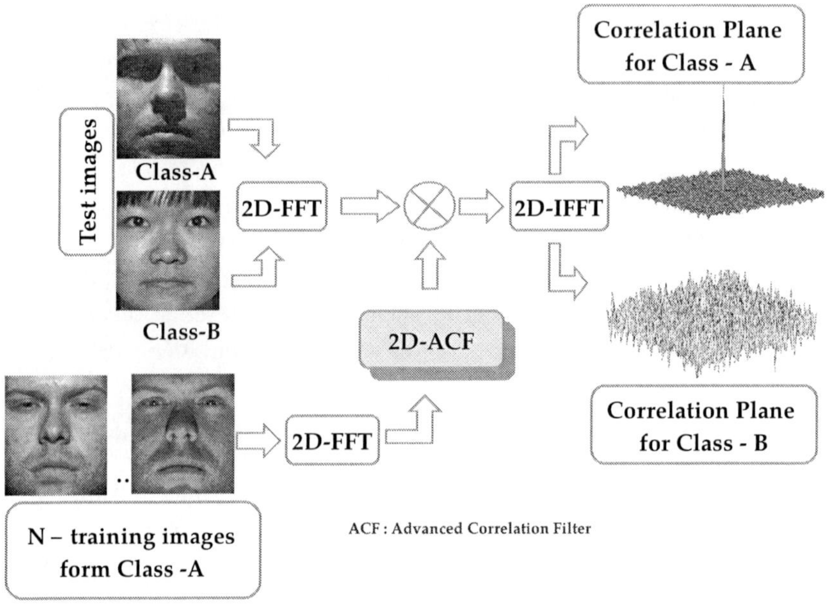

Figure 1. Frequency domain correlation technique for face recognition using correlation filter.

The approach of using CFs offer several advantages over model-based approaches. Firstly, it has built-in shift-invariance, i.e. if the input image is translated with respect to training images, the shift can be easily detected in the correlation plane as shown in Fig(2). Secondly, correlation filters are based on integration operation and thus offer graceful degradation in any impairment to the test face image. Thirdly, correlation filters can be designed to exhibit attributes such as noise tolerance and high ability for discrimination. Finally, design of correlation filter is derived from closed form expressions and thus physically realizable.

2. Mathematical background of correlation filters

The classical synthetic discriminant function (SDF) [13] filter is designed for two-class problem where the correlation values at the origin is set to 1 (may be selected to other values for multi-class problem) for training images from one class, generally authentic or true class, and to 0 for the training images from other class or false class. SDF can be formulated by a single matrix- vector notation denoted as,

$$\mathbf{X}^{+}\mathbf{h} = \overrightarrow{u} \tag{2}$$

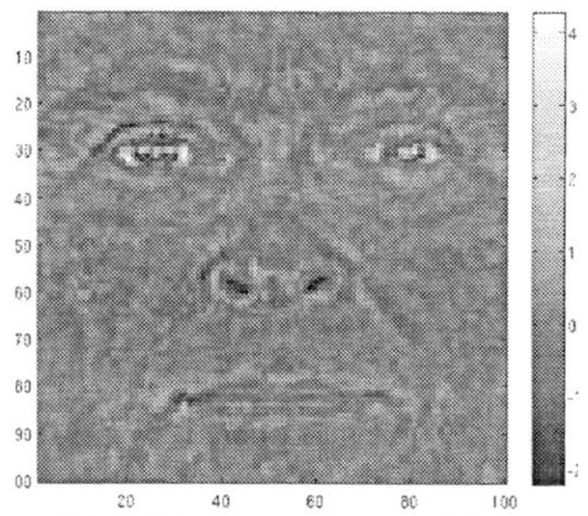

(a) PSF of correlation filter

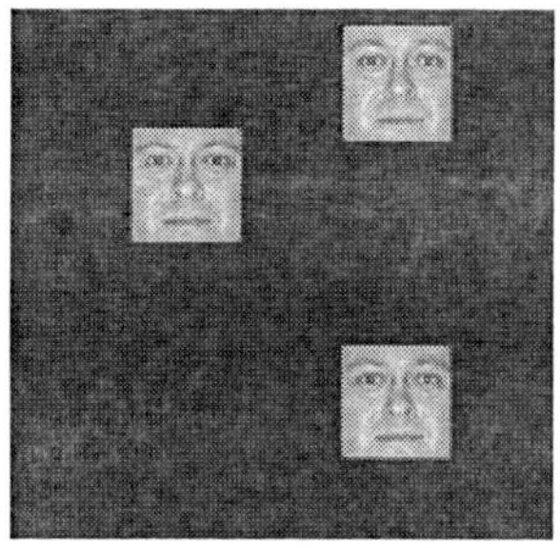
(b) Target image

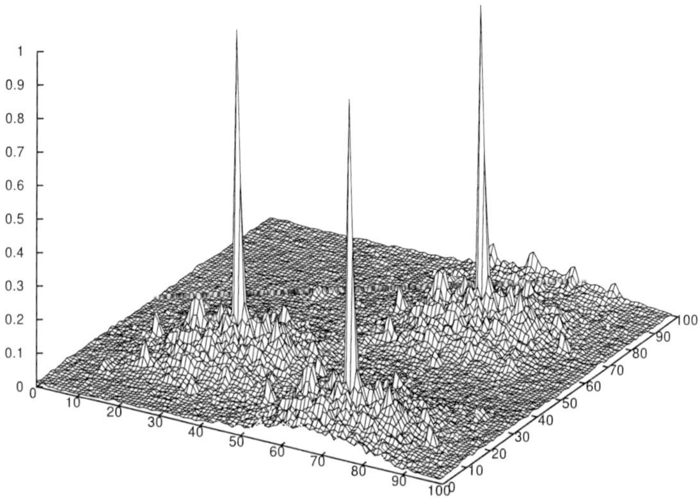

(c)Mesh plot of output correlation plane with detectable peaks at the position authentic image in (b)

Figure 2. Shows that the shift invariant property of correlation filter. The peaks on correlation plane (3D plot) indicate shifting of authentic image in target image.

where, $\mathbf{X} = [\mathbf{x}_1, \mathbf{x}_2, ..., \mathbf{x}_N]$ is a $d \times N$ matrix with N training vectors (lexicographically ordered versions of 2D Fourier transform of N images) as its columns, and $\overrightarrow{u} = [c_1, c_2, \ldots, c_N]^T$ is an $N \times 1$ vector containing the desired peak values at the correlation plane origin for the desired class, d is the total number of pixels present in one image, $\mathbf{h}$[1] is the desired frequency domain correlation filter of size $d \times 1$ and the superscript $+$ indicates the complex conjugate transpose.

The side lobe region around the peak on the correlation plane (Fig(5a)) of SDF filter may be often higher than the target response at the origin, as SDF is designed only by controlling the origin value of the correlation output. To overcome this problem Mahalanobis et al proposed a popular version of SDF filter called MACE filter [6] by minimizing the average correlation energy (ACE) of the correlation output planes for the training images of the

[1]Scalar vectors and matrices are denoted by light face lower and upper cases with an arrow on the top while frequency domain vectors and matrices are denoted by simple bold face lower and uppercases respectively

desired class while satisfying the correlation peak amplitude constraints. More specifically, the average energy of the correlation output is $\mathbf{h}^{+}\mathbf{D}\mathbf{h}$, where $\mathbf{D}$ is the diagonal matrix of size $d \times d$, whose diagonal entries are the average power spectrum of all N training images from a desired class, is minimized subject to the linear constraint $\mathbf{X}^{+}\mathbf{h} = \overrightarrow{u}$. This constrained quadratic optimization problem can be solved using Lagrangian multipliers which yields the optimum solution given by,

$$\mathbf{h}_{MACE} = \mathbf{D}^{-1}\mathbf{X}(\mathbf{X}^{+}\mathbf{D}^{-1}\mathbf{X})^{-1}\overrightarrow{u} \tag{3}$$

Due to the minimization criteria of ACE of MACE-filter, sharp correlation peak is possible by suppressing the side lobes for the target images. However, MACE filter can result in poor intraclass recognition of images which are not included in the training set as this filter emphasizes the high frequency components. Moreover, MACE filter is often excessively sensitive to noise as there is no in-built immunity to noise. Kumar proposed the minimum variance synthetic discriminant functions (MVSDF) [11] which minimizes the correlation output noise variance (ONV) $\mathbf{h}^{+}\mathbf{C}\mathbf{h}$, where $\mathbf{C}$ is the diagonal matrix whose diagonal entries are the noise power spectral density while satisfying the correlation peak amplitude constraints. The solution of MVSDF can be found in [11] as

$$\mathbf{h}_{MVSDF} = \mathbf{C}^{-1}\mathbf{X}(\mathbf{X}^{+}\mathbf{C}^{-1}\mathbf{X})^{-1}\overrightarrow{u} \tag{4}$$

To get the sharp correlation peak with suppressed noise, MACE filter is combined with MVSDF, thus emphasizing low spatial frequencies to reduce noise. The technique resulted in evolving an optimal trade-off function (OTF) [32]. The optimum solution of OTF is given by,

$$\mathbf{h}_{OTF} = \mathbf{T}^{-1}\mathbf{X}(\mathbf{X}^{+}\mathbf{T}^{-1}\mathbf{X})^{-1}\overrightarrow{u} \tag{5}$$

where $\mathbf{T} = \alpha\mathbf{D} + \sqrt{1-\alpha^2}\mathbf{C}$, $0 \leq \alpha \leq 1$. α is used as controlling trade-off parameter i.e. for $\alpha = 0$ leads to MVSDF and $\alpha = 1$ leads to MACE filter.

In face recognition problem OTF is widely used in [12, 16]. Another phase of approach of designing correlation filter is to remove the hard constraint at the correlation plane. Justifications [10] behind the removal of hard constraint are

- there is no relationship between the constraint imposed on the filter and its ability to tolerate distortions
- non-training images always yield different values from those specified for training images during synthesizing the filter.

Some correlation filters [8, 7, 19, 5, 34] are designed based on soft constraints. Maximum average correlation height (MACH) filter [8] is an example of unconstrained filter which maximizes the peak intensity of the average training image. It also minimizes the similarity between average training image correlation output and those outputs due to all training images from the desired class. This similarity measure is known as average similarity measure (ASM) and expressed as,

$$ASM = \mathbf{h}^{+}\mathbf{S}\mathbf{h} \tag{6}$$

where $\mathbf{S} = \frac{1}{N}\sum_{i=1}^{N}(\mathbf{X}_i - \mathbf{M})^{+}(\mathbf{X}_i - \mathbf{M})$. Here $\mathbf{X}_i$ is the diagonal matrix (of size $d \times d$) containing $\mathbf{x}_i$ (2D Fourier transformed image lexicographically ordered) along its main diagonal and $\mathbf{M}$ is a diagonal matrix (of size $d \times d$) containing $\mathbf{m}$ along its diagonal, where $\mathbf{m} = \frac{1}{N}\sum_{i=1}^{N}\mathbf{x}_i$ is the Fourier transform of the average of the N training images.

In the design of MACH filter it is kept in mind that the filter should yield a high peak on average over the training set images. To satisfy this condition the average correlation height (ACH) is set to be maximized. The ACH can be expressed by matrix vector notation as,

$$ACH = \mathbf{m}^{+}\mathbf{h} \tag{7}$$

It has been shown [33, 8] that MACH filter and its other variants, most notably optimal trade off MACH (OTMACH) is very powerful correlation filter algorithm. In practice, other performance measures like average correlation energy (ACE), the output noise variance (ONV) are also considered to balance the system performance for different application scenario. Refregier [33] introduced the optimal trade off approach by relating correlation plane metrics such as ONV, ACE, ASM and ACH. The performance of OTMACH-filter can be improved by minimizing the energy function $E(\mathbf{h})$ of the correlation filter $\mathbf{h}$, given by,

$$E(\mathbf{h}) = \alpha(ONV) + \beta(ACE) + \gamma(ASM) - \delta(ACH) \tag{8}$$

$$= \alpha\mathbf{h}^{+}\mathbf{C}\mathbf{h} + \beta\mathbf{h}^{+}\mathbf{D}\mathbf{h} + \gamma\mathbf{h}^{+}\mathbf{S}\mathbf{h} - \delta|\mathbf{m}^{+}\mathbf{h}|^{2} \tag{9}$$

These considerations lead to the expression for OTMACH filter as

$$\mathbf{h} = \frac{\mathbf{m}}{\alpha\mathbf{C} + \beta\mathbf{D} + \gamma\mathbf{S}} \tag{10}$$

where α, β and γ are the nonnegative optimal trade off (OT) parameters.

For a particular application, OT parameters can be controlled to get the best performance of the filter. Another important approach of correlation filter design is carried out by relaxing the constraint on the correlation values at the origin and considering the entire correlation plane [7]. The formulation of this filter is different from the previous correlation filters as in the later case the distance between the peak height of a certain class from the peak height of the overall representation of classes is maximized. Fig(3) shows schematically three class problems where $\mathbf{m}_1$, $\mathbf{m}_2$ and $\mathbf{m}_3$ represent the class centers, $\mathbf{m}$ is the overall class mean and $\mathbf{z}$ represents the test input which is to be classified. The transformation matrix $\mathbf{H}$ is to be designed in such a way that the class compactness is achieved by shrinking the class boundaries and simultaneously moving the class centers apart to make classes more distinct. Thus the unknown input $\mathbf{z}$ will be properly classified (here class-1 as the distance d_1 is the smallest one). To increase the interclass distances the following measure is performed

$$\begin{aligned} A(\mathbf{h}) &= \frac{1}{C}\sum_{k=1}^{C}|\mathbf{m}_k^{+}\mathbf{h} - \mathbf{m}^{+}\mathbf{h}|^{2} \\ &= \frac{1}{C}\sum_{k=1}^{C}\mathbf{h}^{+}(\mathbf{m} - \mathbf{m}_k)(\mathbf{m} - \mathbf{m}_k)^{+}\mathbf{h} \\ &= \mathbf{h}^{+}\mathbf{M}\mathbf{h} \end{aligned} \tag{11}$$

where, $\mathbf{M} = \frac{1}{C}\sum_{k=1}^{C}(\mathbf{m}-\mathbf{m}_k)(\mathbf{m}-\mathbf{m}_k)^+$, is a $d \times d$ full matrix with rank $\leq (C-1)$. The criterion of class compactness can be obtained by minimizing the objective function as

$$\begin{aligned} B(\mathbf{h}) &= \frac{1}{C}\sum_{k=1}^{C}\frac{1}{N}\sum_{i=1}^{N}\mathbf{h}^+(\mathbf{X}_{ik}-\mathbf{M}_k)(\mathbf{X}_{ik}-\mathbf{M}_k)^+\mathbf{h} \\ &= \mathbf{h}^+\mathbf{S}\mathbf{h} \end{aligned} \tag{12}$$

The objectives of maximizing $A(\mathbf{h})$ and minimizing $B(\mathbf{h})$ can be obtained by maximizing the ratio

$$J(\mathbf{h}) = \frac{A(\mathbf{h})}{B(\mathbf{h})} = \frac{\mathbf{h}^+\mathbf{M}\mathbf{h}}{\mathbf{h}^+\mathbf{S}\mathbf{h}} \tag{13}$$

with respect to $\mathbf{h}$. The dominant eigenvector of $\mathbf{S}^{-1}\mathbf{M}$ gives the optimum solution of the

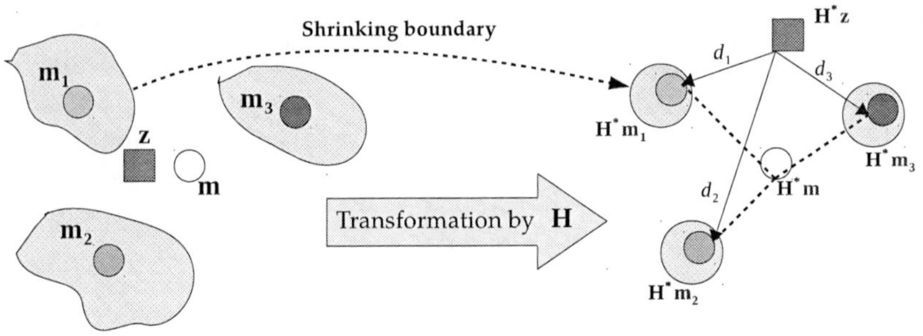

Figure 3. Transformation by **H** makes classes more compact and increases the interclass distances.

desired DCCF ($\mathbf{h}$). The solution of $\mathbf{h}$ (can be found in [7]) is different from that of the classical MACH filter as $\mathbf{M}$ in the numerator of $J(\mathbf{h})$ is not a vector but a full matrix.

3. Performance evaluation of correlation filters in face recognition

3.1. Performance metric and parameter setup

Peak-to-side lobe ratio (PSR) [10] of the correlation output is generally used as performance metric for both constrained and unconstrained filters. The PSR is a measure of peak sharpness.An authentic test image should yield large PSR, and impostors very low PSRs. The correlation output is obtained as,

$$S_{corr} = FFT^{-1}[\mathbf{T}\cdot\mathbf{H}^*] \tag{14}$$

where, **T** is the Fourier transform of test image and **H** represents the designed filter obtained by reshaping **h** in proper row-column order.

The test image is cross-correlated with the synthesized correlation filter and the resulting correlation output is searched for the largest value of peaks (simply called the peak value). A rectangular region (20×20 pixels) centered at the peak is extracted and used to compute the PSR. A 5×5 rectangular region centered at the peak is masked out and the remaining annular region defined as the side lobe region is used to compute the mean and standard deviation of the side lobes. The peak-to-side lobe ratio (PSR) is then calculated as,

$$psr = \frac{peak - mean}{std} \tag{15}$$

where std stands for standard deviation.

The performance evaluation of different unconstrained correlation filters like UMACE, MACH, OTMACH, QPUMACE and POUMACE has been made by setting different optimal trade-off parameters. UMACE filter is designed with the help of the equation, $\mathbf{h}_{UMACE} = \mathbf{D}^{-1}\mathbf{m}, (\alpha = 0, \beta = 1, \gamma = 0)$. Similarly MACH and OTMACH are designed as $\mathbf{h}_{MACH} = \mathbf{S}^{-1}\mathbf{m}, (\alpha = 0, \beta = 0, \gamma = 1)$ and $\mathbf{h}_{OTMACH} = (\alpha\mathbf{C} + \beta\mathbf{D} + \gamma\mathbf{S})^{-1}\mathbf{m}, (\alpha = 0.2, \beta = 0.5, \gamma = 0.3)$ respectively.

POUMACE is obtained as the full phase extension of $\mathbf{H}_{UMACE}$[2] i.e. $\mathbf{H}_{POUMACE} = e^{j\angle \mathbf{H}_{UMACE}}$. In designing QPUMACE filter each element in the filter array will take on ± 1 for the real component. The imaginary component $\pm j$ is calculated in the following manner:

$$\mathbf{H}_{QPUMACE} = \begin{cases} +1 & \Re\{\mathbf{H}_{UMACE}(u,v)\} \geq 0 \\ -1 & \Re\{\mathbf{H}_{UMACE}(u,v)\} < 0 \\ +j & \Im\{\mathbf{H}_{UMACE}(u,v)\} \geq 0 \\ -j & \Im\{\mathbf{H}_{UMACE}(u,v)\} < 0 \end{cases}$$

PSR values are used to make the decision of verification accuracy of the above correlation filters for each database. The decision of authentication by DCCF is made by the following way: the distance to be computed between the transformed input and the ideal shape for class k is $d_k = |\mathbf{H}^*\mathbf{z} - \mathbf{H}^*\mathbf{m}_k|^2$. The input is assigned to the class to which the distance from the test image is *smallest*.

3.2. Databases

The databases have been divided into different categories according to their conditions. AMP database is used to test face images of variable expressions. For face images with illumination variations Cropped Yale and PIE databases are used. For face images having both expression and Illumination variations AR database is used. AMP database contains 13 different persons, each one with 75 images consisting of different facial expressions. All the faces are of gray scale frontal face images of size 64×64. The face images of AMP database contain only expression variations. PIE database contains two illumination subsets containing 65 subjects with 21 images per subject. Each subject is facing the central (frontal) camera with a neutral expression. One dataset is captured with room lights on (referred as RL-PIE) and the other dataset is captured with room lights off (referred as NRL-PIE). Since only the intensity information is used the original 640×486 pixel color images are converted into gray scale images. The images are cropped to the size of 100×100 pixels from the original 640×486 gray scale images. All cropped 100×100 pixels images contains the important facial features like eyes, nose and mouth. Fig.(4a) shows example

[2] $\mathbf{H}_{UMACE}$ is obtained by reshaping $\mathbf{h}_{UMACE}$ by proper row-column arrangement

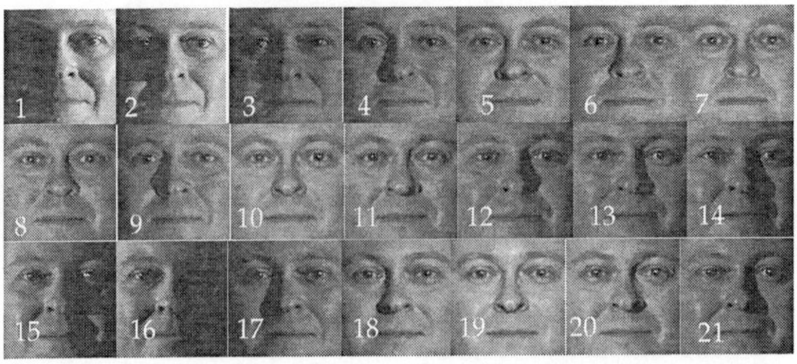

(a)

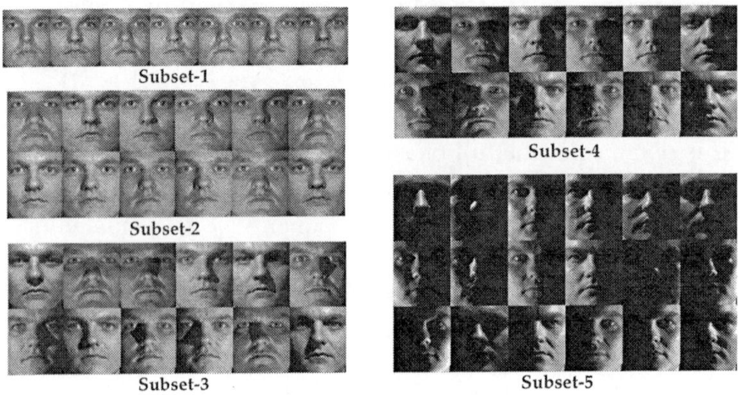

(b)

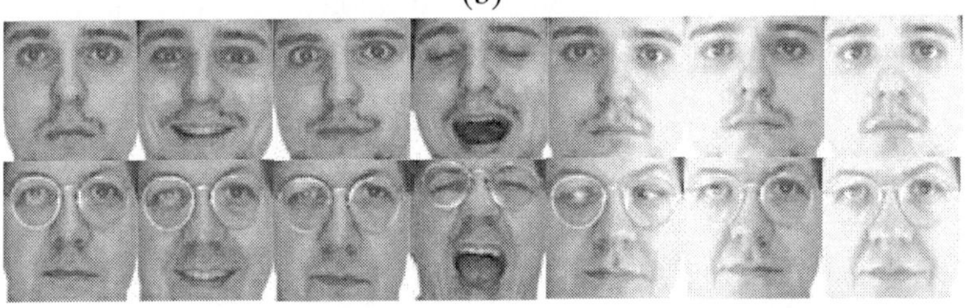

(c)

Figure 4. (a) Shows sample images of person-3 from the illumination subset of PIE database with no background lighting (b) Different subset images of YaleB database (c)Sample images of two individuals of AR face database.

images of person-3 of PIE dataset.

Cropped YaleB database[2] contains 10 different persons and each person contains 64 differently illuminated grey scale frontal face images of size 192×168 containing eye, nose and mouth. A subset of 476 images of AR face database has been used where all the color images are gray scale normalized. All facial images are normalized according to the eye coordinates for scaling, translation and rotation, such that the eye centers are in fixed position. All the images are cropped to the size of 64×64. No preprocessing has been done. Total 68 individuals are taken, each one with 7 images. Fig(4c) shows 7 sample images of two different individuals from AR database.

4. Tests and results

During performance analysis of correlation techniques for face recognition two types of tests may be performed. (1) Identification test - where the class is labeled based on the filter that scores a relative maximum PSR and (2) Verification test- where an authentic test images must achieve a score above a preset threshold. Here face recognition performance of correlation filters (unconstrained) is measured based on verification approach and it is maintained for every experiments on each database. Only the performance evaluation of unconstrained filters have been made in this study. The study of constrained filters performances are excluded due to the following reasons. The two well known constrained filters are ECPSDF and MACE and its output correlation planes [3] for an authentic persons are given in Fig(5). It may be noted from the Fig(5) that high side lobe values are obtained in

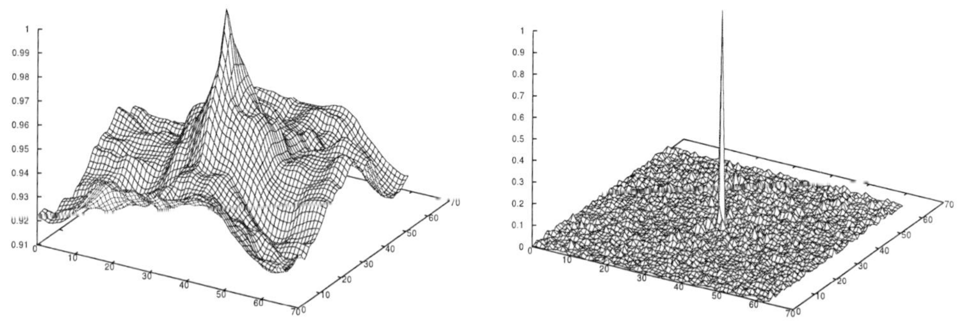

(a) (b)

Figure 5. (a) SDF filter (b) MACE filter correlation outputs.

case of SDF filter comparing to MACE. In MACE filter output a sharp and distinct peak with suppressed side lobes is obtained. Hence, MACE filter gives better discrimination between authentic and impostors comparing to ECPSDF which is also justified form Fig(6). The PSR performance of MACE filter for AMP database of person-1 having training image indices, 1,21,41)is similar to results given in [10], and is almost same for the PSR distribution of UMACE (see Fig.(7c). Hence instead of MACE, the unconstrained MACE is used through the study. Another advantage of UMACE over MACE is that only one inversion of a diagonal matrix **D** is needed.

All unconstrained filters have been synthesized with same number of training images (1,21,41) from Person-1 of AMP database and tested over the whole database. Fig(7) shows the performance of different filters in terms of PSR values. The separation margin between authentic and impostor is calculated by subtracting the minimum PSR value of the authentic class and the maximum PSR value among the impostor classes. The largest distance of separation (DoS) is achieved for UMACE filter compared to others. UMACE filter is also tested where the training images (1,21,41) from Person-2 are used. The results degrades as reduced DoS is found for UMACE. Hence the phase extension of UMACE is considered since phase contains more information than magnitude in an image. It is interesting to ob-

[3]these two filters are synthesized with 1,21,41 images of Person-1 of AMP database

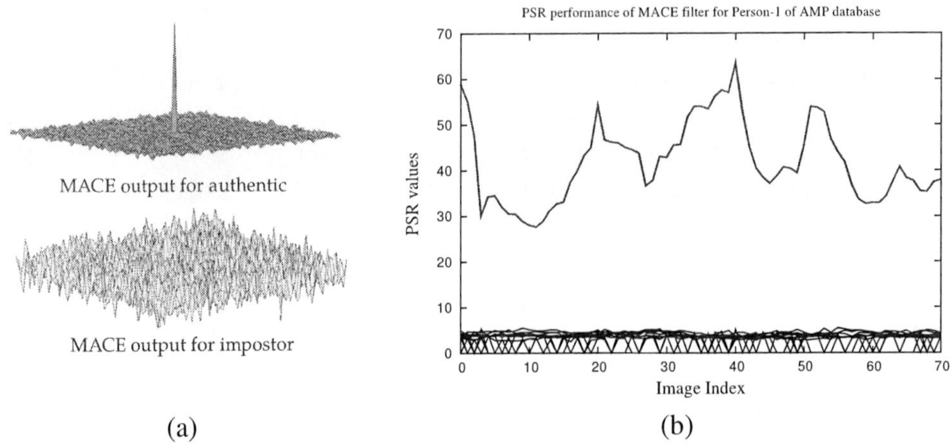

Figure 6. MACE filter performance on AMP database (a) verifies the discrimination ability of MACE filter (b) Shows a clear margin of separation between authentic (blue line) PSR and impostor (black lines) PSRs.

serve that while the full phase [4] instead of quad phase of UMACE is considered, the DoS is increased indicating the better performance for face recognition task. Table(1) summarizes the %mean recognition rate with corresponding %false acceptance rate (FAR). In Table(1) the preset threshold is taken as 7. Table(2) shows the %mean recognition rate at zero FAR. In case of DCCF the minimum distance is observed and the test image is labeled into the corresponding class.

Table 1. The performance of different filters in face recognition on a facial expression database.

Training images	**MACH** %rec,%far	**UMACE** %rec,%far	**OTMACH** %rec,%far	**QPUMACE** %rec,%far	**POUMACE** %rec,%far	**DCCF** %rec,-
1,21,41	90.124,0.9269	99.89,1.76	99.89,2.89	99.37,0.46	100,1.169	99.79
3,22,28	90.124,0.926	99.58,2.48	99.58,3.17	99.16,0.87	99.37,1.89	99.49
46,50,55	64.13,0	99.68,1.69	99.79,2.61	98.75,0.74	99.27,1.75	99.79

During the testing on Cropped YaleB database, each correlation filter is synthesized with each subset and correlated over the whole database. Hence $10 \times 9 \times 64 (= 5760)$ number of impostor scores (PSR) and $10 \times 64 (= 640)$ authentic scores for Cropped yale for each filter and for PIE databse $65 \times 64 \times 21 (= 87360)$ number of impostor scores and $65 \times 21 (= 1365)$ authentic scores for each filter are obtained. From the PSR distribution %mean recognition rate are evaluated according to the verification method and the

[4] the full phase extension of test image is also taken during correlation

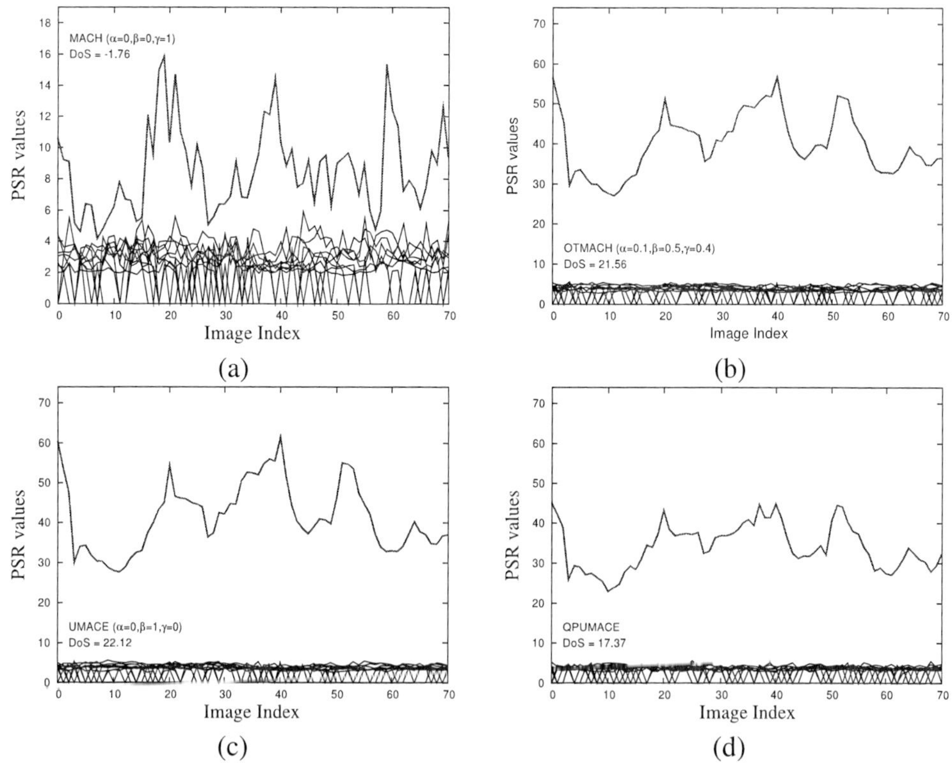

Figure 7. Shows the PSR performance of different unconstrained filter while tested over AMP database.

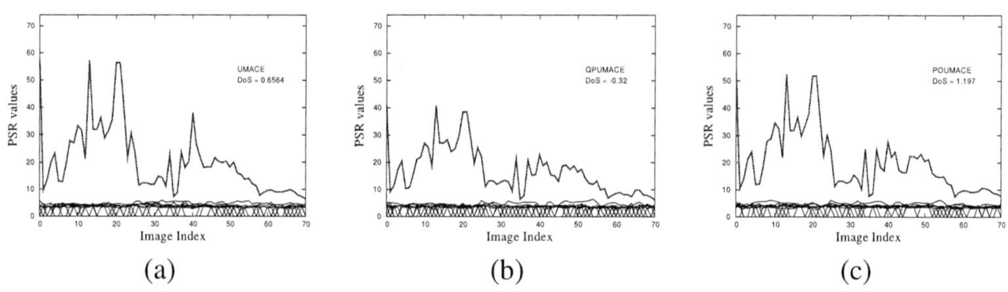

Figure 8. Shows the PSR performance of UMACE and its two types phase extensions (Quad-phase and Full-phase) while tested over AMP database with Person 2.

corresponding %FAR are recorded. Table(3) summarizes the %mean recognition rate of correlation filters while tested over YaleB database. It is observed from the Table(3) the recognition results are greatly affected according to the choice of different lighting directions. Overall performance of the correlation filters shows the best result when subset-4 has been chosen for training purpose. It is due to the fact these training set has images with wide variation of lighting or in other words these images have illumination distributed evenly over the camera's visual field.

Table 2. The %mean recognition rate obtained by different filters when FAR = 0.

Training images	**MACH** %rec	**UMACE** %rec	**OTMACH** %rec	**QPUMACE** %rec	**POUMACE** %rec
1,21,41	53.43	97.50	97.61	96.04	97.92
3,22,28	62.68	98.75	99.06	98.12	98.24
46,50,55	64.13	92.72	92.203	87.00	89.91
1,2,3,10,74	90.85	98.64	98.75	98.33	98.44

Table 3. The %mean recognition rate along with the %far obtained by different filters while the threshold is fixed at 10 (with no illumination compensation).

Filters	**UMACE** %rec,%far	**QPUMACE** %rec,%far	**POUMACE** %rec,%far	**OTMACH** %rec,%far
Subset-1	69.53,0.1042	71.1,0.0174	76.4,0.1215	89.22,16.99
Subset-2	73.28,0.2431	69.37,0.086	73.90,0.257	89.06,21.2
Subset-3	87.34,0.43	82.96,0.086	87.5,0.2431	94.68,10.42
Subset-4	92.81,1.42	87.65,0.26	91.56,0.78	97.65,12.17
Subset-5	92.18,2.06	73.9,0.69	82.03,1.54	98.59,18.92

It is observed that OTMACH filter provides the better %recognition rate comparing to others but from this result it cannot be concluded that OTMACH gives the best performance as %far is very high. Hence by considering both %rec and %far it is observed that the performance of POUMACE is slightly better than the other filters. It is also observed that the best performance of each filter is obtained while subset-4 is used as training set.

One of the very efficient ways to observe the classifier performances is plotting receiver operating characteristics (ROC).The performance of correlation filters can be characterized, as in detection systems, in terms of the probabilities of correct detection (P_D) and false alarm (P_{FA}). In general low detection thresholds improve the probability of correct recognition, while larger thresholds decrease false alarm probabilities by rejecting erroneous peaks (or specifically PSRs). The relationship of P_D and P_{FA} with threshold PSR can be represented by ROCs. ROCs are calculated with increasing PSRs as threshold. When comparing ROC-curves of different tests, good curves lie closer to the top left corner and the worst case is a diagonal line. The diagonal line represents $P_D = P_{FA}$. The curves nearer to the diagonal line represents the worst detection performance. Fig(9) shows that in general the average filter performance is best when subset-4 is used as a training set. This can be explained as the subset-4 includes the training images having wide illumination variation comparing to others. Hence any face image that lies in the convex hull of these training images should be perfectly recognized. Table(4) summarizes the mean %recognition rate of PIE database at FAR = 0. In this test PSRs of 87360 impostor images and PSRs of 1365 authentic face images are normally distributed i.e. a Gaussian model is fit to both the impostor and authentic scores. From the normally distributed data, probability of detection is

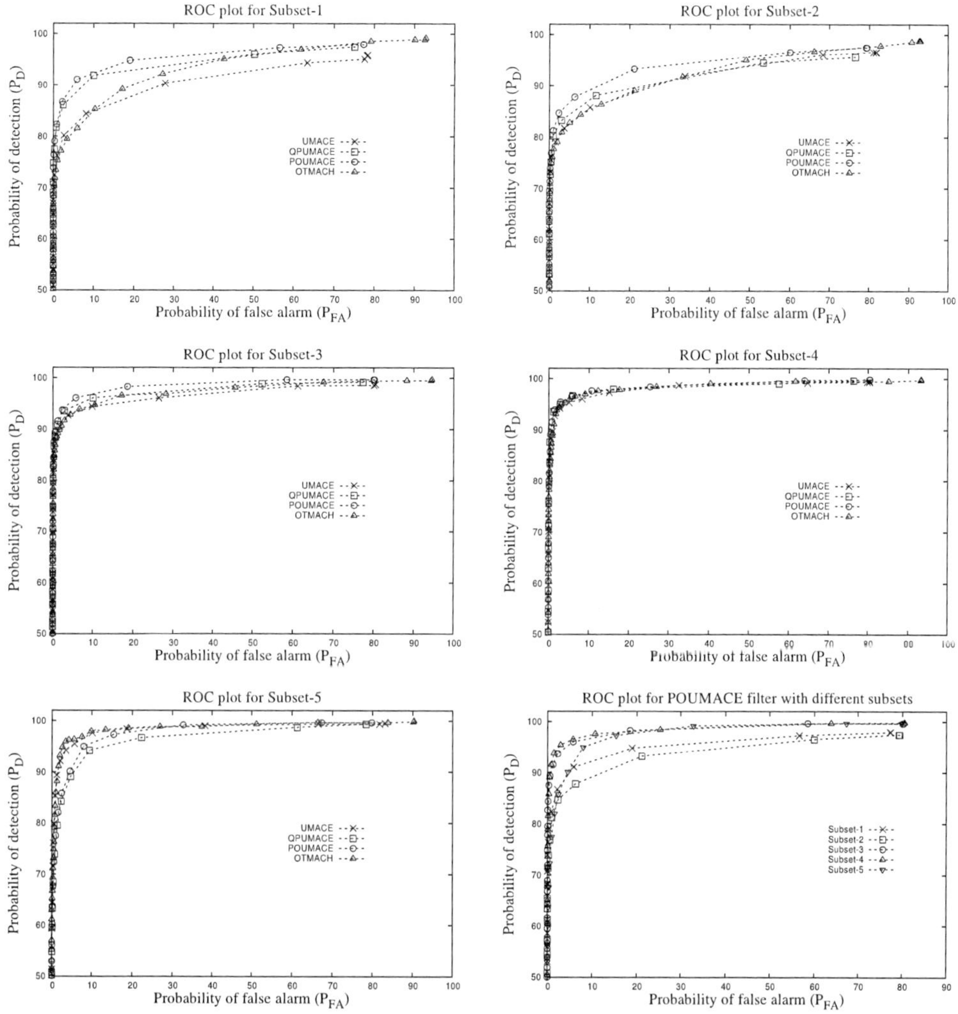

Figure 9. ROC plots of different correlation filters for different subsets. The performance of POUMACE filter is also observed for 5 subsets training.

calculated at zero probability of false alarm. The correlation filters are also designed with randomly taken 4 and 5 face images from an authentic individual and tested over whole database. Fig(10) shows the filter performances on face recognition in AR database. From the Fig(10) it may be noted, that the correlation filters do not give an acceptable amount of recognition accuracy (about 70% recognition rate at 0% FAR, while 5 training images are used for synthesis) on AR database.

5. Photonic Implementation

The interest in the optical implementation of correlators is mainly due to the pioneering work by VanderLugt [4], who used a so-called $4f$ architecture to produce sharp correlation

Table 4. The %mean recognition rate at FAR=0, while near frontal lighting images (with background lights off) are taken as training images

Training images	**UMACE** %rec	**QPMACE** %rec	**POUMACE** %rec	**OTMACH** %rec
5,6,7,8,9,10 11,18,19,20	96.57	95.32	98.83	96.96
18,19,20	91.73	90.16	95.16	91.64
5,6,7,8,9,10	91.73	88.84	96.96	92.2
7,10,19	87.04	91.022	94.77	86.1
8,9,10	93.75	92.27	97.26	94.22

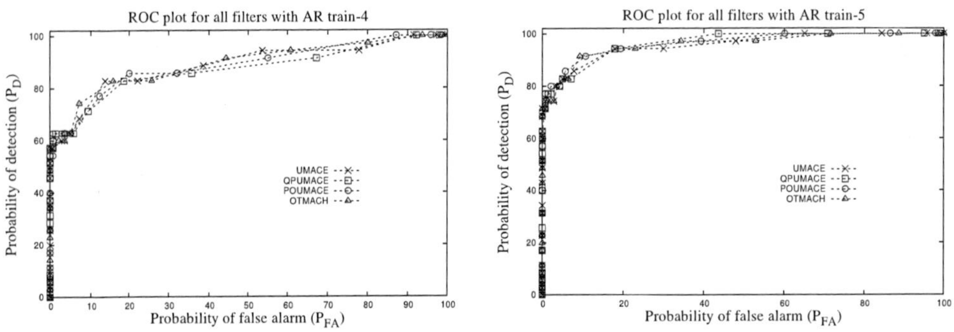

Figure 10. ROC plots for different correlation filters with AR 4 train and 5 train.

peaks for matching input targets even if they are subject to certain distortions or noises. The system shown in Fig(11) attracted a considerable amount of interest for its ability of taking advantage of the inherent parallel processing capabilities of performing the optical Fourier transform (FT). However, such an optical architecture requires a stringent alignment of

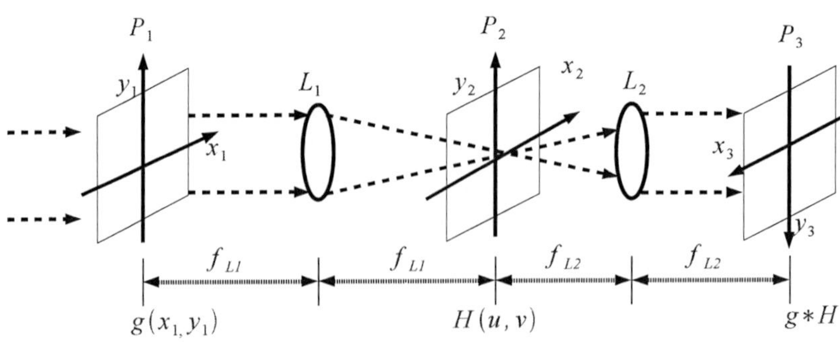

Figure 11. Schematic diagram of optical frequency plane correlator.

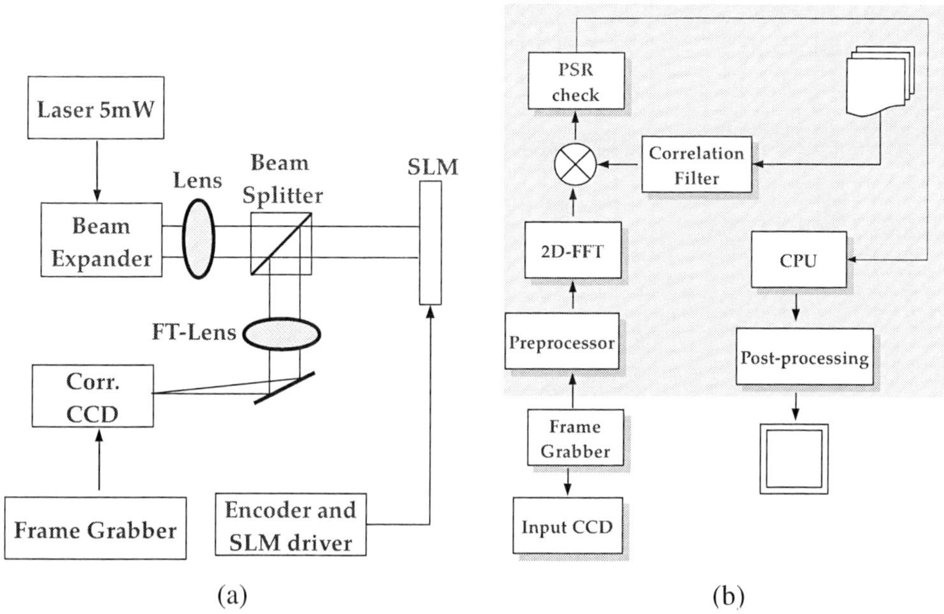

Figure 12. (a) Photonics architecture of hybrid correlator (b) signal flow diagram.

the optical components, typically with micrometer accuracy, in order to achieve correlation [44]. Though such family of systems are supposed to work in theory at the speed of light, yet the speed is limited due to variety of factors. In a practical optical correlators, the input scene is recorded by a CCD camera and displayed on a spatial light modulator (SLM). The SLM is illuminated with a coherent beam of light and optically Fourier transformed, which is then optically mixed with a filter in the Fourier plane [9, 20]. The filter is usually displayed on a second SLM. This is again optically Fourier transformed to obtain the correlation between the reference and input images. Bringing the test images and reference images into the optical correlators and transferring the correlation outputs from the optical correlators for viewing correlation peaks prove to be bottlenecks, mainly because of device constraints for electro-optic conversions and vice versa. The present development of image registration onto a high speed spatial light modulator (SLM) and recording the correlation peak on a high frame rate CCD camera have somewhat eased the problem, but such improvements have to go a long way before the all pervasive advantages of speed and parallel processing capability of optical beam are exploited.

To overcome some of the engineering problems of basic $4f$ VanderLutt correlator, many hybrid digital-optical correlators have been proposed. Young and co-workers in 1993 [43] outlined an optical-digital hybrid correlator system that allows the potential for a multi kilohertz reference template search on data acquired at video rates. In hybrid photonic correlator, the input scene captured by a CCD camera, instead of being displayed on the input SLM, is digitally Fourier transformed using suitable FFT algorithm. The complex data are then mixed digitally with pre-synthesized filters and displayed onto an SLM. The SLM is illuminated with a coherent collimated laser beam and the wavefront is optically Fourier transformed to obtain the correlation peaks. The correlation peak is captured by another

CCD camera and displayed in a monitor. The hybrid approach exploits the asymmetry that exists between the speed requirements for performing the FT of input signal and that required for template search. The schematic of experimental set-up used is shown in Fig(12). A beam from a laser diode source is passed through a spatial filter and then through a col-

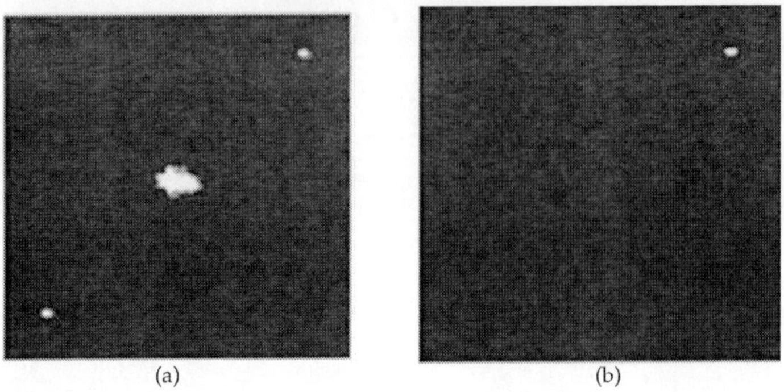

Figure 13. (a) Optical cross correlation pair with central dc in optical experiment (b) dc and one cross correlation peak are removed.

limating lens, which expands and collimates the beam. A face image is digitally Fourier transformed and mixed with the pre-synthesized filter. This results in a complex function, which needs to be encoded onto an electrically addressed binary reflective SLM [17, 18]. The encoded complex data are then displayed on the SLM to obtain the optical Fourier transformation through the Fourier-transform lens. The transformed intensity is then captured using a high frame rate CCD camera connected to a personal computer through a frame-grabber card. The optical Fourier transformation results in 2 orders of diffraction: zero and ± 1. The zero order of diffraction gives rise to DC, and the ± 1 orders correspond to the two autocorrelation peaks as shown in Fig(13a). It is necessary to discard the strong DC and one of the autocorrelation peaks to get a single peak at the output plane (Fig(13b)).

6. Discussions

In this chapter, formulations and performances of frequency domain correlation techniques with respect to different filters are analyzed with different face databases. Table(2,4) and ROC plots (refer Fig.(9)) show the best performance obtained by POUMACE (except subset-5) and the performance of UMACE is closely behind. This is due to the fact the UMACE filter $\mathbf{h} = \mathbf{D}^{-1}\mathbf{m}$ can be rewritten as $\mathbf{h} = \mathbf{D}^{-1/2}(\mathbf{D}^{-1/2}\mathbf{m})$, where $\mathbf{D}^{-1/2}$ is used as preprocessor of signal and noise.

This preprocessor attenuates the frequency (Fig14)components with high energy i.e. major image features and amplifies the frequency components with low energy i.e. the fine details of face image. It can thus be concluded that illumination tolerance is achieved since most images have most concentration of energy in the lower frequency spectrum and the $\mathbf{D}^{-1/2}$ step will emphasize higher frequencies in the test image, where the effects of illumination variation are not so predominant. It may be mentioned that illumination

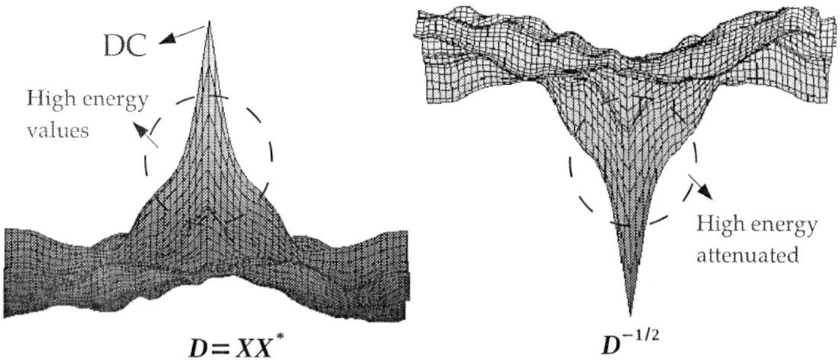

Figure 14. Shows that the UMACE preprocessor attenuates the frequency components of high energy values. These plots are the original average energy distribution of the training images.

variations are mostly predominant in the lower frequency spectrum. As phase contains more information than magnitude, POUMACE is a judicial choice for face recognition without any pose variations. In the design methodology of DCCF filter no correlation plane energy minimization is considered and hence is is not very efficient under variations in illumination conditions. Limitations of photonics implementations of the system where two FFTs are to be performed in an optical or photonics domain is difficult to achieve and therefore hybrid photonics implementations are attempted.

References

[1] Advanced multimedia processing lab web page at electrical and computer engineering department at cmu, http://amp.ece.cmu.edu.

[2] http://vision.ucsd.edu/ leekc/extyaledatabase/extyaleb.html.

[3] Ramzi Abiantun, Marios Savvides, and B. VK Vijayakumar. Generalized low dimensional feature subspace for robust face recognition on unseen datasets using kernel correlation feature analysis. In *IEEE ICASSP*, 2007.

[4] A.B.VaderLugt. Signal detection by complex filters. *IEEE Transaction on Information Theory*, IT-10:139–145, 1964.

[5] A.Mahalanobis and B.V.K.V.Kumar. Polynomial filters for higher order and multi-input information fusion. In *Proc. 11th Euro American Opto-Electronic Information Processing Workshop*, pages 221–231, Spain, 1997.

[6] A.Mahalanobis, B.V.K.V.Kumar, and D.Casassent. Minimum average correlation energy filter. *Applied Optics*, 26(17):3633–3640, 1987.

[7] A.Mahalanobis, B.V.K.V.Kumar, and S.R.F.Sims. Distance classifier correlation filters for distortion tolerance, discrimination and clutter rejection. In *Proc. SPIE 2026*, pages 325–335, 1993.

[8] A.Mahalanobis, B.V.K. Vijaya Kumar, S.Song, S.Sims, and J.Epperson. Unconstrained correlation filter. *App.Opt.*, 33:3751–3759, 1994.

[9] P. M. Birch, G. Li, F. Claret-Tournier, R. Young, D. Budgett, and C. Chatwin. Optical design of a miniature fourier transform lens system for a hybrid digital-optical correlator. *Optical Enginnering*, 41:1650–1654, 2002.

[10] A.Mahalanobis B.V.K. Vijaya Kumar and R.Juday. *Correlation Pattern Recognition*. Cambridge University Press, 2005.

[11] B.V.K.V.Kumar. Minimum variance synthetic discriminant functions. *J.Opt.Soc.Am.*, 3, 1986.

[12] B.V.K.V.Kumar, M.Savvides, and C.Xie. Correlation pattern recognition for face recognition. In *Proc. IEEE*, volume 94, 2006.

[13] C.F.Hester and D.P.Casasent. Multivariate technique for multiclass pattern recognition. *Applied Optics*, 9(11), 1980.

[14] C.K.Ng, M.Savvides, and P.K.Khosla. Real time face verification on a cell phone using advanced correlation filters. In *Proc. of IEEE Workshop on Automatic Identification Advanced Technologies*, volume 57, 2005.

[15] C.Xie and B.V.Kumar. Face class code based feature extraction for face recognition. In *Fourth IEEE Workshop on Automatic Identification Advanced Technologies*, 2005.

[16] C.Xie, M.Savvides, and B.V.K.V.Kumar. Redundant class-dependence feature analysis based on correlation filters using frgc2.0 data. In *Proc. IEEE Int.Conf. of CVPR*, 2005.

[17] J. A. Davis, D. M. Cottrell, J. Campos, M. J. Yzuel, and I. Moreno. Encoding amplitude information onto phase-only filters. *Applied Optics*, 38:5004–5013, 1999.

[18] J. A. Davis, K. O. Valadez, and D. M. Cottrell. Encoding amplitude and phase information onto a binary phase-only spatial light modulator. *Applied Optics*, 42:2003–2008, 2003.

[19] D.W.Carlson. *Optimal tradeoff composite correlation filters*. PhD thesis, Dept. of ECE, Carnegie Mellon University, Dec. 1996.

[20] S. Goyal, N. K. Nishchal, V. K. Beri, and A. K. Gupta. Wavelet-modified maximum average correlation height filter for rotation invariance that uses chirp encoding in a hybrid digital-optical correlator. *Applied Optics*, 45:4850–4857, 2006.

[21] J.Heo, M.Savvides, and B.V.K Vijaya Kumar. Performance evaluation of face recognition using visual and thermal imagery with advanced correlation filters. In *Proc. of IEEE ICCVPR*, volume 9, 2005.

[22] B.V.K.Vijaya Kumar, M.Savvides, K.Venkataramani, and C.Xie. Spatial frequency domain image processing for biometric recognition. In *IEEE ICIP*, 2002.

[23] A.R. Martinez and R. Benavente. The ar face database. Technical report, Computer Vision Center (CVC), Barcelona, 1998.

[24] M.Savvides and B.V.K.Kumar. Efficient design of advanced correlation filters for robust distortion-tolerant face recognition. In *Proceedings of the IEEE Conference on Advanced Video and Signal Based Surveillance (AVSS03)*, 2003.

[25] M.Savvides and B.V.K.Kumar. Illumination normalization using logarithm transforms for face authentication. In *Proc. of Int. Conf. on Advances in Pattern Recognition, Springer*, 2003.

[26] M.Savvides, B.V.K.Kumar, and P.K.Khosla. Robust shift invariant biometric identification from partial face images. In *Proc. of SPIE Defense and Security Symposium*, volume 156, 2004.

[27] M.Savvides, B.V.K.V.Kumar, and P.Khosla. Face verification using correlation filters. 2002.

[28] M.Savvides, J.Heo, R.Abiantun, C.Xie, and B.V. Kumar. Partial and holistic face recognition on frgc-ii data using supportvector machines. In *Proc. of IEEE ICCVPR*, volume 48, 2006.

[29] M.Savvides, B.V.K Vijaya Kumar, and P.K.Khosla. Authentication invariant cancellable correlation filters for illumination tolerant face recognition. In *Proc. of SPIE Defense and Security Symposium*, 2004e.

[30] M.Savvides, Venkataramani, and B.V.K Vijaya Kumar. Incremental updating of advanced correlation filters for biometric authentication systems. In *Proc. of IEEE Int. Conf. on Multimedia and Expo*, volume III, page 229, 2003.

[31] J. Phillips, H Moon, S Rizvi, and P Rauss. The feret evaluation methodology for face-recognition algorithms. *IEEE Transactions on Pattern Analysis and Machine Intelligence*, 22(10), October 2000.

[32] P.Refregier. Filter design for optical pattern recognition: multi-criteria optimization approach. *Opt.Lett.*, 15, 1990.

[33] Ph. Refregier. Optimal trade-off filters for noise robustness, sharpness of the correlation peak, and horner efficiency. *Optics Letters*, 16(11):829–831, 1991.

[34] R.Shenoy and D.Casasent. Correlation filters that generalize well. In *Proc. SPIE 3386*, pages 100–110, 1998.

[35] Marios Savvides, B.V.K.Kumar, and P.K. Khosla. corefaces- robust shift invariant pca based correlation filter for illumination tolerant face recognition. In *Proceedings of the 2004 IEEE Computer Society Conference on Computer Vision and Pattern Recognition (CVPR04)*, 2004.

[36] T. Sim, S. Baker, and M. Bsat. The cmu pose, illumination, and expression database,. *IEEE Transactions on Pattern Analysis and Mlachine Intelligence*, 25(12):1615–1618, 2003.

[37] Jason Thornton, Marios Savvides, and B.V.K. Vijaya Kumar. Linear shift-invariant maximum margin svm correlation filter. In *IEEE ISSNIP*, 2004.

[38] Chunyan Xie and B.V.K. Vijaya Kumar. Comparison of kernel class-dependence feature analysis (kcfa) with kernel discriminant analysis (kda) for face recognition. In *IEEE*, 2007.

[39] Chunyan Xie, Marios Savvides, and B.V.K. Vijaya Kumar. Quaternion correlation filters for face recognition in wavelet domain. In *IEEE ICASSP*, 2005.

[40] Chunyan Xie, Marios Savvides, and B.V.K. VijayaKumar. Kernel correlation filter based redundant class-dependence feature analysis (kcfa) on frgc2.0 data. *LNCS, Springer*, 3723:32–43, 2005.

[41] Yan Yan and Yu-Jin Zhang. 1d correlation filter based class-dependence feature analysis for face recognition. *Pattern Recognition*, 41:3834–3841, 2008.

[42] Yan Yan and Yu-Jin Zhanga. Tensor correlation filter based class-dependence feature analysis for face recognition. *Neurocomputing*, 71:3434–3438, December 2007.

[43] R. Young, C. Chatwin, and B. Scott. High-speed hybrid optical-digital correlator system. *Optical Enginnering*, 32:2608–2615, 1993.

[44] F. T. S. Yu and S. Jutamulia, editors. *Optical Pattern Recognition*. Cambridge University Press, 1998.

In: Face Recognition ISBN: 978-1-61942-663-4
Editors: Adamo Quaglia and Calogera M. Epifano

Chapter 10

Forensic Face Recognition: A Survey

Tauseef Ali,* *Luuk Spreeuwers*† *and Raymond Veldhuis*‡
Biometrics Group, Chair of Signals and Systems,
Faculty of EEMCS, University of Twente,
Netherlands

Abstract

The improvements of automatic face recognition during the last 2 decades have disclosed new applications like border control and camera surveillance. A new application field is forensic face recognition. Traditionally, face recognition by human experts has been used in forensics, but now there is a quickly developing interest in automatic face recognition as well. At the same time there is a trend towards a more objective and quantitative approach for traditional manual face comparison by human experts. Unlike in most applications of face recognition, in the forensic domain a binary decision or a score does not suffice as a result to be used in court. Rather, in the forensic domain, the outcome of the recognition process should be in the form of evidence or support for a prosecution hypothesis verses a defence hypothesis. In addition, in the forensic domain, trace images are often of poor quality. The available literature on (automatic) forensic face recognition is still very limited. In this survey, an overview is given of the characteristics of forensic face recognition and the main publications. The survey introduces forensic face recognition and reports on attempts to use automatic face recognition in the forensic context. Forensic facial comparison by human experts and the development of guidelines and a more quantitative and objective approach are also addressed. Probably the most important topic of the survey is the development of a framework to use automatic face recognition in the forensic setting. The Bayesian framework is a logical choice and likelihood ratios can in principle be used directly in court. In the statistical evaluation of the trace image, the choice of databases of facial images plays a very important role.

Keywords: Forensics, face recognition, Bayesian framework, biometrics.

*E-mail address: t.ali@utwente.nl
†E-mail address: l.j.spreeuwers@utwente.nl
‡E-mail address: r.n.j.veldhuis@utwente.nl

1. Introduction

Face recognition is one of the most important tasks of forensic examiners during their investigations if there is video or image material available from a crime scene. Forensic examiners perform manual examination of facial images or videos to match a trace with an image of a suspects face or with a large database of mug-shots. The use of automated facial recognition systems will not only improve the efficiency of forensic work performed by various law enforcement agencies but also standardise the comparison process. However, until now, there is no automatic face recognition system that has been accepted by the judicial system. A face recognition system must be thoroughly evaluated and verified before it can be utilised for forensic applications. Biometric face recognition has of course been used for secure building access, border control, Civil ID and login verification. However, to date no automatic system exists for identification or verification in crime investigation tasks, such as the comparison of images taken by CCTV with available databases of mug-shots. State-of-the art face recognition systems such as [27, 25] could in principle be used for this purpose, but there are several issues, specific to the forensic domain, which have to be addressed.

First and foremost, the consequences of a wrong decision made by forensic face recognition are far more severe than for most other biometric face recognition applications. Current face recognition solutions [28] are generally not sufficiently robust [18] to the variability in appearance of faces due to variations in pose, lighting conditions, facial expression and caused by imaging systems such as image quality, resolution and compression.

Secondly, a score or binary decision based biometric recognition system is not suitable to the judicial system where the objective is to give a degree of support for one hypothesis against another incorporating the prior knowledge about the case at hand [9, 12].

Finally it should be mentioned that in the forensic scenario the quality of images available is generally low, e.g. images of a crime scene recorded using CCTV. These images usually have a low resolution and depicted faces are often not frontal and may be partly occluded.

The recognition task in the forensic framework can be carried out "offline" in contrast to other applications where a decision has to be made in real-time, e.g. user access for a building or border control. Forensic face recognition therefore has fewer time constraints and to a certain extent human involvement is allowed and does not effect the overall objectivity of the system.

A related field of forensic facial recognition is forensic facial reconstruction which aims to reproduce a lost or unknown face of an individual for the purpose of recognition or identification [8]. Well known is the approach to reconstruct a face starting from the skull and using pins to model the thickness of the muscle tissue, then filling in the muscle tissue using clay and thus reconstruct the facial surface [26]

In this survey, we review existing literature on forensic face recognition. There are relatively few papers focusing on the forensic application of face recognition as most effort is put into the improvement of the technology itself. However, as the performance of face recognition systems improves the demand for application in the forensic domain also increases and, hence, there is a great need for integration of the technology with the legal system and a uniform framework for application of face recognition technology in forensics.

The remainder of the chapter is organised as follows: in section 2, the techniques and methodologies used by forensic examiners for the purpose of facial comparison are discussed. Section 3 presents a literature review of forensic face recognition. In section 4 we discuss the Bayesian framework and how it can be applied to forensic face recognition. Section 5 discusses reliability and court admissibility issues associated with forensic facial recognition. Section 6 presents conclusions.

2. Forensic Facial Identification

Facial identification refers to manual examination of two face images or a live subject and a facial image to determine whether they are of the same person or not. Facial identification methods generally can be classified into the following four categories:

1. *Holistic Comparison*: In this approach faces are compared by considering the whole face at once.
2. *Morphological Analysis*: In this approach individual features of the face are compared and classified.
3. *Photo-anthropometry*: This approach (sometimes referred to as photogrammetry) is based on the spatial measurements of facial features as well as distances and angles between facial landmarks.
4. *Superimposition*: In this approach, a properly scaled version of one image is overlaid onto another. The two images must be taken from the same angle.

The choice of a specific approach is usually dependent on the face images to be compared and generally combinations of these methods are applied to reach a conclusion. Apart from the above described general categorisation of facial comparison approaches, currently there are no standard procedures and agreed upon guidelines among forensic researchers. The process is very subjective and the opinion of one forensic examiner may vary from those of others.

2.1. Working groups

There are several working groups active in this area the aim of which is to standardise the procedure of forensic facial comparison as well as the proper training of facial comparison experts. One of the best efforts towards developing standards and guidelines for forensic facial identification is currently carried out by the Facial Identification Scientific Working Group (FISWG) [2]. It works under the Federal Bureau of Investigation (FBI) Biometric Center of Excellence (BCOE). FISWG is focusing exclusively on facial identification and developing consensus, standards, guidelines, and best practices for facial comparison. Currently they have developed drafts of several useful documents in this regard which include a description of facial comparison, a facial identification practitioner code of ethics and guidelines for training experts to perform facial comparison. These documents are available for public review and comments [2]. Some other working groups active in developing standards and guidelines for forensic facial comparison include the International Association for Identification [4] and the European Network of Forensic Science Institutes (ENFSI) [1]. The standardisation of the process of facial comparison and specific guidelines which are agreed upon by forensic community is, however, still a largely unsolved problem.

2.2. Manual facial comparison by the forensic expert

In this section we briefly review the forensic experts' way of facial comparison. The discussion is based on the guidelines set forward by the workgroup on face comparison at the Netherlands Forensic Institute (NFI) [5, 13] which is a member of ENSFI [27]. The facial comparison is based on morphological-anthropological features. If possible, for comparison images are used with faces depicted at the same size and with the same pose. The comparison mainly focuses on:

- Relative distances between different relevant features
- Contours of cheek- and chin-lines
- Shape of mouth, eyes, nose, ears etc.
- Lines, moles, wrinkles, scars etc. in the face

When comparing facial images manually, it should be noted that differences may be invisible due to underexposure, overexposure, low resolution, out-of-focus and distortions in the imaging process. On the other hand, due to similar limitations in the image formation process (low resolution, difference in focus and positions of the cameras used to record the images relative to the head and other distortions in the imaging process) may lead to different appearance of similar features in the facial images to compare. Due to the aforementioned effects, which complicate the comparison process, the anthropological facial features are visually compared and classified as: *similar in details*, *similar*, *no observation*, *different* and *different in details*. Apparent similarities and differences are further evaluated by classifying features as: *weakly discriminating*, *moderately discriminating*, and *strongly discriminating*. The conclusion based on the comparison process is a in the form of a measure of support for either of the hypotheses (images show faces of the same person vs. images show faces of different persons) and can be stated as: *no support*, *limited support*, *moderate support*, *strong support* and *very strong support* . The process is subjective and often different experts reach different conclusions. There is a great need to standardise the process. Use of automatic face recognition systems will considerably improve the speed and objectiveness of facial comparison and may also be helpful in standardising the comparison process.

3. Literature Overview

In this section we briefly review existing literature on forensic face recognition. This review focuses on work discussing forensic aspects rather than on work describing techniques for biometric face recognition. Surveys on the latter subject can be found in [28, 19].

3.1. Forensic biometrics from images and videos at the FBI

Forensic Biometrics from Images and Videos at the Federal Bureau of Investigation (FBI) is described in [20]. The paper gives a description of FBI's Forensic Audio, Video and Image Analysis Unit (FAVIAU) and the forensic recognition activities that they perform. Many of these activities are performed manually. Types of manual tasks include voice comparison, facial comparison, height determination, and other side by side image comparisons. Two types of examinations that involve biometrics are photographic comparisons and photogrammetry [7]. Currently, in both cases, the forensic examinations are performed manually. Photographic comparison means a one-to-one comparison of a trace facial image to facial images from suspects. The characteristics used in photographic comparison can be categorised into class and individual characteristics [24]. Class characteristics such as hair colour, overall facial shape, presence of facial hair, shape of the nose, presence of freckles, etc. place an individual within a class or group. Individual characteristics such as the number of and locations of freckles and scars, tattoos, the number of and positions of wrinkles etc. are unique to an individual and can be used to individualise a person. Photogrammetry [7] determines spatial measurements of objects using photographic images. It is used to determine e.g. the height of a subject or the length of a weapon used in a crime. In [20] several current and past research projects in the field of forensic recognition are discussed and also directions for future research on forensic recognition are proposed.

3.2. Facial comparison by experts

In [21] the need for facial comparison experts, their role in biometric face recognition development and their training are described. The paper describes the need for facial comparison experts to verify the results of future automatic forensic face recognition systems. It emphasises the systematic training of experts who will be working with these systems. For any future application of an automated face recognition system, the ultimate judgment will be the manual verification of the outcome of the system. Because the implications of an incorrect decision are severe the verification of the outcome of an automated system by an expert is very important. In case of fingerprint technology, there are many experts available working in association with the automated process. Compared to fingerprint technology, forensic application of face recognition is still immature and, therefore, requires even more this manual verification of the results by experts. This means in the near future more experts will have to be trained in order to use automatic face recognition systems. Comparison of images taken under controlled conditions such as passport photos or photos for arrest records requires less expertise compared to images taken under uncontrolled conditions such as snapshots and images from surveillance cameras. The experts also need training in legal issues because they will be working in the judicial system and will present their conclusions in court. The facial image examiners should be trained in three main areas:

1. General background on facial recognition approaches, which includes the history of person identification, current methods in biometrics, underlying principles of photographic comparison [24] and basic knowledge of image formation and processing.
2. Specific knowledge regarding the properties of the face such as the aging process,

temporary changes (e.g., makeup and hair change), permanent changes (e.g. formation of scars, loss of hair, cosmetic or plastic surgery), structure of bones and muscles, facial expressions and the involved muscle groups and comparison of ears and iris.

3. Understanding of the judicial system, awareness of the implications of a testimony, admissibility issues of facial comparison in court, presentation of facial comparison results and processes in court and to laymen.

3.3. Forensic individualisation from biometric data

In [14] basic concepts of forensic science are reviewed. Also a general forensic face recognition framework is proposed based on the Bayesian likelihood ratio approach. Although this work is a comprehensive review of forensic concepts and provides a general description of the system, there is no experimental work described to prove the effectiveness of the proposed framework.

In forensic literature there is confusion between the terms identification and individualisation. If the class of individual entities is determined to be the source, it is called identification or classification. If a particular individual is determined to be the source, it is called individualisation. In the former case, the identity is called *qualitative identity* while in the later case the identity is called *numerical identity*.

In forensic science, the individualisation process is usually considered as a process of rigorous deductive reasoning, as a syllogism constituted of a major premise, a minor premise, and a conclusion. The major premise here in forensic face recognition context is the general principle of uniqueness applied to the source face and trace face. However, it is based on inductive reasoning which cannot be considered as a form of rigorous reasoning, because what is true for one instance is not necessarily true for all. While the demarcation criteria of empirical falsifiability reject the uniqueness of properties used for individualisation from face, this does not imply that face recognition cannot be used in forensic individualisation. It rather just puts a limit on the reliability depending on the quality of the images and method used.

To describe the likelihood ratio approach based on the Bayes theorem, two mutually exclusive hypotheses, the prosecution hypothesis (H_p) and defence hypothesis (H_d), can be defined as the set of all possible hypotheses for the inference of the identity of the source of a trace. Let I represent the background information about the case at hand and E the evidence. The likelihood ratio approach requires computation of E, *between-source variability* (BSV) and *within-source variability* (WSV). Fig.1 and 2 show how to incorporate the likelihood ratio approach into forensic individualisation as described in [14]. A more detailed description of the Bayesian framework and its application to forensic face recognition is presented in section 4.

3.4. Automatic forensic face recognition from digital images

Automatic forensic face recognition from digital images is addressed in [16]. This paper describes small scale experimental work carried out by the Forensic Science Service in the UK, exploring the performance of an existing automatic face recognition system [3] in the forensic domain. The paper investigates the application of the Bayesian framework

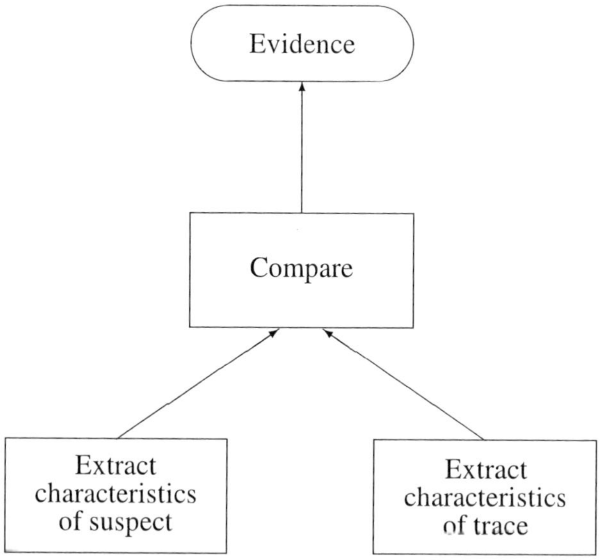

Figure 1. Obtaining evidence in the Bayesian framework.

for forensic facial comparison and decision making. Experiments are carried out using the Image Metrics OptasiaTM [3] software package for face recognition.

The approach of the Image Metrics OptasiaTM software used for experiments is straightforward. Active shape and appearance models [22], based on a general dataset of faces, are fitted to a new facial image. The fitted model consists of local information around landmark points in the facial image and forms a face template. To compare two faces, the similarity of the two face templates is determined. In [16] the similarity is expressed in a percentage (0-100%) and is called *recognition probability*. Given a database of n facial images, then a query image results in n recognition probabilities. Query images of persons included in the database are presented to the system and for each query image all n similarity scores are computed. The authors carried out three tests for evaluation of the system.

In the first test they used the same images as those in the database for benchmarking to get an idea of the the maximum performance of the technique. Twenty pictures chosen at random from the database were used as query images and a similarity score of greater than 95% was obtained for the correct match for each of the query images. The recognition probability sharply drops after the nearest match.

The second test was a feasibility test. For five persons in the database, new images, not present in the database, were obtained and captured exhibiting variation in pose, illumination, age, facial expression, resolution and image quality and used as query images to the system. In this experiment, illumination turned out to have the strongest effect on

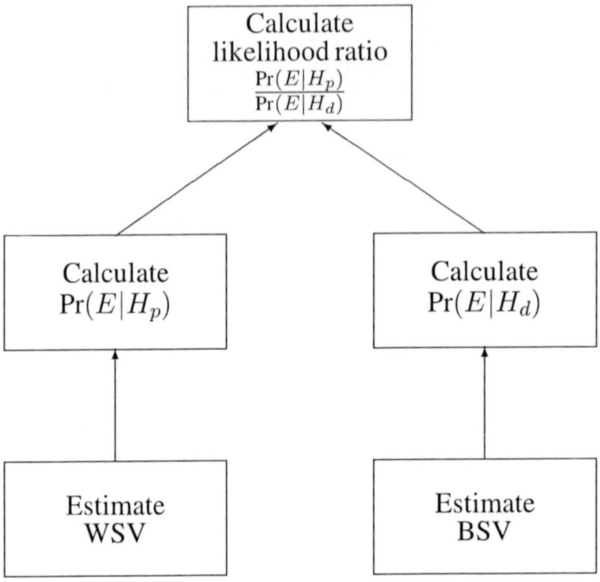

Figure 2. Using the evidence to calculate the likelihood ratio.

the recognition probability. The other variations had smaller but significant effects on the recognition probability.

Finally, for evaluation testing, the applicability to the forensic framework was investigated. To be able to calculate likelihoods, the WSV and BSV are needed. Five people of whom images were present in the database were photographed under similar conditions as those used to record images for the database in order to estimate the WSV and the BSV of the database. Of each person 10 images were recorded, resulting in a set Q if 50 images. From this set Q, the WSV for each person was determined from the matching scores resulting from comparing the templates of the person to the template of the same person in the database. The BSV was obtained by matching all images in the set Q to all images in the database. Using the WSV and BSV, the likelihood ratio for a matching score can be calculated. For the set Q in 58% of the cases the comparison to the correct person in the database resulted in the highest likelihood.

The evaluation test provides a small scale, very limited assessment of the expected value or performance of the system in the forensics domain. There is no discussion on how the population size may influence the results.

3.5. Face matching and retrieval using soft biometrics

Although it does not directly focus on the forensic aspects of face recognition, the techniques and methodology proposed in [15] seem very attractive for forensic application of face recognition. Soft biometrics (ethnicity, gender and facial marks), if combined with a traditional face recognition system such as [23, 10] can improve the recognition accuracy as well as the ease of use and interpretation of the outcome in the forensic domain.

In [15] first facial landmarks are detected using an Active Appearance Model (AAM) [22]. Using these landmarks primary facial features are extracted and excluded in the subsequent facial marks detection process. First the face image is mapped to a mean facial shape to simplify the subsequent processing. The Laplacian of Gaussian (LoG) operator is utilised to detect facial marks. Each detected facial mark is classified in a hierarchical fashion as linear vs. not linear and circular vs. irregular. Furthermore, each mark is also classified based on its morphology as dark vs. light. In this way, each of the facial marks can be classified as a mole, freckle, scar etc.

Although the demonstrated performance of the proposed approach, using facial marks detection is not robust, facial marks nevertheless give a more descriptive representation of facial recognition accuracy compared to the numerical values obtained from traditional face recognition systems. This representation may be particularly useful in forensic applications. In such an approach semantic based queries can be issued to retrieve a particular image from a database. Furthermore, the facial marks can be used for facial comparison of partly occluded faces, which are quite common for surveillance cameras, and may even allow differentiation of identical twins. In [15] experimental results are presented, based on the FERET [17] database and a mug-shot database that show that using the soft biometrics in combination with existing face recognition technology can improve the overall performance of the system and is more useful to forensic applications.

4. A Bayesian Framework for Forensic Face Recognition

The aim of a forensic biometric system is to report a meaningful value or expression in court to assess the strength of forensic evidence. The output of a biometric system cannot be used directly in forensic applications as discussed in detail in literature on forensic speaker recognition [9, 12, 6]. Systems using a simple threshold to decide between two classes resulting in a binary decision are not acceptable in the forensic domain [6]. For the purpose of forensic applications, the likelihood ratio framework is agreed upon as a standard way to report evidential value of a biometric system. This framework has been discussed in detail in the speaker recognition domain [9, 12] and the theory presented here benefits from it However, unlike for forensic speaker recognition, there are very few published works which focus on the forensic aspects of face recognition and there is a serious need for reliable facial comparison and recognition systems which can assist law enforcement agencies in investigation and can be used in courts.

The Bayesian framework is a logical approach and can be applied to any biometric system without change in the underlying theory. The likelihood ratio (LR) assessed from a score based biometric system can be used directly in court. While in commercial biometric systems, the objective is to present a score or decisions in a binary form, in forensic applications, the objective is to find the degree of support for one hypothesis against the other. Using the Bayes theorem, given the prior probabilities, the posterior probabilities can be calculated as:

$$\Pr(H_p|E,I) = \Pr(E|H_p,I)\Pr(H_p|I) \tag{1}$$
$$\Pr(H_d|E,I) = \Pr(E|H_d,I)\Pr(H_d|I) \tag{2}$$

where H_p and H_d are the prosecution and defence hypotheses respectively and E represents forensic information (evidence), while I is background information on the case at hand. The prosecution hypothesis H_p states that the suspect is the source of the trace (in this case a facial image) while the defence hypothesis H_d states that someone else in a relevant population is the source. Equations 1 and 2 give the posterior odds required by judicial systems given the prior odds (background knowledge on the case) and likelihood ratio of the evidence E. The likelihood ratio

$$\text{LR} = \frac{\Pr(E|H_p,I))}{\Pr(E|H_d,I))} \tag{3}$$

gives a measure of degree of support for one hypothesis against the other, taking into consideration the circumstances of the case (background information I), and the result of the analysis of the questioned face. It calculates the conditional probability of observing a particular value of evidence with respect to two competing hypotheses [11]. The numerator of the LR requires the WSV while the denominator requires the BSV to be calculated. This calculation of the LR from the WSV and BSV for a given matching score or evidence E is illustrated in Figure 3.

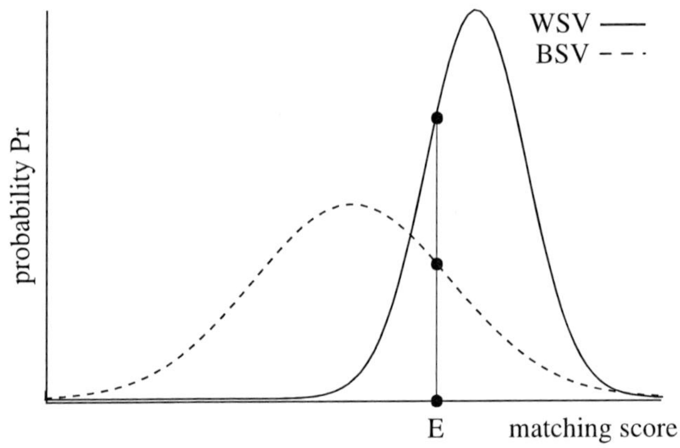

Figure 3. Calculation of the LR from the WSV and the BSV. The solid curve represents the WSV or $\Pr(E|H_p,I)$ and the dashed curve the BSV or $\Pr(E|H_d,I)$. If a trace results in a matching score or evidence E, the LR is obtained by dividing the values of $\Pr(E|H_p,I)$ by $\Pr(E|H_d,I)$. Here the LR would be about 2.

The task of a forensic scientist is to evaluate the LR which is then used by the judicial system to reach a conclusion. In order to use a score based biometric face recognition system, in order to calculate the LR we thus need the following:

- The evidence E, a score obtained by comparing a trace face and a suspect face.

- A distribution of matching scores obtained by comparing facial images of the suspect taken under similar conditions to that of suspect facial image (control database): the within-source variability (WSV). The WSV is then used to estimate the numerator,$\Pr(E|H_p, I)$ of the likelihood ratio.

- A distribution of matching scores obtained by comparing facial images of a relevant population taken under similar conditions as that of the suspect facial image (relevant population database): the between-source variability (BSV). The BSV is then used to estimate the denominator, $\Pr(E|H_d, I)$ of the likelihood ratio.

Figure 4 illustrates the complete procedure.

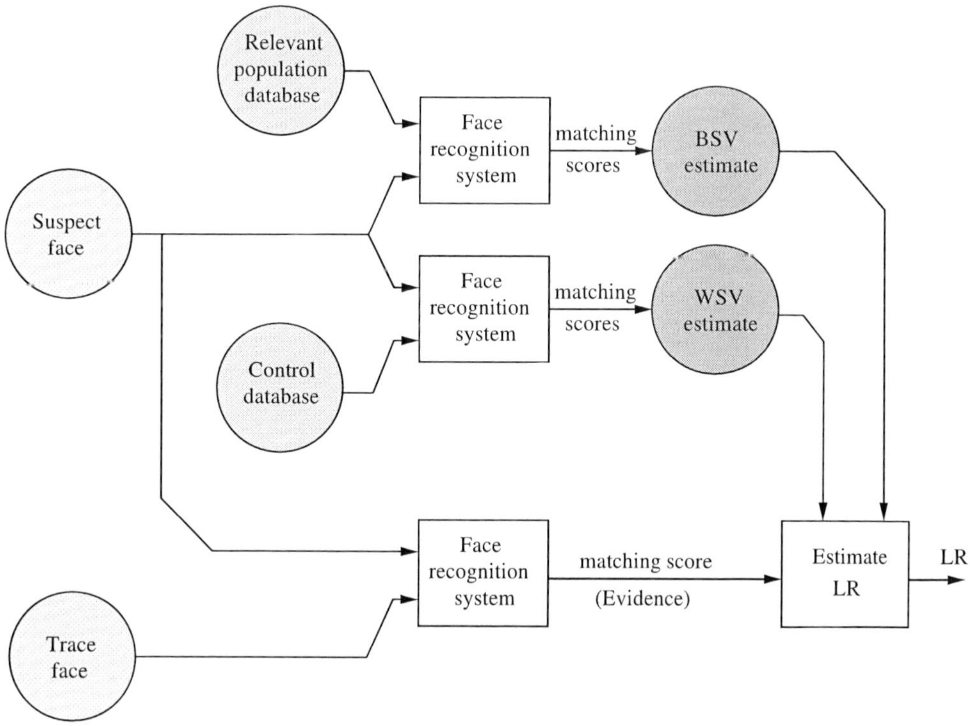

Figure 4. Estimation of the LR. First the WSV and BSV are estimated using a Control database and a Relevant population database with images recorded under the same circumstances as the suspect facial image. Then the LR can be computed by comparing the trace facial image with the suspect facial image and using the WSV and BSV.

5. Reliability and Court Admissibility Issues

The reliability of forensic face recognition is more critical compared to biometric face recognition where an incorrect decision at most results in e.g. a denial of access for a person to a building or a login restriction, the consequences of which are usually not very serious. In the forensic case, however, the consequences are far more severe as an incorrect decision can convict a person as a criminal while he is innocent. While it is agreed upon that future application of automatic facial recognition systems must be assisted by human experts for the final verification [21], the reliability of these systems themselves is also very important as it will reduce manual efforts and help standardise the process of facial comparison. In order to assess the reliability of forensic face recognition systems, several factors such as lighting conditions, facial expressions and pose etc., which are widely explored in the biometric domain should be considered here as well. If the Bayesian framework is used, other factors such as the number of images used to compute the BSV and WSV must also be taken into consideration. Apart from the sizes of the databases, it should also be ensured that the databases sufficiently cover the variations in imaging conditions (such as lighting conditions, image quality etc.) and facial appearance (such as pose, facial expressions etc). The Bayesian framework is the most logical framework, however it is sensitive to the methods used to determine the BSV and WSV. In particular, the distribution of H_p and H_d scores are probability density functions and their estimation is sensitive to the underlying mathematical model chosen. Therefore, a different modelling method can easily lead to different likelihood ratio values.

As a general rule, in order for the evidence extracted from forensic face recognition to be admissible in a court of law, the employed technology must be thoroughly tested and evaluated. In the United States this was ensured by application of the "Frye rule". It states that the judges should be acting as "gatekeeper" to asses if the technology on which the evidence is based is generally accepted in a relevant scientific community or not. Nowadays, in the United States, mostly a revised version of Frye rule called "Daubert" is in practice. It ensures that, in addition to general acceptance of the technology, the employed technology is tested and can be challenged in some objective way, the technology or theory must be peer-reviewed and a description of the error rate of the technology must be available. Finally, the technology must be maintained and adhere to standards.

In the European judicial system, there is no specific admissibility rule described regarding the scientific evidence. The judges are responsible for the evaluation of the scientific evidence pertaining to the case at hand.

6. Conclusion

At the moment there are no generally accepted standards for facial comparison by human forensic experts. However, several working groups are working on documents for standardisation and training.

Although much research and effort is put into improving state-of-the-art face recognition systems performance, far less effort is devoted to integrating face recognition technology with the legal system of court and justice. Only few papers have been published on the subject of how automatic face recognition can be adopted to forensic purposes. The output of a biometric face recognition system is not suitable for use in forensic applications and the output of a conventional score based biometric system must be processed in order to render it more useful and acceptable by the court.

Although the likelihood ratio value is subjective since it depends on the databases used for the estimation of the WSV and BSV and the underlying mathematical model of their distribution, it still provides the most logical framework for the judicial system to incorporate biometric evidence and background information on the case to reach a conclusion.

There is an urgent need for "tuning" and integration of face recognition systems or development of new systems which can fulfil the requirements of law enforcement agencies and legal systems of court and justice.

References

[1] European network of forensic science institutes, http://www.enfsi.eu/.

[2] Facial identification scientific working group, http://www.fiswg.org/.

[3] Image Metrics OptasiaTM operating instructions, 2002, www.image-metrics.com.

[4] International association for identification, http://www.theiai.org/.

[5] Netherlands forensic institute (nfi), http://www.forensicinstitute.nl/.

[6] C.G.G. Aitken. *Statistics and evaluation of evidence for forensic scientists.* John Wiley & Sons, 1997.

[7] D. Alspaugh. *A brief history of photogrammetry*, pages 1–14. 2004.

[8] M. Y. Aulsebrook, W. A. Iscan, and J. H. Slabbert. Superimposition and reconstruction in forensic facial identification: a survey. *Forensic Science International*, 75:101–102, 1995.

[9] C. Champod and D. Meuwly. The inference of identity in forensic speaker recognition. *Speech Communication*, 31:193–203, 2000.

[10] http://www.cognitec-systems.de Cognitec Systems GmbH. Facevacs software developer kit.

[11] F.i. Botti et al. An interpretation framework for the evaluation of evidence in forensic automatic speaker recognition with limited suspect data. In *Proc. ODYSSEY*, pages 63–68, 2004.

[12] J. Gonzalez-Rodriguez, J. Fierrez-Aguilar, and J. Ortega-Garcia. Forensic identification reporting using automatic speaker recognition systems. In *Proc. ICASSP*, 2003.

[13] Netherlands Forensic Institute. General method of facial comparison. addendum #:1. internal document.

[14] D. Meuwly. Forensic individualization from biometric data. *Science & Justice*, pages 205–213, 2006.

[15] U. Park and A. K. Jain. Face matching and retrieval using soft biometrics. *IEEE Transactions on Information Forensic and Security (TIFS)*, pages 406–415, 2010.

[16] C. Peacock, A. Goode, and A. Brett. Automatic forensic face recognition from digital images. *Science & Justice*, pages 29–34, 2004.

[17] J. Phillips, H. Wechsler, J. S. Huang, and P.J. Rauss. The Feret database and evaluation procedure for face recognition algorithms. *Image and Vision Computing*, pages 295–306, 1998.

[18] P. J. Phillips, W. T. Scruggs, A. J. OToole, P. J. Flynn, K. W. Bowyer, C. L. Schott, and M. Sharpe. FRVT 2006 and ICE 2006 large-scale results. *IEEE Transactions on PAMI*, 2010.

[19] A. Samal and P. A. Iyengar. Automatic recognition and analysis of human faces and facial expressions: A survey. *Pattern Recognition*, page 6577, 1992.

[20] N. A. Spaun. Forensic biometrics from images and video at the federal bureau of investigation. In *Proc. BTAS*, pages 1–3, 2007.

[21] N. A. Spaun. Facial comparisons by subject matter experts: Their role in biometrics and their training. In *Proc. ICB*, pages 161–168, 2009.

[22] Cootes T.F., Edwards G.J., and Taylor C.J. Active appearance models. *IEEE Transactions on PAMI*, pages 681–685, 2001.

[23] M. Turk and A. Pentland. Eigenfaces for recognition. *Journal of Cognitive Neuroscience*, pages 71–86, 1991.

[24] H. Tuthill and G. George. *Individualization: Principles and Procedures in Criminalistics, 2nd Ed.* Lightning Powder Company, Inc., Jacksonville, FL, 2002.

[25] F. Wang, J. Wang, C. Zhang, and J. T. Kwok. Face recognition using spectral features. *Pattern Recognition*, pages 2786–2797, 2007.

[26] C.M. Wilkinson and R.A.H. Neave. Skull re-assembly and the implications for forensic facial reconstruction. *Science & Justice*, 41(3):233–234, 2001.

[27] L. Wiskott, J.-M. Fellous, N. Kruger, , and C. von der Malsburg. Face recognition by elastic bunch graph matching. *IEEE Transactions on PAMI*, pages 775–779, 1997.

[28] W. Zhao, R. Chellappa, P. J. Phillips, and A. Rosenfeld. Face recognition: A literature survey. *ACM Computing Surveys*, pages 399–458, 2003.

In: Face Recognition
Editors: Adamo Quaglia and Calogera M. Epifano
ISBN 978-1-61942-663-4

Chapter 11

CORRELATION AND INDEPENDENT COMPONENT ANALYSIS BASED APPROACHES FOR BIOMETRIC RECOGNITION

P. Katz[1], A. Alfalou[1], C. Brosseau[2] and M. S. Alam[3]
[1] ISEN Brest, L@bISEN, France
[2] Université Européenne de Bretagne, Université de Brest, France
[3] Department of Electrical and Computer Engineering, University of South Alabama, US

ABSTRACT

Independent component analysis (ICA) models, describing a given signal as a linear combination of various independent sources, have proven to be a fruitful endeavor. One prominent example deals with audio applications in order to separate the speaker's voice from environmental noises disturbing it. However, very few ICA based systems are available for biometric encryption applications. For that specific purpose, the ICA method can be easily adapted to add noise to a target image in order to encrypt it. In this chapter, at first, we discuss biometric recognition systems based on the ICA and correlation approaches. Next, we explore an ICA-based algorithm for face recognition. Basically, it consists of building a base of independent components using a learning database that contains several chosen reference images. Then, the target image (image to be recognized) is projected on the independent component base, and the similarity between the target image and each of the reference images is studied. Discrimination tests between the proposed technique and alternate methods are conducted by using the Pointing Head Pose Image Database (PHPID). In this chapter we report some of the recent developments dealing with the ICA method for face recognition applications. As part of our analysis, we precisely determine a set of metrics aimed at better understanding the role of the number and choice of the reference images on the performance of the proposed technique.

INTRODUCTION

Over the last two decades tremendous advances has been made in face recognition techniques. This interest partly stems from potential applications in many diverse fields such as identification of wanted people in public areas, automation of passport registration at airports, and nonintrusive monitoring of activities of daily living, especially for the elderly [1]. Much progress has been made in the realm of face recognition techniques. A number of techniques can be employed based on optical correlation such as VanderLugt correlation (VLC), or on numerical methods such as eigenfaces [2], wavelets [3], principal component analysis (PCA) [4], and independent component analysis (ICA) [5]. Overall, ICA and PCA are versatile techniques allowing us to decompose any arbitrary image or signal into a linear combination of independent variables. The main difference between ICA and PCA arises from the fact that the former leads to independent images while the latter deals with uncorrelated images. This is an important issue in face recognition [6]. Assessing the performance of recognition techniques by relevant metrics is essential for understanding the advantages and limitations of these techniques.

In this chapter we report some of the recent developments dealing with the ICA method for face recognition applications. On the one hand, we consider a hybrid technique using ICA and correlation methods that was proposed recently by some of the authors [6]. On the other hand, a method based on ICA solely is investigated. Our main goal is to evaluate the receiver operating characteristic (ROC) [7] for characterizing the performances and limitations of this technique. Emphasis has been placed on the optical correlation methods using composite and segmented phase only filters (POFs) [8] and detection criteria of the correlation peak. In order to compare the performances of both methods, we report an extensive series of simulations aimed at better understanding the role of the number and choice of the reference images, and the pre-processing of the target images. Most importantly, the real power of the new method presented here is its high discrimination level for face recognition applications.

GENERALITIES

We start by discussing two standard approaches for face recognition approaches. The first method is based on VLC [9]. Single correlation, i.e. classical matched filter, POF, and multicorrelation, i.e. composite and segmented composite filters, approaches are considered [8]. Several correlation criteria are defined along with a performance metric of a classifier, i.e. the ROC [7]. Another hybrid method based on optical correlation and ICA will be introduced [8]. The method is designed to take advantage of the robustness of ICA and the discrimination of optical correlation.

VLC Technique for Face Recognition

VLC technique is based on the multiplication of the target image spectrum (image to be recognized) with a correlation filter H, fabricated with a reference image, as shown schematically in Figure 1.

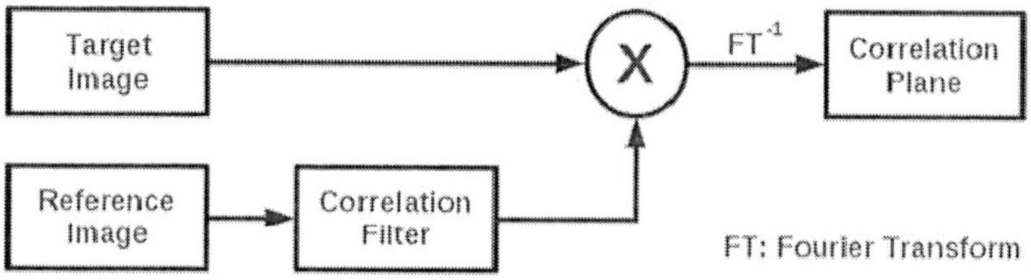

Figure. 1 Schematic diagram of the VLC method.

The scene containing the object to be recognized, called the input plane is multiplied by the correlation filter after applying the Fourier transform (FT) operation. Remarkably, the result obtained by applying the inverse Fourier transformation (FT-1) shows a central correlation peak (close to a two-dimensional sine cardinal), which is more or less narrow and intense depending on the resemblance between the target and reference images. The main advantage of this technique is that it can be easily implemented optically. Different filters have been designed for the purpose of increasing the discrimination and robustness of the VLC, originally based on the classical matched filter (CMF) [9]. For example, POFs have been largely explored by the image processing community since the early 1960s. Since, other methods were proposed to deal with multicorrelation [8]. That is to compare a target image with a set of reference images in order to be able to recognize a given subject for every position in space and face expression. The transfer function of the CMF takes the form

$$H_{CMF}(u,v) = \frac{\alpha S_{R_1}^{*}(u,v)}{N(u,v)}, \tag{1}$$

where $S_{R_1}^{*}$ corresponds to the reference image spectrum, N is the spectral density of the noise, and α is a constant. This filter is robust but cannot be used in practice since it is not discriminating.

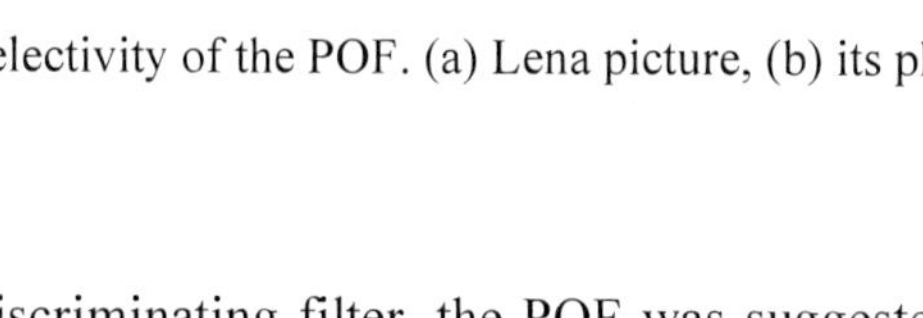

Figure 2. Illustrating phase selectivity of the POF. (a) Lena picture, (b) its phase representation.

Phase Only Filter

To provide a better discriminating filter, the POF was suggested [8]. The choice of this filter is based on the fact that the phase of a spectrum contains the necessary information to reconstruct the target image [10]. Hence, the spectrum amplitude which displays a fast dynamics but contains little information is unnecessary. To provide a better appreciation for this important property, an example of image is shown in Fig 2, with the original image (Figure 2a) and its phase (Figure 2b). The most distinct feature in Figure 2b is that it contains the information on the contours of the image. This allows us to get much more discriminating filters than the adapted filter.

The POF's transfer function reads as

$$H_{POF}(u,v) = \frac{S_{R_1}^*(u,v)}{\left|S_{R_1}(u,v)\right|}. \tag{2}$$

In contrast with CMF, POF leads to a very narrow correlation peak. This leads to a more discriminating filter with low robustness due to the strong sensitivity to image variations.

Composite Filter

In an attempt to overcome the shortcomings of CMF and POF, multicorrelation analysis was introduced. Its basic principle, shown in the diagram of Figure 3, is to fabricate a filter with several reference images, e.g. to deal with several face orientations. This permits to decrease the necessary number of correlations, and consequently the computation cost.

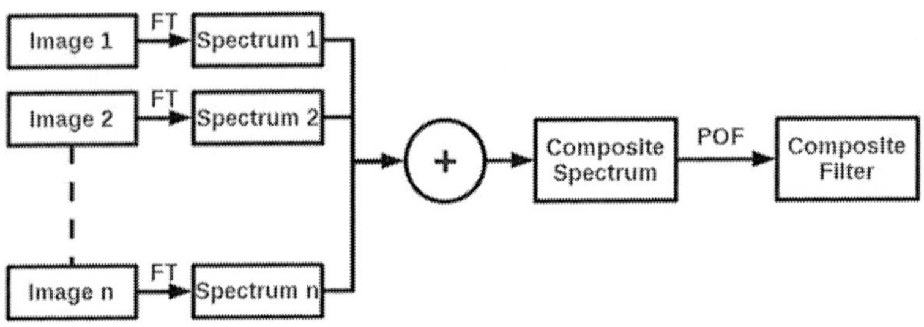

Figure 3. Schematic diagram of the composite filter.

The composite filter is simply a linear combination of the n reference images. Its transfer function is

$$H_{COMP} = \sum_{i}^{n} a_i R_i, \tag{3}$$

where a_i is a weight coefficient. One advantage of this filter is that the correlation peaks of the reference images are additive, rendering it more robust to the rotation effects of the target image, allowing subject identification thanks to a larger face area analysis. However, it can lead to a saturation of the correlation plane when one considers too many reference images or when these images have high energy [11].

Segmented Composite Filter

The segmented composite filter, shown in Figure 4, can be used to deal with the correlation plane saturation of the composite filter. The segmentation of the Fourier plane is realized by assigning each pixel according a specific segmentation criterion, e.g. its energy, its spectrum gradient, its phase gradient, or its real part.

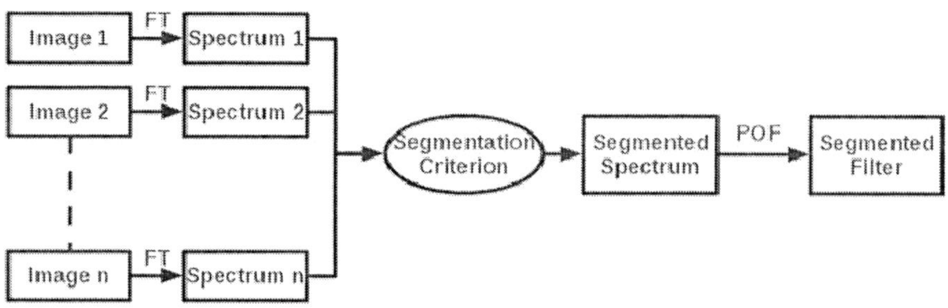

Figure. 4 Schematic diagram of the segmented composite filter.

The choice on the pixel is done according the inequality

$$a_i Crit^i_{(u,v)} \leq a_j Crit^j_{(u,v)} \ \forall j \in [\![1, n]\!] \ and \ j \neq i. \tag{4}$$

where $Crit^i_{(u,v)}$ corresponds to the segmentation criterion of the Fourier plane. For example, if one uses the image energy as segmentation criterion, the relative energy of each pixel after Fourier transforming each reference image is compared with the other images of the reference base. The resulting spectrum considers the high energy components of the base for each pixel. This filter, obtained after selection of the phase of the segmented image, allows us to use multicorrelation for a large set of reference images while avoiding the saturation of the Fourier plane.

Detection Criteria

Before turning to the presentation of face recognition methods, we discuss important prerequisite for a useful detection scheme.

Correlation Peak Detection Criteria

The comparison of the different algorithms used for implementing VLC [9] requires some useful ways to quantify and assess the correlation performances. We first offer a general discussion of the different metrics encountered in the literature for characterization of the correlation peak, e.g. signal-to-noise ratio (SNR), peak-to-correlation energy (PCE) [12], and their variants PCE' and PCE'' [13].

The SNR, and its counterpart expressed in dB, SNR_{dB}, are commonly employed metrics in signal processing. The simple definition of SNR is

$$SNR = \frac{Signal\ Power}{Noise\ Power} = \frac{C(Peak)}{\sqrt{\sum_{u=0}^{W}\sum_{v=0}^{H}|C_n(u,v)|^2}}, \tag{5}$$

where $C(Peak)$ is the maximal value of energy, (Peak denoting the coordinates of the correlation peak), $\sum_{u=0}^{W}\sum_{v=0}^{H} C_n(u,v) = \sum_{u=0}^{W}\sum_{v=0}^{H} C(u,v) - C(Peak)$ denotes the noise, i.e. the entire correlation plane $C(u,v)$ except the correlation peak, while W and H characterize the size of the Fourier plane. The SNR_{dB} reads as

$$SNR_{dB} = 10\log_{10}(SNR). \tag{6}$$

Concurrently, there are numerous efforts to develop other metrics to probe and understand the correlation performances. For example, PCE is defined as the energy of the correlation peak normalized to the overall energy of the correlation plane [13]. The explicit definition follows a variant of the metric suggested by Dickey and Romero [14] :

$$PCE = \frac{\sum_{u=0}^{W} E_{Peak}(u,v)}{\sum_{u=0}^{W}\sum_{v=0}^{H} E_{Correlation\ \ Plane}(u,v)} = \frac{C(Peak)^2}{\sum_{u=0}^{W}\sum_{v=0}^{H} C(u,v)^2}, \tag{7}$$

where E_{Peak} and $E_{Correlation}$ denote respectively the energy of the correlation peak and of the correlation plane. Consequences of Eq. (7) are as follows. The energy of an intense correlation peak is much larger than the energy of the correlation plane. Hence, the value of the PCE will be large. In contrast, a wide correlation peak has a PCE value close to 0. It is worth observing that the correlation plane can have secondary peaks, which are not important in case of strong correlation, but which generate false alarms when the peak is not intense.

Two other convenient parameterizations to quantify and assess face recognition performances, i.e. PCE' and PCE'', were suggested by Horner [13]. The PCE' is chosen as a compromise between SNR and PCE

$$PCE' = \frac{C(Peak)}{\sum_{u=0}^{W}\sum_{v=0}^{H}|C_n(u,v)|^2}. \tag{8}$$

The PCE" is defined as

$$PCE'' = \frac{PCE}{1-PCE}. \tag{9}$$

Receiver Operating Characteristic

We next focus on the ROC representation. In practical calculations, face recognition can be modeled as a two-class prediction problem (binary classifier system). Either, the subject is recognized as that chosen for the fabrication of the filter, or it is not recognized. For our purpose, we define the vector $\underline{w}$, also termed the observation vector, composed of n observations $w_1, \cdots, w_n$. The basic idea is to make the best decision from a set of observations according to a criterion $\hat{\theta}(\underline{w})$ which is the best estimate of the parameter θ. We first define $\underline{Y}$ as the vector formed by the ensemble of values taken by the evaluation criterion when the target image corresponds to the reference subject, and $\underline{Z}$ the vector formed in the opposite case. From basic discrete random variable (pi, yi) theory it follows that the expected value of $\underline{Y}$ is given by

$$E[\underline{Y}] = \mu = \sum_{i=1}^{n} p_i y_i = \frac{1}{n}\sum_{i=1}^{n} y_i, \tag{10}$$

and the standard deviation is $\sigma = \sqrt{E[\underline{Y}^2] - E[\underline{Y}]^2}$. When $\underline{Y}$ and $\underline{Z}$ are Gaussian distributed, one posits that $\underline{Y} \sim \mathcal{N}(\mu_Y, \sigma_Y^2)$ and $\underline{Z} \sim \mathcal{N}(\mu_Z, \sigma_Z^2)$ (Figure 5). Four cases can occur: detection, non-detection false alarm, and false non-detection. To evaluate graphically the performance of the classifier, the remaining task is now to determine the ROC curve [7], which is a graphical plot of the true positive rate TPR (called also sensitivity, or probability of true detection) versus false positive rate FPR (called also 1-specificity, or false alarm probability) as its discrimination (detection) threshold is varied. Lets us call H_0 the hypothesis such that the target image is that of subject 0, H_1 is that of subject 1, D_0 that subject 0 is detected, and D_1 that subject 1 is detected. We have

$$FPR = P(D_1|H_0) + P(D_0|H_1) \tag{11}$$

and

$$TPR = P(D_0|H_0) + P(D_1|H_1). \tag{12}$$

Now if we consider that a decision is made by comparing the estimator $\hat{\theta}(\underline{w})$ with a given threshold s [7], i.e.

$$\hat{\theta}(\underline{w}) \underset{\mathrm{H}_{1-\mathrm{i}}}{\overset{\mathrm{H}_\mathrm{i}}{\gtrless}} s, i \in \{0,1\}. \tag{13}$$

we immediately obtain FPR and TPR as

$$FPR = P(\hat{\theta}(\underline{w}) > s|H_1) + P(\hat{\theta}(\underline{w}) < s|H_0)$$

and

$$TPR = P(\hat{\theta}(\underline{w}) > s|H_0) + P(\hat{\theta}(\underline{w}) < s|H_1). \tag{14}$$

In practice, s is varied between 0 and 1. According the values of the estimation $\hat{\theta}(\underline{w})$ and threshold s, the classifier makes a decision, D_0 or D_1, leading to a 2×2 confusion matrix, or contingency table (Table 1).

Finally, we define the false positive (FPR) and true positive (TPR) rates as

$$FPR = \frac{FP}{FP + TP} \text{ and } TPR = \frac{TP}{TP + FN}. \tag{15}$$

The ROC curve is obtained by plotting the FPR versus the TPR for each threshold value s (Figure 6). The perfect classification, corresponding to the case for which the densities of probability of $\underline{X}$ and $\underline{Y}$ have disjoint supports, would yield a point in the upper left corner of the ROC space, i.e. representing 100% sensitivity (no false negatives) and 100% specificity (no false positives).

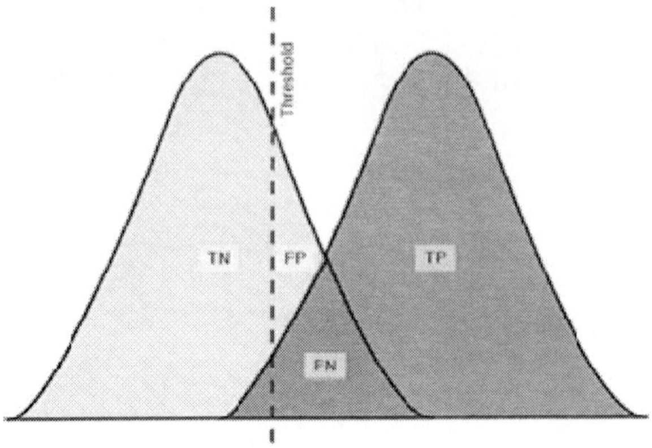

Figure 5. Gaussian curves. TP is the true positive, TN is the true negative, FP is the false positive, and FN is the false negative.

Table 1. Confusion matrix or contingency table

	Positive	Negative
Positive	TP	FP
Negativee	FN	TN

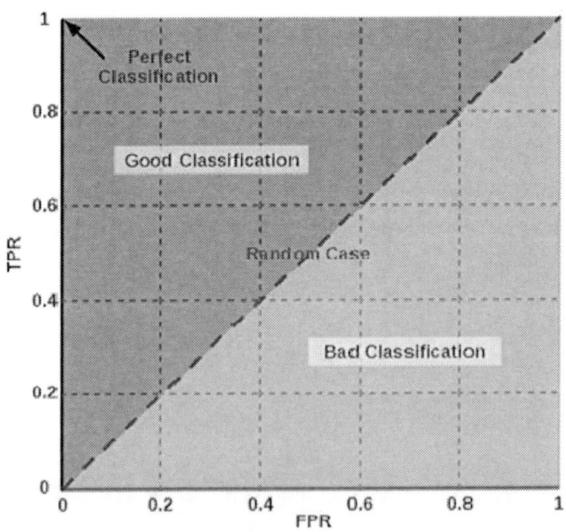

Figure 6. The ROC space.

An important property of this representation is that the diagonal line corresponds to random guess. This diagram discriminates between a region of good classification (points above the diagonal) and a region of poor classification (points below the diagonal). An alternative way for representing the performance of a classifier is to consider the area under curve (AUC) [15]. In the case of a random classification $AUC = 5$ whereas $AUC > 5$ for a good classification.

Robust and Discriminating Method for Face Recognition Based on Correlation Technique and ICA Model

It is well established that optical correlation techniques are very sensitive to face rotation. The segmented composite filter was proposed to deal with this problem but its performance decrease as the number of reference images is increased [11]. To overcome this problem, several computational strategies have been suggested, including ICA [5]. Other fields of research where such ICA-based approaches have been fruitfully applied are acoustics [16], cognitive sciences [17-19], optical encryption [20], and recognition [21-22].

Principle of ICA

In its simplest form, the ICA method predicts, from a set of n observations, $S_1, \cdots, S_n$, statistically independent components $C_1, \cdots, C_n$, such the observations can be represented by a linear combination of the different components. Hence, for the vectors $\underline{S}$ and $\underline{C}$, of dimension n, and A being the coefficient matrix of dimension n^2, the decomposition of $\underline{S}$ reads as

$$\left| \begin{array}{l} s_1 = a_{1,1}c_1 + a_{1,2}c_2 + \cdots + a_{1,n}c_n \\ s_2 = a_{2,1}c_1 + a_{2,2}c_2 + \cdots + a_{2,n}c_n \\ \quad\vdots \\ s_n = a_{n,1}c_1 + a_{n,2}c_2 + \cdots + a_{n,n}c_n \end{array} \right. , \tag{16}$$

with

$$\underline{S} = \begin{pmatrix} s_1 \\ s_2 \\ \vdots \\ s_n \end{pmatrix}, \underline{C} = \begin{pmatrix} C_1 \\ C_2 \\ \vdots \\ C_n \end{pmatrix}, \mathrm{A} = \begin{pmatrix} a_{1,1} & a_{1,2} & \cdots & a_{1,n} \\ a_{2,1} & a_{2,2} & \cdots & a_{2,n} \\ \vdots & \vdots & \ddots & \vdots \\ a_{n,1} & a_{n,2} & \cdots & a_{n,n} \end{pmatrix}, \tag{17}$$

or, can be expressed in the entirely equivalent matrix form

$$\underline{S} = A\underline{C}. \tag{18}$$

The basic objective of this method is to find the linear combination which minimizes the statistical dependence between its components. For that specific purpose, one is searching from the knowledge of $\underline{S}$ the matrix W such $W \times A$ is diagonal.

These components are given by

$$\underline{C} = W\underline{S}. \tag{19}$$

Several algorithms, adapted for ICA, were proposed in the literature, e.g. fastICA [23], using criteria such as kurtosis, negentropy, and minimization of mutual information.

ICA and Correlation Based Method

We now turn our attention to the numerical procedure involving both ICA and VLC [6]. Most interestingly, in this analysis the system still retains the robustness of ICA and the high discrimination of VLCs. The basic principle of this analysis is to recognize a target image by using a set of reference images. The ICA is used as pre-processing stage of the reference base. Image recognition is realized thanks to a simple 1-reference POF. It is worth noting that this method can be implemented optically or numerically.

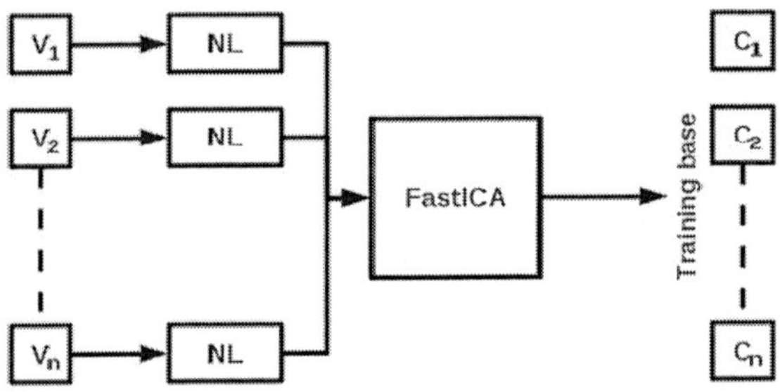

Figure 7. Definition of the independent component learning base.

Our algorithm can be summarized as follows. The first step [6], shown graphically in Figure 7, consists in fabricating a reference base from a learning base of n different images $(V_1, \cdots, V_n)$ of subject X. Here, we used the fastICA algorithm [23]. The use of a specific nonlinear function over the learning base is also necessary to ensure that the algorithm is convergent [20]. The next step consists to correlate each image V_i of the learning base to the different POFs, fabricated from the base of independent components C_j. From these correlation planes, we get

$$PCE_{ij} = f\left(V_i \otimes pof_j\right), \tag{20}$$

where f denotes is a specific function, and pof_j is the inverse FT of the POF fabricated from C_j (Figure 8).

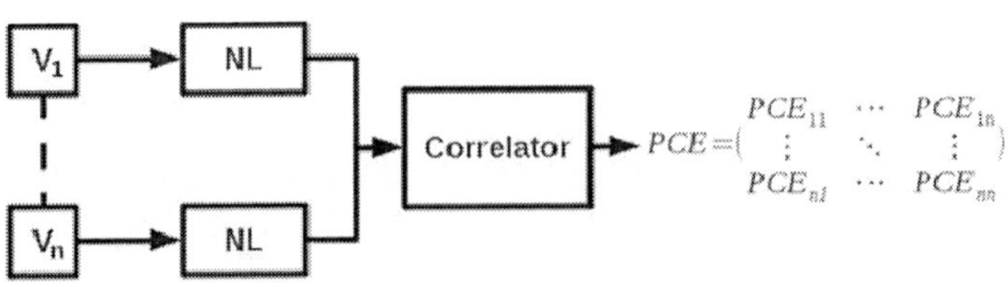

Figure 8. Definition of the PCE matrix.

The last step of the algorithm, displayed in Figure 9 consists of the comparison and recognition of the target image. We consider a target face $V_?$ of a given subject. Next, we decompose it in a linear combination of independent components of the reference base. In a first step, this target image is correlated with every pof_j of the base. Then, we get a vector called Val_{Corr}, such that $Val_{Corr} = (PCE'_1, \cdots, PCE'_n)$, with $PCE'_j = f\left(V_? \otimes pof_j\right)$. Finally, we define the components of the as

$$\varepsilon_i = |PCE'_1 - PCE_{i1}| + |PCE'_2 - PCE_{i2}| + \cdots + |PCE'_n - PCE_{in}|. \tag{21}$$

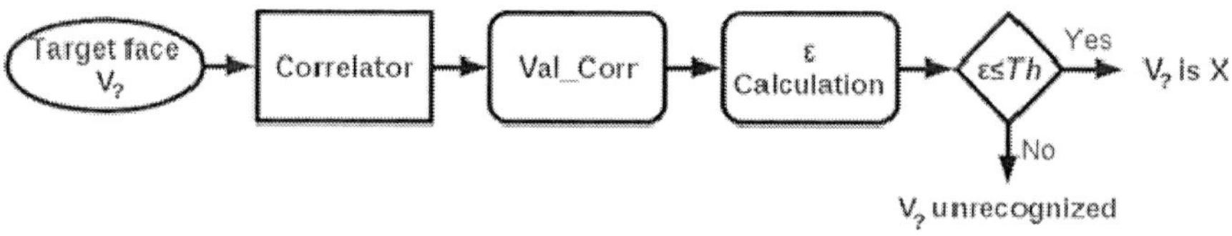

Figure 9. Illustration of the recognition procedure.

Finally, the arithmetic mean ε of the components of the error vector is compared to a given threshold Th. The target image $V_?$ is recognized as arising from subject X when ε is smaller than the threshold and is not recognized otherwise. This technique offers many advantages. Firstly, the architecture is both optically and numerically implementable.

Secondly, it leads to better results than those obtained with a simple composite filter [6], using a simple 1-reference POF, i.e. a single matrix of independent components. Thus, outstanding performances are expected for a multicorrelation implementation.

ICA Based Biometric Recognition

Previously, we have introduced a method allowing us to fabricate an image base of statistically independent references and applied it to an optical correlation technique such as VLC in order to improve the face recognition performances. Now, we consider a purely numerical technique based on ICA which is found to be robust for biometric recognition such as face recognition [24].

Method

Principle

Below we describe in detail one of our pervisoly algorithms [24] which is central to our analysis. Firstly, a learning base of reference images is fabricated. Secondly, the ICA method is applied over this base leading a coefficient matrix A and a matrix of independent components C: each line of A corresponds to a specific reference image. Thirdly, $V_?$ is written as a linear combination of the $C_j's$. Fourthly, the coefficients encoded in $\underline{A'}$ are compared with those obtained from the decomposition of the target image with each line of the matrix A, leading to the error between the target image $V_?$ and each reference image. Finally, the smallest error corresponds to the most resembling reference image to the target image. That is, if the error is less than a threshold, then the image corresponds to the reference subject. The central point of our analysis, shown in Figure 10, is to decompose a base $\underline{V}$ of reference images of a subject X with the fastICA method [23]. Then, we get a vector $\underline{C}$ of independent components and a matrix A of coefficients (Figure 10).

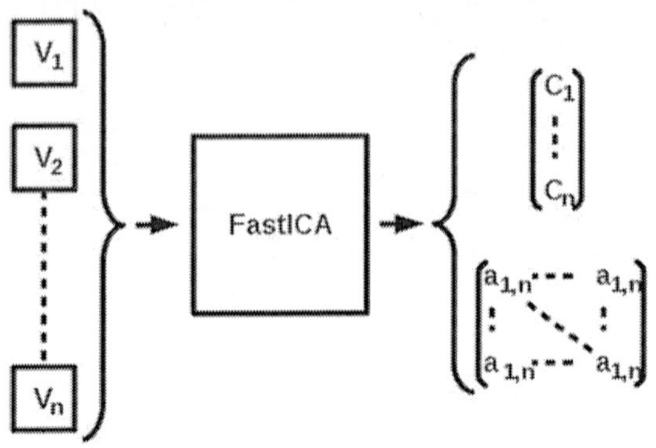

Figure. 10 Principle of decomposition.

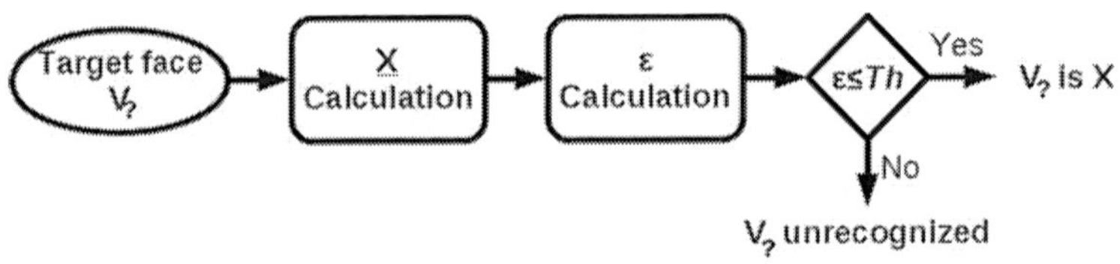

Figure. 11 Recognition procedure.

The second step of the algorithm, with reference to Figure 11, considers a target image $V_?$ corresponding to an unknown subject. This image will be written as a linear combination of independent components forming $\underline{C}$ calculated within the learning base. Then, $V_?$ is written in the form

$$V_? = \underline{A'C}, \tag{22}$$

where $\underline{A'}$ of size n, i.e. $\underline{A'} = (a_1', \cdots, a_n')$, summarizes the set of coefficients allowing us to reconstruct $V_?$ from the components of $\underline{C}$. In this way, we find $\underline{A'} = V_? C^{-1}$. In order to a make decision, the differences between the vector $\underline{A'}$ and each line of the matrix A are calculated (Eq. 21). Minimizing the error function leads to the most resembling image of the reference base to the target image $V_?$.

$$\left| \begin{array}{lcl} \varepsilon_1 & = & |a_1' - a_{1,1}| + |a_2' - a_{1,2}| + \cdots + |a_n' - a_{1,n}| \\ \vdots & & \vdots \\ \varepsilon_n & = & |a_n' - a_{n,1}| + |a_2' - a_{n,2}| + \cdots + |a_n' - a_{n,n}| \end{array} \right. . \tag{23}$$

In a similar fashion as was mentioned above the error is defined as $\varepsilon = (\varepsilon_i + \cdots \varepsilon_n)/n$. When the error is less than a given threshold the target image $V_?$ is considered as representing subject X, otherwise it is not recognized. On the one hand, this algorithm relies on the strong robustness of the ICA method. On the other hand, it allows a precise quantification of the resemblance of the target image with the reference base.

Protocol

Next, we validate this approach by a series of tests using subjects 1 and 2 of the PHPID [25]. This base has 15 subjects, 93 references per subject, and the angle characterizing the face orientation varies every 10°, either horizontally or vertically. Here, we shall consider only 53 images per subject, i.e. the first 20 and last 20 images have been removed. In addition, the face images were reframed (215 × 215 pixels), to minimize the background noise of the images (Figure 12). The images of subject 1 were chosen for fabricating the reference base (Figure 12 (a)). The recognition procedure is tested for both subjects 1 and 2 (Figure 12 (a-b)).

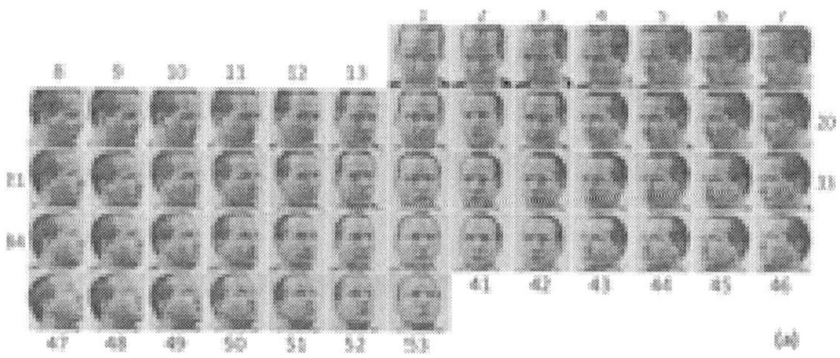

Figure. 12 Database 1 : (a) Subject 1 and (b) Subject 2.

As concerns the study of the noise of the input image, 8 target images of the PHPID will be considered (Figure 13). Here, the images were not reframed. Two kinds of test were performed. In the first test, subject 1 was the reference subject (Figure 13 (a-f)). For the second we test used two images (Figure 13 (g-h)), i.e. the two faces are similar to the reference face (Figure 13 (g)), or one face is different than the reference one (Figure 13 (h)).

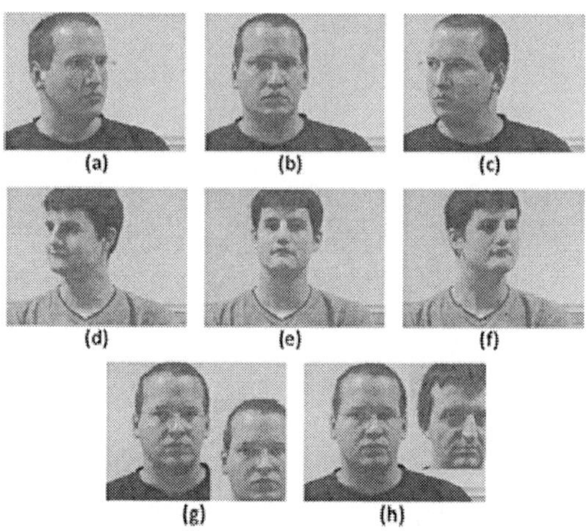

Figure. 13 Database 2: (a-c) Subject 1, (d-f) Subject 2, (g-h) Mixed images.

Experimental Results

Influence of the Reference Images

The influence of the choice of the reference images is illustrated in Figure 15. Four ROC curves are shown and were obtained from using different sets of reference images of Figure 14, i.e. images 1, 27, and 53 for Figure 15 (a-b), images 26, 27, and 28 for Figure 15(c-d), images 27, 30, and 36 for Figure 15 (e-f), and images 9, 27, and 45 for Figure 15 (g-h).

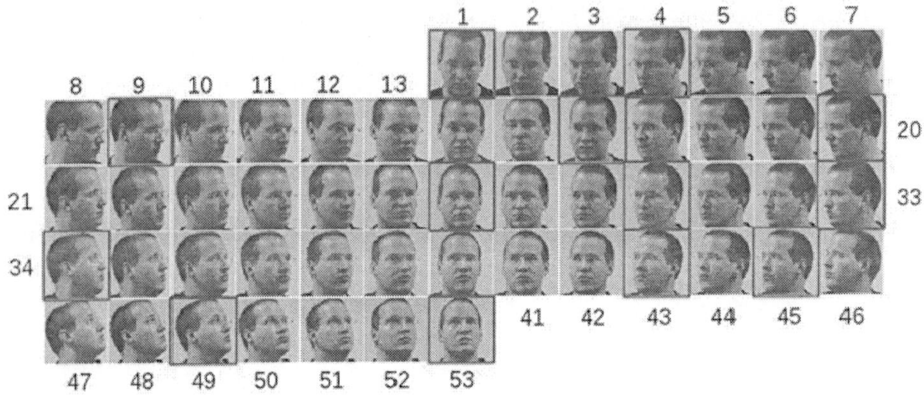

Figure. 14 Subject 1. The images framed in red are the reference images.

We can immediately observe that some image configurations lead to poor results. For example, choosing the images 1, 27, and 53 as reference images gives a ROC curve (Figure 15 (a)) going well below the random guess line, with a true recognition rate of 30% for a false alarm rate of 60%. If the *FPR* is set to 10% the true recognition rate is only of 19%. Additionally, choosing images 27, 26, and 28 gives a ROC curve (Figure 15(c)) close to the random guess line and a *TPR* of 19% when the *FPR* is set to 10%. The situation is quite different if the images 27, 30, and 36 (Figure 15(e)); or the images 9, 27, and 46 (Figure 15(h)) are selected, the ROC curve is now above the random guess line. The former case leads to a *TPR* of 52% when the *FPR* is set to 10%, while the latter case gives a *TPR* of 40% for a *FPR* set to 10%. These numerical results prove that the choice of the reference images has a strong influence on the performances of this ICA-based algorithm.

Influence of the Number of Reference Images

To further characterize the influence of the number of reference images we shall use 1, 5, 11, and 13 reference images among those of subject 1 (Figure 16). Figure 17 summarizes the behavior of the ROC curves corresponding to these assumptions.

From visual inspection, the classification is less efficient as the number of references is increased, i.e. we get a *TPR* of 64% for a *FPR* set to 10% and a single reference and a *TPR* of 51% for a *FPR* set to 10% and 5 references. This may be due to the specific choice of reference images, or to the saturation of the filter (the image 27 is used as reference for both filters). If the number of reference images is increased, the *TPR* increases to respectively 75% and 68% for 11 and 13 reference images and *FPR* set to 10%.

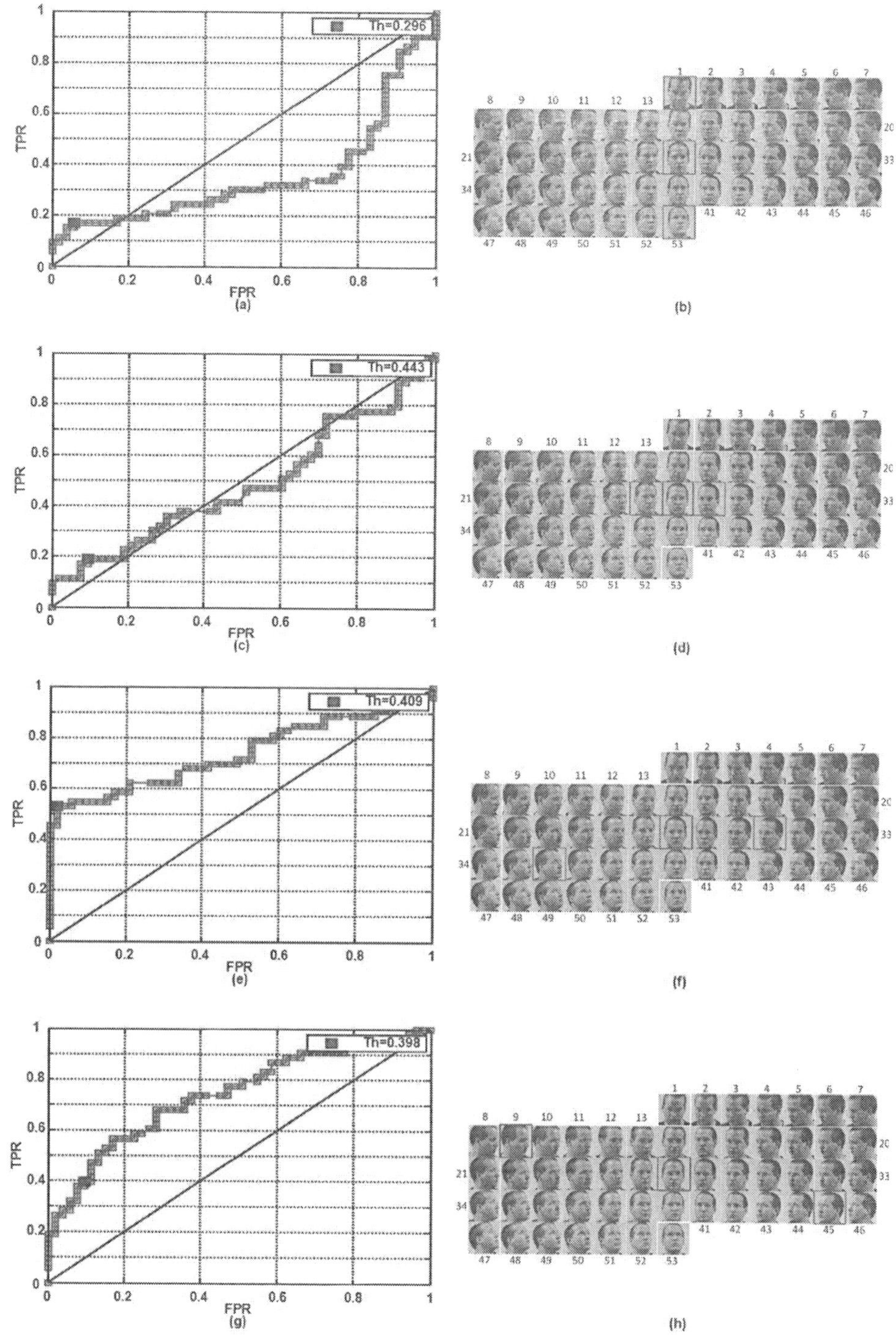

Figure. 15 Simulation results. (a-b) ROC plot and the three references chosen (references 1, 27, and 53). (c-d) The same as in (a-b) with references 26, 27, and 28. (e-f) The same as in (a-b) with references 27, 30, and 36. (g-h) The same as in (a-b) with references 9, 27, and 45.

Other keys to this work are the fabrication and recognition times of the reference base which depend of the number of images used. For a base containing a single reference the fabrication time is found to be 2.7 s and the recognition time is 0.43 s. When 13 reference images are used these times they are respectively equal to 5.3 s and 0.6 s. We interpret this behavior to be due to the size of the matrix of independent components which increases as the number of images is increased.

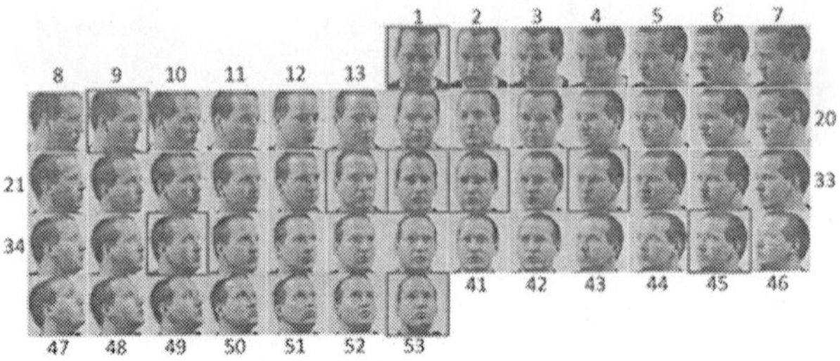

Figure. 16 Subject 1. The images in red are the references.

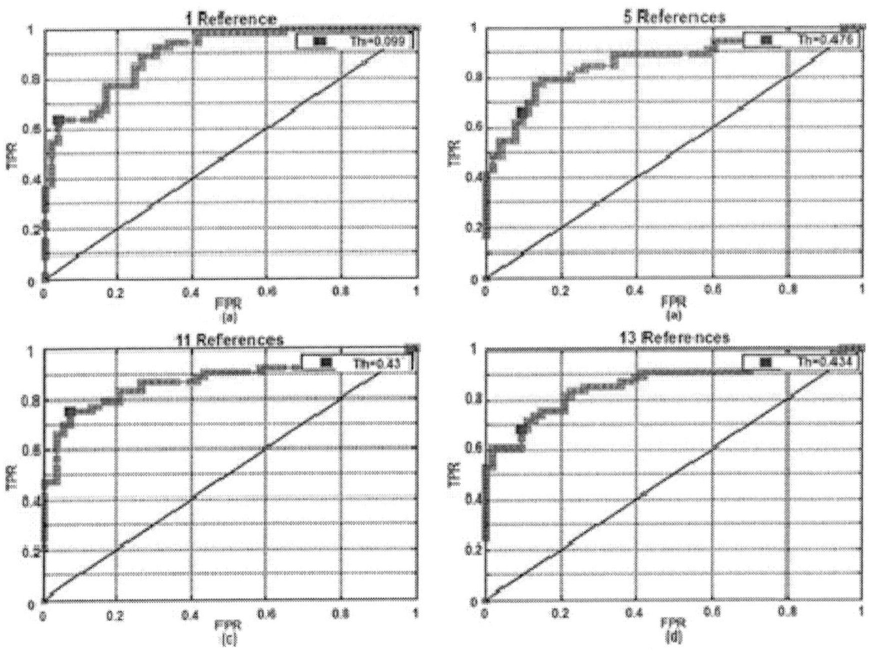

Figure. 17 Simulation results. (a) ROC plot using 1 reference. The blue square represents the best TPR value for a FPR set to 10%. (b), (c) and (d) are the same as in (a) for respectively 5, 11 and 13 references.

Effect of Noise in the Target Image

The effect of the background of the target images is first investigated. The images shown in Figure 13 are used as target images of the algorithm and the first 3 images (Figure 13 a-c) are taken as references. The results of our investigation are listed in Table 2. The first line of this table corresponds to the target images, the second line shows the reference images with minimal error (RIME), and the third line contains the error. We observe that the ICA-based method is strongly robust for distinguishing the two subjects (when the target image has only one face). The error is found of the order of 10^{-31} when the target and reference images are identical and of 10^{-6} otherwise. Although both errors are very weak the 25 orders of magnitude difference between these numbers lead to an efficient recognition technique. When a second face is introduced in the target image the error is found to increase significantly up to 10^{-6} even if both faces correspond to the same reference subject. This is an example of the low robustness to noise of the ICA-based method.

Table 2. ICA errors using target images shown in the first line. RIME means reference image with minimal error

Target image								
RIME								
Error	$1.3 \cdot 10^{-61}$	$1.3 \cdot 10^{-31}$	$2.7 \cdot 10^{-33}$	$7 \cdot 10^{-6}$	$1.7 \cdot 10^{-6}$	$7.3 \cdot 10^{-6}$	$2.7 \cdot 10^{-6}$	$1.1 \cdot 10^{-6}$

Comparison between ICA Model and VLC Using an Optimized Composite Filter for Face Recognition

We now describe the recognition performances of the ICA and VLC methods. Our first aim is to examine different filters used to implement the VCL. Our second aim is to present the results. The two approaches based on ICA and VLC will be compared and their performances discussed below.

Filter Fabrication

Phase Only Filter

Following the definition of the POF shown in section 2, the algorithm was tested with subjects 1 and 2 of the PHPID [24] (Figure 12). In order to compare with the ICA-based algorithm, the effect of the noise of the input image will be also studied as above (Figure 13). The image of the central position of subject 1 (Figure 18) is used as reference image for the fabrication of the filter.

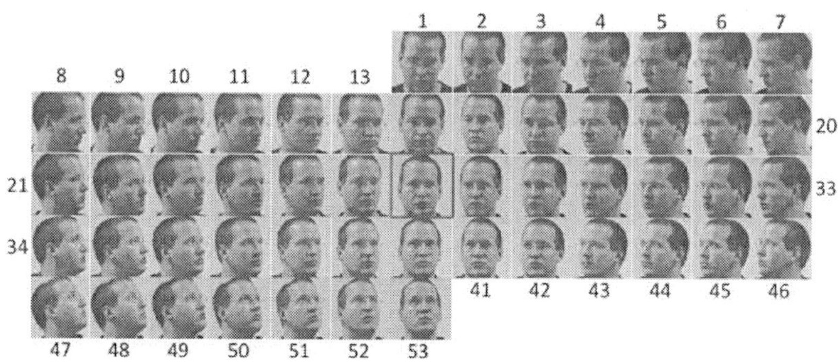

Figure. 18 Subject 1. The reference image is framed in red.

Segmented Composite Filter

As described previously, the segmented composite filter is a filter composed of many reference images. The principle of this method is to choose, for all spectra of the reference images, pixels containing most of the information for the given application. Each pixel of the reference base will be compared to the others for each image, in order to select the one corresponding to the segmentation criterion. For a given position (u,v) in the Fourier plane, the energy of the pixel is compared for the entire set of reference images, and is given by $E_{(u,v)} = I^2_{(u,v)}$. $I_{(u,v)}$ is the amplitude of the pixel and $E_{(u,v)}$ is its energy at coordinates (u,v). Note that the energy of each pixel is normalized by the overall energy of the image in the spectral domain. Hence, the spectrum of the segmented composite filter is composed of the most energetic pixels of the entire set of reference mages. The energy criterion reads

$$a_i \frac{E^i_{(u,v)}}{\sum_{u=0}^{W}\sum_{v=0}^{H} E^i_{(u,v)}} \geq a_j \frac{E^j_{(u,v)}}{\sum_{u=0}^{W}\sum_{v=0}^{H} E^j_{(u,v)}},$$

$$\forall\, j \in [\![1,n]\!] \text{ and } j \neq i, \tag{24}$$

where $E^i_{(u,v)}$ denotes the energy at coordinates (u,v) of the ith image and $\sum_{u=0}^{W}\sum_{v=0}^{H} E^i_{(u,v)}$ represents the energy of the ith image. The major drawback of this criterion is that it does not take into account of the phase [10]. In order to consider the phase information one can use the complex gradient of the spectrum, given by the partial derivatives of the spectrum with respect to coordinates u and v

$$\nabla \mathrm{S}_{(\mathrm{u,v})} = \begin{pmatrix} \dfrac{\partial \mathrm{S}_{(\mathrm{u,v})}}{\partial u} \\ \dfrac{\partial \mathrm{S}_{(\mathrm{u,v})}}{\partial \mathrm{v}} \end{pmatrix} \tag{25}$$

where $S_{(u,v)} = A_{(u,v)} e\char`^(i\varphi)$ denotes the spectrum at coordinates (u,v). The square of gradient modulus,

$$\left|\nabla S_{(u,v)}\right|^2 = \left|\frac{\partial S_{(u,v)}}{\partial u}\right|^2 + \left|\frac{\partial S_{(u,v)}}{\partial v}\right|^2, \tag{26}$$

strongly depends on the phase. The segmentation is now realized according the criterion

$$a_i\left|\nabla S^i_{(u,v)}\right| \geq a_j\left|\nabla S^j_{(u,v)}\right|, \forall\, j \in [\![1,n]\!] \text{ and } j \neq i. \tag{27}$$

For each pixel of the overall reference base, the one having the largest magnitude of the gradient will be selected for fabricating the segmented composite filter. In contrast with the energy criterion, the phase and the modulus of the spectrum are taken into account for fabricating the filter. It is also instructive to investigate the phase gradient defined as the phase derivative with respect to the pixel

$$\nabla\varphi_{(u,v)} = \begin{pmatrix} \dfrac{\partial\varphi_{(u,v)}}{\partial u} \\ \dfrac{\partial\varphi_{(u,v)}}{\partial v} \end{pmatrix}, \tag{28}$$

where $\varphi_{(u,v)}$ denotes phase at coordinates (u, v).The segmentation is now realized according the gradient modulus, leading to

$$a_i \left|\nabla\varphi^i_{(u,v)}\right| \geq a_j \left|\nabla\varphi^j_{(u,v)}\right|, \forall\, j \in [\![1, n]\!] \text{ and } j \neq i. \tag{29}$$

In contrast with the energy criterion, the gradient criterion does not consider the modulus of the spectrum, and thus has a slow dynamics. Another segmentation criterion considers the real part of the pixel. The pixel selection is done according the condition

$$a_i \frac{A^i_{(u,v)} \cos\left(\varphi^i_{u,v}\right)^2}{\sum_{u=0}^{W} \sum_{v=0}^{H} E^i_{(u,v)}} \geq a_j \frac{A^j_{(u,v)} \cos\left(\varphi^j_{u,v}\right)^2}{\sum_{u=0}^{W} \sum_{v=0}^{H} E^j_{(u,v)}},$$

$$\forall\, j \in [\![1, n]\!] \; and \; j \neq i. \tag{30}$$

Note that, in a similar way as is done for the energy criterion, a normalization of the pixel by the overall energy of the image is realized. The main advantage of this criterion is to consider both phase and modulus.

Experimental Results

Our simulation scheme of the VLC is now used to explore the performances of the POF for the target image base composed of subjects 1 and 2 (Figure 12).

Phase Only Filter

In order to assess the POF performances, two filters fabricated with the central images of the reference subject for the two bases 1 and 2 (Figure 19) have been applied to all target images shown in Figure 12. The results are shown in Figure 19. The corresponding ROC curve (Figure 19 (b)) indicates a TPR value of 20% for a FPR set to 0%. When the FPR is set to 9 %, the TPR is equal to 58 %. These low values are consistent with the PCE values shown in Figure 19 (a), i.e. the value of the PCE for the reference image, corresponding to a high correlation, is very large ($4.4 \cdot 10^{-3}$) compared to the values of the PCE for the other images of subject 1 ($2 \cdot 10^{-4}$). Consequently, the values of the PCE are very similar for most of the images of subject 1, even smaller than the values of the PCE for the images of subject 2, thus leading to classification mistakes. POF is very sensitive to small changes in face rotation: it has a high discrimination power but has a low robustness.

Next, we have investigated the effect of background noise of the target and reference images. For that purpose, the images shown in Figure 13 have been used for characterizing the performance of the POF. The first image (Figure 13 (a)) is taken as reference. The data are presented in Table 3.

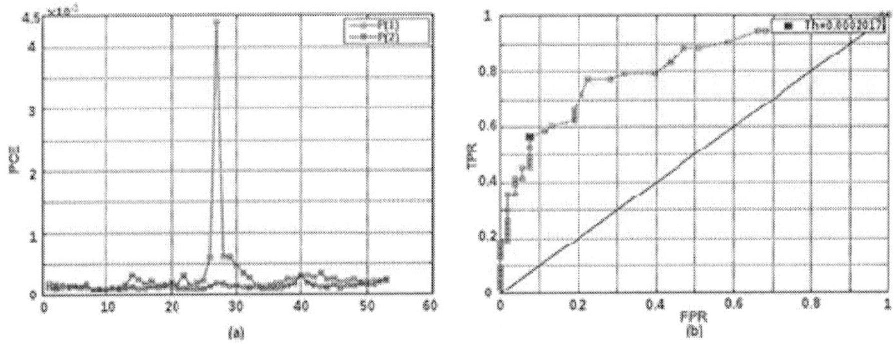

Figure. 19 Results using a POF, (a) PCA values, (b) ROC curve.

Table 3. Correlation planes using target images shown in the first line

Target image								
POF	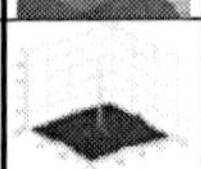	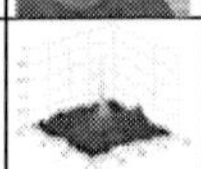	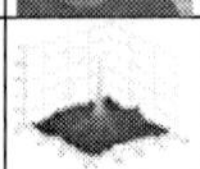	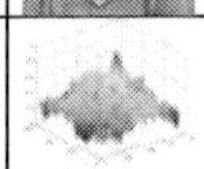	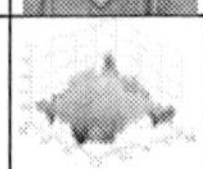			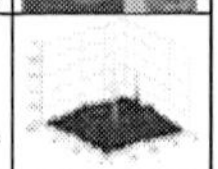
PCE	$3.4 \cdot 10^{-4}$	$9.1 \cdot 10^{-4}$	$9 \cdot 10^{-4}$	$6.9 \cdot 10^{-5}$	$7.3 \cdot 10^{-5}$	$5.8 \cdot 10^{-5}$	$3.7 \cdot 10^{-4}$	$2.1 \cdot 10^{-4}$

Table 4. TPR and FPR values for the different peak detection criteria

Criterion	Threshold	TPR (%)	FPR (%)
PCE	$2 \cdot 10^{-4}$	56.6	7.6
PCE'	$2.4 \cdot 10^{-4}$	58.5	7.6
PCE''	$2 \cdot 10^{-4}$	56.6	7.6
SNR	$1.2 \cdot 10^{-3}$	56.6	9.4
SNR_{dB}	62	56.6	7.6

The first line corresponds to the target images, the second and third lines contain, respectively, the correlation planes and the values of the PCE. For the first 3 target images of Table 3 (identical reference and target images), it is to be noted that the correlation planes have an intense correlation peak with low level of noise. In contrast, when the target and reference subjects are different the correlation peak broadens and is characterized by a high level of noise. Although the value of the PCE is smaller for the second target face than for the first one, a correlation peak is observed when the target and reference subjects are different. The values of the PCE are close whether correlation is effective or not. As a result, this causes the increase of the false alarm rate. By contrast, the results obtained with the images containing background noise are interesting. When the target images contain a second face (the last two images of Table 3) we find that the correlation planes have an intense peak with low level of noise and PCE values which are comparable with those of the first 3 images of

Table 3. To summarize, the background noise of the target image has little effect on the correlation result. The POF is strongly robust to the noise related to the background of the image.

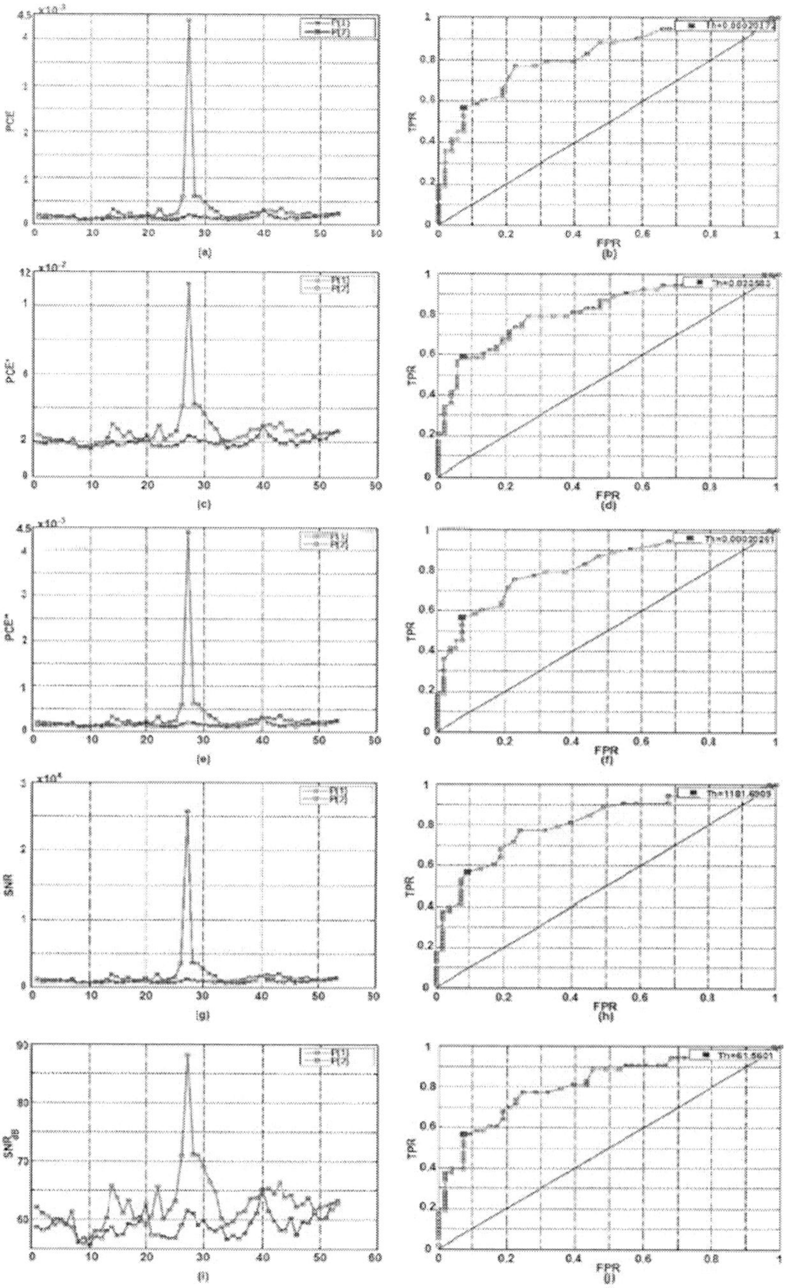

Figure. 20 Simulation results using a POF and different metrics. (a) PCE, (c) PCE', (e) PCE'', (g) SNR, (i) SNR_{dB}. The corresponding ROC curves are shown in (b), (d), (f), (h) and (j).

A POF fabricated with the central image of subject 1 (Figure 18) has been applied to the base of reference images (Figure 12). The correlation peak was characterized by the different criteria. The results, shown in Figure 20, are very similar. In addition, the ROC curves shown in Figure 20 show the same trend. That is, for a *FPR* set to 0%, the *TPR* is close to 20% for every criterion. It should be noted that only small differences are noticeable in Table 4. Note that the *SNR* is less performing than the other criteria. Combined to its robustness to noise, the *PCE'* is the most efficient criterion [13].

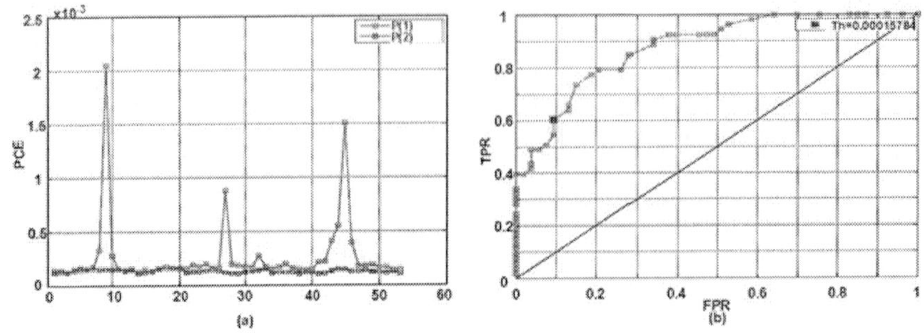

Figure 21. PCE results and ROC curve using a segmented composite filter.

Segmented Composite Filter

The segmented composite filter, fabricated with images 9, 27, and 43 of the reference subject (Figure 16) was applied to the set of target images shown in Figure 12. The segmentation criterion chosen was the energy of the spectrum. As was shown in Figure 19 (a), the values of the *PCE* for the set of target images are weak. We find that several values of the *PCE* corresponding to the target images of the reference subject are less than the values of the *PCE* of the target images of the second subject. This has for effect to decrease the performances of this filter. Consequently, one may introduce a couple of supplementary reference images to increase the robustness of this filter. Figure 21 shows the results obtained with a segmented composite filter using 3 reference images. The recognition performances are well compared to those of the POF since the *TPR* is now equal to 40% when the *FPR* is set to 0%. This is due to the large increase of the *PCE* corresponding to the added reference images as is evidenced in Figure 21 (a). Increasing the number of reference images has for effect to enhance the performances of the classifier. In addition, the recognition time remains identical since only one correlation is needed, even if the fabrication time of the filter is a little bit larger.

From a trial and error method we noted that 13 reference images were sufficient to recognize a large part of the base. Several implementation of this 13-reference correlation were tested, e.g. a single filter segmented with all 13 references, or several filters containing some of these 13 references. The filters were fabricated using the images shown in Figure 16. They were segmented with the energy criterion and a weighting factor set to 4 for the central image. Several tests were made with 6 filters with 3 references, 3 filters with 5 references, 2 filters with 7 references, and 1 filter with 13 references (the image 27 having the central position is systematically used for fabricating the filters). The results shown in Figure 22 lead to better performances than those obtained previously (Figure 21) and using 3 reference images, i.e. a minimum value of 62% is obtained for the *TPR* when the *FPR* is set to 0% (Figure 22 (d)). In addition, the minimum value of the *TPR* is 79% when the *FPR* is set to 10%, to be compared with the 60% obtained earlier. The effect of the number of filters on the recognition performance is noticeable. For example, if the *FPR* is set to 0% the *TPR* is respectively of 79%, 62%, 83%, and 77% for 6, 3, 2, and 1 filter. If the *FPR* is set to 10% these numbers are 89%, 79%, 89%, and 83%. Using 6 filters with 3 references and 2 filters with 7 references lead to the best results. The weak performances of the filter with 13 references are due to a saturation effect. Using a combination of 2 filters with 7 references requires 2 correlations while using a combination of 6 filters necessitates 6 correlations. Hence, it is the best compromise between accuracy in the recognition and computational expense.

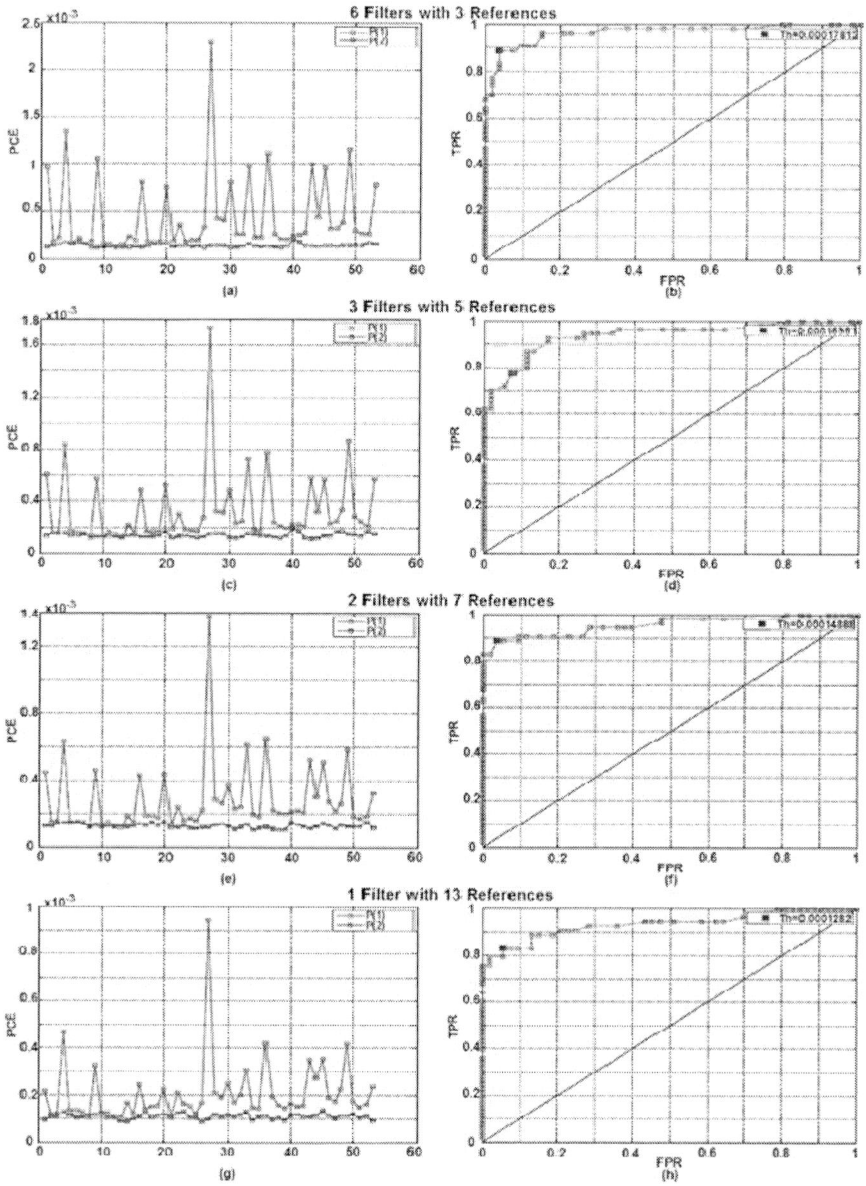

Figure. 22 PCE results and ROC curves using a segmented composite filter for 6 filters and 3-reference filters (a-b), 3 filters and 5-reference filters (c-d), 2 filters and 7-reference filters (e-f), 1 filter and 13-reference filters (g-h).

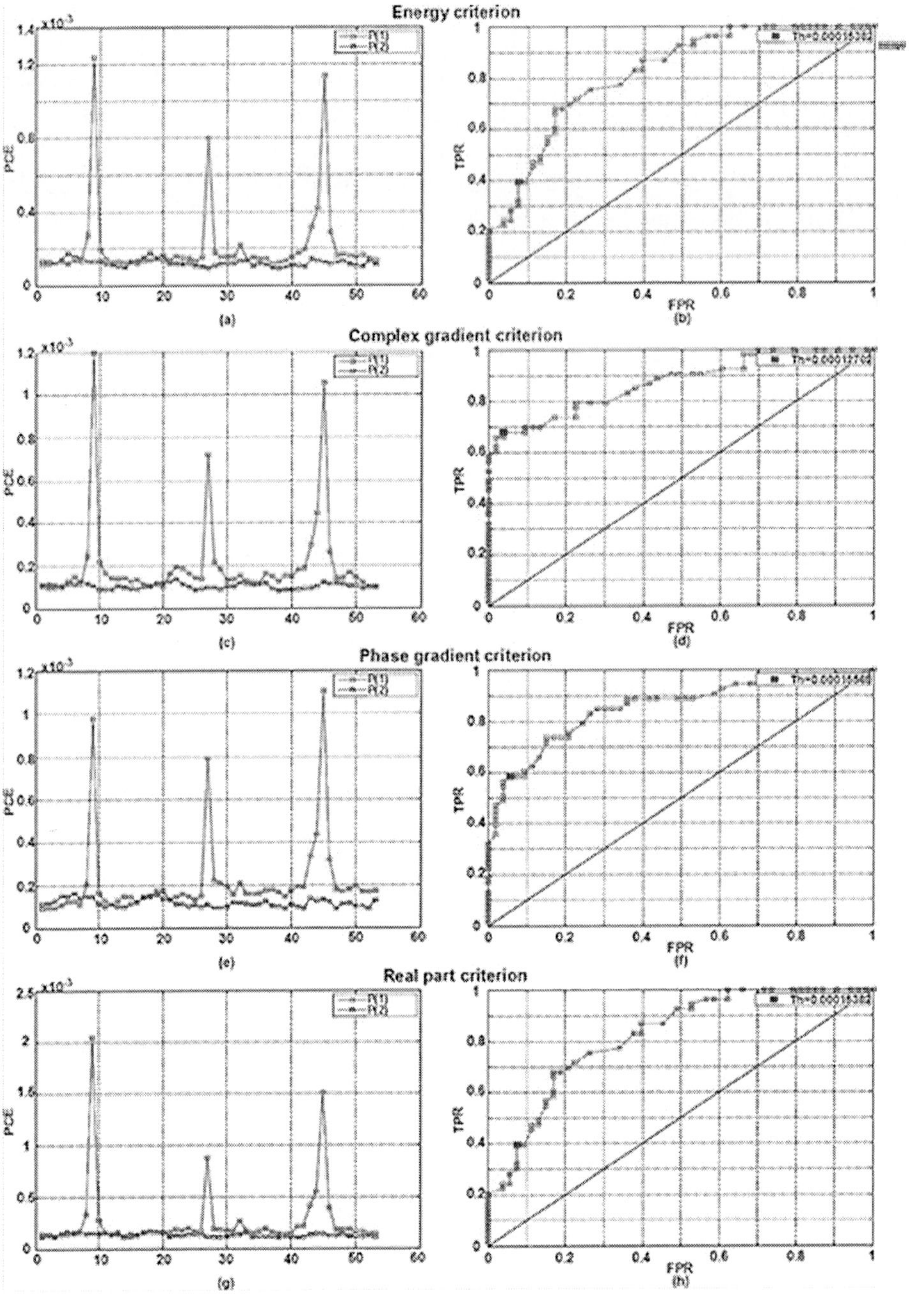

Figure. 23 PCE results and ROC curves using a segmented composite filter for the energy criterion filter (a-b), the complex gradient criterion (c-d), the phase gradient criterion (e-f), and the real part criterion (g-h).

As mentioned earlier, different segmentation criteria can be used for the fabrication of the segmented composite filter, i.e. energy of the spectrum (Figure 23 (ab)), its complex gradient (Figure 23 (cd)), its phase gradient (Figure23 (ef)), and its real part (Figure 23 (gh)). It is seen that the segmentation criterion has a significant impact on the performance of the filter, as exemplified by calculations of the recognition rates which are respectively equal (for $FPR = 0\%$) to 22% for the energy, 60% for the complex gradient, 32% for the phase gradient, and 21% for the real part. If the *FPR* is set to 10%, this recognition rate is respectively of 40%, 70%, 59%, and 39%. Although the phase gradient has a low *TPR* for *FPR* set to 10% its recognition rate is largely increased when the *FPR* is set to 0% contrasting with the energy and real part criteria. This is due to the fact that the phase contains most of the information. The most efficient criterion is that of the complex gradient leading to high robustness and discrimination. The results obtained with the complex gradient are similar to those obtained with the energy criterion and 13 reference images.

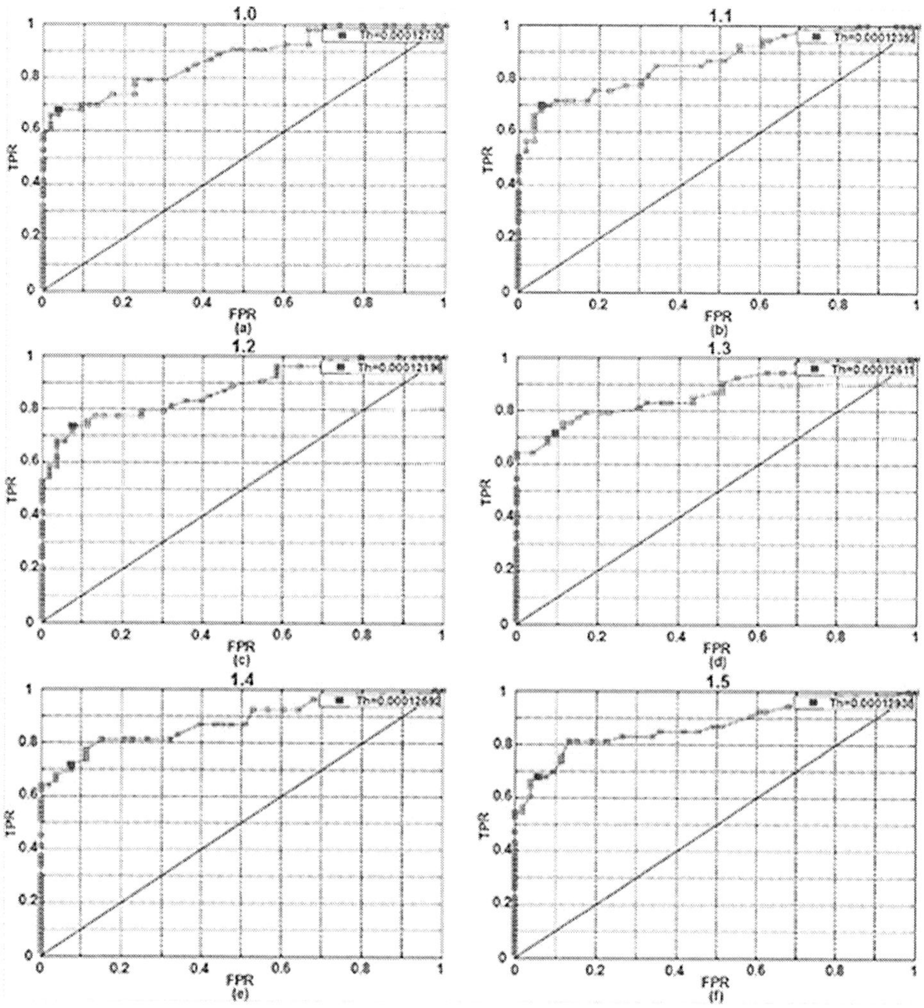

Figure. 24 Results using a segmented composite filter with different weight coefficients: (a) 1.0, (b) 1.1, (c) 1.2, (c) 1.3, (d) 1.4, (e) 1.5, and (f) 1.6.

As also indicated above, a weighting factor may be applied to some references allowing us to increase the face recognition performances. Several weighting factors were considered, when using a 3-reference filter (images 9, 27, and 45) segmented with the gradient spectrum. The effect is illustrated in Figure 26 with respective weighting factor 1.0 (Figure 24 (a)), 1.1 (Figure24 (b)), 1.2 (Figure 24 (c)), 1.3 (Figure24 (d)), 1.4 (Figure 24 (e)), and 1.5 (Figure 24 (f)). This weighting factor plays a significant role in the recognition performance. Comparing the *TPR* with a *FPR* set to 0% we pass from 51% (weighting factor=1.1) to 64% (weighting factor=1.3 and 1.4). When the *FPR* is set to 10% the *TPR* values are close to 70%.

COMPARISON

Finally, we turn to a comparison of the performances of the ICA (Sec. 3) and VLC (Sec. 4) methods focusing our attention on the role of the number and choice of the reference images, and the effect of the background noise of the target image.

Table 5 compares the results obtained via the two methods on the effects of the background noise of the image and the presence of a second face in the target image. The first line shows the target images used; the second line shows the reference images with minimal error obtained with the ICA-based method; the third line contains the error obtained; the fourth line shows the correlation plane, and the fifth line indicates the *PCE* value obtained with VLC-based method. For the ICA-based method, the three first images of the first line of Table 5 (subject 1) were used. The filter used for the VLC-method considers the first image of Table 5. As mentioned above, the ICA-based method allows us to recognize efficiently the subject when the background of the image does not contain any face. The 3 first images of Table 5, corresponding to the reference subject, lead to an error of the order of 10^{-31}, while the next 3 ones, corresponding to the second subject, lead to an error of the order of 10-6. The POF lead to very intense correlation peaks for the first 3 images, allowing a good recognition of the subject, i.e. the *PCE* values are of the order of 10^{-3} in case of recognition and 10^{-6} otherwise, while the errors of the ICA-based method are respectively of the order of 10^{-31} and 10^{-6}. While both methods have good recognition results, the ICA-based method leads to a more efficient discrimination. Now, as concerns the last 2 target images of Table 5 in which a second face has been introduced in its background, it is interesting to observe that the ICA-based method cannot recognize the subject in sharp contrast with the VLC-based method, i.e. the error is of the order of 10^{-6}, the POF has a high magnitude correlation peak, and the *PCE* value is of the order of 10^{-3} in a similar way when the reference subject is taken as the target image. Remarkably, VLC allows us to obtain results with much stronger robustness.

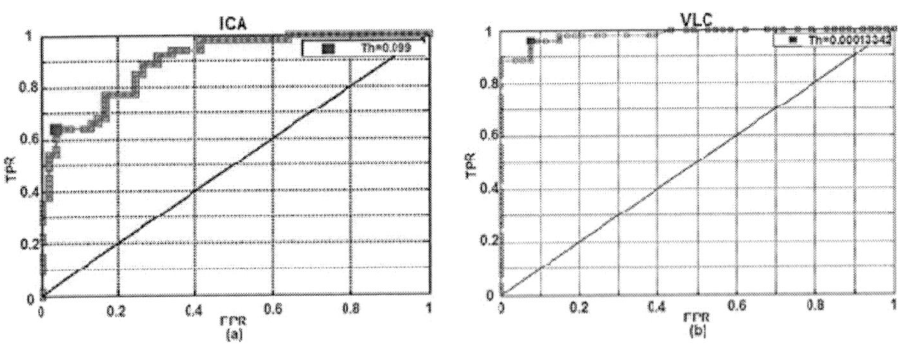

Figure. 25 ROC curves using 13 references for (a) the ICA-based method, and (b) the VLC method using a segmented composite filter.

Finally, Figure 25 shows the results for both approaches. For VLC we use two segmented composite filters with 7 references, the complex gradient of the spectrum criterion, and a weighting factor of 1.4. The ICA-based method uses a single reference, i.e. image 27 (Figure 18). We note that these two methods present significantly different performances. For example, the ROC curve for VLC shows a good classification, with a *TPR* of respectively 90% and 97% when the *FPR* is set to 0% and 8%. In contrast, the ICA-based method leads to *TPR* values of respectively 39% and 64% when the *FPR* is set to 0% and 8%. Hence, VLC leads to the best results with a good classification with only 2 correlations. The fact that this architecture is optically implementable makes this technique well suited for image processing systems since it is quasi-instantaneous, contrasting with the ICA method which is computationally intensive.

Table 5. ICA errors and correlation planes using target images shown in the first row. RIME means reference image with minimal error

Target image								
RIME								
Error	$1.3\ 10^{-31}$	$1.3\ 10^{-31}$	$2.7\ 10^{-33}$	$7\ 10^{-6}$	$1.7\ 10^{-6}$	$7.3\ 10^{-6}$	$2.7\ 10^{-6}$	$1.1\ 10^{-6}$
POF	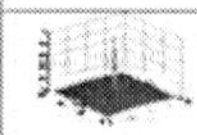	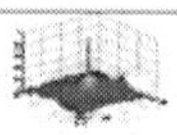	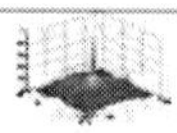				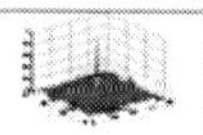	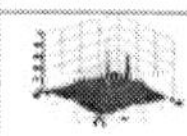
PCE	$3.4\ 10^{-3}$	$9.1\ 10^{-4}$	$9\ 10^{-4}$	$6.9\ 10^{-5}$	$7.3\ 10^{-5}$	$5.8\ 10^{-5}$	$3.7\ 10^{-3}$	$2.1\ 10^{-3}$

Conclusion

In this chapter, we proposed and validated a novel ICA-based approach for face recognition. The performance of the proposed techniques was compared with that of alternate techniques, such as the VLC. We have reported an extensive series of first principles numerical studies aimed at better understanding the role of the number and the choice of reference images.

As mentioned earlier, one of the motivations of our study is to consider the effects of different criteria on the correlation peak detection and segmentation of the reference images for assessing the performance of the VLC. Additionally, we described a performance probabilistic metric for our classifiers i.e., the receiver operating characteristic (ROC). These two methods show different performances in terms of robustness and discrimination. Importantly, the ICA-based technique possesses the best discriminating power, i.e. errors are on the order of 10^{-31} for the comparison of the subject with itself, and on the order of 10^{-6} for the comparison with a different subject. By comparison, the VLC-based technique is robust enough to treat the background noise of images. From the previous discussion we conclude that this technique is the most efficient for recognition of the entire database of 53 images for each subject.

Hence, the VLC allows us to get good classification performances, i.e. typically 90% of true recognition for 0% false alarm with a segmented composite filter using the gradient of spectrum and a weighting factor of 1.4, while the ICA-based method offers weaker results.

These findings may initiate future research efforts to improve the robustness of face recognition methods involving extremely large databases.

References

[1] P. Glascock and D. M. Kutzik. Behavioral telemedicine: A new approach to the continuous nonintrusive monitoring of activities of daily living. *Telemedicine Journal*, 6(1):33–44, 2004.

[2] M. Turk and A. Pentland. Eigenfaces for recognition. *Journal of Cognitive Neuroscience*, 3(1):71–86, 1991.

[3] L. Shen and L. Bai. A review on gabor wavelets for face recognition. Pattern Analysis and Applications, 9(2):273–292, 2006.

[4] T. Joliffe. Principal component analysis. New York: *Springer-Verlag*, 1986.

[5] P. Comon. Independent component analysis, a new concept? Signal Processing, 36(3):287–314, 1994.

[6] Alfalou and C. Brosseau. Robust and discriminating method for face recognition based on correlation technique and independent component analysis model. *Optics Letters*, 36(5):645–647, 2011.

[7] M. Barret. Traitement statistique du signal. 2009.

[8] Alfalou and A. Mansour. Double random phase encryption scheme to multiplex and simultaneous encode multiple images. *Applied Optics*, 48(31):5933–5947, 2009.

[9] VanderLugt. Signal detection by complex spatial filtering. *IEEE* Journals, 10:139–145, 1964.

[10] V. Oppenheim and J. S. Lim. The importance of phase in signals. Proceedings of the IEEE, 69(5):529–541, 1981.

[11] Alfalou, G. Keryer, and J.-L. de Bougrenet de la Tocnaye. Optical implementation of segmented composite filtering. *Applied Optics*, 38(29):6129–6135, 1999.

[12] V. K. V. Kumar and L. Hassebrook. Performance measures for correlation filters. Applied Optics, 29(20):2997–3006, 1990.

[13] J. Horner. Metrics for assessing pattern-recognition performance. Applied Optics, 31(2):165–166, 1992.

[14] F. M. Dickey and L. A. Romero. Dual optimality of the phase-only filter. Optics Letters, 14(1):4–5, 1989.

[15] J. A. Hanley and B. J. McNeil. The meaning and use of the area under a receiver operating characteristic roc curve. Radiology, 143(1):29–36, 1982.

[16] M. A. Casey and A. Westner. Separation of mixed audio sources by independent subspace analysis. In University of Michigan, International Computer Music Conference, 2000.

[17] S. Makeig, M. Westerfield, T.-P. Jung, J. Covington, J. Townsend, T.J. Sejnowski, and E. Courchesne. Functionally independent components of the late positive event-related potential during visual spatial attention. The *Journal of Neuroscience*, 19(7):2665–2680, 1999.

[18] J. Onton, M. Westerfield, J. Townsend, and S. Makeig. Imaging human eeg dynamics using independent component analysis. Neuroscience and Biobehavioral Reviews, 30(6):808–822, 2006.

[19] M. Wang and Y. Mo. Face recognition method based on independent component analysis and by neural network. Proceedings of the SPIE, volume 5267, pages 214–219. SPIE, 2003.

[20] Alfalou and A. Mansour. All-optical video-image encryption with enforced security level using independent component analysis. *Journal of Optics A: Pure and Applied Optics*, 9(10):787, 2007.

[21] Alfalou, M. Farhat, and A. Mansour. Independent component analysis based approach to biometric recognition. In Information and Communication Technologies: From Theory to Applications, 2008. ICTTA 2008. 3rd International Conference on DOI - 10.1109/ICTTA.2008.4530111, pages 1–4, 2008.

[22] X. Guan, H. H. Szu, and Z. Markowitz. Local ICA for the most wanted face recognition. In H. Szu Harold, Vetterli Martin, J. Campbell William, and R. Buss James, editors, Proceedings of the SPIE, volume 4056, pages 539–551. SPIE, 2000.

[23] Hyvärinen and E. Oja. A fast fixed-point algorithm for independent component analysis. *Neural Computation*, 9(7):1483–1492, 1997.

[24] A. Alfalou, M, Farhat, A. Mansour, "Independent Component Analysis Based Approach to Biometric Recognition," *Information and Communication Technologies: From Theory to Applications, 2008. ICTTA 2008. 3rd International Conference on*, vol., no., pp.1-4, 7-11 April 2008. doi: 10.1109/ICTTA.2008.4530111.

[25] N. Gourier, D. Hall, and J.L. Crowley. Estimating face orientation from robust detection of salient facial structures. In Proceedings of Pointing 2004, ICPR, International Workshop on Visual Observation of Deictic Gestures, 2004.

INDEX

D

G

H

I

J

K

L

M

N

O

P

Q

R

T

U

V

W

X

Y

Z